DATE DUE

DEMCO 38-296

Themistius and the Imperial Court

Themistius and the Imperial Court

Oratory, Civic Duty, and *Paideia* from Constantius to Theodosius

John Vanderspoel

Ann Arbor

THE UNIVERSITY OF MICHIGAN PRESS

Copyright © by the University of Michigan 1995
All rights reserved
Published in the United States of America by
The University of Michigan Press
Manufactured in the United States of America
⊗printed on acid-free paper

1998   1997   1996   1995   4   3   2   1

A CIP catalogue record for this book is available from the British Library.

Library of Congress Cataloging-in-Publication Data

Vanderspoel, John, 1954–
    Themistius and the imperial court : oratory, civic duty, and
    Paideia from Constantius to Theodosius / John Vanderspoel.
        p.   cm.
    Includes bibliographical references and index.
    ISBN 0-472-10485-3 (hc. : acid-free paper)
    1. Themistius. 2. Themistius—Relations with Roman emperors.
    3. Rome—Kings and rulers. 4. Rome—Politics and
    government—284–476. I. Title.
    B708.T7V36   1995
    185—dc20   95-12268
                                                       CIP

For Teresa

οὐδὲν δεινὸν ἐγκεῖσθαι βιβλίοις παρούσης
γυναικός, τοῦτο μὲν οὖν ἥδιστον παρ' ᾗ
βούλοιο ἂν εὐδοκιμεῖν, καὶ ταύτης ὁρώσης
καλόν τι ποιεῖν.
(Libanius, *Ep.* 379.7)

Preface

Themistius was one of the most important individuals in the fourth century A.D. Yet his life and work are poorly understood. No detailed account of the life, work, and influence of this philosopher, orator, and politician has ever appeared. The study by W. Stegemann in the *Real-encyclopädie*, published in 1934, is out of date, and G. Dagron's treatment, in *Travaux et Mémoires* 3 (1968), focuses primarily on one aspect of Themistius' thought, his concept of Hellenism and its relation to the views of his contemporaries. Both works, especially that of Dagron, remain valuable, but a new treatment of Themistius' life and work is necessary. This is the goal that I have chosen to pursue; the end result is, I hope, a new foundation for further study of Themistius. Three things above all, it seems to me, required attention. First, a precise chronology for Themistius' life and speeches is needed. To that end, I have reexamined all the evidence for chronology. Second, because the work of Themistius is not widely known, I have summarized, at least briefly, virtually every speech he delivered during his career. I trust that this allows Themistius himself to outline the guiding principles of his life. Third, and perhaps most important, I have attempted to assess and evaluate without prejudice Themistius' role and actions in the terms of the fourth century. In consequence, Themistius is no longer the self-serving flatterer of other portraits; rather, his use of praise is a fourth-century phenomenon employed as a device to achieve political ends. Similarly, Themistius was above all a civic leader and civic orator whose work has imperial significance because his city was Constantinople. His interactions with emperors and court stem from this perspective. I have not discussed in detail Themistius' work as an academic philosopher; this lies outside the parameters of this book. I have, however, been conscious at every turn that Themistius was a philosopher and that this has an important bearing on his work and career.

I have learned much from others since I began, a long time ago, to study Themistius. Many to whom I owe much are named in the notes; I have often gained much insight from scholars whose views I did not adopt. Scholars and friends alike offered encouragement and expressed a desire to see the finished product. Some deserve individual mention. First among these is Professor T.D. Barnes, who guided my first steps as a student of the fourth century and supervised my Ph.D. thesis "Themistius and the Imperial Court," on which this book is based. I shall never forget the congenial student-teacher relationship nor the attention to detail and the fresh approach that he espoused in his teaching, thesis supervision and scholarship. As a member of my thesis committee, Professor C.P. Jones contributed much by comments on drafts of the dissertation, and his books have been in some ways models for my own. Professor W.E. Kaegi, external examiner of the thesis, offered some important suggestions in what was a rather pleasant forum and kindly lent me a copy of G. Downey's unpublished translation of Themistius' speeches. This has been useful, though the translations in this book are my own except where noted. Since that time, now so long ago, others too have shown interest. Two colleagues in particular have been helpful. Michael Dewar read an earlier draft and contributed some valuable thoughts. And for almost a decade now, Waldemar Heckel has been a fellow traveler in quest of historical truth, about Themistius and much else. (How often has Themistius participated at lunch and over coffee?) As a colleague and friend, he has read drafts and made many suggestions on content and writing, usually in the midst of some important work of his own. To move to a different category of contribution, two readers for the University of Michigan Press persuaded me to add considerable material to chapter 1, to add chapter 3, and to recast some other parts of this book; the end result is an improvement. While I was doing this, Ellen Bauerle exhibited patience with the delay, and more recently she has cheerfully answered far too many questions. To all, named and unnamed, I offer my sincere gratitude.

Finally, a more personal conclusion. I had no idea, Teresa, how supportive and encouraging a wife could be. Now I do. You were the latest participant, but by no means the least. Even an ocean cannot dampen your enthusiasm or that of a family who made so much possible. Truly, nothing is more pleasant than writing a book in such circumstances.

Contents

Abbreviations

The following abbreviations are used frequently throughout the notes to the following chapters. For other works, I give complete bibliographical information for books at their first citation and a shortened form thereafter. Articles are cited by author, abbreviated journal title, volume number, year and page numbers, and except for items included here, all references are fully listed in the bibliography, where abbreviations are expanded. For speeches of Themistius, I use the Teubner edition of Downey-Norman and usually give only the number of the speech and, as is standard practice, a reference to page and section of the Harduin edition (Paris, 1684; Downey-Norman include these in their edition); the Arabic *Risâlat*, edited and translated by I. Shahîd, is cited by page number from Volume 3 of this edition. Where a reference is part of a sentence or where confusion might otherwise result, I generally give a more complete citation.

Baret, *Themistio*	E. Baret. *De Themistio sophista et apud imperatores oratore.* Paris, 1853.
Bouchery, "Contribution"	H.F. Bouchery. "Contribution à l'étude de la chronologie des Discours de Thémistius." *L'Antiquité Classique* 5 (1936): 191–208.
Bouchery, *Themistius*	H.F. Bouchery. *Themistius in Libanius' Brieven.* Publication de l'Université de Gand 78. Antwerp, 1936.
CAG	*Commentaria in Aristotelem Graeca.* Ed. by various hands. Berlin, 1883–1907. Cited by volume and part.
CTh	*Codex Theodosianus.* Ed. T. Mommsen and P.M. Meyer. Berlin, 1905.
Dagron, *Thémistios*	G. Dagron. "L'empire romain d'Orient au IVème siècle et les traditions

                                       politiques de l'hellénisme: Le
                                       témoignage de Thémistios." *Travaux et*
                                       Mémoires 3 (1968): 1–242.

Gladis, *Themistii*   C. Gladis. *De Themistii Libanii Iuliani in*
                                       Constantii Orationibus. Breslau, 1907.

Jones, *LRE*   A.H.M. Jones. *The Later Roman Empire*
                                       284–602: A Social, Economic and Admin-
                                       istrative Survey. 3 vols. Oxford, 1964.
                                       (The volume and page numbers are
                                       those of the 3 volume English edition,
                                       but the page numbers are the same as
                                       the 2 volume edition.)

Méridier, *Le philosophe*   L. Méridier. *Le philosophe Thémistius*
                                       devant l'opinion de ses contemporains.
                                       Rennes, 1906.

PLRE, 1   A.H.M. Jones, J.R. Martindale, and
                                       J. Morris. *The Prosopography of the Later*
                                       Roman Empire. Vol. 1. A.D. 260–395.
                                       Cambridge, 1971.

RIC   *The Roman Imperial Coinage.* 9 vols. Vol-
                                       ume 8, ed J.P.C. Kent. London, 1981.
                                       Volume 9, ed J.W.E. Pearce. London,
                                       1933.

Scholze, *Temporibus*   H. Scholze. *De temporibus librorum*
                                       Themistii. Göttingen, 1911.

Seeck, *Briefe*   O. Seeck. *Die Briefe des Libanius zeitlich*
                                       geordnet. Leipzig, 1906.

Seeck, *Regesten*   O. Seeck. *Regesten der Kaiser und Päpste*
                                       für die Jahre 311 bis 476 n. Chr.
                                       Stuttgart, 1919.

Stegemann, "Themistios"   W. Stegemann. "Themistios (2)." *RE*
                                       V, A 2 (1934): 1642–80.

Themistius and the Imperial Court

1

Introduction

The author of the *Philopolis*, a summary of *Oration* 4,[1] calls Themistius a "political philosopher" (*politikos philosophos*), an apposite description if understood correctly. As the writer indicates, this term applies to an individual whose most important goal was to benefit the state while living a noble life. Themistius never regarded himself as a political philosopher in the modern sense, that is, as purely a theorist of political philosophy. Instead, he was a philosopher involved in the public life of the eastern part of the Roman Empire for most of the second half of the fourth century A.D.[2] A philosopher and a politician,[3] he operated in both spheres at once, which made him unique among his contemporaries and caused a debate about the role of the philosopher in society.[4]

Any complete study of Themistius must come to grips with both aspects of his career. It is not enough to consider him as politician alone. A detailed biographical study, even if it delves deeply into the panegyrics, will not do him justice. Much of his political life depends on philosophy and, to a lesser extent, rhetoric. Conversely, a study of his philosophy will contribute to an understanding of the trends in

---

1. So L. Philippart, *Serta Leodiensia.* Bibliothèque de la Faculté de Philosophie de l'Université de Liége 44 (1930): 269–75. O. Seeck and H. Schenkl, *RhM* 61 (1906): 554–66, had argued that the hypothesis summarizes the lost panegyric of Julian.

2. For the title of her book, *Seneca: A Philosopher in Politics* (Oxford, 1976), M.T. Griffin has adopted a phrase that could be the subtitle of the present work as well. Themistius mentions Seneca by name only once (13.173b), when remarking that Nero did not heed the Stoic philosopher much.

3. Throughout this book, I use terms like *politician* and *politics* to describe participation in the civil administration and public life of the empire at all levels below that of emperor, not the modern concept of political activity.

4. See later in this chapter, chapters 4 and 8, and appendix 2 for the details.

philosophical thought in the fourth century,[5] but will necessarily fail to assess Themistius the man completely. An account of debates with contemporaries in philosophical terms alone is inadequate precisely because his role as a politician lies at the center of these debates. Differing approaches to philosophy undoubtedly played a part, but the philosophical disputes need not have developed into public controversy and did so precisely because Themistius refused to remain an academic only. His political career forced both sides to propound their arguments openly,[6] a dissemination of views that, he states in an early speech (*Or.* 24), was one of his goals.[7] Themistius must surely have realized that his audiences were forced, by respect for the emperors, to attend his panegyrics. The use of a captive audience displeased his opponents, who lacked or avoided similar opportunities. Politics and philosophy are thus inexorably linked in the life and career of Themistius.

Not everyone has seen this connection or finds the legitimate use of flattery attractive.

Fuit aulicus adulator uersipellis, uanus iactator suae philosophiae, specie magis quam re cultae, ineptus et ridiculus uexator et applicator Homeri et ueteris historiae, tautologus et sophista: in omnibus orationibus paene eadem, et ubique argutiae longe petitae.

So wrote J.J. Reiske[8] in his assessment of Themistius. J. Geffcken[9] was, if anything, even less favorable:

---

5. This book is less concerned with the actual philosophy of Themistius than with the presence of philosophy in his speeches; it therefore contains no systematic treatment of his philosophy, but only some general remarks later in this chapter. Some other items appear in the succeeding chapters as they are relevant. A complete survey of his writings, including the philosophical works, can be found in appendix 1.

6. It is thus unfortunate that the opponents have not left an extant record of their views and that most of the information derives from Themistius himself, with the exception of Julian's *Letter to Themistius*.

7. See the discussion in chapter 2, where the relevant passage is quoted.

8. Quoted in the preface of W. Dindorf, *Themistii Orationes* (Leipzig, 1832; reprint Hildesheim, 1961), xii.

9. *The Last Days of Greco-Roman Paganism*, trans. S. MacCormack (Amsterdam, 1978), 167–68.

Many rulers made this well-known rhetor into an instrument of their imperial glory; he considered himself a philosopher because he was skillful at paraphrasing Aristotle, and therefore thought that he had to defend himself against attacks on his activities as a Sophist. This panegyrist, who satiated what he regarded as philosophy with the perfume of the court, who thought he could see a philosopher or at least a friend of philosophers in almost every one of the emperors whom he celebrated, who proclaimed Jovian and Valens, one after the other, as Plato's ideal ruler, who was filled only with the consuming fire of ambition, is hardly a sympathetic figure.

Much the same sentiment is expressed by A. Alföldi:[10]

He calls himself a philosopher, it is true, but in reality he was no more than a rhetorician, with a taste for moralizing. But how enthusiastically does Constantius II celebrate him in a letter addressed to the Senate of Constantinople.

A. Piganiol, discussing Themistius' statement, in a panegyric of Theodosius, that he did not intend to flatter, remarks:[11]

Il nous paraît bien au contraire qu'il flatte impudemment la tendance de l'empereur à l'inertie, et, pour tout dire, son «défaitisme».

These assessments are typical of attitudes toward Themistius. He is often regarded as a false philosopher and a flatterer of emperors for the sake of personal glory. Some of his contemporaries would have agreed. Their views are treated in later chapters. Others clearly did not. In a letter to Themistius (*Ep.* 241), Libanius expressly declines to comment on philosophy, but calls his correspondent the leading orator of the day. It matters little that Libanius is attempting (unsuccessfully) to secure Themistius' influence on behalf of a friend. The remark must contain some positive assessment based on reality, even if

---

10. *A Conflict of Ideas in the Late Roman Empire: The Clash between the Senate and Valentinian I* (Oxford, 1952), 109.

11. *L'Empire chrétien*, 2d ed. (Paris, 1972), 234.

Libanius means only that Themistius was the most prominent Greek panegyrist or that he was the leading orator at Constantinople: Libanius did not possess the virtue of modesty to any great degree and undoubtedly reserved some prominence for himself, in either the style or the Antiochene location of his own oratory.[12] Since only four panegyrics antedate Libanius' remark, the deliberate exclusion of comment on philosophy could indicate that the sophist was aware of private speeches (Or. 20, 21, 23, 24, 26, 29) where Themistius discusses the relation of philosophy, rhetoric, flattery, and public life. If so, Libanius' assessment is based on a thorough knowledge of the speeches delivered before the year 360. Gregory of Nazianzus, whose level of acquaintance with Themistius' speeches cannot be determined, calls him the "king of words" (Ep. 24), and elsewhere notes that words mark him out just as ivory shoulders mark out the Pelopidae (Ep. 38). Gregory had once been a pupil of Basil of Neocaesarea, under whom Themistius too may have studied.[13]

The view that Themistius was merely a flatterer ignores his own account of his purposes as an orator. Throughout his life, he insisted that he was a philosopher and that he chose a political (or public) expression for his philosophy to benefit the state and society at large. This consisted largely of attempts to influence emperors to practice mildness, philanthropy, justice, and similar virtues. Naturally, he felt that his social and political views were more useful than those of contemporaries, and in this he may be correct. Emperors found his suggestions useful, or at least not particularly dangerous. The view that acquaintance with the literature and philosophy of the past engenders moral rectitude in society is hardly harmful, though not all contemporary Christians would be as easily persuaded as Christian emperors clearly were.[14] An attempt to create an upright society was Themistius' greatest concern. His speeches, imperial and private,

---

12. Missing here is any consideration of Himerius. I suggest later in this chapter (and in appendix 2) that Themistius had a low regard for the type of oratory represented by this contemporary. Libanius would have been more impressed, but professional rivalry stood in the way of any admission of this.

13. See chapter 2 for this suggestion.

14. I.e., those Christians who denied any utility to study of the ancient classics. Emperors naturally had less choice: some subjects were not Christians, and some form of accommodation with at least some of them was necessary.

were vehicles to spread philosophical perspectives learned early in life.[15]

That Themistius flattered emperors cannot be denied, but a (reasonable) distaste for panegyric has highly colored modern attitudes. Neither the philosopher nor the emperors, nor, indeed, most contemporaries, found the practice objectionable in and of itself. Panegyric was, after all, endemic in the fourth century and possessed a long history, with roots as much in the philosophical as in the rhetorical tradition. Further, Themistius' flattery was not flattery pure and simple: it was didactic, filled with ideals for emperors to emulate and with stimulants to further action. On occasion, he used flattery, or generous interpretations of events, to incline emperors favorably to his requests. That he failed on occasion is not surprising: he was only one adviser to emperors who held views of their own and had other advisers as well.

As a panegyrist, Themistius is unparalleled in the fourth century, and the nature and background of his speeches require some treatment here. The volume of his output places him at the top of the profession. No orator even comes close to his total. Himerius delivered more speeches, but few are imperial panegyrics.[16] Libanius, too, was prolific as an orator, but even the sum of his panegyrics and his speeches as a representative of Antioch does not exceed the number by Themistius. The same is true in the Latin tradition: not until the verse panegyrics by Claudian and Sidonius Apollinaris, among others, do we find the delivery of numerous panegyrics by a single author.[17]

The contrast with Libanius goes beyond numbers. The bulk of Libanius' imperial speeches were addressed to Julian, and most other emperors escape his praise. Jovian and Valens did not experience his eloquence, while Theodosius heard requests for social change, not panegyrics. Moreover, Libanius intimates that his panegyric of Constantius and Constans was delivered on request (Or. 59.4–6).[18] He avoided Christian emperors or was not asked to perform for them very often. One reason is his political and religious stance. In contrast,

---

15. For Themistius' education and early life, see chapter 2.

16. On the career of Himerius, cf. T.D. Barnes, CP 82 (1987): 206–25.

17. The extant collection of Latin prose panegyrics does contain speeches by different hands addressed to the same emperor, e.g., Constantine.

18. Cf. R. Foerster, Libanii Opera, vol. 4 (Leipzig, 1908), 202.

Themistius delivered panegyrics of all emperors in the East from Constantius to Theodosius and traveled to the West to speak in honor of Gratian. His own religious attitudes, though important, did not prevent him from addressing Christian emperors. His basic views inclined toward tolerance and acceptance, not opposition.[19] Naturally, he preferred emperors to adopt this perspective.[20]

Most importantly, Themistius differs from contemporary panegyrists in the content and structure of his speeches. By the fourth century, a standard form for the imperial oration, based on a tradition of great antiquity,[21] had emerged. In treatises on rhetoric ascribed to Menander Rhetor, a panegyric was to contain sections devoted to the native country or region of the emperor; his family, birth, upbringing, and education; his accomplishments and actions in war and peace, with some attention to the virtue that each exhibits; and a comparison of his reign with those of his predecessors.[22] This structure can be observed in most panegyrics of the fourth century, with minor deviations that do not detract from the prescription as a whole. No panegyric by Themistius follows this structure in even a general way, though the prescribed subjects occasionally appear in a different form. Themistius' panegyrics focus on philosophical themes, with other topics introduced to support his remarks. In one sense, they are exactly the reverse of the standard. Whereas Libanius or Julian can draw a philosophical conclusion about an emperor's sense of justice, for example, from a list of his actions, Themistius prefers to begin with an abstract discussion of justice before indicating that an emperor possesses this quality by adducing an instance or two.[23] Themistius' method makes his panegyrics less historical, and thus sometimes more difficult to analyze, than most other imperial speeches of the fourth century. Philosophical themes predominate, a fact noted already by contemporaries. The author of the hypothesis to *Oration* 2 wrote that Themistius established a philo-

---

19. Dagron, *Thémistios*, in too many places to cite individually, discusses the opposing views held by Libanius and Themistius. See also the brief discussions at various points in later chapters.

20. See the discussion of Themistius' religious views later in this chapter.

21. For example, Xenophon's *Agesilaus* is very similar. Cf. the remarks of D.A. Russell and N.G. Wilson, *Menander Rhetor* (Oxford, 1981), xv.

22. Cf. Russell and Wilson, *Menander Rhetor*, 76–95.

23. Gladis, *Themistii*, discusses and compares the panegyrics of Constantius by Themistius, Libanius, and Julian at some length.

sophical goal for his praise and drew everything in the speech to that end (2.24b). Themistius thus differs from Libanius, Julian, and Pacatus, who offer more traditional panegyrics. Not surprisingly, Claudius Mamertinus develops some philosophical themes in his *gratiarum actio* to Julian, but falls far short of the practice of Themistius. In the fourth century, the Christian Eusebius of Caesarea is perhaps closest to Themistius in the nature of his subject matter, but his themes naturally differ in some important ways.[24]

Consequently, Themistius is unique by the standards of the fourth century, though his work is not entirely without precedent. In speeches *On Kingship* to Trajan (*Or.* 1–4),[25] Dio Chrysostom develops philosophical themes and structures his speeches around these rather than the historical topics of most other panegyrics. At one level, the procedure is precisely the same. Dio Chrysostom, above all in *Oration* 3, describes the ideal emperor in Platonic terms, while implying that Trajan is an example of the ideal. Indeed, the characteristics of Trajan become important elements of the model ruler.[26] Themistius often adopts the same approach, most clearly in the panegyric of Gratian (*Or.* 13), but the technique is found throughout his work.[27] Moreover, he derives some ideas in his orations from Dio Chrysostom.[28]

Comparison with Dio Chrysostom is useful for a second aspect of Themistius' career. In *Oration* 3, Dio Chrysostom inveighs against the suggestion that he flattered for personal gain. In part, his description of an ideal emperor is designed to counter this view,[29] and Themistius,

---

24. Cf. F. Dvornik, *Early Christian and Byzantine Political Philosophy: Origins and Background* (Washington, D.C., 1966), 2:614–26, on Eusebius and his similarity to Themistius; also G.A. Kennedy, *Greek Rhetoric under Christian Emperors* (Princeton, 1983), 32–33. Dagron, *Thémistios*, 135–38 and passim, notes that there is no direct influence of Eusebius on Themistius.

25. Cf. C.P. Jones, *The Roman World of Dio Chrysostom* (Cambridge, Mass., 1978), 115–23.

26. Cf. Jones, *Dio Chrysostom*, 116–20, especially his comparison of details found in both Dio Chrysostom and Pliny.

27. Themistius mentions Dio Chrysostom several times in his speeches, each time with Trajan, in the context of emperors who honored or heeded the advice of philosophers, e.g., 5.63d, 11.145b, 13.173c.

28. Cf. J. Scharold, *Dion Chrysostomus und Themistius* (Burghausen, 1912) [which I have not seen]; J. Mesk, *Phil. Woch.* 54 (1934): 556–58; Dagron, *Thémistios*, 85–87, 126–28.

29. So Jones, *Dio Chrysostom*, 119–20.

who faced the same charge,[30] perhaps learned his similar response from this predecessor. Beginning with his first panegyric of Constantius, Themistius insists that his words were not gratuitous flattery but truth, which was visible only to a true philosopher.

In his career, Themistius also faced the charge that he was a sophist. That term should be examined here, in the context of similarity to Dio Chrysostom. Early in the fifth century, Synesius composed his *Dio*, which accused his subject of sophistry before a conversion to philosophy. Philostratus, however, considered Dio Chrysostom a philosopher who displayed sophistic tendencies in speeches (*VS* 1.7, pp. 486–88). This was probably closer to the truth and reflected the biographer's willingness to include philosophers who were considered sophists.[31] The disjunction of views indicates different meanings for the same term. While appellations of status were sometimes used loosely in the Second Sophistic, generally the word *rhetor* is applied to teachers of rhetoric and to those who used rhetoric to achieve practical goals. The name *philosopher* was reserved for teachers of philosophy. The term *sophist* was given to brilliant rhetors or philosophers whose characters were flawed and whose speeches were merely words devoid of intellectual content.[32]

The same distinction appears in the fourth century. Libanius was regarded as a "sophist" in a positive way, but the term was applied to Themistius negatively, forcing him to argue that he was not a sophist by Plato's definition. Contemporaries were not convinced, because they did not recognize Plato's definition as the operative meaning in the fourth century, at least in its application to philosophers. It appears, from Synesius and from Themistius' own remarks at various points, that rhetorical adornment in philosophy was disliked, especially by Neoplatonists, if Synesius can be taken to represent this point of view. As outlined in his early *Oration* 24, Themistius willingly uses rhetoric to make philosophy palatable.[33] In *Oration* 23, he coun-

---

30. See chapters 4 and 8 for discussions of debates with contemporaries.

31. Cf. Jones, *Dio Chrysostom*, 10–12, and now A. Cameron and J. Long, *Barbarians and Politics at the Court of Arcadius* (Berkeley and Los Angeles, 1993), 62–69.

32. For discussion, cf. G.W. Bowersock, *Greek Sophists in the Roman Empire* (Oxford, 1969), 10–14; C.P. Jones, in *Approaches to the Second Sophistic*, ed. G.W. Bowersock (University Park, Penn., 1974), 12–14; and idem, *Dio Chrysostom*, 9.

33. See the discussion of this speech in chapter 2.

ters charges of sophistry by examining himself in the light of Plato's definition and accuses opponents of innovation in their refusal to accept Plato's view.[34] A negative attitude toward the use of rhetoric in philosophy is thus evident by the middle of the fourth century and undoubtedly existed earlier.

Consciously or unconsciously, Themistius used orators of the Second Sophistic as models. Dio Chrysostom holds pride of place. Both Themistius and Dio were philosophers and orators who used rhetoric to adorn speeches of mainly philosophical content. One might include Themistius, as Philostratus apparently included Dio Chrysostom, among the "philosophers who were not, but seemed to be, sophists" (VS 1, p. 484), not because he was charged with sophistry, but because he reflects this practice of the Second Sophistic. In this context, it is interesting that Eunapius does not mention Themistius, though he promises to include the best philosophers and orators (VS, pp. 453, 454). Eunapius, it seems, fell prey to suggestions of contemporaries that Themistius was not a true philosopher or an outstanding orator, views by no means universal in the fourth century.[35]

In keeping with his knowledge of the Second Sophistic, Themistius was also familiar with Aelius Aristides.[36] This is hardly surprising, since Aristides and Dio Chrysostom were the most influential and copied Greek orators in the fourth century. Libanius, Julian, Synesius, and others were similarly influenced. For Themistius, however, structure was less influential than the style and content which he used as sources for his own speeches. He adopts and adapts items from the speeches of Aelius Aristides when, for example, he uses ideas on the unity of the empire from the panegyric of Rome (Or. 26 Keil) in his first panegyric of Valens and Valentinian (6.83c–d).[37] His remarks in the same speech on the harmony between emperors are based on Aristides' treatment of Marcus Aurelius and Lucius Verus (Or. 27 Keil, esp. §§22–39).

---

34. See chapter 4 for discussion of this speech and Or. 21 on a similar theme.

35. R.J. Penella, *Greek Philosophers and Sophists in the Fourth Century A.D.: Studies in Eunapius of Sardis* (Liverpool, 1990), 134–37, suggests that the biographer omitted Themistius, because, in addition to a difference in point of view, he was not linked professionally to the individuals who do appear.

36. Cf. Dagron, *Thémistios*, 82, 90, 118, n. 197.

37. Cf. Dagron, *Thémistios*, 90, with nn. 40–40 *bis*.

More striking is Themistius' knowledge, in *Oration* 5, of the *On Kingship* (*Or.* 35 Keil), whose authorship and date have been discussed since the beginning of this century.[38] These questions lie beyond the scope of this book, but it is reasonably safe to state that Aristides was regarded as the author in the fourth century.[39] Only a few months after Themistius uses this panegyric, he employs other speeches of Aristides (*Or.* 26, 27 Keil) in his first extant panegyric of Valens and Valentinian (*Or.* 6), which suggests that he read or reread the works of Aristides about this time.

Most notable in their similarity are the descriptions of the characters of the respective emperors. After an introduction, Aristides remarks in his *On Kingship* (*Or.* 35 Keil) that his emperor was worthy of the empire before his accession (§5), as Themistius also states of Jovian (5.65b). Both emphasize the peacefulness of uncontested accessions and the constancy of characters before and after that event (§§7–9; 5.66d–67a). Themistius (5.67a–b), like Aristides (§§15–19), mentions an imperial concern with justice, though Themistius does so in the context of Jovian's selection of his associates. The speeches are largely concerned with dissimilar topics, but one similarity remains. Each closes with a reference to the emperor's son and a request that the son follow in the footsteps of his father (§39; 5.71b). Themistius thus includes many of the topics of the *On Kingship* and discusses them in the same sequence, which suggests that he used Aristides' panegyric when he wrote his praise of Jovian, who is not likely to have recognized this fact. In this single instance, Themistius adopts, in part, the structure of a speech by Aristides. Most often, his use is limited to ideas and style.

With an inclination toward edifying oratory, Themistius had a low regard for speeches by orators like Himerius. For this reason, he was not interested in becoming a sophist as defined by the ability to speak ex tempore. On one occasion, he discusses an inability to do so,

---

38. For brief surveys, cf. C.A. Behr, *P. Aelius Aristides: The Complete Works.* Vol. 2, *Orations XVII–LIII* (Leiden, 1981), 399–400; C.P. Jones, *JRS* 62 (1972): 134.

39. The contention that the speech was added to the corpus of Aristides' work considerably after his death becomes increasingly difficult as one approaches and enters the fourth century, since time for diffusion of copies from an archetype that included the speech would be too short. Jones, *JRS* 62 (1972): 139, n. 42, suggests that Libanius may have known the speech as well.

without apparent regret, and emphasizes, almost certainly in imitation of Aristides, that true art demands time for composition.[40] His view is clear in *Oration 24*, where he describes sophists as interested only in applause (24.302a). Elsewhere, he displays a negative attitude toward the "singing"[41] sophists (22.265b, 27.336c, 28.341c), noting that their primary interest was euphony and adornment of speeches, with little regard for content. Themistius' concern was utility, in imperial and other speeches. Adornment and resulting pleasure are welcome if they make philosophy palatable to audiences, but should not be the primary goal. Finally, in Themistius' view, philosophers were obliged to deliver speeches to improve the lot of humanity and to play a greater role in society in their efforts to reach as many people as possible.[42] Most often, he supports this assertion by rehearsing the names of past philosophers, including Socrates, Plato, and Aristotle, who took an active role in public life and attempted to expound their views publicly. They, Themistius reminds audiences in debates about his position, had acted as he was acting, both in politics and in attempts to stir the populace to virtue.[43] Occasionally, he uses this activity of predecessors to attack his opposition, who had withdrawn from society.[44]

The recollection of philosophers of the past had a further purpose. As panegyrics, Themistius' speeches belong to the *epideictic* branch of oratory, devoted to the application of praise and blame. So it was classified in the earliest treatments of rhetoric, and so too by

---

40. See chapter 7 on the circumstances surrounding the delivery of *Or.* 25. On Aristides, cf. Philostratus, *VS*, pp. 582–83, for an occasion when he asked for a day for composition as Themistius does in *Or.* 25, and C.A. Behr, *Aelius Aristides and the Sacred Tales* (Amsterdam, 1968), 46, n. 21.

41. A technical term that Himerius applies to his own oratory; cf. Méridier, *Le philosophe*, 10–14, for discussion. On Himerius' oratory, cf. Kennedy, *Greek Rhetoric*, 141–49.

42. On these and the following points, see the discussion of *Or.* 24 in chapter 2 and appendix 2. Cf. G. Fowden, *JHS* 102 (1982): 33–59, for the normal withdrawal of fourth-century philosophers from society at large.

43. For discussion of *Or.* 21, 23, 26, 29, 31, and 34, see chapters 4 and 8 and appendix 2.

44. This helps to date *Or.* 23, 26, and 29 to the reign of Constantius, since at any later date Themistius could have used the examples of Priscus and Maximus as evidence that philosophers other than himself were involved with the imperial court.

Menander Rhetor: "Epideictic speeches, then, fall under the two headings of blame and praise."[45] Speeches of this type were delivered by both philosophers and orators, in treatments at first, like Gorgias' *Helen*, largely confined to mythology and fantasy. Not until Isocrates' *Evagoras* and Xenophon's *Agesilaus* do speeches on contemporary or near-contemporary individuals occur.[46] Interestingly, Isocrates was an orator and Xenophon a philosopher; that Themistius refers only to Xenophon symbolizes the dispute that had long ago arisen between rhetors and philosophers, with each group claiming their own profession as the more qualified to deliver epideictic oratory. To put it simply, the disagreement centered on the relative validity of form and content.[47]

The application of praise and blame for virtues and faults of contemporaries was a sensitive matter, especially when the subject possessed imperial power, and occasionally wrath. This left the practitioners of the craft open to charges of flattery when they were successful; Themistius felt the sting of rebuke on this account several times. A valid, if not always effective, counterattack was the statement that he spoke the truth, which cannot be flattery. A second argument was his career as philosopher. By virtue of their profession, philosophers spoke the truth only. "I thought that it was unlawful for you to flatter or deceive," wrote Julian (*Ep. ad Them.* 254b), chastising the philosopher for exceeding the bounds of moderation in his *protrepticus* to the Caesar. In his first panegyric, Themistius makes the same point from a different angle. As a philosopher, he could see the truth about Constantius and his virtues; others perceived it only dimly. To drive his point home, the philosopher describes the perceptions of different observers of Constantius, in terms that recall Alcibiades' description of Socrates in Plato's *Symposium*.

Themistius is claiming that the description and discussion of virtues is most properly the preserve of philosophers and voicing his view on a long-standing dispute between rhetoric and philosophy. By the fourth century, panegyric had largely become the preserve of rhetors, while philosophers tended to withdraw from society and

---

45. Trans. Russell and Wilson, *Menander Rhetor*, 3.
46. Cf. Russell and Wilson, *Menander Rhetor*, xiii–xv, for brief discussion.
47. There is no need to rehearse here the long history of this dispute, which goes back to Plato at least.

public life. Themistius' perspective is an attempt to reclaim a division of epideictic oratory for philosophy. His views on this point, combined with his willingness to engage in the public life of the empire, bring to mind some philosophers of the first and second centuries. Musonius Rufus and many of his pupils, such as Dio Chrysostom, Epictetus, and Euphrates of Tyre, were philosophers who also possessed great eloquence and, in addition, were involved in public life.[48] This coincides with the suggestion that Themistius' oratory has its nearest antecedents in the second, not the fourth, century. Like his predecessors, Themistius undertook civic obligations.[49] Though he was not a benefactor, like Herodes Atticus, it should never be forgotten that he used his oratory not only to praise emperors, but also as an official representative of his (adopted) city.

Apposite here is a newly developed model of at least some rhetoric of the fourth century: the suggestion that panegyric and other forms of public oratory are careful reminders to emperors and imperial administrators of the need to rule in accord with the strictures of *paideia* and that philosophers inherently possessed the *parrhésia*—not so much freedom of speech as independence of status—to voice such reminders appropriately.[50] Themistius' frequent claims to philosophy and appeals to the traditions of the past can best be seen in this light. He needed to establish his position as philosopher to have the full weight of the classical tradition behind him in his struggle to achieve the cooperation of emperors. This tradition sought to ensure that rulers governed their subjects with mildness and temperance, with benevolence and kindness, and with tolerance and sometimes deference. Collectively, these constitute a *paideia* based on a knowledge and awareness of the classical authors, philosophical as well as others. Thorough grounding in these principles would create rulers and officials who could govern in accord with what might almost be called proper etiquette.[51]

---

48. For brief discussion, cf. Jones, *Dio Chrysostom*, 13. Themistius mentions each of these, except Euphrates, at least once, and some of his views have antecedents, if not always their origin, in Dio and Musonius.

49. On the responsibilities of orators and sophists to their cities, cf. Bowersock, *Greek Sophists*, 26–29.

50. P. Brown, *Power and Persuasion in Late Antiquity: Towards a Christian Empire* (Madison, 1992), esp. chap. 2. His discussion of *parrhésia* is at 61–70.

51. This is not so very different from the program of reading outlined by, e.g., Thomas Elyot in his *Boke named the Gouernour*, published in England in

Themistius was perhaps unfortunate to live in an age when the principles of *paideia* had largely been forgotten by the throne. With the exceptions of Constantius and Julian (and Gratian in the West), his emperors, and their advisers too, were men of military background, often devoid, if contemporary writers are worthy of belief, of the advantages of a classical education. Precisely for this reason, Themistius at times seems too insistent. He needed to remind the emperors of principles they ought to have had by training and of the traditional position that he, as philosopher, occupied. Lack of the appropriate education in the fourth century was perhaps not the only reason. The instability of the third century lay between Themistius and his most successful predecessors in imperial times. It is not surprising, possible loss of material notwithstanding, that imperial panegyric emerges once again with the new stability established by Diocletian and Constantine.[52] In the third century, when traditional government was not as evident as it had been earlier, or even possible, appeals to the injunctions of *paideia* offered little utility, precisely because these requests demanded a shared sense of intellectual heritage. This tradition had been broken and needed reaffirmation. To do this, orators went back to the most recent models available to them: Dio Chrysostom and Aelius Aristides in Greek, Pliny in Latin.[53] It might even be suggested that the treatises of Menander were composed out of necessity in Diocletianic times precisely because a new period of classicizing Greek oratory had just begun.[54] Like many of his counterparts, Themistius was attempting to repair the tradition; unlike them, he found it necessary to reestablish the philosophical underpinnings of this perspective. His fondness for Dio Chrysostom was a result of his own inclination toward a philosophical approach and of the fact that Dio had previously fulfilled a similar role.

It was no easy task. A century or more of government by different

---

1531: the sons of the nobility and the gentry would almost inherently become suitable civil servants and representatives of the King by following a proper course of education.

52. For remarks, with a different emphasis, about the directions for panegyric under the Tetrarchy, cf. S. MacCormack, *Art and Ceremony in Late Antiquity* (Berkeley and Los Angeles, 1981), 3–5.

53. Examples of the use of Greek models earlier in this chapter; for the use of Pliny, cf. S. MacCormack, *REAug* 22 (1976): 29–77.

54. On authorship and date, Russell and Wilson, *Menander Rhetor*, xxxiv–xl.

standards had created new expectations on the part of the governed as well as their rulers. Some no doubt preferred this to a return to more ancient values. At the same time, even among those who, like Themistius, preferred the old, differences of opinion existed. Themistius was more willing to adapt to the new reality than, for example, Libanius or Julian, whose speeches mirror the prescripts of Menander Rhetor more closely.[55] Meanwhile, the period of Themistius' own life witnessed the emergence of yet another new direction, as emperors adopted Christianity and attempted to rule in accord with the injunctions of that perspective. In the early part of Themistius' career, Christianity did not so much affect rhetoric itself as engender a greater unwillingness of emperors to adopt traditional *paideia*: ecclesiastics began more and more to seduce, and sometimes to turn by force, the emperors' ears to their perspective.

The effect of Eusebius was negligible: he can in no way be considered a part of the public life of the empire.[56] While his thoughts on the nature of government exercised some influence on Christian thinkers, any similarity of perspective shared by Eusebius and Themistius was a consequence of the times in which they lived. Christians and non-Christians alike were compelled to rethink their attitudes to the imperial administration, and similar responses to the same situation naturally resulted. It was not so very remarkable that emperors took an active part in the religious life of the empire. They had often done that, as the example of Elagabalus makes absolutely clear. The greatest difference was the extent to which personal religious perspective was successfully integrated into the administration. Elagabalus, as high priest, attempted to insinuate his own Baal into the Roman pantheon of deities. He was ridiculed, not least because the Emesene divinity had few adherents outside the Lebanon. Wholesale mockery was not possible in the fourth century: Christians were everywhere and in large numbers.[57]

---

55. MacCormack, *Art and Ceremony*, 5–6, points out that late Roman panegyrists were selective in their adherence to the rules of the rhetorical tradition exemplified by Menander Rhetor.

56. Cf. T.D. Barnes, *Constantine and Eusebius* (Cambridge, Mass., 1980), 265–67. See comments earlier in this chapter for Eusebius' lack of influence on Themistius.

57. The extent of Christianization is still a matter of debate and beyond the purpose of this book, but I incline to the view that it was already significant by

Christians also, as the career of Themistius progressed, began more and more to adapt the old education to their own purposes. Leading individuals of talent, Prohaeresius, Basil of Neocaesarea and his homonymous son Basil of Caesarea, Gregory of Nazianzus, Gregory of Nyssa, and later John Chrysostom, for example, all received a thoroughly classical training in rhetoric. Except for John Chrysostom, they shared a Cappadocian origin, though Prohaeresius, who was not an ecclesiastic, does not quite fit in with the rest of the group. Clearly, Christians could receive the basics of rhetorical training in that region, probably because of the influence of Gregory Thaumaturgus.[58] In the fourth century, Basil of Neocaesarea enjoyed considerable success, offering a combination of rhetoric and philosophy at the first levels of rhetorical training (his students typically furthered their education in rhetoric and philosophy elsewhere).[59] Only Prohaeresius and Basil of Neocaesarea developed and prosecuted traditional careers; the others abandoned or never attempted to follow the old pattern, choosing instead the episcopate to display their considerable talents for oratory. For such men, sermon and theological disputation replaced rhetorical exercise and display of talent on public occasions. Naturally, they could operate on traditional lines. Gregory's *epitaphios* for his father is not very different, in terms of rhetorical background and prosecution of argument, from Libanius' long lament over Julian in *Oration* 18.[60] Examples could be multiplied, but the point is clear: Christian orators used the same techniques, but normally for a different purpose. They were no less capable of capitalizing on an audience's keen interest in

the reign of Constantine and continued to be more so during the life of Themistius.

58. The tradition may have begun with an unidentifiable student of Herodes Atticus attested at Neocaesarea; cf. P. Moraux, *Une imprécation funéraire à Néocésarée*. Bibl. arch. et hist. de l'Inst. franc. d'Archéol. d'Istanbul 4 (Paris, 1959), and J. Robert and L. Robert, *Bulletin Épigraphique* (1960), no. 387.

59. On the effects of this, it would be foolish to attempt an improvement on R.R. Ruether, *Gregory of Nazianzus: Rhetor and Philosopher* (Oxford, 1969). Ruether offers, first of all, a useful account of the background to rhetoric in the fourth century (1–17), then, in later chapters, shows in great detail Gregory's use of classical rhetoric and philosophy in his life and work. Her discussion is applicable to the other Cappadocians as well and, indeed, to Themistius, since a suggestion that he too received some training in rhetoric from Basil of Neocaesarea appears in chapter 2.

60. Cf., for discussion of this speech, Ruether, *Gregory of Nazianzus*, 112–15.

displays of rhetoric. Whether this is now Christian rhetoric or classical rhetoric employing Christian themes is less important than the recognition that a transformation was underway.[61]

A difficult question is that of the new Christian orators' influence on public affairs. More to the point, was Themistius in direct competition with them? And did any of his opponents belong to this group? The answer to the first question is apparently negative, certainly before the reign of Theodosius. No evidence indicates that Christian orators in the East habitually practiced their oratory on those occasions when a Themistius or a Libanius might be persuaded or expected to display his talents, to make known his views (most often on behalf of a larger group) on issues of public policy, or to argue for a specific course of action.[62] That bishops commented, sometimes fulminated, on such issues from the pulpit need not be doubted. Their influence was in consequence limited, because the audience consisted primarily of coreligionists, not the entire citizen body. Within the group, the effect was perhaps more powerful. Even without usurping the role of the philosopher, the power of the episcopate generally gave these pronouncements greater authority than even a philosopher with *parrhésia*. In some cases, theological disputes or other factors may have relegated bishops to levels of little power, but under normal circumstances, a position of authority combined with an emperor's willingness to attune his ear to the injunctions of an ecclesiastic had a profound effect. Such incidents as Gratian's refusal, on episcopal advice, to wear the pontifical robe, Ambrose's reaction to the massacre at Thessalonica,[63] or, in an earlier generation in the East,

---

61. On the Cappadocian fathers, cf. most recently, J. Pelikan, *Christianity and Classical Culture: The Metamorphosis of Natural Theology in the Christian Encounter with Hellenism* (New Haven, 1993) [which reached me too late for detailed reference here].

62. Synesius is an obvious exception, but he represents a later development some years after the death of Themistius, quite in line with Brown's recent suggestion in *Power and Persuasion* that Christians, especially bishops, began to usurp more and more of the traditional role of the philosopher. On his involvement with the imperial court, before he became bishop, cf. Cameron and Long, *Barbarians and Politics*.

63. Cf. Brown, *Power and Persuasion*, 109–13, though I am less inclined than he is to regard the result as Theodosius' capitulation to traditional values and more as an attempt by Ambrose to control the throne—especially in the context of frequent attempts by Symmachus and others to have state subsi-

Constantius' quick reinstatement of Athanasius after receiving a threat of civil war and sensing the inevitable with the see vacant[64] reveal the power of the new hierarchy. The willingness of the Alexandrians and Milanese to support their bishops against the throne in these confrontations gave the prelates even greater authority.

Tantalizing hints in his work indicate that Themistius was aware of the new reality and its negative possibilities. The praise he receives from Christian orators indicates that he was not in direct competition with them on public issues and perhaps that his views were more innocuous to their classically trained ears than the ideas they heard elsewhere. Or it might be an attempt to disarm him, to dissuade him from a program that is generally well hidden, but occasionally rises close enough to the surface to be seen. Early in his career, he already suggests that Christian religion was one of the factors drawing people away from philosophy.[65] During the reign of Valens, he begins to refer to Christian scripture, in part because this ruler was not as willing as Constantius, for example, to give even the appearance of accepting older values. Themistius was clever and flexible enough to realize that a concept common to Homer and Christian scripture could be expressed in terms of the latter rather than the former if the opportunity to achieve his intended result, some vestigial preservation of traditional values, was enhanced. Continued influence in several reigns indicates a measure of success in his attempt to forge an alliance between two groups on the basis of elements common to both. To do so, he needed to combat extreme elements in each camp; dissidents on both sides opposed him. Non-Christians like Libanius and Julian were unable or unwilling to accept concessions and reacted unfavorably. Christians, too, offered opposition, though less identifiably as individuals in the fourth century, partly because even the leading exponents used the tools and traditions of rhetoric to justify and promote their distaste for classical oratory, and partly because the work of others has not survived. The task of separating the Christian

---

dies and the images of Roman religion restored. Ambrose calculated the risk very carefully and won.

64. Cf. now T.D. Barnes, *Athanasius and Constantius: Theology and Politics in the Constantinian Empire* (Cambridge, Mass., 1993), 89–92.

65. See the discussion of *Or.* 24 in chapter 2. The other factors are rhetoric for rhetoric's sake and Iamblichan theurgy.

perspective from the oratorical is, accordingly, sometimes difficult. Julian's so-called school law attempted to do exactly this; one bizarre response, the attempt of Apollinares and his homonymous son to rewrite the Pentateuch in hexameter verse, reveals both the depth of the problem and Christian need for the old training.

During the career of Themistius, the continuing development of a Christian rhetoric was a problem he had to face. It did not, however, spill over extensively into the public arena. Christian orators still tended to exercise their talents in a different forum, though their effect on the imperial court was not always less powerful as a result. Notably, during the fourth century in the East, appeals to traditional values devolved entirely upon practitioners of the old religion. The efforts of a Eusebius failed in this period to engender a Christian twin to classical rhetoric, so immersed was the fourth century in the values and culture of second-century oratory. The blinkered vision of hind-sight saw an earlier age as the zenith of a *paideia* common to elite and throne. Trajan, Antoninus Pius, and Marcus Aurelius were emperors who ruled within the limits prescribed for them by the leading orators of the day, and a longing for the imagined past in some quarters is not surprising during a period of transformation. But too much had changed. Julian could no more be a Marcus Aurelius[66] than Libanius an Aelius Aristides (in spite of common medical complaints) or Maximus of Ephesus an Apollonius of Tyana. Julian's failure to achieve consensus is evidence enough. Even a more moderate position, Themistius' attempt to establish new philosophical foundations along old lines, failed in the end to gain universal appeal. His occasional success may also be an illusion, if his emperors, or some of them (Valens is the leading candidate), merely feigned acceptance in an effort to appease, for political reasons, a still significant portion of the governing elites. A world in flux engenders different responses; Themistius offered a bridge between old and new and was more successful than most non-Christians in maintaining a high level of influence during a long career. In a significant way, the values of rhetoric, Christian or traditional, have little to do with it. More to the point is a sense of practical reality and a desire to offer an alternative based on ideals that all could accept. That was, after all, precisely the

66. Cf. C. Lacombrade, *Pallas* 14 (1967): 9–22, for Julian's inclinations in this direction.

reason for the imagined success of Dio Chrysostom and Aelius Aristides.[67]

The suggestion that Themistius is uncharacteristic of his own century in oratory applies to philosophy as well. A few aspects of his thought indicate that he was in some ways the last true Peripatetic,[68] but he reveals an extensive knowledge of Plato as well and employed this in panegyrics. Even a cursory examination of the source apparatus in the Teubner text shows that Themistius uses Aristotle rarely and employs Plato's dialogues much more often.[69] The most frequent references are to the *Republic* and the *Laws*, but Themistius alludes to more than twenty dialogues of Plato and uses many passages of a given work.[70] Most references are verbal echoes of no great philosophical importance, but the scope of his knowledge of Plato is evident.[71] He himself claims to have studied Plato's work in some detail (10.130d–131a).

It is not enough to hold that Themistius was a late Peripatetic and nothing more.[72] He praises his father for a desire to harmonize Plato and Aristotle, and his own extensive use of Plato points in the same direction.[73] Consequently, he can be regarded as an eclectic, at least in a limited sense. But there is more. His approach to Aristotle and Plato does not reflect the philosophical preoccupation of his age. The *Para-*

---

67. The fourth century seems to have forgotten that these representatives of the Second Sophistic had their share of detractors as well.

68. H.J. Blumenthal, *Phronesis* 21 (1976): 82–83; idem, in *Arktouros: Hellenic Studies presented to Bernard M. W. Knox on the occasion of his 65th birthday*, ed. G.W. Bowersock, W. Burkert, and M.C.J. Putnam (Berlin, 1979), 391–400 (revised in *Aristotle Transformed: The Ancient Commentators and Their Influence*, ed. R. Sorabji [London, 1990], 113–23).

69. Professor R.B. Todd kindly made available to me a few pages of B. Colpi, *Die paideia des Themistios: Ein Beitrag zur Geschichte der Bildung im vierten Jahrhundert nach Christus* (Bern, 1988), who lists and discusses Themistius' use of Plato (85–93) and Aristotle (95 ff.) in his speeches.

70. For knowledge of Plato's dialogues in the second century A.D., cf. P. De Lacy, in *Approaches to the Second Sophistic*, ed. G.W. Bowersock (University Park, Penn., 1974), 4–10. For the works of Plato most used by the Neoplatonists, cf. R.T. Wallis, *Neoplatonism* (London, 1972), 19.

71. Blumenthal, *Arktouros*, 393, points out that Themistius tends to use parts of Plato's philosophy which the Neoplatonists left aside.

72. Cf. the remarks of F.M. Schroeder and R.B. Todd, *Two Greek Aristotelian Commentators on the Intellect* (Toronto, 1990), 34.

73. On his father's influence, see chapter 2.

phrases indicate that he was concerned with the discovery and dissemination of Aristotle's original views on their own terms. Though no
direct evidence is available, his view on Plato was probably the
same.[74] The Neoplatonists tended to focus on the exposition of their
own philosophical views, a valid but very different approach to the
study of philosophy. Plato and Aristotle were useful to them primarily
as sources to be pillaged for phrases and ideas that supported, in or
out of context, their own views.[75]

Themistius' inclination to harmonize Plato and Aristotle and his
desire to elucidate their original meanings reflect, more than anything
else, the preoccupations of the Middle Platonists, a nebulous group of
philosophers about whom too little is known to form an accurate
picture.[76] Generally, however, this group represents a wide variety of
attitudes toward Aristotle and the relation of his philosophy to Plato.
Some were hostile toward Aristotle and the Peripatetics; others, including some who accepted many of Aristotle's views, regarded the
Lyceum as little more than an alternate form of Platonism and attempted to harmonize the two schools on this basis. Another group
was more or less indifferent on the question of harmony. Given this
range, it is difficult to locate Themistius' philosophy accurately, but
his preoccupations, as well as the problems that he did not address,
make him more a late Middle Platonist than a Neoplatonist. The label
is useful largely because it transposes his views from the fourth century to a period before Neoplatonism.[77]

A few remarks on the *Paraphrase* of the *de anima* may clarify
Themistius' philosophical position. Essentially, he rewrites Aristotle's
treatise in his own words, adding his own commentary throughout.[78]

---

74. Note his attempt to reaffirm Plato's definition of the sophist in *Or.* 23.

75. I do not mean to imply that the Neoplatonists did nothing else or that
they never understood Plato and Aristotle accurately, but the basic approach
to Plato and Aristotle was different from that of the Middle Platonists. On this
question, cf. Wallis, *Neoplatonism*, 16–25.

76. J. Dillon, *The Middle Platonists* (London, 1977), is a recent survey.
Again, the Neoplatonists were not necessarily against harmonization, if it
was on their own terms.

77. Neoplatonists—a term that is accurate enough if its use is limited to a
general approach to Plato in a specific period—were naturally not an entirely
homogeneous group.

78. Cf. Schroeder and Todd, *Two Greek Aristotelian Commentators*, 35–36, for
a more detailed treatment of Themistius' procedure in several *Paraphrases*.

Most of this is designed to elucidate and, more importantly, to defend Aristotle. To do this, Themistius frequently discusses the views of other philosophers, including Aristotle's predecessors and later writers. Thales, Anaxagoras, Empedocles, Democritus, Zeno, Theophrastus, Plato, Alexander of Aphrodisias, and Porphyry are among those named. Recent research has suggested that Themistius knew and was occasionally influenced by Neoplatonist views on the soul and intellect, including those of Plotinus; the resultant approach was not purely Aristotelian at certain points.[79] But the primary objective of elucidating and accepting Aristotle's views remains always visible. Unlike contemporaries, Themistius harmonizes Plato with Aristotle, rather than Aristotle with Plato, and his *Paraphrases* are generally of Aristotelian counterparts to works of Plato favored by the Neoplatonists.[80] Precisely this approach makes Themistius so different as a philosopher and so difficult to classify accurately. The label "Peripatetic" is perhaps most applicable, if it is regarded as a general adherence to Aristotle, not to a school of philosophy in the normal sense.

One point deserves further comment. Themistius insisted throughout his life that he was a true philosopher, deserving by that position the status of *parrhésia*. Yet there was little interaction between Themistius the academic philosopher and Themistius the politician. It might be thought, and indeed it has been suggested,[81] that Themistius was doing little more than posing as a philosopher, that he pretended to be one to avoid charges of insincerity in his speeches to emperors. That he did face such accusations is not a sufficient reply; in any case, other factors, some outlined earlier in this chapter, were as much responsible. Similarly, that he wrote his *Paraphrases* and taught students does not absolve him: academics even today are not averse to intimating that some contemporaries are mere poseurs. In contrast, Themistius began his career as a philosopher and first entered the realm of imperial politics from that position. Present-day politicians normally first prosecute another occupation and are not automatically castigated, to choose one example, as incompetent lawyers when they embark on public life. The reverse is often true, since competence in

---

79. Cf. ibid., 35, with n. 115, and the literature cited there, as well as notes to the translation of the *Paraphrase* of *de anima*, 3.4–8, in that volume.

80. E.g., the *Paraphrase* of the *de anima* as a counterpart to the *Timaeus*.

81. See the quotations at the beginning of this chapter.

one field frequently provides the opportunity to enter another, provided that the ambition and the will exist. Themistius was both able and willing; other philosophers of his generation, those he characterizes as elusive figures in the shadows, were not. A peculiar concession to the view of these latter individuals has led some to a negative view of Themistius, who continued to be appreciated for philosophy after his entry into politics. That appreciation is evident from the actions of Celsus,[82] who volunteered to join the Senate in 359 to obtain an association with Themistius as philosopher (Lib. *Ep.* 86).

Themistius was hardly unique in the fourth century, but few others with similar views are known. His father Eugenius, if Themistius does not credit him with too many of his own views, had the same perspective, and Maximus of Byzantium is perhaps to be included as well. Basil of Neocaesarea may be another example, but to a Christian other ideas were more important. A philosopher of Sicyon who abandoned the teaching of Iamblichus can be included,[83] while Themistius' popularity as a teacher suggests that others existed, though some of these may have turned away: Themistius complains on one occasion that his opposition in the debates included former students.[84] These had perhaps come under the influence of philosophers more characteristic of the fourth century.

In one area, Themistius was obliged to depart some distance from a second-century perspective. With Christianity dominant at the imperial court, it is not surprising that Themistius discussed matters of religion in his speeches.[85] In his speech to Jovian, the philosopher attempts to convince the emperor to allow all religions to exist without threat of persecution. This is as much a reaction to the policies of Julian as fear for the future of pagans. Themistius was concerned with freedom of religious expression and promoted religious plural-

---

82. On whom, cf. J. Vanderspoel, *Historia* 36 (1987): 383–84.

83. This philosopher of Sicyon abandoned the teachings of Iamblichus for the Academy and the Lyceum (23.295b). Themistius' use of these terms may imply that he was not averse to the ancient labels. On this philosopher, see the article cited in n. 82, the brief discussion later in this chapter and chapter 4.

84. See chapter 4.

85. I discuss his views on religious plurality here, because it permeates his life and work, even before he delivered his panegyric of Jovian.

ity vigorously. That the concept was basic to his philosophical position and not a reaction to specific circumstances is evident from his attempt to deflect Valens' persecution of non-Arian Christians. He employed the same arguments in that speech, known only from a summary by Socrates (*HE* 4.32),[86] as he does with Jovian. Byzantine and Arabic sources record a similar attempt to persuade Julian to abandon persecution of Christianity, but no details survive. The only indication of success is recorded by Socrates, who states that Valens heeded the philosopher to some extent. Jovian died not long after Themistius' plea, and some rescripts on religious matters are more likely the work of Valentinian.[87] Julian never abandoned his persecution.

Themistius' argument for religious plurality is similar to that of Symmachus. He argues that God created a diversity:

> He wants Syrians to be citizens of one type, Greeks to be citizens of another type, and Egyptians citizens of a third type; even the Syrians he does not want to be alike, but he has actually broken them down into small units.[88] For there is not one person who understands matters in exactly the same way as a neighbor, but one thinks in this way, another in that way. Why do we then compel the impossible? (5.70a)

Symmachus expresses much the same sentiment:

> Everyone has his own customs, his own religious practices; the divine mind has assigned to different cities different religions to be their guardians. Each man is given at birth a separate soul; in the same way each people is given its own special genius to take care of its destiny. (*Rel.* 3.8; trans. Barrow)

Both Themistius (5.68d) and Symmachus (*Rel.* 3.10) focus on the existence of multiple paths to the divine. The shared ideas seem to indi-

---

86. The Latin version found in some texts of Themistius is a Renaissance forgery. Cf. R. Foerster, *NeueJbfürPäd* 6 (1900): 74–93.

87. See chapter 6 for discussion.

88. κατακερματίζω is often used in philosophical contexts to denote the division of large units into smaller, separate items; cf. *LSJ*, s.v.

cate that Themistius and Symmachus used a common source, even if these advocates of pagan tradition exchanged views when Themistius was at Rome in 357 and 376.[89]

The source is probably Porphyry, some of whose work was known in the West in translations by Marius Victorinus.[90] Symmachus almost certainly owes much to Porphyry,[91] and there is, prima facie, no reason to deny the Neoplatonist some credit for the views of Themistius, who may have known Porphyry's arguments without accepting them in their entirety. While his attitude toward Neoplatonist philosophy may counsel caution, other considerations suggest that Themistius had some of Porphyry's views in mind when he wrote *Oration* 5. The reference to Syrians, Greeks, and Egyptians may denote the three major views of the fourth century, with the Syrians and Greeks denoting Christianity and Hellenism, respectively. The Egyptians would then represent Iamblichan theurgy, if Themistius had in mind Porphyry's *Letter to Anebo*, where Egypt is the symbolic home of mystery religion.[92] Naturally, Iamblichus' own *de mysteriis Aegyptiorum* is relevant: he draws extensively on the Hermetic tradition and notes its links with Egypt.[93] The remark about divisions among the Syrians is then a pointed statement on the prevalence of theological dispute between groups of Christians. Just after the passage quoted, Themistius refers to an Empedocles who is a poor interpreter of the divine laws, but specifies that the philosopher of old is not his target (5.70b). In his speech for Gratian (13.178a), Themistius praises the Roman Senate for holding to tradition and not yielding to Empedocles, who seems to

---

89. Some of Themistius' work was known in the West. Vettius Agorius Praetextatus, who died in 384, translated into Latin Themistius' *Paraphrase* of the *Analytica* (Boeth. *de interpret. ed. sec.* 1.289).

90. Cf. P. Hadot, *Porphyre et Victorinus* (Paris, 1968).

91. P. Courcelle, *REA* 64 (1962): 131, notes the debt in one sentence. In *Grace, Politics and Desire: Essays on Augustine*, ed. H.A. Meynell (Calgary, 1990), 179–93, I discuss this question from a different angle and reach the conclusion that Augustine retracted (*Retract.* 1.4.3) a statement on religious plurality that he had made at *Soliloq.* 1.13.23 (*sed non ad eam* [i.e., *sapientiam*] *una via pervenitur*) precisely because he withdrew from his (Porphyrian) Neoplatonist views as he developed as a Christian thinker.

92. The view of Dagron, *Thémistios*, 154–56.

93. The Hermetic tradition has been elucidated by G. Fowden, *The Egyptian Hermes: A Historical Approach to the Late Pagan Mind* (Cambridge, 1986). Cf. esp. 131–41 on Iamblichus.

represent Christianity or a Christian figure in some way.[94] In contrast to Themistius' generally milder approach to Christianity, this section of *Oration* 5 may adopt the attitude of Porphyry, and some of the arguments may derive from the Neoplatonist.

The details of Porphyry's views cannot be established with certainty. Because he wrote a treatise *Against the Christians*, it is clear that he was, at one point in his life,[95] opposed to Christianity. This opposition did not necessarily include the desire to see Christians persecuted out of existence. Certainly, some pagans attacked Christianity; an example is an unnamed philosopher, perhaps a pupil of Iamblichus,[96] at Nicomedia in 303 (Lact. *Div. Inst.* 5.2). Similarity of argument in Themistius and Symmachus leads to the conclusion that Porphyry had also argued for religious plurality on some occasion. If the two views, on opposition and plurality, can be dated to different periods in Porphyry's life (this is hardly certain), the problem of holding both attitudes disappears. If not, a desire for persecution of Christians is not incompatible with a view that Christians, not pagans, ought to be more tolerant of different religions. In other words, Porphyry could argue for religious plurality and for hostility toward Christianity at the same time. If so, he perhaps offered an ideal situation and a practical solution, which Themistius, as would be his nature, may have adopted. From whatever source Themistius developed his views on religious plurality, however, his attitude did not cause serious problems for a series of Christian emperors.

Themistius' probable use of Porphyry on this point indicates a willingness to adopt some aspects of contemporary philosophy. It indicates, too, a respect for Porphyry as a philosopher.[97] His view of Iamblichus was different. Themistius praises a philosopher of Sicyon

---

94. There is no evidence to establish this positively, but Themistius can hardly mean anything else. Dagron, *Thémistios*, 159–63, suggests that Themistius means Jesus. But the bishop of Rome or Ambrose in the later instance may represent other possibilities. W. Portmann, *Geschichte in der spätantiken Panegyrik* (Frankfurt am Main, 1988), 270, n. 18, and 181, rejects this for *Or.* 5 and accepts it for *Or.* 13.

95. The date of this treatise is a vexatious problem; cf. T.D. Barnes, *JTS* 24 (1973): 424–42, with references to earlier treatments.

96. So T.D. Barnes, *GRBS* 19 (1978): 105, with n. 28.

97. Dagron, *Thémistios*, passim, sees a few other echoes of Porphyry's philosophy. Porphyry is named in the *Paraphrase* of the *de anima*, 31.2–3.

who had been a student of Iamblichus (23.295b) for abandoning the teachings of his master for the Academy and the Lyceum,[98] implying that Iamblichus was not worthy to be called a philosopher. At the beginning of *Oration* 24, Themistius notes that the "the song from the Lebanon" (24.301b) is one of the pursuits that draw people away from the study of rational philosophy. This too is a reference to Iamblichus, born at Chalcis ad Libanum.[99] These passages reveal Themistius' awareness of contemporary philosophy and religious belief, even if he did not adopt them as his own views.

Born ca 317 in the reign of Licinius,[100] Themistius lived his formative years during the sole reign of Constantine. He saw with his own impressionable eyes the changes that the defeat of Licinius engendered and grew up in an empire that had become Christian at the most important level of administration. To this, others may have been impervious, but Themistius and his family, though pagan, accommodated themselves to the new empire. The result of his rhetorical training under Basil of Neocaesarea ca 330, reinforced by his father's influence, was a true commitment to religious toleration. By the time of Constantine's death in 337, Themistius had become a student of philosophy, training under his father and others at Constantinople.

During the reign of Constantius, but probably not until the 340s and outside the capital, Themistius began to teach philosophy. By the late 340s, he had returned to Constantinople, where he began or continued work on *Paraphrases* of some works of Aristotle. Within a few years, he had become a senator and a leading figure in the intellectual life of the capital. He served as an ambassador for Constantinople and, as *princeps senatus* or its equivalent, was charged with finding suitable candidates for adlection to the Senate. Four public speeches (*Or.* 1, 2, 4, 3; in chronological order) date to this reign. Harassed by contemporaries for this involvement with the court and public life, Themistius justified himself in a series of speeches (*Or.* 20, 21, 23, 26,

---

98. For an attempt at identification, cf. Vanderspoel, *Historia* 36 (1987): 383–84.

99. Rather than the city of the same name in northern Syria (Chalcis ad Belum). For this interpretation, cf. J. Vanderspoel, *Hermes* 116 (1988): 125–28.

100. The details on the various points raised in the rest of this chapter can be found at the appropriate places in later chapters, to which further reference is not made.

29) outlining views already evident in a speech delivered earlier (*Or.* 24). He is not particularly defensive, instead attacking his accusers with arguments drawn from the history of philosophy and the injunctions of Plato and Aristotle to prove that he had done nothing contrary to tradition. He faced similar problems during the reign of Theodosius, when he became even more actively involved in political life, holding office for the first and only time in his career. In response, he uses the same arguments from a tradition that allowed him to be a public figure and to express his philosophy in the public domain.

Themistius' stance, if nothing else, remains constant, even in the face of adversity. He experienced difficult relations with the court during the reign of Julian, because the emperor held views different from his own in important ways. Nevertheless he attempted to effect change, first in a *protrepticus* sent to Julian, at that point the new Caesar in Gaul, and second in a panegyric after Julian became sole emperor. This oration, which satisfied Libanius, is no longer extant in Greek, but is arguably to be equated with the Arabic *Risâlat*. The composition of such a panegyric in strained circumstances is a testament to his political resilience and his inclination to achieve harmony whenever possible. More to the point in this reign is Themistius' effort to change Julian's mind on the persecution of Christians. While this cannot be dated and was perhaps little more than private discussion with Julian, Themistius must have known that it would not endear him to an emperor whose open letter to the East (*Ep. ad Them.*) had already revealed his attitude. Emboldened by his convictions, Themistius nevertheless made an attempt. Conversely, he did not hesitate to plead for religious tolerance for pagans from the short-lived Jovian in *Oration* 5 or to ask Valens to abandon his persecution of some Christians with the same arguments, in a speech known only from a report by the ecclesiastical historian Socrates. One cannot help but notice that his main perspective was the very humane view that all forms of all religions should be regarded with equal tolerance.

His views on peace, expressed during the reigns of Valens and Theodosius, were similarly humane. Peace both prevented the slaughter of humanity and obviated the need for increases in taxes to support the war effort. It allowed humans to live in security and to farm land once uninhabitable because of constant threats of war. Perhaps even more important is the extension of the concept of humanity to include peoples regarded as barbarians by contemporaries and, for that matter, modern writers. The quest for peace on the borders and within the empire was not favored by all; some, apparently including Valens at first, preferred the destruction of the enemy. For Themistius, who on occasion celebrated military victories, it was perhaps fortunate that Theodosius preferred to buy the loyalty of the Goths. Though the emperor may have had little choice, the philosopher could proclaim the victory of humanity over barbarism within the empire. Events soon proved that peace was tenuous at best, but Themistius could retire from active participation in political life with the satisfaction of a goal achieved. He probably died before the renewed violence occurred.

One other theme, that of mildness, is very much evident in the reign of Valens. Whether Themistius pleads for harmony between Valens and Valentinian (Or. 6), asks Valens to be mild toward adherents of Procopius (Or. 7 and sometimes in other speeches), expresses his desire for peace with the Goths (various places in Or. 8–11), or simply praises the emperor, his main purpose is to convince Valens to be mild, no easy task given the accounts of the emperor's irascibility in other sources. Themistius later boasted of his success with Valens, but his career did not advance during that emperor's reign. He retained his prominence as a senator and as a representative of the eastern Senate, and his influence no doubt increased as time wore on. There is little else, except a second bronze statue, undoubtedly a reward for a particularly pleasing panegyric, and, more importantly, a commission from Valens himself in 376 to deliver a panegyric of Gratian (Or. 13, nauseating in its insistence on the emperor as Beauty personified) in the Senate at Rome, an oration designed to deflate the rising tension between the Senate and the court in the West. Valens could not have a chosen better representative: for a dozen years, he had heard of the need for harmony and mildness from Themistius' lips.

The philosopher was more at ease with Theodosius, whose perspectives, like those of Constantius, coincided more nearly with his own. His public speeches of the reign (Or. 14–19, to which 31 and 34 should be added) reveal this beyond doubt. Though Themistius is aware of some disharmony between East and West early in the reign, he was much happier with the new emperor than he was with the old. Some of that pleasure was due to the easing of relations between court and capital. (Among his other roles, Themistius was always a representative of a city.) By the end of his reign, Valens had alienated the citizens of Constantinople to the point that he threatened to plough the city under. In contrast, Theodosius cultivated good relations with the city and achieved some success in this regard. He was more good-natured in other ways too, generally adopting the stance of the benevolent ruler. For a willingness to proclaim this publicly, Themistius was rewarded with the prefecture of Constantinople in 384. His two efforts to combat the approbation for his acceptance of office (*Or.* 31, 34) are essentially further panegyrics of Theodosius. Soon after the delivery of *Oration* 34, Themistius disappears from the public record, except for a single reference in a letter of Libanius in 388. No doubt he died soon after, though that event is, perhaps oddly, not recorded anywhere, not even in the correspondence of Libanius, who wrote often to friends at Constantinople in the next few years until his own death, probably in 393. One might wonder whether Themistius did not slip into gentle retirement in 385 or 387, after thirty years as senator or *princeps senatus*, and outlive his Antiochene contemporary. In any case, he lived into his seventies, with a long career of public service as a teacher and a politician.

At any point, it would have been easy for Themistius to give in to the demands of others whose views differed from his own or were jealous of his success. He did not. He had decided to live in accordance with precepts of Plato and Aristotle and devoted his life to civic activity and philosophy. All the Neoplatonists of the fourth century together were unable to prevent him. Because they withdrew from public life, their names, so far as they relate to Themistius and the political life of the East, are largely unknown. The name and writings of Themistius, whose stance on the relation between philosophy and politics was for several reasons increasingly anachronistic even in his own day, have survived. The next seven chapters detail his life, circumstances, and thought.

2

The Early Life of Themistius

The year and place of Themistius' birth can be determined within reasonable limits from his own statements. Because he remarks (1.18a) that his philosophy is contemporary with Constantius, born on 7 August 317,[1] Themistius' birth is often dated to the same year.[2] With no evidence to disprove this, the suggestion may be retained, though it must remain uncertain. The location of his birth has occasioned disagreement. He was Paphlagonian, but some have placed his birth at Constantinople (Byzantium), citing his own remarks that he had been brought up in the city and spent his childhood there.[3] The evidence indicates another birthplace. In a letter to the eastern Senate, Constantius (*Ep. Const.* 21d) praises Themistius for preferring the city to his native town and for acting and thinking like a citizen even before he became one. This statement should be conclusive:[4] however young Themistius was when he first came to the city, he was born elsewhere and became a citizen of Constantinople later in life.

The corpus of Julian's correspondence may place Themistius' father in Paphlagonia. Some letters, not authored by Julian, were written from the court of Licinius in the 310s, when the eastern emperor was under severe pressure from Constantine.[5] If the letter (*Ep.* 193)

1. For the date of Constantius' birth, cf. T.D. Barnes, *The New Empire of Diocletian and Constantine* (Cambridge, Mass., 1982), 45, where the evidence is listed.

2. Seeck, *Briefe,* 292; Stegemann, "Themistios," 1642, where "Konstantin" should read "Konstantios"; *PLRE,* 1:889; and a good many other works.

3. Themistius refers to his Paphlagonian origins at 2.28d and 27.333c–d and seems to indicate an upbringing at Constantinople at 17.214c and 34.12, 16. Seeck, *Briefe,* 291, followed by Stegemann, "Themistios," 1642, and *PLRE,* 1:889, suggests that the orator was born at Constantinople, while his birth is placed in Paphlagonia by F. Schemmel, *NeueJbfürPäd* 22 (1908): 153, and Dagron, *Thémistios,* 5.

4. So already Schemmel, *NeueJbfürPäd* 22 (1908): 153.

5. Cf. Barnes, *GRBS* 19 (1978): 99–106, with notes.

addressed to Themistius' father Eugenius belongs to this group,[6] it may have been sent to Paphlagonia: the author expresses a desire to fly to the foothills, presumably near his correspondent's residence. An appropriate location in Paphlagonia can be found.[7] Two places, Gangra and Cimiata, seem suitable. The former is south of the mountains running through Paphlagonia and Galatia; the latter lies between this range and the Olgassys Mountains in the middle of Paphlagonia. Because Strabo (12.3.41) places Cimiata at the foothills of the Olgassys, that town is the stronger possibility.[8] Another letter in this correspondence, a complaint to Iamblichus about difficult times, has been dated to 316;[9] the wish to fly to Paphlagonia may have been motivated in part by circumstances. The letter to Eugenius could belong to the same period, placing him in Paphlagonia about the time of Themistius' birth.

Few details about Themistius' early life survive. It may be assumed that he enjoyed a comfortable childhood: his family was not rich, as he himself points out (20.233d; 23.288d, 291c), but neither was it afflicted with poverty.[10] It had achieved some distinction for philoso-

---

6. For identification with Themistius' father, Seeck, *Briefe*, 133–34. Themistius' eulogy (*Or*. 20) was composed in 355; see the discussion later in this chapter and in chapter 4. On Lib. *Ep*. 1192, see chapter 4. For discussions of authenticity generally, cf., e.g., W. Schwarz, *De vita et scriptis Iuliani imperatoris* (Bonn, 1888), 22 ff.; and F. Cumont, *Sur l'authenticité de quelques Lettres de Julien*. Université de Gand, Recueil de Travaux 3 (Gand, 1889), 12 ff., who suggests that many letters were penned by the correspondent of Iamblichus and Sopater. Most of the addressees can be identified as philosophers and teachers if the letters are redated earlier in the fourth century.

7. Abonutichus, suggested by Baret, *Themistio*, 5–7, and F. Wilhelm, *ByzneugrJb* 6 (1929): 452, 482, is doubtful; it is on the coast, not in the foothills, and Themistius refers (27.333c–334a) to an oracle that had recently ceased to prophesy in a nearby town; Harduin (p. 701 Dindorf) correctly identified this with Abonutichus. On the town's oracle, cf. L. Robert, *À travers l'Asie mineure*, Bibl. des Écoles franç. d'Ath. et de Rome 139 (Paris, 1980), 393–421.

8. Cimiata is also much closer to Abonutichus, described as nearby at 27.333c–d, provided that Themistius delivered this speech in his native town; see the discussion later in this chapter. Note also that Themistius decries the desire of the young man he is addressing to seek his rhetorical education in an ancient city with many old myths (27.332a), and cf. Robert, *À travers l'Asie mineure*, chap. 8, on the antiquity of Gangra and its myths. This perhaps also makes Gangra a less likely possibility.

9. Barnes, *GRBS* 19 (1978): 104.

10. As Constantius remarks at *Ep. Const*. 22a.

phy in a previous generation, when Diocletian honored the founder of Themistius' family.[11] Themistius compares this with imperial recognition of other philosophers: Augustus of Arius, Tiberius of Thrasyllus, Trajan of Dio Chrysostom, and Antoninus Pius and Marcus Aurelius of Epictetus (5.63d). The comparisons are generous and, for Marcus Aurelius, anachronistic. Themistius repeats the list, with some changes,[12] in a speech to Valens (11.145b), concluding with a Byzantine philosopher honored by Diocletian.[13]

Almost nothing is known about other members of Themistius' family. His mother and brothers are mentioned only in *Oration* 20, and the latter are sometimes thought, on the basis of a passage in this speech, to have predeceased their father.[14] When Philosophy saw Themistius overcome by grief at the death of Eugenius, she

> bore it hard and threatened to do some terrible and pernicious things to me, to exclude me immediately from my paternal inheritance (and I don't mean from land, fields, and flocks, but from what I alone of my brothers strive after, lay claim to, and attempt to inherit) and to strike me from the catalog of her own attendants. (20.233d–234a)[15]

There is here no reference to the death of Themistius' brothers. Rather, it appears that they were more interested in property, while Themistius himself almost lost the legacy of his father's philosophy because he did not deserve it.

---

11. Probably his grandfather rather than Eugenius; cf. Seeck, *Briefe*, 132.

12. Philip and Aristotle, Alexander and Xenocrates, and Marcus Aurelius and Sextus are included, while Epictetus disappears completely.

13. Another reference to Themistius' grandfather; cf. Schemmel, *Neue-JbfürPäd* 22 (1908): 153. He is not, however, the unnamed philosopher who attacked Christians in Nicomedia in 303, as Schemmel suggests. Lactantius implies that this occurred at Nicomedia (*Div. Inst.* 5.2), while Themistius places the philosopher in Byzantium. Lactantius' philosopher was rich, dining better at home than at the imperial palace. Most likely, the philosopher of Nicomedia had been a student of Iamblichus; cf. Barnes, *GRBS* 19 (1978): 105, with n. 28.

14. Seeck, *Briefe*, 133, followed by Stegemann, "Themistios," 1643. This suggestion misunderstands "alone of my brothers" in the passage as "bereft of my brothers."

15. At 26.324a, Epicurus is struck from the catalog of philosophers.

Themistius perhaps began his education in Paphlagonia, from in-
structors whose names are unknown.[16] His training in rhetoric took
place in a small city in Pontus, near the Phasis River, where, despite
barbarian surroundings, one man made the place Greek and a mis-
tress of the Muses (27.332d–333a).[17] Themistius admits that he had
not chosen this school and that his father had sent him (27.333b). His
description of the school's location, near the Thermodon River and
the plain of Themiscyra, once peopled by Amazons, virtually guarantees that he studied rhetoric at Neocaesarea,[18] a city in Pontus
Polemoniacus (Am. Mar. 27.12.9), the furthest of the Pontic provinces, which stretched nearly to Phasis. Themistius does not state
why he was sent to Neocaesarea, but his father presumably trusted
the competence of the rhetor. Possibly, he too had studied there or the
instructor was a friend.[19]

Themistius does not name his instructor, but the location of the
school permits reasonable conjecture. Basil of Neocaesarea, father of
Basil of Caesarea, taught rhetoric in the region for a number of years.
Although he lived for a time in Cappadocia, where his wife Emmelia
originated, his own family was from a Pontic province, either Polemoniacus or Helenopontus.[20] Lack of specific evidence obscures Basil's

16. Themistius names no teacher, not even his father, whose identity is
known only from *Ep. Const.* 23a. Since Libanius once advises Hierocles (*Ep.*
517.3) to learn from Themistius whom he had once taught, some have argued
that Hierocles was Themistius' teacher of grammar or rhetoric; cf. Seeck,
Briefe, 176; Schemmel, *NeueJbfürPäd* 22 (1908): 154; Stegemann, "Themistios,"
1643; *PLRE*, 1:431–32, 889. But Themistius had recently been to Antioch, and
the letter informs Hierocles that he could have news about Libanius from
Themistius, as Themistius had earlier brought Hierocles' news to Antioch and
Libanius; cf. Bouchery, *Themistius*, 80; also Dagron, *Thémistios*, 6, with n. 7.

17. The passage is translated later in this chapter.

18. At 27.333a, Themistius uses the word που, suggesting an approximate
location. Neocaesarea is not near Phasis, but he is exaggerating to make his
point.

19. Wilhelm, *Byz-neugrJb* 6 (1929): 458, followed by Stegemann, "Themistios," 1643, suggested that Eugenius had studied at the same place, while
Seeck, *Briefe*, 292, and Schemmel, *NeueJbfürPäd* 22 (1908): 154, hold that the
instructor was a friend. There is no evidence for either view, and they are not
mutually exclusive.

20. The unknown location of Annisa causes the uncertainty. Cf., among
others, A. Jülicher, *RE*, III, 1 (1899), 52; Y. Courtonne, *Saint Basile: Lettres*, vol.
1 (Paris, 1957), vii–viii; and P.J. Fedwick, in *Basil of Caesarea: Christian, Human-*

career, but enough survives to indicate that he spent much time near his mother, a follower of disciples of Gregory Thaumaturgus, a former bishop of Neocaesarea (Greg. Naz. *Or.* 43.9–12 = *PG* 36.504–512). Basil certainly taught rhetoric at Neocaesarea and was likely there during the late 320s and early 330s, when Themistius took his training.

In his funeral oration for Basil of Caesarea, Gregory of Nazianzus makes a few remarks about his subject's father (*Or.* 43.9–12 = *PG* 36.504–512). Well-versed in literature, he put this to good use when he taught the principles of rhetoric to his own son and to Gregory. He also had an interest in philosophy. This combination perhaps appealed to Eugenius, who is himself praised for his breadth of learning in *Oration 20*, and it may have had an effect on Themistius, who learned partly from Basil the combination of rhetoric and philosophy that permeates his own work.[21] This dual interest, which bridged the often hostile relations between the two pursuits, undoubtedly began with the training received from his father and was reaffirmed at Neocaesarea. Lessons from Basil also fostered Themistius' knowledge of Christian beliefs and practices. His life and career reveal an ability to use this to good advantage, as he ignored differences of religious persuasion and concentrated on similarities. This enabled him to maintain good relations with Christians, including emperors and other important individuals.

Themistius' arrival at Constantinople is usually placed in 337.[22] He mentions, in a passage that has been needlessly emended,[23] that his embassy to Rome in 357 took place after twenty years at the capital.[24]

---

ist, Ascetic, ed. P.J. Fedwick (Toronto, 1981), 5, with n. 15, on Basil's early life, with implications for the residence of his father.

21. For the same approach in Gregory of Nazianzus and other Cappadocian fathers, cf. Ruether, *Gregory of Nazianzus*.

22. Seeck, *Briefe*, 292; Stegemann, "Themistios," 1643 (where 377 is surely a misprint for 337); Dagron, *Thémistios*, 6; *PLRE*, 1:889.

23. *Or.* 23.298b: ἐν εἴκοσιν ὀλίγοις (ὅλοις [Petau]) ἐνιαυτοῖς. All manuscripts read ὀλίγοις, but editors have adopted the conjecture of Petau. Themistius' point is the same whether he speaks of "merely" twenty years or twenty "complete" years. Bouchery, "Contribution," 196, n. 3, denies the value of the passage for the chronology of Themistius' life.

24. *Or.* 23 has also been dated to 377/8 (cf. Méridier, *Le philosophe*, 23–24; Scholze, *Temporibus*, 76, with n. 475 disputing Seeck's view, *Briefe*, 292), though this makes nonsense of the reference to twenty years at the capital. *PLRE*, 1:889, cites the speech to show that Themistius had been at Constantinople for twenty years in 357, but later (893) accepts Scholze's date for the speech.

The manuscript reading is difficult only if his point is misunder-stood.[25] Themistius emphasizes that his speech at Rome included contrasting elements, a combination of items he had learned in merely twenty years at Constantinople and of others drawn from the long tradition of literature and philosophy, in short, his own work combined with that of the ancients.

A more serious problem arises in considering Themistius' age, be-cause he would be about twenty in 337, if he was indeed born ca 317. Students often began to study philosophy much earlier, at fifteen or sixteen.[26] If Themistius began his philosophical training under the tutelage of his father, a transfer to Constantinople in 337 implies ei-ther that he began his training late or that Eugenius, who was his teacher, moved to the city at the same time. Yet the twenty years of residence at Constantinople before his first embassy to Rome need not have been continuous. Themistius almost certainly taught else-where during the 340s; during this period, he cannot be regarded as residing in the city.[27] Since Themistius represented Constantinople on the embassy, he is pointing out that twenty years of residence had instilled sufficient civic pride to allow him to fulfill his duties appropri-ately. If these twenty years of residence were cumulative, not continu-ous, some corollary conclusions are possible. First, it allows a sugges-tion that Themistius began his study of philosophy at the normal age of fifteen or sixteen. Second, any period outside Constantinople dur-ing the 340s can be accommodated. Third, it is easier to explain state-ments about his presence in the city during his youth (17.214c; 34.12, 16) if he first arrived as an adolescent rather than as a young man of twenty. Moreover, Eugenius, who was well known at Constantinople

---

25. Cf. Dagron, *Thémistios*, 210–11, for discussion. His translation ("égale-ment de tout ce que j'ai pu acquérir chez vous en vingt ans de séjour à peine") indicates acceptance of the text as transmitted (cf. 210, n. 37), but he does not note the contrast between Themistius' own work and long tradition.

26. On normal ages for different subjects of study, cf. A.D. Booth, *Florilegium* 1 (1979): 1–14; for a specific instance, idem, *Byzantion* 53 (1983): 157–63.

27. Seeck, *Briefe*, 292–93, and Dagron, *Thémistios*, 7, both suggest periods spent outside Constantinople as a teacher without realizing the chronological consequences of the twenty years in the city: παρ' ὑμῖν ἐνθένδε (23.298b), in a speech delivered at Constantinople, cannot mean Nicomedia or Ancyra. It is possible, of course, that Themistius is ignoring this period.

(*Ep. Const.* 22d–23b), might then be placed there as early as 330;[28] Themistius, meanwhile, took his training in rhetoric, away from home, at the normal age of twelve or thirteen.[29]

On this reconstruction, Themistius began his education in philosophy about 332/333, at the age of fifteen or sixteen,[30] under the tutelage of his father, who was by then resident in Constantinople. From his father, he learned the peculiar brand of philosophy that characterizes his own thought.[31] Eugenius' ability to expound philosophy for a general audience, praised in *Oration* 20, was undoubtedly one factor that induced Themistius to pursue the same goal and, probably, to write *Paraphrases* of some works of Aristotle. These consisted, on Themistius' own admission, mostly of knowledge he gained from his father and grandfather. Precise dating is impossible, but Themistius notes that he had written the *Paraphrases* as a young man (23.294d). He perhaps wrote them between assuming a teaching post at Constantinople and joining the Senate, but he may have begun them earlier and completed them later.[32]

Two speeches in particular reveal aspects of Themistius' education and his own attitude toward that training.[33] *Orations* 20 and 27 were delivered in the autumn of 355, when he traveled to Paphlagonia for his father's funeral. *Oration* 20 is a celebration of his father, but also an important document relevant to his debate with contemporaries

---

28. Schemmel, *NeueJbfürPäd* 22 (1908): 152–53, also places Eugenius at the capital earlier than 337.

29. Cf. Booth, *Florilegium* 1 (1979): 1–14; idem, *Byzantion* 53 (1983): 157–63.

30. There is no need to think that Themistius undertook full training in rhetoric. Booth, *Byzantion* 53 (1983): 161, argues that Libanius might have been expected to devote himself completely to rhetoric from the age of fifteen to eighteen. Even if Themistius studied rhetoric until he was eighteen, he would have begun to study philosophy in 335, two years before he is normally placed at Constantinople.

31. See the discussion of Themistius' attitude toward his training later in this chapter.

32. Stegemann, "Themistios," 1651–52, cf. also 1644, opts for 345–355, accepting the earlier date (following Seeck, *Briefe*, 292) as the beginning of his teaching career; Dagron, *Thémistios*, 7, suggests 348 or 349, proposing a later date for the professorship at the capital; Scholze, *Temporibus*, 81–85, suggests 345–360. Seeck, *Briefe*, 292, and Schemmel, *NeueJbfürPed* 22 (1908): 154, offer 337–355.

33. *Or.* 28 is not discussed here; see the translation in appendix 2.

about the role of the philosopher in society, as is *Oration* 27, delivered to a young Paphlagonian[34] who preferred famous schools in the large cities. Themistius advises him not to ignore schools in his own area, assuring him of their adequacy, and emphasizes quality of training, not its location. He admits that contemporaries would reject and despise both his teacher and himself, because neither had been educated at famous schools, but does not hesitate to state that the value of his training was evident in his speeches. The central argument of the speech follows:

> I myself learned rhetoric, most noble youth, in a place far more removed than this one, not a civilized or Greek place, but at the furthest reaches of Pontus near the Phasis River, where, poets marvel, the Argo arrived safely from Thessaly and where heaven took it up. There too are the Thermodon River, the lands of the Amazons, and the plain of Themiscyra. Nevertheless, the wisdom and excellence of a single man made so barbaric and uncivilized a place Greek and a temple of the Muses. Located in the middle of Colchians and Armenians, he did not teach archery, the casting of the javelin, or horsemanship, according to the educational system of the neighboring barbarians, but skill in rhetoric and what is suitable on festive occasions.[35] Whether I speak the truth will be immediately obvious when I say anything. I did not go there out of my own inclination or decision, but my father, as loving as a father could be and testing me correctly as only a philosopher could, sent me. You will, no doubt, wholly despise him [the teacher] because he himself acquired his much discussed philosophy there, but me perhaps even more since I was initiated into the mysteries at home upon the hearth. (27.332d–333b)

Implicit here is the view that schools in the major cities did not necessarily offer the right kind of training. Themistius does not state this directly, but implies as much with numerous examples of excellence arising in obscure places.

To some extent, Themistius is apologizing for his own education,

---

34. Cf. 27.332d, 340b–d. On date and occasion, Scholze, *Temporibus*, 72.
35. One might detect here an emphasis toward panegyric and epideictic oratory.

against contemporaries who preferred the major centers. His emphasis on quality instead of location is designed to deflect criticism. The funeral speech for his father, delivered in the autumn of 355,[36] addresses some similar points, though he focuses on philosophy more than rhetoric. Since little is known about Eugenius, it is not immediately obvious whether Themistius' assessment of his father's praiseworthiness is accurate or whether the philosopher had an ulterior purpose. The speech, like *Oration* 27, was written and delivered soon after he joined the Senate at Constantinople, an event that stirred up a debate about the role of the philosopher in society and politics. Portions of both speeches are relevant to the debate, especially the funeral speech, with its emphasis on philosophy at the expense of rhetoric. The most obvious point is Themistius' attribution of his own combination of philosophy and rhetoric to his father, as if to remind contemporaries that his approach was not entirely new.

The philosopher begins by noting that neither his father nor Philosophy allowed him to be overcome by grief. Philosophy, in fact, threatened to take his paternal inheritance of philosophy away and remove him from the catalogue of her admirers because he was briefly overcome. This threat forced him to dry his eyes (20.233d–234a). After a brief discussion of Eugenius' return to heaven and his presence at the side of Socrates, Plato, and Aristotle, the praise of his eclecticism begins. Eugenius was a better interpreter of Aristotle than Bacis and Amphilytus were of Loxian Apollo. But this ability was not his sole excellence. He was a student of every other philosophy, from Pythagoras and Zeno to Plato, and was especially concerned with harmonizing the views of Plato with those of Aristotle. He disliked the tendency to divide their views into separate schools and was not entirely fond of Epicurus (20.234b–236b), though he considered him a philosopher. In addition to skill at philosophy, Eugenius knew literature very well, specifically Homer, Menander, Euripides, Sophocles, Sappho, and Pindar, and engaged in agriculture. Following Musonius perhaps,[37] he regarded agriculture as the only suitable pursuit for a

---

36. See chapter 4 for the date.

37. Musonius, fr. 11, extols the philosopher-farmer; cf. A.C. van Geytenbeek, *Musonius Rufus and Greek Diatribe*, trans. and rev. B.L. Hijmans (Assen, 1973), 129–34.

philosopher, especially one advanced in years,[38] and as a metaphor of the difference between rhetoric and philosophy. Sophists planted plane trees and cypresses, since they cared only for pleasure and nothing for the nourishment of grains and vine, as philosophers do (20.236b–237d). Eugenius compared sophists to people who gathered all the herbs and medical advice necessary for healing illness, but did not use them when they were ill, and to athletes who did not train, but preferred instead to sit in the bath to discuss the outcome of the matches. Philosophy does not need display of words, but practice of virtue for its own sake, not for money or glory. Of all this, Eugenius held Socrates, whom he emulated, to be a good example, because he did what he thought right despite the circumstances surrounding him. Like Heracles and Socrates with whom he is compared (he experienced domestic discord like Socrates [20.239a]), Eugenius fought evil on earth and reminded humanity of virtuous life. Themistius closes with his desire to follow in his father's footsteps and asks for his help (20.238a–240d). We cannot determine to what extent he accomplished this desire: Eugenius remains for us an enigma.

Probably after his education was complete, Themistius married for the first time. His wife's father was a philosopher (21.244b), but his name is not stated. Themistius reports that his father-in-law taught him philosophy (21.244b–d), though it is not clear whether this occurred at Constantinople. He did marry after he had arrived at the city: Constantius remarks that Themistius conceived an interest in marriage and procreation "while among us" (*Ep. Const.* 22a). The marriage produced children, including a son named Themistius who died in 356/7 (Lib. *Ep.* 575). Since he trained in the principles of Isocrates' rhetoric under Libanius,[39] who moved to Antioch in 353/4,[40] the son was born before the late 340s.[41] The marriage thus

38. For the view that Themistius wrote his praise of agriculture (*Or.* 30) in the late 340s or early 350s, when Eugenius may have retired to his farm, see chapter 4.

39. Not necessarily the normal course. Bouchery, *Themistius,* 103, suggests that Libanius had merely spoken to him about rhetoric on an informal basis, making his age somewhat, though not entirely, irrelevant.

40. Another possibility for the training is 356, when Themistius was in Antioch on a lecture tour.

41. For discussion, Bouchery, *Themistius,* 102–3. There is no need to assume that the younger Themistius was the oldest of the philosopher's children.

took place before Themistius' final transfer to the capital. Precision is impossible, but he presumably did not marry until the 340s. Constantius' statement suggests, but does not force, the conclusion that Themistius' father-in-law resided at Constantinople. On this view, Maximus of Byzantium, an Aristotelian philosopher, is a prime candidate.[42]

Some evidence for the date of his marriage and the birth of his children may come from a speech delivered in Constantinople.[43] *Oration* 32, responding to opponents,[44] discusses the right of philosophers to have and care for children. Themistius argues that they, especially students of Aristotelian philosophy (32.358a–b), not only have the right, but are best able to approach parenthood with the equanimity required. Philosophers should have normal lives and ought not to withdraw from society in any way.[45] His main theme of moderation in passions is Aristotelian and anti-Stoic, since *metriopatheia* is the opposite of Stoic *apatheia*.[46] Themistius discusses the grief that children can bring, but the speech need not follow the death of his own son.[47]

Evidence for the date of the speech may come from Constantius' apparent reference to it in the letter announcing Themistius' adlection to the Senate at Constantinople. The emperor remarks:

> While among us he gave thought also to marriage and procreation, which preserve the succession of the race. This is praiseworthy in another, but extremely useful in a philosopher. (*Ep. Const.* 22a)

---

42. Cf. J. Vanderspoel, *AHB* 1 (1987): 71–74.

43. Scholze, *Temporibus*, 69–70, 86, dates the speech to 346/350, regarding it as early because it shows a lack of technical maturity.

44. 32.361b, quoted later in this section.

45. Some of these ideas might derive from Musonius, though this cannot be shown from the fragments that survive.

46. Cf. Diog. Laert. 5.31: ['Αριστοτέλης] ἔφη δὲ τὸν σοφὸν ἀπαθῆ μὲν μὴ εἶναι, μετριοπαθῆ δέ. Cf. J.M. Rist, *Stoic Philosophy* (Cambridge, 1967), 26–27, and idem, in *The Stoics*, ed. J.M. Rist (Berkeley, 1978), 259–64, on *apatheia* and children. The speech bears the title Μετριοπαθὴς ἢ Φιλότεκνος.

47. Recently, O. Ballériaux, *Byzantion* 58 (1988): 33–35, has argued this, but his arguments are not compelling, since Themistius does not seem to refer to his own grief.

It appears that Constantius knew *Oration* 32 or the sentiments of the speech when he wrote to the Senate.[48] Though he only needed to know that Themistius had children, a comparison of his statement with the view that philosophers are the ideal parents for children is revealing. The possibility that the emperor heard the speech when it was first delivered is worth considering. Between 350, when he traveled toward the West to engage Magnentius, and 359, Constantius was not in the East,[49] and the speech may belong to the previous period. If it was delivered at Constantinople,[50] it could date to 349 or 350.[51]

One passage in particular suggests that Themistius was a father at the time. Launching an explanation of the reasons that philosophers are the best parents, he writes:

Good gentlemen, I have spoken at length to you about this because I suspect that you laugh at and despise philosophers when you see them attached to their sons and daughters just like the masses. Therefore I tell you that this indeed is their most philosophic experience. And if many endure it, they endure it for no other reason than because nature has sown some trace of philosophy in every man. (32.361b–c)

Themistius seems to be discussing personal experience, and while he makes the general point that all philosophers have the right to procreate and to become involved emotionally with the lives of their children, he is answering charges against himself as well. Themistius was thus married and a father by the late 340s, though how much earlier is impossible to state.

By the late 340s, Themistius had begun teaching. While the details of his early career remain uncertain, there are hints that he held other

48. See chapter 4 for further discussion of Constantius' letter.

49. Seeck, *Regesten*, 196–207, and now Barnes, *Athanasius and Constantius*, 220–23.

50. The standard view, though nothing in the text forces this conclusion.

51. Cf. T.D. Barnes, *Phoenix* 34 (1980): 164, for Constantius at Constantinople. Barnes, *Athanasius and Constantius*, 220, now suggests a possible visit in 343 and casts some doubt on that of 349, but 343 is probably too early for Themistius' speech (and the birth of his children), and I suggest later in this chapter that Themistius was elsewhere at the time.

teaching positions before he taught at the capital.[52] *Oration 24*, which summons Nicomedia to consider and adopt philosophy, inaugurated a course of lectures and suggests that Themistius taught there briefly before 344.[53] Libanius arrived in that year, but first met Themistius at Constantinople in 350; the philosopher had no doubt departed before the sophist arrived.[54] Themistius seems to indicate residence, not a series of guest lectures.[55] At the outset,[56] he attacked rhetoric (*Or.* 24), in a city that Libanius calls the "nurse of eloquence" (*Or.* 1.48), and contemporary philosophy.

His *protrepticus* to the people of Nicomedia is designed to stimulate interest in philosophy.[57] Throughout, he discusses the relationship of rhetoric to philosophy. While he intends to show the possibility of harmony, his opening words hardly promote it. He contrasts Socrates with Gorgias and Prodicus, then requests the indulgence of his audience for his inability to speak like the sophists to whom it was accustomed.[58] These sophists, he remarks in his complaint about the attractions of pursuits other than rational philosophy,

> always set up a Sicilian table and concoct many variegated schemes against us.[59] Some by singing the native song, others the Assyrian song and that from Lebanon, bewitch you with domestic and foreign harmony. (24.301b)

52. Cf. Bouchery, "Contribution," 192–96; Dagron, *Thémistios*, 7, 25.

53. Dagron, *Thémistios*, 7.

54. In *Ep.* 793, dating to 362, Libanius refers to a twelve-year acquaintance.

55. 24.302c. Cf. Bouchery, "Contribution," 193. Seeck, *Briefe*, 293, suggests that the speech was delivered on a visit to Nicomedia, as does Scholze, *Temporibus*, 73, who dates it to late 355, when Themistius traveled through it to his native Paphlagonia.

56. The view that Themistius lived and taught at Nicomedia may be strengthened by his remark (24.302c) about a god who wished him to go to the city, stirred up love for the city in him, and did not want him to speak like others fond of the city (i.e., sophists).

57. Some of Themistius' ideas are found in Dio Chrysostom, e.g., in *Or.* 32 and 33.

58. Compare Dio Chrysostom's similar remarks at *Or.* 32.1.

59. So the Teubner text of Downey-Norman, with the reading μηχανὰς ἡμῖν of ms. A; variants include ὑμῖν ἡδονὰς and ἡδονὰς ὑμῖν in other manuscripts.

The items that draw people from the study of philosophy are, in Themistius' view, rhetoric (native song), Christianity (Assyrian song), and Iamblichan theurgy (the song from Lebanon).[60]

Themistius' procedure, an attack on pursuits responsible for a lack of interest in rational philosophy, seems to be the approach of a young man, not yet able to disguise his criticisms. At the same time, youthful exuberance, with inadequate consideration of alternate possibilities, may have played an important role. The view that the speech inaugurated a series on philosophical topics and the concomitant view that Themistius taught at Nicomedia, combined with this youthful exuberance, are the only reasons for dating the speech to the 340s. Many of the arguments, especially the descriptions of the role of rhetoric in explaining philosophical problems, reappear in later speeches that examine the relationship between the two, but his approach is different in those speeches. His education in rhetoric and philosophy under his father and Basil had taught him a suitable relationship. Training produced arguments, but time produced the maturity in other speeches on similar topics.[61]

His words, Themistius states, are children of Mnemosyne and Zeus (the Muses), just like the words of the sophists, but they differ from their siblings (24.301c). He outlines this difference:

> And so some, whenever they enter the theater of the Muses—they do this often and continuously—smile and fawn upon you, and effusively embrace the leader of the claque. Others, however, stay at home most of the time and want to take thought for amelioration in private, but if the god stirs them into public, they are rather austere and not particularly pleasant, and so much shun flattery that they often even censure the listeners whenever they recognize some fault in them.[62] In my case, however, since I am addressing men who are friends and, for the most part, sound of mind, I must imitate the wiser doctors, who ad-

---

60. On the implications of the passage, cf. Vanderspoel, *Hermes* 116 (1988): 125–28; see also chapter 1. The term *Assyrian* denotes Christians, from its use to describe Aramaic and related languages. On this last point, cf. J. Matthews, *The Roman Empire of Ammianus* (London and Baltimore, 1989), 69.

61. E.g., *Or.* 20, 21, 23, 26, and 29. See also appendix 2 for *Or.* 28.

62. Cf. Dio Chrysos. *Or.* 32.10–11, for similar remarks.

minister a draught of the more bitter medicines after covering the cup with honey.[63] As a result, you too would perhaps offer yourselves more submissively to a speech that nurtures pleasingly, just as a charioteer who is skilled at his trade attempts to drive the chariot with the reins and uses his goad and whip sparingly. With what kind of words will I then help you and please you at the same time? For there is a great need for me to honor this method of addressing you. (24.302a–c)

Themistius' attitude toward the faults of rhetoric and philosophy in contemporary practice is evident. Sophists offer relaxation and pleasure, but practice their craft for personal enjoyment and have no concern for improvement of the human race. Philosophers refuse to support their interest in human improvement by public speeches to large audiences, preferring to teach and study in small groups. When they deign to appear publicly, they frighten audiences with the severity of their appearance and speech. Themistius, who reiterates his ideas in *Oration* 28,[64] regards both approaches as unsuitable and develops a theory and practice from the best elements of each, suggesting that the honey of rhetoric must sweeten the bitter pill of philosophical concern. This theme emerges often in debates of the 350s, when he replies to charges that he was merely a sophist,[65] but his explanation here, with no indication of accusations, suggests again that this speech was delivered earlier. The tone of the opening remarks may have been partly responsible for later attacks.

The philosopher continues with a new metaphor:

The court of philosophy is not completely bereft of the graces, nor do the goddesses camp at all far apart from our shrines. I would never place before you a chorus that takes no part in chaste pleasure, but I will always be eager to weave Aphrodite

---

63. At *Or.* 33.10, Dio Chrysostom has nurses use this technique for their charges. A more interesting parallel is Lucretius, 4.8 ff., where the poet adds the honey of the Muses (i.e., his poetry) to his philosophy to make it palatable: he too compares the practices of physicians to his own approach, and note Themistius' reference to the Muses. If the source is Epicurus, the parallel is striking, given an ambivalence toward Epicurus.

64. See appendix 2.

65. See chapter 4 and appendix 2.

together with the Muses. For they are sisters of one another and welcome their association. (24.302d–303a)

Harmony is possible, because rhetoric and philosophy inhabit Themistius. He compares each to female figures (24.303a–304d).[66] Philosophy is tall and august in a decorous robe, with no excess of adornment in clothing or toiletry.[67] Somewhat severe, she displays reverence that engenders the same in a beholder as well, so that Polemon of Athens, for example, once he had seen her, abandoned a life of revelry and turned to philosophy, as a student of Xenocrates.[68] Rhetoric is a girl very beautiful in her own right, but wears embroidered clothing and longs for the application of external beauty. She can guide youths to involvement in public life and often leads a chorus in a beautiful dance, as long as the brothers (adherents of rhetoric and philosophy) dance with, not apart from, one another.[69] Whenever rhetoric attempts to lead alone, the result is a disarray of Bacchic frenzy. The presence of philosophy is thus necessary for the most beautiful of choruses to be a possibility.

As further evidence of this harmony, Themistius adopts yet another metaphor, the myth of Eros and Anteros. In his version, appar-

---

66. This passage almost certainly owes something to Dio Chrysostom's description of Kingship and Tyranny as two women at *Or.* 1.67–82 and to similar allegorical oppositions, such as Prodicus' myth of Heracles. On this, cf. M.C. Waites, *HSCP* 23 (1912): 1–46, who cites (17–18) *Or.* 22.280a–d, where Themistius discusses Prodicus' story, and notes the influence of Dio Chrysostom, but ignores the present passage. On the use of the technique by Dio Chrysostom and Lucian, cf. Jones, *Dio Chrysostom*, 116–17, and idem, *Culture and Society in Lucian* (Cambridge, Mass., 1986), 9. Note also, e.g., Ovid, *Amores* 3.1, where the poet contrasts Elegy and Tragedy as different female figures.

67. Boethius, *Cons.* 1.1, has a similar description of Philosophy as tall. Interestingly, Gregory of Nyssa, following the typical Christian equation of philosophy with asceticism (cf. A. Cameron, *Christianity and the Rhetoric of Empire* [Berkeley and Los Angeles, 1991], 158), in his *Life of Macrina* calls his sister Philosophy personified. The image, as well as the comparison of two different females, perhaps arises from personification in art.

68. Cf. Diog. Laert. 4.16–17.

69. Themistius has changed the sex of his subject; previously he was discussing the parentage of rhetoric and philosophy, but he is now discussing the adherents of each. The reference is to the typical separation of the two pursuits into two separate disciplines.

ently known only from this speech,[70] Aphrodite, distressed that her son refused to grow after birth, approached Thetis, who informed her that Love could only grow if Reciprocal Love were present. Soon thereafter, Aphrodite gave birth to Anteros, and both boys grew rapidly (24.304d–305c). Themistius omits the more familiar depiction of Anteros wresting a palm branch from Eros' hand,[71] countering the normal view by arguing that the myth concerns harmony more than dispute.

Themistius next reveals that he went to Nicomedia precisely to show that rhetoric and philosophy are related, not because the city was beautiful, pointing out that he would not have come if the city were not amenable to learning (24.305c–306c). At the same time, he was there because he wanted the city to become better than all others[72] in learning and to grow in concern for the soul (24.307c). He states that the acquisition of learning is like a wall that protects those within, built by Apollo and so strong that it cannot fall down.[73] This leads him to Troy and the Trojan War, where Agamemnon asked the gods not for ten warriors like Achilles, but for ten counselors like Nestor. Wisdom, in the view of Homer, was more important than brute strength, evident in the behavior of Achilles. A final example of the efficacy of learning is Odysseus. Stripped of everything by a storm and "clad in virtue instead of a cloak," he approached Nausicaa, impressing her with words alone. His training had given him the strength of a mountain-bred lion, removing any need to act as a beggar or a suppliant (24.308a–309c).

The basic view that informs the rest of Themistius' speeches, public and private, is evident in this short and early programmatic speech. The practice of rhetoric or philosophy by itself was not sufficient. Rather, the two disciplines were to act in harmony, each supporting the other. Rhetoric was to serve philosophy by being a vehicle to allow moral correction to reach as many people as possible and become

---

70. Cf. G. de Tervarent, *Journ. War. & Court. Institutes* 28 (1965): 205–8.

71. Cf. Paus. 6.23.5, and de Tervarent, cited in n. 70.

72. Surely another indication that Themistius intended to be at Nicomedia for some time.

73. Themistius' remark that it is legitimate to grieve at misfortunes (24.308a), in the context of shaken walls, may suggest a recent disaster. This is not the earthquake of 358, since he mentions the amenities that were apparently still standing. No other earthquakes at Nicomedia are known.

useful. Conversely, philosophy needed to abandon its esoteric nature and give attention to reaching more people, a view perhaps originating in Themistius' education and not entirely dissimilar to the delivery of sermons by bishops.[74] Speeches ought to provide moral instruction as well as pleasure, though the latter is often necessary to reach the audience. In accordance with this view, Themistius regarded himself as a philosopher first and an orator second, and a follower of the precedents established by Socrates, Plato, and Aristotle, in his insistence on the need for philosophers to emphasize moral correction. These points emerge at every opportunity, particularly in other speeches where he discusses his role as a philosopher.[75]

After a brief stay at Nicomedia, where sophists were more popular than philosophers because their words pleased audiences more,[76] Themistius probably held another post before returning to the capital. Reasonable conjecture places him in Ancyra. While direct evidence for a teaching position is lacking, he delivered his first panegyric of Constantius there, probably in March 347.[77] It would be odd for Themistius to travel to Ancyra to deliver the speech after his installation at Constantinople, if the emperor were traveling to or through the city, as he did in 350. The view that Themistius wanted to deliver the speech away from rivals and other panegyrists[78] is unsatisfactory. Delivery at Ancyra is easier to explain if, among the cities on Constantius' itinerary, Ancyra was the nearest to Themistius' residence in 347. It is reasonable, then, to suggest that he was teaching at Ancyra itself at the time. In the mid 350s, before he decided to remain at Constantinople permanently, he had offers from Antioch and Ancyra (23.299a), the former perhaps due to his acquaintance with Libanius,[79] the latter for reasons unknown. Previous residence offers a suitable pretext.

---

74. Cynic preaching may have had its effect as well.

75. Cf. R. Maisano, *Koinonia* 10 (1986): 29–47, for some remarks on Themistius' views, especially those expressed in *Or.* 24.

76. Bouchery, "Contribution," 193, citing 24.302d.

77. While Constantius undoubtedly passed through Ancyra each time he traveled between the East and Constantinople during the late 340s, evidence places him at Ancyra only on 8 March 347 (*CTh* 11.36.8). For an extended discussion of the date, see chapter 4.

78. So Seeck, *Briefe*, 294.

79. Cf. Lib. *Ep.* 402, 407 (to Themistius), and Bouchery, *Themistius*, 38–40.

It is thus possible that Themistius moved to the capital from Ancyra. If so, his first panegyric of Constantius was perhaps responsible for an imperial appointment. A partially preserved speech, *Oration* 33, sometimes regarded as his inaugural oration at the capital,[80] can be dated with reasonable precision because it contains a reference to a new coin type, the product of a reform of the bronze currency in 348.[81] The appointment may therefore date to the autumn of that year. The reconstruction offered here accords well with Themistius' remark that he had resided at the capital for twenty years in 357 and allows him to have begun his study of philosophy at something close to the normal age. He arrived at Constantinople ca 332 and was absent for about five years, while teaching at Nicomedia ca 342/343 and at Ancyra ca 344/347, before returning in 348. Neither post is directly attested, and both must remain the result of conjecture and inference. The lack of evidence is odd, but Themistius is generally silent about his life, especially his youth. He almost certainly did not begin his teaching career at Constantinople. On the slender evidence available, Nicomedia and Ancyra are the most likely sites for his early appointments.

---

80. Dagron, *Thémistios*, 7. In the speech, Themistius points out that he is not an orator, but a philosopher, and that the citizens ought not to expect frequent displays of pure oratory from him.

81. Seeck, *Briefe*, 293, with n. 1; on the date of the reform, idem, *ZfN* 17 (1890): 132; *RIC*, 8:34–39. Scholze, *Temporibus*, 68, accepts this view. H.R. Baldus, *JNG* 34 (1984): 77–106, has recently discussed the coinage of this decade. The speech itself announces an intention to discuss the names of emperor and consul, which may be odd when Constantius was not consul in either 348 or 349 (nor in 347, 350, or 351). A solution is perhaps available: in the autumn of 348, Constantius may have contemplated a consulship in 349 to celebrate twenty-five years as Caesar and emperor (or perhaps Themistius was speaking in anticipation of such an event). Though his *dies imperii* was 8 November 324 and a consulship in 348 was possible, he celebrated his fifteenth year with a consulship in 339 instead of 338; on Constantius's *vota* and consulships, cf. R.W. Burgess, *NC* 148 (1988): 82–83, 91.

3

Constantinople

Constantinople was, in the late 340s, a young city. Founded officially on 8 November 324 and dedicated about the time that Themistius began his training in rhetoric,[1] it occupied the more ancient site of Byzantium[2] and guarded an important crossing of the Bosporus. Constantine no doubt chose the site largely for this reason. His experience of civil war had taught him the importance of preventing an opponent from crossing into his own territory. Just as some Balkan cities controlled mountain passes in their regions and could hinder a rival's access either to the West or to the Danubian legions (depending on the point of origin), the new city of Constantinople could prevent the eastern armies from joining the Thracian military in a challenge to an emperor in the western part of the empire or hold the Bosporus for an emperor resident in the East.[3] This intent, coupled with a not uncommon desire to establish a new city with his own name,[4] was a sufficient, though not necessarily the exclusive, reason for the foundation. A new capital for the East was not absolutely required; Constantinople was, in any case, on the wrong shore to be founded primarily for this purpose.[5] Nicomedia, or perhaps Nicaea, was much better suited to be the eastern capital, in terms of cultural development and perhaps in location as well: it was less exposed and a safer haven.

Constantine's ultimate intention for his new city remains unclear.

---

1. Themistius (*Or.* 4.58b) states that city was founded on the same day that Constantius became Caesar. It was dedicated on 11 May 330.

2. On this site, cf. the brief surveys of G. Dagron, *Naissance d'une capitale: Constantinople et ses institutions de 330 à 451* (Paris, 1974), 13–19; and C. Mango, *Le développement urbain de Constantinople (IVe—VIIe siècles).* Travaux et Mémoires, Monographies 2 (Paris, 1985), 13–21.

3. On the strategic value of the site, cf. Dagron, *Naissance,* 68–69.

4. Cf., e.g., Eus. *VC* 3.48, and Soz. 2.3.2, for this wish of Constantine.

5. So Dagron, *Naissance,* 68, citing Herodian, 3.1.6 and 4.3.5–6, to show that Byzantium's primary purpose was to guard the Bosporus.

The interpretations offered by some writers from antiquity would seem to support the general modern view that the emperor wanted to create a new capital in the East.[6] The emperor's own name for the city, New Rome, attested as late as 334, seems to require the same view.[7] But Constantine had stated that Serdica was "his Rome" when he reached an agreement with Licinius in 317 and resided frequently at that city thereafter.[8] For Constantine, then, *Rome* hardly meant "capital city" in a modern sense, and Constantinople cannot automatically be considered a new capital designed to coexist with Rome or replace it, despite the emperor's preferred name for his foundation. Constantine's interment of his mother's body is a telling indication. The sarcophagus of Helena, who had herself founded two churches in Palestine, was brought to Rome in a military procession, with the emperor himself perhaps in attendance, and was placed in a mausoleum at one of that city's churches.[9] She was not buried in her son's city, although several churches may already have been under construction. Consequently, even the view that Constantinople was intended to be a "dynastic capital" becomes difficult, though more than one source offers this interpretation.[10]

To ascertain the most significant features of Constantinople's development into the capital it eventually became, the concept ought to be

---

6. The sources are surveyed by Dagron, *Naissance*, 19–27. There is no need to rehearse the bibliography of scholars who adopt this view, since almost every treatment of Constantine or Constantinople does so.

7. Note *CTh* 13.5.7: *urbis, quam aeterno nomine iubente deo donauimus*.

8. The sole source for this is the so-called Continuator of Dio, fr. 15: ἡ ἐμὴ Ῥώμη Σαρδικὴ ἐστιν. Cf. Dagron, *Naissance*, 27, with n. 7; Barnes, *Constantine and Eusebius*, 72; for Constantine's residence at Serdica, idem, *New Empire*, 73–74.

9. Cf. Barnes, *Constantine and Eusebius*, 221.

10. Anon. Vales. 6.30: *quam uelut patriam cultu decorauit ingenti et Romae desiderauit aequari*; Eus. *VC* 4.51: οἷά τινα πατρῴαν οὐσίαν. Themistius several times calls Constantinople the sister of Constantius (see chapter 4). Dagron, *Naissance*, 27–29, citing these sources, argues cogently that the establishment of a "dynastic capital" was Constantine's true intention. Depite the difficulty mentioned in the text, I find the suggestion attractive, if not necessarily conclusive. The sources, after all, belong some years after 8 November 324, when the city's rapid development and continued imperial attention might have influenced their views. The disposition of Helena's body presumably owes something to her own wishes, and she had lived mainly at Rome for about twenty years.

examined briefly in its Roman context. In many ways, the capital was wherever the emperor happened to be, since a significant part of the administration was done at and from the imperial court. In that sense, the empire did not have a capital at all, but merely a series of imperial residences. Constantine's name for Serdica is a public recognition of that fact.[11] Rome was, however, something more than simply an occasional imperial residence (which it became less and less). The so-called Eternal City was, until the founding of Constantinople and indeed much later, the ideological center of the empire that bore its name.

The features that separated Rome from imperial residences in general are precisely those that made Rome the original capital of the empire and eventually transformed Constantinople into a second one. Other residences were centers of administration, but in the absence of the emperor, the government was of provinces, dioceses, and/or prefectures rather than the empire. The existence of a bureaucracy is thus not the salient feature that separates residence from capital, nor is it the bureaucracies' sphere of competence: the civil servants at local centers of administration must have contributed to the central government when the emperor was in residence. By the same token, the size of the civil service quartered in a given city is insignificant, though Rome's was no doubt the largest.[12]

The institution that most signifies the distinction between local centers of administration and Rome is the Senate. Though the centuries of empire had effectively silenced its Republican thunder, the Senate of Rome was still an institution of great importance. Its province was no longer the appointment of the mighty (Tacitus had long before absolved distant soldiers of the need to feel guilt on that account), but its approval of accession continued to be desirable, if not always necessary. Occasionally, as with the young Gordian, it offered its own rival to a plethora of candidates vying for a firmer hold on the throne or threw its collective support behind a specific candidate. At other times, candidates chosen elsewhere sought and obtained, sometimes by force, a belated ratification of their selection. Meanwhile, emperors still thought it important to consult and address the Senate

11. As Dagron, *Naissance*, 27, discussing Constantine's remark, points out: "Là où réside l'empereur, là est le center de l'Empire."

12. Cf. Jones, *LRE*, 2:563–606, and esp. 1057, for the size of the civil service.

from time to time, as Constantius did in 357.[13] By this time, inclusion of the best men from the entire empire in preceding generations, to be followed by their descendants, had made the Senate in theory a collective of the imperial aristocracy, dominated, naturally, by Roman and Italian elements within it.[14]

Essentially, its cosmic governing class, which served also as the local council, distinguished Rome from the other cities of imperial importance. Local councils were a feature of every city in the empire, but Rome's council alone, larger than the rest and more prestigious, exercised influence and authority over the empire as a whole, however limited these prerogatives had become. In a manner not dissimilar to a metropolis of a province, Rome was the metropolis of the empire and is celebrated as such. Its history and Roman expansion had made it so, and even cities of greater antiquity paled in comparison.

Soon after its founding and/or dedication, Constantinople became an important eastern imperial center. Cultural and social development proceeded with some alacrity, as the powerful and those wishing to be, as well as intellectuals, flocked to the site. In combination with these factors, frequent imperial visits and lavish imperial attention increased the city's *potential* as a capital. By the late 340s, when Themistius arrived to take his position as a teacher, Constantinople was hardly yet a serious rival for Rome's status, not even in part. Its eternity had not yet been proved, and its cultural and social institutions were still in the early stages of development, where they existed at all. The city was not immediately the metropolis of anything, least of all the empire or a significant portion of it. Nor, as noted, was this indubitably Constantine's intent. The view, often found in treatments of the period, that Constantine founded his city as the capital of the East joins two separate facts (i.e., that Constantine founded the city and that it became the capital of the East) into a single one of dubious merit. If Constantine actually intended his city to be the eastern capital of the empire, he did not see his dreams come to fruition.

The transformation of Constantinople occurred during the reign of Constantius, and the process was not complete until near the end of his reign. Nor is it entirely clear that this was the emperor's intent

13. See chapter 4.

14. For some remarks on the Senate in late antiquity, Jones, *LRE*, 2:523–62. On the domination of Italy, idem, *LRE*, 2:525.

immediately after his father's death. Constantius was rarely at Constantinople in the decade after 337: the military situation on the frontier with Persia necessitated his presence in that region and his customary residence at Antioch. Certainly, the emperor continued and completed the building program begun by his father.[15] In fact, much of the adornment of the city ascribed to Constantine ought rather to be credited to his son.[16] Naturally, the city became larger, more prosperous, and more beautiful; its stature increased, but its status did not immediately change.

Only in the late 350s could Constantinople boast a Senate comparable in size to that of Rome, and the city was not governed by a city prefect until 359. These features changed Constantinople from an imperial city to a capital. The specific moment of the transformation is Constantius' decision to alter the nature of the eastern Senate. Before 357, senators who lived in the East or were there for some reason met as an organization that had, at best, a semiformal status as an eastern Senate. Adlections presumably occurred with some frequency, but few are known, as the addition of Themistius in 355 is. Everything changed in 357, when Constantius established a new Senate in the East. The jurisdiction of senators meeting at Constantinople now became the East, as Rome had once governed the entire empire. To accomplish this, the emperor appointed Themistius to find additional members for this new Senate throughout the East.[17]

This shift in the city's status is not immediately obvious from the terminology used by Themistius.[18] He employs various terms to describe Constantinople, but rarely describes it as a "metropolis." His first use of that term to describe a city[19] occurs as "metropolis of trophies," still designating Rome, in *Oration* 3 (42b),[20] in the middle of a passage that emphasizes the joint status of Rome and Constantinople

15. Well described by Mango, *Le développement urbain*.

16. Cf., e.g., the comments of A. Cameron and J. Herrin, *Constantinople in the Early Eighth Century: The PARASTASEIS SYNTOMAI CHRONIKAI*. Columbia Studies in the Classical Tradition 9 (Leiden, 1984), 268.

17. See the further discussion later in this chapter.

18. Cf. Dagron, *Naissance*, 52–54, for more extensive discussion of terminology.

19. In 355, Themistius had used "metropolis" in *Or.* 20, the *epitaphios* on his father, to describe the parentage of vines.

20. On the date of *Or.* 3, see chapter 4.

as participants in the festival celebrated by Constantius in May 357 at Rome. Earlier in the paragraph, Themistius had mentioned "ruling cities," and he goes on to discuss various relationships between the two cities, such as age, size, and primacy. He clearly envisions close ties between the two cities and considers them of virtually equal status. It is less clear whether he intends to convey the reality of an existing situation or is simply attempting to bring the concept and thus a subtle request to Constantius' attention. Given Themistius' later reports of this embassy and its achievements,[21] the latter may be more likely; the request certainly fell on willing ears.

Even in 358, just before he briefly mentions his embassy to Rome the previous year, he talks about Rome as "our metropolis," pointing out specifically that he does not mean the mother city Megara, from which Byzantium was originally colonized, but the "ruler of the other cities, the one ruling together with yours" (Or. 23.298a–b; he is addressing residents of Constantinople in this speech). By the reign of Theodosius, his attitude has apparently changed; in one breath, he is quite willing to consider the two cities as equal in status, before the Council of 381 put a religious stamp on what had become the civic view. In Oration 14, delivered no later than the spring of 379,[22] he links the capitals in no uncertain terms, using the Greek dual to do so. He speaks of the "two métropoleis of the world—I mean that of Romulus and that of Constantine" (14.182a). This conjunction would hardly be surprising after the Council of 381, and it is interesting that Themistius' single use of the word métropolis after 381 is a reference to Rome in the context of the expulsion of foreigners (Or. 18.222b). Perhaps the precedence among equals granted to Rome by the Council has affected Themistius' terminology here. More likely, since Oration 14 includes the request that Theodosius reconfirm the city's earlier privileges, the virtual equality of the two cities was more on Themistius' mind in 379 than in the mid 380s. Naturally, Valens' threat in 378 to plough the site of the eastern city raised some fears for civic security.[23] In the late 350s and mid 380s, when status was not an immediate issue because the matter had recently been settled, Themistius was quite willing to grant some form of precedence to Rome. Interestingly, he uses "the beautiful city"

---

21. See chapter 4.
22. See chapter 8 for the date.
23. See the brief discussion in chapter 8.

(*kallipolis*, a favorite term, possibly adopted from Eusebius)[24] half a dozen times during the reign of Constantius in *Orations* 21, 4, and 3 (in chronological order), all delivered within the space of six to eight months between late 356 and spring 357 and only seven more times in all the rest of his speeches.[25]

Libanius is, perhaps oddly, more helpful, since his terminology for Constantinople changes in the 350s. He does not, in his *Letters*,[26] use the word *métropolis*, but, with a single exception in his correspondence, begins in 357 to use "the Great city" with some frequency in references to Constantinople,[27] and occasionally refers in derision to "the big city in Thrace" (*Or.* 18.177). The exception occurs in a letter (*Ep.* 454) to his uncle Phasganius, normally dated to 355/6, where Libanius refers to the attempt of a madman, seemingly Photius as proconsul, to deprive him (hardly unfairly) of the salary and benefits he was still collecting from Constantinople after he moved to Antioch. The letter mentions the sophist Acacius of Caesarea, a rival of Libanius and apparently in Palestine at the time. Other letters that treat Acacius or were written to him fall between 361 and 365, except for two possible instances in letters of 357 (*Ep.* 50) and 358/9 (*Ep.* 560), and he may appear in *Oration* 31 of 360 or 361.[28] The enumeration in the manuscripts that places *Ep.* 454 with other letters from 355/6, the reference in the letter to Strategius Musonianus, who was praetorian prefect from 354–358, and the death of Phasganius in the autumn of 359 all prevent a radical redating of *Ep.* 454 to the very late 350s, though 357 is possible, apart from the problem of enumeration. More likely, this is an early indication, in a private letter to an uncle, of the sarcastic attitude to Constantinople and its citizens that is evident

---

24. Cf. *VC* 3.55, where Eusebius uses the term for the city. Possible adoption of a word does not mean that Themistius was otherwise much influenced by Eusebius.

25. Once during the reign of Jovian (5.70c), twice under Valens (6.83b; 11.151b), and four times in the reign of Theodosius, three of them in so-called private speeches (14.181d; 31.354d; 34.9, 12).

26. No concordance is available for his speeches, but Dagron, *Naissance*, 56, n. 3, cites some passages relevant to the sophist's usage.

27. Μεγάλη is conveniently capitalized by Foerster in his edition.

28. The date was established by P. Wolf, *Vom Schulwesen der Spätantike: Studien zu Libanius* (Baden-Baden, 1950), 94–95. The speech had previously been dated to 355.

throughout the work of Libanius. He uses "the big city" for other cities, including Antioch, but in reference to Constantinople, "the Great city" always seems to contain an element of disapproval. More significant for the present argument is his frequent use of the term beginning in 357, which implies a change of some sort in the status of Constantinople. His failure to use *métropolis* is simply another indication of his attitude.

Julian, too, briefly discusses the city's status. In his first panegyric of Constantius, he considers Constantinople to be as far above other cities as it is surpassed by Rome. He finds greater advantage, however, in regarding it as the second city after Rome than as the first among the rest (*Or.* 1.8c). Earlier in the speech, Julian had stated that Rome ruled the entire empire (*Or.* 1.5c), and the eastern city, where Julian had been born, is thus no more than an important foundation. The speech cannot be dated later than summer 357: Julian could hardly have failed to mention the victory of 357 after that date; he may, however, allude to the campaign of 356 (*Or.* 1.45b). Early in the panegyric (*Or.* 1.6b–c), Julian forbears to discuss Rome's virtue, stating that Constantius had done so himself. If this refers to the emperor's visit to Rome, which it might not do, Julian cannot have known of changes enacted for Constantinople's Senate during that visit, since his treatment of the city would signify disapproval. In short, Julian's treatment is unhelpful in the attempt to discover a change in the city's status.

One further category of evidence suggests that Constantine's city was not a capital before 357. Though it may be imprudent to place too much weight on manuscript illustrations, the *Calendar of 354* offers depictions of four cities.[29] Rome is clearly depicted as the ruling city: a helmeted Roma is sitting on a throne and holds a globe with a standing victory in one hand, a spear in the other; a sack of money lies at her feet and to her right, a small figure is scattering coins from a second sack. A turreted Alexandria, as is fitting, carries grain, while a

---

29. Cf., for reproductions of these illustrations, M.R. Salzman, *On Roman Time: The Codex Calendar of 354 and the Rhythms of Urban Life in Late Antiquity* (Berkeley and Los Angeles, 1990), figs. 2–5; Dagron, *Naissance*, 64–65, pl. V; J.M.C. Toynbee, *JRS* 37 (1947), fig. 1 for Constantinople and pl. VIII.2 for Rome. The following discussion owes much to both Toynbee and Dagron, though with some modifications.

helmeted Trier has a captive barbarian by his hair. A standing, turreted Constantinopolis carries a spear[30] and a wreath, and a pair of
cherubs (Erotes) holds a wreath above her head. The bag of money at
her feet is numbered M instead of Rome's MCCCC. She has been
identified as a typical city Tyche and a representation of Anthousa,
goddess of prosperity.[31] Her status is clearly similar to that of Rome
who nevertheless takes first place; just as clearly, Constantinopolis
has precedence over the other two cities.[32]

An ancient map, the *Tabula Peutingeriana*, originating in the fourth
century, reveals a change of status.[33] It depicts three cities, Rome,
Constantinople, and Antioch, all seated on thrones. Rome is clearly
the most important imperial city; once again, the helmeted figure
holds a globe. A number of roads lead from her, and she holds a
scepter instead of a spear. Antioch protects an individual who has
sought protection, presumably from Persians.[34] Constantinople wears
military attire, with a helmet instead of a crown, and, more signifi-
cantly, her right hand is stretching toward a column topped by a
figure holding a spear and a globe; this is Constantine's column in
his city.[35] Clearly, Constantinople is now a military or triumphal city,

---

30. Salzman, *On Roman Time*, 28, calls this a scepter, but it is clearly a
spear.

31. Cf. Toynbee, *JRS* 37 (1947): 143.

32. Interpretations differ markedly. Toynbee, *JRS* 37 (1947): 143, holds that
Constantinople is not much raised above the two other cities; Dagron, *Naissance*, 59, gives Constantinople equal status to Rome, though not equal dignity.

33. K. Miller, *Itineraria Romana: Römische Reisewege an der Hand der Tabula
Peutingeriana* (Stuttgart, 1916; reprint 1964), is the standard work. Cf. also
E. Weber, *Tabula Peutingeriana: Codex Vindobonensis 324*, 2 vols. (Graz, 1976),
who offers one volume of facsimiles and one of discussion; and A. Levi and
M. Levi, *Itineraria picta: Contributo allo studio della Tabula Peutingeriana* (Rome,
1967) [which I have not seen]. Brief discussions may be found in O.A.W.
Dilke, *Greek and Roman Maps* (London, 1985), 113–20; and idem, in *The History
of Cartography*. Vol. 1, *Cartography in Prehistoric, Ancient, and Medieval Europe
and the Mediterranean*, ed. J.B. Harley and D. Woodward (Chicago, 1987), 238–
42. Illustrations are also reproduced in Toynbee, *JRS* 37 (1947): pl. IX; Dagron,
Naissance, 64–65, pl. IV.

34. Cf. Dagron, *Naissance*, 58. Dilke, *Greek and Roman Maps*, 116, thinks
that this figure may be a personification of the Orontes. The suggestions are
not mutually exclusive.

35. Cf. Dagron, *Naissance*, 57–58; Toynbee, *JRS* 37 (1947): 143. Levi and
Levi, *Itineraria picta*, 153–54, regard it as a lighthouse.

and the column of Constantine points to its dynastic connections. The original map is often dated to 365/366, on the grounds that the three cities are meant to be imperial centers, Rome in the West, Antioch for Valens, and Constantinople for the usurper Procopius.[36] This is hardly appropriate, since Procopius was never recognized as legitimate.[37] Caution may be in order here, but a conjecture is perhaps not entirely out of the question. In 357, Constantius visited Rome, Persian envoys for peace were at Antioch, and Themistius proclaimed the familial ties of Constantius and Julian with Constantinople.[38] In other words, each city was prominent in that year in exactly the way depicted on the *Tabula*. More to the point for this discussion, the status of Constantinople has changed. Not simply a prominent city, in second place after Rome, it has become a *sovereign* city and a dynastic one, still second to Rome: Constantinopolis is not herself holding a globe, but the figure on the column does. The imagery reflects exactly Themistius' remarks on the city's status at *Oration* 3.41–42. Constantinople is a sovereign city like Rome, by the wish of the emperor, though it yields to Rome in some ways. Whether it has also become a capital is more difficult to judge;[39] within a few years, however, both its Senate and its civic authority, a prefect rather than proconsul, matched that of Rome.

Another issue intrudes upon discussion of these last points. Coins and medallions of the 340s and early 350s portray Rome and Constantinople as virtual equals. In the earliest appearances, dating from 343, the cities, with slightly different iconography, appear in tandem, but Constantinople is soon found alone as well. Rome clearly occupies pride of place, but the eastern city is not far behind. The imagery has

---

36. Suggested by Miller, *Itineraria Romana*, xxx–xxxii; followed by Toynbee, *JRS* 37 (1947): 143, and Levi and Levi, *Itineraria picta*, 65 ff.

37. Dilke, in *History of Cartography*, 239, points out that Valens never reached Antioch, but turned to challenge Procopius. This is surely less important than the fact that Procopius was a usurper.

38. See chapter 4 for more detailed discussion of these points. Dilke, *Greek and Roman Maps*, 116, notes that the temple beside the figure of Antioch may be that of Apollo at Daphne which was damaged by fire in 362 and suggests that the date of the original map may be earlier than that year. Even more importantly perhaps, Nicomedia, which was destroyed by an earthquake in 358, is depicted as still standing.

39. Dagron, *Naissance*, 58, answers this in the negative.

been studied often enough,[40] but one aspect requires further discussion. Though the *Tabula Peutingeriana* suggests that Constantinople is a sovereign city only in 357, the coins and medallions seem to portray this earlier. The solution is perhaps simple. During the 340s and early 350s, Constantius was master over only the eastern part of the empire, while Constans and then Magnentius held the West. With no access to the capital, Constantius chose to promote the claims of Constantinople, but he let these die down somewhat when he gained the West. It is significant, surely, that these coins and medallions were struck with the cooperation of Constans in both East and West (but mainly in the East) during the 340s, by Magnentius in the West when he was still negotiating with the emperor, and by Constantius, first alone and then in conjunction with Gallus, in the East from 350.[41] Later use of the same types merely advertises the dynastic link with Constantinople, especially after Julian became Caesar. Constantius, it seems, advanced the claim of Constantinople more forcefully when he needed the city to balance Rome. Since this had become unnecessary, the prominence of Constantinople after 357 was a consequence less of imperial design than of civic effort. Much of the credit must fall to Themistius, who maintained a close watch on emperors' attitudes and occasionally reminded rulers to keep the city's status equal or very close to that of Rome.

Two items, both already mentioned, were instrumental in the transformation of Constantinople from an important eastern city and dynastic center into an administrative capital. The new Senate created by Constantius in 357 gave the city a governing body equivalent to that of Rome, but hardly as prestigious. The groups may have become equal numerically as well. Though the number of Roman senators is not known with certainty, Constantius increased the size of the eastern Senate to two thousand members and perhaps provided for the enlargement of the older establishment; at the minimum, he needed to ensure that Rome's senators numbered no fewer than those in the East. Replacements for senators transferred to the East were necessary to guarantee performance of the games and perhaps to buy land in Italy that was vacated or sold by senators with new positions in the

40. Cf., e.g., Toynbee, *JRS* 37 (1947): 137–42, with plates; Dagron, *Naissance*, 49–51, with plates.

41. For the details, Toynbee, *JRS* 37 (1947): 137–42.

enlarged Senate at Constantinople.[42] Unfortunately, direct evidence for the enlargement of the Roman Senate is lacking; the single rescript possibly relevant to an increase in the number of senators focuses on games and the search for current senators who avoided their duties by absenteeism (*CTh* 6.4.11). The only other statement is a remark of Ausonius in praise of a teacher of rhetoric, Tiberius Victor Minervius, who "gave one thousand youths to the forum and added two thousand to the number of the Senate and the purple togas" (*Prof.* 1.9–10). Though Minervius taught at Bordeaux, Constantinople, and Rome, he was hardly responsible personally for two thousand new senators,[43] not even in the East and West combined. Most likely, Ausonius simply means that all senators at Rome were once students of Minervius, because they had "heard him"; he had doubtless delivered at least one speech in the Roman Senate. This would indicate a body of two thousand members, not necessarily when Minervius spoke, but when Ausonius wrote the work.[44]

By contrast, Themistius offers clear evidence that the Senate in the East was enlarged in 357; he speaks of his own responsibility to find 1,700 new senators,[45] an immense task that occupied him for some years. The three hundred existing senators present a different problem, since their provenance is unknown. Some had certainly been added to an existing eastern senatorial group. Themistius himself is an example; in his announcement of the adlection in 355, Constantius eschews any mention of the Roman Senate. Similarly, Constantius addressed the body as "the Senate" on the subject of praetorian

---

42. Unfortunately, the available evidence does not allow a conclusion on when and if the requirement that senators own land in Italy elapsed, but many certainly owned large estates in the region; cf. J.F. Matthews, *Western Aristocracies and Imperial Court* A.D. 364–425 (Oxford, 1975), 17–31.

43. H. Sivan, *Ausonius of Bordeaux: Genesis of a Gallic Aristocracy* (London and New York, 1993), 83, taking the passage very literally, suggests that Minervius had three thousand students.

44. Cf. A. Chastagnol, *La préfecture urbaine à Rome sous le Bas-Empire* (Paris, 1960), 38, with reference to J. Sundwall, *Weströmische Studien* (Berlin, 1915), 150–52, and Alföldi, *Conflict of Ideas,* 59, on the number of senators at Rome. Sivan, *Ausonius of Bordeaux,* 165, provides a table of the different dates, from 367–389, assigned to this work of Ausonius by different scholars; Minervius, according to Jerome, *Chron.* s.a. 353, was active in Rome in the 350s.

45. I make some general remarks here; for the details of Themistius' role and position, see chapter 4.

games in 340 (*CTh* 6.4.5, 6); the rescripts were sent from Antioch when requests from Rome were the responsibility of Constans. Some structured existence must therefore be accorded to the eastern Senate from an early point of the city's history, perhaps from 340, when the empire was divided between Constans and Constantius.[46]

That much is certain, even if these senators were Roman senators who happened to meet at Constantinople; less clear is the status of the three hundred existing senators in 357. Had they all been part of this body regularly, or were some of them newly transferred from Rome in that year? Too little is known about them, but worth noting are the regions mentioned by Constantius in 357 (*CTh* 6.4.11): Achaea, Macedonia, and Illyricum. These areas had been under the jurisdiction of Constans during the 340s; their senators presumably met at Rome during that period. The rescript offers compensation to Rome for privileges given to the eastern Senate and states unequivocally that some senators had chosen to avoid senatorial service at Rome[47] and their Italian estates. A few senators had perhaps migrated to the East, and these, with others who had abandoned responsibilities entirely, were ordered by Constantius to return to their Roman senatorial seats.[48] The rescript thus removed senators from Constantinople, though some, perhaps many, Roman senators of eastern origin were reallocated to the new Senate.[49] The single known example from the

---

46. Cf. Jones, *LRE*, 1:132, for the view that Constantius instituted the Senate in Constantinople in 340 because Constans now had sole possession of Rome.

47. "Furthermore, if any persons should artfully avoid the Senate House of the City of Rome, though endowed with the title of Most Noble, We have issued orders that they shall be sought out throughout Achaea, Macedonia, and all Illyricum, since they rarely or never frequent the seat of their own dignity" (trans. Pharr).

48. Cf. Dagron, *Naissance*, 127–29, for a very similar view. P. Petit, *Ant. Class.* 26 (1957): 357, has a somewhat different view.

49. This is an inversion of the standard view, which holds that senators from these areas were transferred to Constantinople and that the rescript exempted them from the requirement to pay for games if they had already done so at Rome. Cf., e.g., Chastagnol, *La préfecture urbaine*, 38, citing the first edition of A. Piganiol, *L'Empire chrétien* (Paris, 1947), 105 (117 in the second edition); Jones, *LRE*, 1:132, 2:546. Since the rescript is addressed simply "To the Senate," it may have been sent to either Senate, or even to both, so that no senator needed to pay for games twice. The first part of the rescript

350s suggests as much. Libanius (*Ep.* 70) refers to the transfer of the Antiochene Olympius, a senator in Rome, to Constantinople and asks Themistius to free his new charge from the requirement to pay the entry fee and the need to live in Constantinople; Olympius had previously gained these exemptions from Rome.[50] Senators were thus normally expected to live in Constantinople, possibly because they served as the city council as well. In later years, this requirement seems to have been relaxed;[51] senators occasionally changed their residences, in the train of emperors like Valens and Theodosius, and doubtless with imperial permission,[52] but these changes seems rare. Even in 384, Celsus, a philosopher from Athens, was granted entrance to the Roman Senate on the recommendation of Symmachus (*Rel.* 5).[53] Clearly, a geographical division of senatorial jurisdiction, with Achaea, Macedonia, and Illyricum allocated to Rome, occurred in 357.

A few corollary conclusions follow. First, the apparent traffic of senators between East and West under a sole emperor in the early 350s suggests that the two bodies had not yet separated, even if the Senate in the East had been granted its existence as a legitimate institution. In short, eastern senators were still Roman senators who happened to hold their meetings in Constantinople; presumably, ethnic and cultural ties with the Greek East made this a desirable venue for some senators from Greek-speaking areas of the empire. Second, some semiformal arrangement had been operative earlier, when two emperors ruled portions of the empire. In this period, senators from every region gathered in the Senate House under the dominion of their own emperor.[54] Finally, and most important, in 357 Constantius divided the empire into two parts for senatorial purposes and formalized the arrangement, basing his partition on the border that had once separated his dominion from that of Constans, with the diocese of

---

mentions Rome specifically. Dagron, *Naissance*, 129, suggests that some nonextant laws to complete the process of transfer were promulgated.

50. For discussion, cf. Petit, *Ant. Class.* 26 (1957): 367–69.

51. Cf. Petit, *Ant. Class.* 26 (1957): 357–58.

52. Cf. Jones, *LRE*, 2:552.

53. This Celsus is not the Antiochene former student of a Sicyonian philosopher who entered the Senate at Constantinople.

54. Cf. Jones, *LRE*, 1:132: "The nucleus of the new senate was presumably formed by the Roman senators domiciled in Constantius' dominions."

Thrace allocated to the East. Precisely at this point, the Senate of Constantinople gained an independent existence; the year 357 thus represents a key point of transition in the administrative history of the Roman Empire. Two Senates, equal in number, equal in status, and soon to be governed in the same way by a city prefect, had replaced the single administrative unit. In one important way, the Byzantine Empire began in 357.[55]

The impetus perhaps came as much from the eastern senators themselves as from the emperor. Though Constantius continued, even after gaining control of the West, to promote both the Senate and the city of Constantinople, he spent most of the 350s in the West. More importantly, senators of eastern origin had become accustomed to serving in Constantinople; many of them might well have preferred the East, where they were much more prominent socially and politically and free of the need to compete with aristocratic Roman families of ancient senatorial heritage. This was particularly true of many new appointees, who, like Themistius himself, had neither the resources nor the desire to rival Roman senators in the traditional center of the empire. A formally instituted Senate in Constantinople was, for senators of this type, a solution to some of the problems associated with membership.

Unfortunately, the exact moment of the decision to create the new Senate cannot be recovered. In *Oration* 3, in May 357, Themistius talks of two ruling cities, but still considers Rome the "metropolis" of the empire; he does not mention the creation of a new Senate in the speech. This may be a politic silence designed to appease a body that had just lost its exclusivity, or possibly the decision had not yet been made. Later, Themistius mentions discussions with Constantius, as a representative of his fellow senators.[56] If these private talks with the emperor introduced the subject of a formally constituted eastern Senate, the proposal fell on willing ears. Equally possible is the suggestion that Constantius announced his intention to Themistius and the other senators who had accompanied the orator. Once this decision had been made, actions followed quickly: Themistius was delegated to find 1,700 new senators. Less certain, but likely, is the suggestion

---

55. The fact that the boundary between East and West shifted occasionally (cf. V. Grumel, *REB* 9 [1951]: 5–46) does not seem to have affected the location of senatorial seats.

56. See chapter 4 for Themistius' visit to Rome.

that Constantius decided at the same time to replace the proconsul of Constantinople with an urban prefect;[57] previous announcement of future proconsuls or the need to find a suitable first incumbent may have forced the delay in implementation.

The new Senate was considerably less prestigious than the Roman institution. Libanius, who in any case never had much regard for the eastern foundation, remarks (*Ep.* 70), in a letter to Themistius, that Olympius had been transferred from the superior Senate to a lesser one, a typical expression of the sophist's attitude and perhaps a slight on the philosopher. In another letter, this time to Iamblichus, Libanius writes that senatorial service "profits nonentities" (*Ep.* 34.4; trans. Norman). Factors other than the antiquity and wealth of the Roman Senate and senators contributed as well. By imperial edict and legislation, the wealthiest and most prominent citizens were bound to serve as decurions in their own cities; they could thus not be selected to serve at Constantinople without exemptions from curial duties, and these exemptions were usually opposed by the cities of origin. Many individuals of this group in any case preferred not to serve at Constantinople. Membership consequently devolved upon a lower class of citizen, as many men, not necessarily all, who had served in various capacities in the civil and military bureaucracies became de facto senators at Constantinople. While the same circumstances affected Rome, the established core of old senatorial families was a much higher percentage of the total. Rhetors, philosophers, and other teachers were also chosen for the new Senate by virtue of their profession. Presumably, their education contributed, if not to the prestige, at least to the quality of the assembly. Generally, then, the quality of possible candidates in the East could not match the Senate in the West. The expectation that it might is unreasonable: the Roman Senate had been formed under an entirely different set of circumstances.[58] Nevertheless, a decision was made in 357 to create a new Senate, equal in number, status, and jurisdiction to the old Senate. Less prestigious or not, this new Senate made Constantinople a second imperial city in the full sense of the word.

---

57. As Chastagnol, *La préfecture urbaine*, 38, proposes.

58. Cf. Jones, *LRE*, 2:546–57, on the class of senators at both Rome and Constantinople with individual examples, and 2:554–56, on the different outlays of money for games at the two cities as an indication of the senators' respective wealth.

The transformation of Constantinople's status continued with the establishment of an urban prefecture. Previously, the city had been governed by proconsuls, perhaps appropriately, since it does not seem to have had a city council or curial class apart from a senate whose members were at first styled *clari*, not *clarissimi* like senators at Rome.[59] Constantinople is perhaps best regarded in its early history as a territory carved out of Thrace for governmental purposes, but separate from it. Few of the proconsuls are known, among them Alexander and Limenius in the 340s, and Justinus, Araxius, and perhaps Anatolius, Flavius Strategius Musonianus, and Photius in the 350s.[60] As long as the city had no formally constituted Senate, government by a proconsul presiding over a senatorial group, in the manner of a governor convening a provincial council, was suitable; the establishment of a large Senate with jurisdiction over the entire East demanded a change.

That change occurred with the inauguration of Honoratus as the first city prefect in late 359, with Constantius present for the installation. The event is dated to both 11 September (*Chron. Pasch.* s.a. 359) and 11 December (*Cons. Const.* s.a. 359), but the later date is preferable. The activities of Constantius in that year and the dates of the ecclesiastical councils in Ariminum and Seleucia require a date in December.[61] Honoratus had served the emperor in several previous positions. He had been *consularis Syriae* ca 350 and *comes Orientis* ca 353/354. Similarly, the next known city prefect, Domitius Modestus had also been *comes Orientis* before he assumed his position at Constantinople.[62] Judging from the careers of other prefects, few candidates, if any, held the prefecture until they had served in some other important capacity in the bureaucracy.[63] This, combined with a preference for longer tenures of office during the early period, makes it unlikely that Themistius was city prefect between Honoratus and

59. For discussion, cf. Dagron, *Naissance*, 123–24. Either a change occurred before 355 or Themistius was an exception: he is named *lamprotatos* by Constantius (*Ep. Const.* 19b).

60. Cf. Dagron, *Naissance*, 220–24.

61. For discussion, Dagron, *Naissance*, 215–17. On the councils, Barnes, *Athanasius and Constantius*, 144–49.

62. Dagron, *Naissance*, 240–73, offers a prosopography of known prefects from 359–452.

63. Cf. Dagron's prosopography at *Naissance*, 240–73, and idem, 274–94, on the career patterns of prefects.

Domitius Modestus and may be part of the reason he did not serve, even though he had been announced.[64] All the evidence points to the conclusion that the prefecture was at first reserved for men who had chosen a career in imperial service.

Like the proconsul before him, the city prefect became the president of the Senate while in office. Themistius himself served in that capacity in 384, apparently referring to his position as the *prohedria*, a standard term used for the office and dignity of the presiding officers of assemblies.[65] To the city prefect, therefore, fell the duties of convening the Senate and guiding its discussions. Comparison with Symmachus at Rome suggests as well that the task of maintaining civic contact with the imperial court fell to the prefect. He was responsible for the government and well-being of the city. The civic bureaucracy was under his control, and his duties, in contrast to those of Rome's prefect, included the maintenance of the food supply. The burden was considerable, and it is not surprising that the office was most often given to men with previous experience in administration.[66]

The city prefect was not, however, the *princeps senatus*. This position of honor was reserved for a different individual, who held it for a long period, perhaps for life. At Constantinople, almost nothing is known of such a position. Yet Themistius claims to have held an honor that he calls a *prostasia* from 357 until at least 385.[67] His fellow senators, he avers, had selected him to be the foremost senator, not

---

64. For the view that Themistius was neither proconsul nor city prefect during the reign of Constantius, see chapter 4.

65. The title in the manuscripts of *Or.* 31 is *peri prohedria*, and Themistius uses the word at the end of the speech (355c) to describe the presidency of Calliope and a man "whom the daughters of mighty Zeus esteem." Cf. *LSJ*, s.v., for the meanings of the term in earlier periods, and, for the extension to presiding presbyters and bishops, G.W.H. Lampe, *A Patristic Greek Lexicon* (Oxford, 1961), s.v.

66. For detailed treatment, cf. Dagron, *Naissance*, 226–39. There is little direct evidence for the prefecture at Constantinople and more for Rome in this period; comparisons have generally been made. For the prefecture at Rome, cf. also Chastagnol, *La préfecture urbaine*. Rome continued to have a *praefectus annonae*, though even there many of his previous responsibilities fell to the city prefect; cf. Chastagnol, *La préfecture urbaine*, 54–63; Dagron, *Naissance*, 228–29.

67. The argument that Themistius became *princeps senatus* is developed more fully in chapter 4.

when he began to enlarge the Senate, but earlier, with his selection to head the embassy to Rome. This claim would seem, prima facie, to indicate a role as *princeps senatus*. A comparison with Rome, because its Senate was structured very similarly, is instructive. Three *principes senatus* are known in the fourth century. In the early 350s, Constantius arrested a certain Nunechius, the *princeps senatus* who had come to negotiate on behalf of Magnentius (Petr. Pat. fr. 16). Both the elder Symmachus and his more famous homonymous son were *principes senatus*, at points in their careers when they were not in office as city prefect.[68] On this model, Constantinople ought to have had a *princeps senatus* as well.[69]

Much changed at Constantinople in the first decade of Themistius' permanent residence. In the late 340s, the city was, for Constantius, an imperial center made more important by Constans' control of Rome. Its walls and public buildings were still under construction, and its Senate was little more than a local council, with a semiformal structure and a proconsul as presiding officer. Schools of rhetoric and philosophy were only beginning to achieve some prominence. Ten years later, Constantinople was a second capital, with the prefecture of the Orient under its jurisdiction. The imperial building program had continued, and the city's amenities had increased considerably. The eastern Senate was now a fully constituted imperial assembly, governing the East as Rome had once ruled the entire empire, and equal to the western Senate in number and, theoretically, in status. The city and its Senate were governed by a city prefect, and the addition of teachers of rhetoric and philosophy to the Senate contributed to the academic prestige of the capital. As Themistius himself noted in a speech of 357 (4.61a–b), the city's harbors now traded in education as well as merchandise.

The population of the city had expanded as well, though the details can no longer be recovered. While enough grain to feed 600,000 persons reached Constantinople during the reign of Justinian in the

---

68. For discussion, cf. Chastagnol, *La préfecture urbaine*, 69–72. P.E. Vigneaux, *Essai sur l'histoire de la praefectura urbis à Rome* (Paris, 1896), 88 [which I have not seen], had argued that the city prefect filled this position.

69. Dagron, *Naissance*, 143–44, with 144, n. 1, suggests that the position at Constantinople was filled by individuals like Aspar and Basiliscus who played a truly political role, but both examples belong to the fifth century, when much had changed.

sixth century, Constantine had established grain distribution for 80,000.[70] This was halved in 342, apparently without serious consequences, as punishment for the murder of Hermogenes and restored to its full amount in 357, when Themistius convinced Constantius to do so.[71] Arguably, the restoration was necessary because the city's population had increased appreciably; it may have reached 100,000 in the 370s or 380s.[72] Though eligibility for the free distribution was not universal, the number of candidates had perhaps surpassed 40,000 by 357, with a total population something in the region of 70,000. To what extent it was Christian is impossible to determine. John Chrysostom speaks of 100,000 Christians and 50,000 poor (some presumably Christians) in the much larger city of the early fifth century (*Hom. XI in Act. Apost.* 3).

When Themistius arrived, Constantinople was just beginning its ascent to greatness. He himself was responsible for some of the changes and contributed his talents in several areas. His oratory contributed to a high imperial regard for the city, and his position as professor added to the educational system. Above all, his role as senator increased both the status and stature of Constantinople. In all three respects, Themistius was a public figure; his important role in these areas must now occupy center stage.

---

70. Most discussions of population start from the grain supply; cf., e.g., J.L. Teall, *DOP* 13 (1959): 89–139; Jones, *LRE*, 2:696–98; Mango, *Le développment urbain*, 53. Dagron, *Naissance*, 518–41, introduces other considerations as well.

71. See the brief discussion in chapter 4.

72. D. Jacoby, *Byzantion* 31 (1961): 102–9, on the basis of the areas enclosed by the walls of Constantine and Theodosius, argues that the first envisioned a population of 100,000–150,000, the second 400,000–500,000, and that the first stage was surpassed by the 380s, with a very rapid increase after 390; cf. also Dagron, *Naissance*, 524–25. Teall, *DOP* 13 (1959): 92, suggests that the population reached 500,000 by 400. Many of the estimates are too high; some of the grain shipped to Constantinople was perhaps sold or diverted for military use.

4

Themistius and Constantius

Themistius first became involved in the public life of the East while Constantius was emperor. His career advanced only in this reign and that of Theodosius. He continued to be important in the intervening years and retained the title of *princeps senatus*, but his relations with emperors were less harmonious, and at times he had considerably less influence. In the reign of Constantius, he was on occasion accused of excessive involvement in politics, but he continually denies this, replying that his harmonious relations with Constantius were the result of the emperor's virtue and character, as he does during the reign of Theodosius, when a similar debate was raging. The harmony began with the delivery of *Oration 1*, but clearly the philosopher had previously considered Constantius a virtuous emperor.[1]

Raised to a share of the throne by Constantine soon after the final victory over Licinius, Constantius and his brothers gained control of the empire between the death of their father on 22 May 337 and 9 September 337.[2] They eliminated all male paternal relatives except Gallus and Julian, who were still too young to be dangerous. Though Julian blames Constantius, all three were involved in the planning and design, though most of the slain lived in Constantius' part of the empire. For the next three years, the brothers governed in apparent peace. In 340, Constantinus, the eldest, invaded the territory of his youngest brother Constans. For his efforts, he was killed, and Constans assumed control of the West; Themistius later praises Constantius for not taking additional territory. For several years, the two were content and preoccupied, Constans with the borders in the West, Constantius with the Persians.[3]

---

1. So G. Wirth, *BF* 6 (1979): 298. Wirth offers a survey of Themistius' relations with Constantius that differs at many points from the views in this chapter.

2. For the dates, cf. Barnes, *New Empire*, 8.

3. For their known movements, Barnes, *Phoenix* 34 (1980): 160–66, now replaced by idem, *Athanasius and Constantius*, 218–26.

Constantius spent much of the period from 337 to 350 at Antioch and near the eastern frontier. He traveled to Constantinople early in 342—because the controversy following the death of the bishop Eusebius resulted in a riot and the lynching of the *magister equitum* Hermogenes—and in the autumn of 343 or 349.[4] In March 347, he was at Ancyra, possibly on his way to Constantinople. His single visit to Macellum, where he had sent Julian and Gallus in 342,[5] probably dates to 347. Almost every year, his military engaged the Persians, though Constantius was not always present.

By the middle of the decade, relations between emperors had deteriorated. Beyond natural rivalry, religious convictions played a major role. The bishop of Alexandria, Athanasius, who had returned to his see after the death of Constantine, was ejected again and fled to the western court in the spring of 339. Some three years later, Constans and Constantius began negotiations; neither these nor the Council of Serdica (343) were immediately successful, since Athanasius did not return to Alexandria until autumn 346. The final resolution of the issue was not a peaceful compromise: frustrated by the delay, Constans wrote his brother a letter in 345, threatening to reinstate Athanasius personally, by force if necessary, and traveling as far as Sirmium (he had been in Italy and Gaul since 340) to lend credence to his threat. Constantius, whose armies and eastern boundaries were under constant danger from Persian invasions (which are well enough attested for both 345 and 346), had little choice but to capitulate.[6] His fondness for his younger brother can hardly have grown. Two years later, relations improved, or perhaps it seemed desirable to portray harmony: the new bronze coinage of 348 was issued in the name of

---

4. Barnes, *Phoenix* 34 (1980): 164, suggested a visit in 349, but more recently considers the possibility that the evidence for this date (*CTh* 12.2.1; 15.1.6) ought to be redated to 343: cf. idem, *Athanasius and Constantius*, 220, with nn. 18 and 25. R. Klein, *Constantius II. und die christliche Kirche*, Impulse der Forschung 26 (Darmstadt, 1977), 74, n. 179, suggests that Constantius was at the Council of Serdica (dated to 343 by Barnes, *Athanasius and Constantius*, 71). For reasons that chapter 2 makes clear, a visit in 349 seems desirable.

5. This account follows the early chronology of Julian's exile, but differs in some details from the view of N.H. Baynes, *JHS* 45 (1925): 251–54. For Constantius' single visit, Jul. *Ep. ad Ath.* 274a.

6. Cf. the detailed account in Barnes, *Athanasius and Constantius*, 34–93. Constans' letter is quoted by Soc. *HE* 2.22.5.

both and proclaimed, among other things, a unified empire.[7] When Constans fell to Magnentius' uprising in January 350, Constantius quickly settled matters in the East and traveled to the West to secure his throne.

Themistius delivered his first panegyric of Constantius in this context, but the evidence for its date is susceptible to varying interpretations. In this speech, as in many others, he concerns himself with philosophical themes and rarely alludes to historical events. Two dates have emerged. Foerster,[8] in the belief that Libanius saw the speech before he wrote his own panegyric of Constantius and Constans (Or. 59), dated Themistius' speech to the 340s, before the death of Constans. He proposed 347, when Constantius was at Ancyra, where the speech was delivered (CTh 11.36.8: 8 March).[9] Seeck[10] noted that Themistius does not refer to Constans at all and concluded that the panegyric must postdate his death. Attestation at Ancyra is not decisive, he argued, since Constantius passed through Ancyra each time he traveled from the eastern frontier to Constantinople. He suggested 350 as the only possibility, given Constantius' lengthy stay in the West.[11]

The rubric prefixed to the text of Oration 1 reports that Themistius was a young man when he delivered the panegyric: "He delivered the speech in Galatian Ancyra, when he first encountered the emperor and was still a young man. For that reason, he is not entirely in control of the form."[12] On its own, "young man" cannot support an argument for 347 as opposed to 350: it is imprecise and can describe a man of thirty-three, as well as thirty, years of age. Initially, the remark

---

7. See the final note of chapter 2 for references.

8. Foerster, Libanii Opera, 4:201–2. Recently, W. Portmann, BZ 82 (1989): 1–18, has challenged Foerster's, and the standard, view that Libanius delivered the speech in 348/9, dating it to 344/5 instead.

9. Recently, few have accepted this date, which, as Gladis, Themistii, 2, with n. 2, points out, was the standard view, held by Harduin, p. 371 (p. 496 Dindorf); Baret, Themistio, 1; G.R. Sievers, Das Leben des Libanius (Berlin, 1868), 56; and others, before Seeck's proposal.

10. Briefe, 293–94.

11. Accepted by Stegemann, "Themistios," 1644; Scholze, Temporibus, 9–10; Bouchery, Themistius, 38; Dagron, Thémistios, 20; Wirth, BF 6 (1979): 299–300; PLRE, 1:889, 893; and others. Gladis, Themistii, 4–5, suggested 348.

12. οὗτος εἴρηται ἐν Ἀγκύρᾳ τῆς Γαλατίας, ὅτε πρῶτον συνέτυχε τῷ βασιλεῖ, νέος ὢν ἔτι· διόπερ οὐδὲ πάνυ κρατεῖ τῆς ἰδέας.

that Themistius delivered the speech when he first encountered the emperor is more promising, since it suggests that Themistius was unknown to the court, acting on his own behalf and perhaps seeking imperial favor. The orator's installation at Constantinople can be dated to the 340s on other grounds,[13] but it is not certain when he first met Constantius, who was perhaps at the capital in 349.[14]

The single allusion to specific military activity of Constantius is imprecise, but may offer a new conclusive argument. After a discussion of the virtuous and philanthropic emperor (βασιλεύς) that contrasts the Persian king as "tyrant" (τύραννος) and "dynast" (δυνάστης) (1.11b–c), Themistius states, "This, then, is what destroyed him [the Persian king], not Mesopotamia, but the virtue of the emperor shining nearby" (1.12a–b). The Persian king obviously suffered a reverse[15] after crossing into Roman territory (Mesopotamia),[16] with Constantius in the vicinity. Festus (*Brev.* 27) reports nine important battles with the Persians in the reign of Constantius. The emperor took part in two, both at or near Singara, in 344 and 348. His direct participation excludes both from consideration as the engagement when he was nearby; neither 344 nor 348 is the *terminus post quem* for Themistius' speech,[17] though Libanius probably wrote *Oration* 59 after the first battle.[18]

Few details of other Roman campaigns against the Persians in the

---

13. For discussion, see chapter 2.

14. συνέτυχε τῷ βασιλεῖ can mean anything from a public appearance before the emperor to a private audience, but the earliest contact with the court seems the most natural interpretation. Constantius appears to have had some knowledge of a private speech delivered at Constantinople; see chapter 2.

15. So too, Gladis, *Themistii*, 4.

16. For Romans, Mesopotamia was Roman; cf. Ammianus' emotional response to the treaty of Jovian that ceded Nisibis to the Persians (25.9). The Persians naturally regarded it as their own. On such perceptions, cf. Matthews, *Ammianus*, 54–56.

17. The standard view, held by Dindorf, *Themistii Orationes*, 499; Gladis, *Themistii*, 4; G. Downey, *G&BS* 1 (1958): 63; and others. Portmann, *Panegyrik*, 261, nn. 3–4, finds the view problematic, but nevertheless dates the speech to 350.

18. So Portmann, *BZ* 82 (1989): 1–18, who dates the first battle to 344 and consequently places *Or.* 59 in 344/5 on the principle applied here, i.e., shortly after his latest datable reference. For problems with sources for the two battles, cf. J.W. Eadie, *The Breviarum of Festus: A Critical Edition with Historical Commentary* (London, 1967), 150, and Barnes, *Phoenix* 34 (1980): 163.

340s are known. Nevertheless, the passage demands an occasion when Constantius was near the frontier for a Roman victory. The siege of Nisibis in summer 337 is too early to merit consideration. In any case, Constantius was nowhere nearby. Shapur invested Nisibis again in 346 and in 350.[19] According to Theophanes (a.m. 5841), the Persians, with elephants among their forces, breached the city wall in three places in 350, but retired without success. Zonaras (13.7) reports that Constantius fortified the city and restored its inhabitants, but only after Shapur, attacked and harassed by the Massagetae, had departed in shame. Ephraem of Nisibis offers further evidence for the emperor's activity in 350. He focuses on theological interpretation of the city's liberation, with historical agents largely forgotten; an impending imperial visit is not a cause of Shapur's departure, as it is in 346. Instead, he attributes deliverance to the prayers of the bishop Vologeses.[20] The *Chronicon Paschale* offers more information. When Shapur asked the inhabitants of Nisibis to surrender, they refused, in the absence of the emperor, who was at Antioch. Because (in a vision) he had seen Constantius standing on the wall, the Persian king failed to understand this response and departed.[21] With the emperor at Antioch or at least nowhere near Nisibis, "shining nearby" cannot describe Constantius's activities in this year.

The siege in 346 was also unsuccessful. Jerome (a. 346, p. 236 Helm) is unhelpful, as is the account of Theophanes (a.m. 5838), who notes only a siege of seventy-eight days and Shapur's departure in shame. Ephraem offers a little more. In a hymn (*Carm. Nis.* 13.15) linking the outcome of the sieges to three successive bishops of

---

19. Eadie, *Festus*, 149–51, lists the sources for the various engagements. Cf., most recently, C.S. Lightfoot, *Historia* 37 (1988): 105–25, for a detailed discussion.

20. Many of the relevant portions of Ephraem and the other sources cited here are available in translation in M.H. Dodgeon and S.N.C. Lieu, *The Roman Eastern Frontier and the Persian Wars (A.D. 226–363): A Documentary History* (London and New York, 1991), 164–207.

21. Edited by J. Bidez-F. Winkelmann, *Philostorgius Kirchengeschichte*, 2nd ed. (Berlin, 1972), Anhang VII, p. 217.12–218.19; less detail in Theophanes, a.m. 5841, also edited in Bidez-Winkelmann, pp. 217.34–218.34. Cf. Theod. *HE* 2.30. The story about Constantius remaining at Antioch is told of both 337 and 350 in the sources; cf. the material collected by Dodgeon and Lieu, *Roman Eastern Frontier*, 166–71, 203–6. Barnes, *Athanasius and Constantius*, 313, n. 27, doubts that Constantius stayed at Antioch in 350.

Nisibis (Jacob, Babu, and Vologeses), he reports that Constantius came near the city and withdrew. While his poem lacks precision, the approach was apparently sufficient to drive away the Persian king. Athanasius (*Apol. sec.* 51.6) seems to confirm that Constantius traveled as far as Edessa in 346.[22]

Only the Syriac poet confirms Themistius' remark that the emperor was once nearby when Shapur departed, and he places this occasion in 346. Because the orator does not refer to Singara in 348, as would be normal if this were the emperor's most recent victory, the panegyric should fall between the two engagements. The emperor's attested presence at Ancyra in March 347 makes this date the most suitable. Some problems remain. Themistius does not refer to Constans.[23] Yet he reveals no knowledge of usurpations in the West either; the omission would be startling in 350.[24] Themistius occasionally refers to the Persian king as a tyrant who rules through fear, in contrast to Constantius' philanthropy (e.g., 1.10c–11b). In 350, Magnentius was the obvious example, as he is in *Oration* 2. His absence and Constantius' preoccupation with Persia are further reasons to prefer a date in 347. The exclusion of Constans results from strained relations between emperors and reveals the orator's perspicacity in matters of politics: after the reform of bronze coinage in 348 and the illusion of harmony, reference to Constans, living or dead, would be required. 348 is thus the *terminus ante quem* for the speech. With this established, silence on the West is not critically important for the date of the speech, though

22. Cf. Barnes, *Phoenix* 34 (1980): 163–64, who cites Ephraem, *Carm. Nis.* 13.4–6, as evidence for an imperial visit to Nisibis in 345; also idem, *Athanasius and Constantius,* 220. This does not preclude the possibility that Constantius approached the city in 346. As Barnes notes (*Phoenix* 34 [1980]: 164, n. 14), Eadie, *Festus,* 150–51, goes too far when ascribing to Ephraem the view that Constantius reached Nisibis, thus inducing Shapur to flee. Rather, the emperor's threatened arrival frightened the Persian king.

23. The major obstacle to an early date, in the view of Seeck, *Briefe,* 293–94; he notes Themistius' remark at 16.200b (1 January 383) that he had first come into contact with the court more than thirty years previously (cf. also *Briefe,* 269–70), which, as Gladis, *Themistii,* 4, points out, means only that he had had dealings with the court for more than thirty years. Both 347 and 350 can fit the phrase.

24. So too Gladis, *Themistii,* 4. Barnes, *Athanasius and Constantius,* 313, n. 21, puts much emphasis on this and suggests a date either in 347 or in whichever of 343 or 349 Constantius visited Constantinople.

Constans' letter to his brother provides a solid pretext for silence and a possible *terminus post quem.*[25] Taken together, the evidence points unequivocally to delivery in 347. In the absence of a complete description of military activity, the only specific allusion should refer to events closely preceding the delivery of the panegyric. Therefore, Themistius delivered *Oration* 1 early in 347 at Ancyra. The example of Himerius is instructive: the sophist delivered a number of speeches, as professor at Athens, for the *aduentus* of governors. Themistius may well have done the same for the emperor when Constantius passed through Anycra in 347.[26] The speech represents Themistius' public service as a teacher and was not commissioned by Constantinople;[27] it may have led to his appointment at the city.

The remark that Themistius had not yet mastered the genre can mean almost anything. It may simply indicate that Themistius' speech did not conform to the standard model for imperial panegyric.[28] A statement broad enough to cover any fault of design or composition may include the omission of a second emperor. This is particularly relevant if Libanius, whose own *Oration* 59 addresses both emperors, but focuses on Constantius, wrote the remark.[29]

In this first imperial panegyric,[30] titled "On Philanthropy or Constantius," Themistius outlines a philosophy of kingship retained

25. For Themistius' silence on Valentinian II, see chapter 8.

26. See chapter 2 for the suggestion that he was teaching at Ancyra in 347.

27. As Gladis, *Themistii*, 4, and most others think. Speeches delivered as a representative normally mention that fact in some way; this panegyric does not.

28. Outlined by Menander Rhetor, pp. 368–77 (= Russell and Wilson, *Menander Rhetor*, 76–94).

29. H. Schenkl, in O. Seeck and H. Schenkl, *RhM* 61 (1906): 560–61, discusses the summaries preceding some of Themistius' speeches, arguing that they were written by the same individual. Since the hypothesis of *Or.* 2, with close verbal parallels to the Φιλόπολις, is attributed to Libanius in one manuscript, he reasonably suggests that Libanius wrote some hypotheses when preparing an edition of Themistius' speeches. Hypotheses are extant only for *Or.* 1, 2, 4, 20, and the *Ep. Const.* (none later than 1 January 357); perhaps these speeches formed part of a collected edition donated early in 357 to the library instituted by Constantius. The orator mentions the donation at 4.61c–d, and *Or.* 3, his next, has no hypothesis. Any number of reasons can explain the lack of hypotheses for *Or.* 21, 24, 27, 30, 32, and 33. On the hypothesis for *Or.* 26, see the discussion later in this chapter and appendix 2.

30. Downey, *G&BS* 1 (1958): 49–69, has translated the speech.

throughout his life. He notes first his difference from other panegyrists who only describe externals. As philosopher, he looks deeper
and, without flattery,[31] repeats what he had heard about Constantius;
truth depends on the accuracy of these reports (1.1a–4a). Though
philosophers alone are true witnesses of virtue (1.3d), they merely
recognize and systematize what all can see dimly, an argument perhaps designed to ensure a receptive audience for a speech that was
not standard fare. In the discourse, Themistius moves between abstract and concrete, with boundaries not always evident. His theme is
philanthropy, the sole requirement for achieving perfect fame (1.4b–
c). The treatise explains and amplifies, describing how other virtues
fall within the scope of philanthropy.

In Themistius' view,[32] the philanthropic emperor is just, moderate,
and courageous, and acts with mildness and gentleness. He knows
that he must exercise self-control before he rules others. Kingship has
its own *areté*, which includes the virtues mentioned, but these are not
sufficient until philanthropy places a seal on them. An emperor must
be calm, not stirred by anger, which is temporary madness. He is
dangerous when angry: Polydamas and Glaucus caused little damage, but tribes and nations felt the madness of Cambyses (1.4a–7c).

Themistius esteems Constantius because he softened his high
spirit, rendering it useful and helpful (1.7c).[33] In consequence, it does
not induce him to proceed without reflection or impel him, like a
horse chewing at the bit, to ignore the charioteer (1.7c).[34] The emperor, Themistius intimates, has made his high spirit helpful. Without
further comment, the orator moves on. Ammianus confirms the lofty
spirit of the emperor. When he entered Rome in 357, Constantius was
as immobile as a statue, not turning to the right or the left, not spit-
ting or wiping his face and nose (16.10.10).[35] The historian, who has

---

31. A theme often repeated; cf., e.g., 3.41b, 4.62a (by implication). Jul. *Ep.
ad Them.* 245a–b, notes that a philosopher ought not to flatter and deceive.

32. Because this speech is Themistius' first on philanthropy, I discuss it at
some length. Earlier treatments include G. Downey, *Historia* 4 (1955): 199–208;
J. Kabiersch, *Untersuchungen zum Begriff der Philanthropia bei dem Kaiser Julian*
(Wiesbaden, 1960), 6–15; and L.J. Daly, *Byzantion* 45 (1975): 22–40.

33. Almost a direct quotation of Plato, *Resp.* 411a–b.

34. The imagery recalls Plato's chariot myth at *Phaedr.* 246a–b.

35. Cf. C.J. Classen, *RhM* 131 (1988): 177–86; Matthews, *Ammianus*, 231–33.

Xenophon's account of Cyrus and his officials in mind,[36] explains: "All this was no doubt affectation, but he gave other evidence too in his personal life of an unusual degree of self-control, which one was given to believe belonged to him alone" (16.10.11; trans. Hamilton). Ammianus here criticizes the emperor's attempt to make himself larger than life and to increase the dignity of the imperial station, but expresses some admiration on this point in his summation of Constantius (21.16.1).[37] Panegyrists and propagandists naturally proclaimed the uniqueness of the emperor's temperament: he had a lofty spirit, but did not give way to anger, employing his spiritedness instead to preserve a suitable station above that of his subjects. Themistius, adopting the imperial view, praises Constantius in his own way, discussing self-control and anger in the context of a philanthropic emperor.

The shift from abstract to concrete is subtle. Collocation of anger and high spirit blurs the distinction; as a result, the qualities of a philanthropic emperor apply to Constantius as well.[38] A theoretical exposition of desirable characteristics has become a treatment of Constantius' virtues. Ammianus offers an interesting counterpoint. After noting that Constantius was not always mild and clement in trials for treason, the historian reports that the emperor made an effort to be considered just and merciful (21.16.11). Themistius continues his treatment of Constantius by returning to philanthropy. This virtue is more kingly than others, since God is called philanthropic, not courageous or moderate. The emperor thus shares in divine virtue. Earlier rulers, who imitated God by compelling subjects to worship them, are amusing. True imitation of God involves pursuit of divine virtue, not divine honors. A suitable offering by an emperor is the attempt to make his soul an image of God. A philosopher pursues the same ideal, but does

---

36. *Cyr.* 8.1.40–42; the similarity was noticed by M.P. Charlesworth, *JRS* 37 (1947): 34–48. For discussion, cf. Matthews, *Ammianus*, 231–33; and S.A. Bradbury, *Innovation and Reaction in the Age of Constantine and Julian* (Ph.D. diss., University of California, Berkeley, 1986), 90–95. Ammianus has perhaps fallen prey to the view common among some pagans that the house of Constantine had destroyed the traditional empire. Themistius' sharp contrast between Constantius and Shapur may be a reply to such criticism.

37. Cf. A.M. Tassi, *CritStor* 6 (1967): 157–80.

38. Evident also from the title: "about philanthropy" or "Constantius."

not pursue power.[39] The perfect image of God rests in a man who has the power to do good and chooses to do so (1.8a–9c).

The orator dwells on this point, suggesting that good deeds alone are insufficient. Just as shepherds and herdsmen must truly care about their flocks and herds, the philanthropic emperor must act from love for his human flock (1.9c–10c). The very name of emperor depends on this, and such actions induce subjects to be concerned about their emperor's well-being (1.10c–d). A tyrant raises himself above the downtrodden by fear, but the philanthropic emperor rules the upright. The former is like a rich man with slaves, but an emperor raises the fallen. The tyrant wants to surpass the wretched, not the fortunate (1.10d–11b). Shapur is an example, treating even his family badly:

> For this reason, I think, the Persian dynast is far from holding the name of king. For he does not only consider and make all his subjects slaves, but even his relatives, his brother and his son, to whom he intends to pass on his empire. Anyone who considers his brother a slave is quite ridiculous to think himself free. (1.11b–c)[40]

This shift from an abstract treatment of tyranny to the Persian king, with a brief discussion of the futility of power without the proper character and soul (1.11c–12a), leads to Shapur's transgression into Roman territory and his defeat by a true emperor shining nearby (1.12a–b). The Persian king was incapable of properly handling the rudder of the "ship of state" and fought badly against Constantius, who had been trained as a helmsman from childhood (1.12b), a reference to an appointment as Caesar at the age of seven.[41] Shapur, too,

---

39. On this, Themistius and his detractors would agree, though the latter would argue that the orator had not lived up to this ideal; see the further discussion later in this chapter.

40. On the family of Shapur, cf. *PLRE*, 1:803 (Sapor II, III), 443 (Hormisdas [Shapur's brother]). The passage may allude to the fact that Hormisdas fled to the Romans after he escaped from prison and his brother (cf. Zos. 2.27, Zon. 13.5). For brief discussion, F. Paschoud, *Zosime: Histoire nouvelle*, vol. 1 (Paris, 1971), 218–19.

41. For Constantius' appointment as Caesar, Barnes, *New Empire*, 8, 45, 85. The remarks about training are similar in spirit to those of Julian, *Or.* 1.10b ff.

had ascended the throne while still young (Zos. 2.27; Zon. 13.5), but Themistius ignores this, preferring to argue that the Persian's training had been inadequate.

The philanthropic emperor reverences the human race. He does not forsake virtue for money and considers praise from his subjects of great value. While every reign needs both gifts of honor and the exaction of vengeance, to increase virtue and curtail wickedness, respectively, the philanthropic emperor gives honor. From earliest times, punishment was entrusted to public officials and honor to rulers, who were to create desire for virtue. After a brief restatement, Themistius notes that Constantius removed capital punishment. Earlier law gave the same (death) penalty to dissimilar crimes and was harsh, but also inexact. A philanthropic emperor recognizes this. Since he both is the law and above it,[42] he removes harshness, substituting exile for death and confiscation for exile.[43] Philanthropy seeks opportunities for clemency, and Constantius deserves praise for achieving this at a young age. Finally, the philanthropic emperor thinks his friends of great value. Through them, the emperor sees and hears far and wide.[44] The orator closes by insisting that his praises are true (1.12c–18b).

The view of kingship espoused here is based, at a distance, on Aristotle,[45] who regarded a ruler's position as that of a father over his children, not of a master over slaves, which is tyranny.[46] However

42. A favorite view with an Aristotelian background; cf. 5.64b, 16.212d, 19.228a. See chapter 6 for discussion.

43. Cf. similar remarks about clemency at 15.192d, 194c–d, discussed in chapter 8. Portmann, *Panegyrik*, 133, with 261, n. 3, suggests that some otherwise unknown commutation of sentences is the reason for this speech. This puts rather too much emphasis on what is merely a depiction of an ideal emperor, but Constantius may have acted in some way to allow Themistius this interpretation.

44. Similarly at 15.196c–197a. One presumes that Themistius does not have men like Paul the "Chain" (on whom, Am. Mar. 14.5.6–9, 15.6.1: *tartareus ille delator*) in mind here. For an earlier discussion of the concept, cf. Dio Chrysos. *Or.* 3.104–107.

45. On Themistius' view of kingship, cf. J. Straub, *Vom Herrscherideal in der Spätantike* (Stuttgart, 1939; reprint 1964), 160–74.

46. Part of the argument of *Pol.* 1; cf. the useful remarks by H. Kelsen, in *Articles on Aristotle*, vol. 2, *Ethics and Politics*, ed. J. Barnes, M. Schofield and R. Sorabji (London, 1977), 170–73.

much his command is tempered by love, concern, and virtue, a father is superior to his children. Adherence to Aristotle is evident in the comparison of Shapur to a tyrant and master of slaves. Plato, in contrast, argues that a philosopher-king is best equipped to rule. This individual is a member of the citizen body, selected at an early age for training in the art of rule. He rules, not by virtue of natural position, as a father over his children, but because talent and trained excellence make him the first among his equals, the citizen body.

Themistius exerts some effort to harmonize the two views of kingship. His comparison of Constantius to Shapur, as noted, casts the Roman emperor as a ruler in the Aristotelian mold and is supported by the comment that the Persian regarded even his family as slaves (1.11b–c), since Aristotle (*Eth. Nic.* 1160b25 ff.) notes that Persian fathers regard their sons as slaves. Shortly thereafter, Themistius refers to Constantius as a helmsman who had been trained from childhood to handle the "ship of state" and points to Shapur's inadequacy (1.12b). This comparison is more Platonic in its emphasis on education and its metaphor of a ship, and Constantius emerges as an emperor with Aristotelian and Platonic characteristics. Most emperors must have appreciated Themistius' ability to consider them the best of both, but Julian, who disputes such claims in his *Letter to Themistius*, reveals that the view was not universally accepted.[47]

His view on kingship makes it easy for Themistius to suggest that the king is semidivine. Apart from epithets such as "loved by Zeus," "born of Zeus," and "nourished by Zeus," which appear with great frequency in the panegyrics and derive largely from the Hellenistic period, the philosopher seems genuinely to believe that kings are in some ways similar to the gods. Aristotle (*Pol.* 1259b13; *Eth. Nic.* 1160b26) cites with approval Homer's description of Zeus as the "father of gods and men" because Zeus is king and kings are like fathers. Themistius (10.132b) mentions Homer's verse but does not quote it exactly; he calls Zeus the "father and king of all" (11.143a), a similar view. For Aristotle (*Pol.* 1187b–1188a and context), monarchy is the best form of government when the individual most preeminent in virtue is king. Themistius had no choice and worked within existing structures. He exhorts emperors to be virtuous and occasionally anticipates his conclusions when praising

---

47. See chapter 5 for discussion.

their virtues; his goal is the continuation of practices that permitted his statements.

Themistius adopts a specific approach to semidivinity. He cites Homer, *Iliad* 24.258–259, Priam's remark that Hector seemed to be the son of a god, in his panegyric of Gratian (13.169a–c) and implies that Alexander and Heracles were semidivine. He compared Julian to Heracles in his *protrepticus* to the Caesar. In the *Eulogy on his Father,* Heracles is a paradigm of virtue (20.240a) and benefactor of the human race. A comparison of kings to Heracles makes kings semidivine, if they were beneficial. Themistius, in his first panegyric, calls some kings ridiculous for forcing their subjects to worship them in temples as if they were gods (1.8d). His approach to divinity goes beyond Aristotle, but is also some distance from the views of the Hellenistic period. It was difficult, even for Christian emperors, who are sometimes reminded that their hearts are in the hand of God,[48] to return to Aristotelian views after centuries of a higher status; Themistius is doing the best he can.

Themistius' activities after this first encounter with the emperor are imperfectly known. Perhaps through imperial favor, he soon moved from Ancyra to Constantinople.[49] He states, in 384 (31.352c–d), that he had served the city and undertaken embassies for nearly forty years.[50] Since *Oration* 1 was delivered at Ancyra and his first official embassy for Constantinople was *Oration* 3 in the spring of 357,[51] less than thirty years before 384, the orator means service "by his oratory," that is, public speeches as a professor; curial service is precluded by status as a philosopher and teacher. The oratory includes *Oration* 32, a treatment of philosophers' right to have children, and *Oration* 33, perhaps his inaugural speech at the capital.[52]

---

48. Themistius cites both Homer, *Il.* 24.527 ff., and Proverbs 21.1 to this effect; cf. 7.89d, 11.147c and 19.229a. On Themistius' knowledge of Christian Scripture, cf. G. Downey, *Studia Patristica* 5 (1962): 480–88 (482–83 on the passage from Proverbs).

49. For his presence at Ancyra and the move to Constantinople, see chapter 2.

50. Since Themistius began to teach at Constantinople in 348, "nearly forty years" means "more than thirty-five years" in an effort to maximize length of service.

51. See the discussion later in this chapter.

52. See chapter 2 on both speeches.

Once installed as a professor, Themistius' fame increased rapidly, but he provides few details about his career, mostly in replies to attacks.[53] A philosopher of Sicyon, who had been a student of Iamblichus, transferred his entire school to Constantinople. Questioned by his students, he sent them to the oracle of Apollo, where they heard that Themistius was the wisest man of his day, just as Socrates had once been so named (23.295b, 296a–b).[54] Celsus, one of the Sicyonian's former students, moved to Constantinople in 359, to enroll in the Senate and to study under Themistius (Lib. *Ep.* 86).[55] The *Paraphrases*, written as notes for the classroom, circulated from place to place until they reached Sicyon (23.294d–295a).

Themistius may have delivered another speech during the early years at Constantinople. *Oration* 30, devoted to praise of agriculture, is usually considered an early speech because of its simplicity.[56] The philosopher's father was very interested in agriculture, as Themistius remarks in his funeral oration (20.236d–237b). Eugenius had perhaps retired from teaching and returned to his estates in Paphlagonia.[57] *Oration* 30 may be linked to his retirement, thus dating to the early 350s at the latest.

Meanwhile, Constantius had gone to the West. An amusing assumption of imperial rank by Magnentius at Augustodunum (Autun) on 18 January 350 was soon followed by the death of Constans. After a dinner for the son of Constans' *comes rei priuatae* Marcellinus, Magnentius left

---

53. On these speeches, see the discussion later in this chapter and appendix 2.

54. Cf. Vanderspoel, *Historia* 36 (1987): 383–84, for the suggestion that the philosopher was Hierius, a former student of Iamblichus and uncle of Aristophanes of Corinth. He may be following the example of Eudoxus of Cnidos, who brought a number of students to Athens; cf. Diog. Laert. 8.87.

55. Celsus is often thought to be the philosopher from Sicyon; cf., e.g., Baret, *Themistio*, 55; Schemmel, *NeueJbfürPäd* 22 (1908): 152; A.F. Norman, in the Teubner edition of Themistius, vol. 2, p. 90, apparatus. But he was a student of the Sicyonian; cf. Vanderspoel, *Historia* 36 (1987): 383.

56. Scholze, *Temporibus*, 70. The speech itself gives no indication of date or place of delivery.

57. Eugenius probably taught at Constantinople for some time; see chapter 2 for his fame. Baret, *Themistio*, 5, citing 24.305d, thinks that Themistius returned to Paphlagonia after completing his education and took over his father's school.

the room on the pretext of relieving himself. On his return, he wore imperial costume and was hailed as emperor. A second usurpation followed on 1 March 350, by the *magister peditum* Vetranio in Illyricum. According to Philostorgius (*HE* 3.22), Vetranio was aided by Constantius' sister Constantina, who had resided in the area with her husband Hannibalianus (slain in 337) and hoped to secure the Balkans for her brother against Magnentius. Vetranio certainly promoted this view, and Constantius seems to have accepted it, at least temporarily. Philostorgius further reports that Constantius sent him a diadem, but this may legitimately be doubted. Moreover, Constantina's purpose is not clear. Later, as the wife of Gallus, she is said to have goaded her husband against Constantius.[58] A third usurper appeared in Rome. Nepotianus, son of a sister of Constantine, was proclaimed emperor on 3 June 350, but agents of Magnentius murdered him, his mother, and other supporters after twenty-eight days, on 30 June.[59]

While settling matters in the East, the emperor sent military aid to Vetranio to forestall his defeat by Magnentius (Jul. *Or.* 1.30b).[60] In the meantime, Magnentius negotiated with his rivals and concluded a treaty with Vetranio (Jul. *Or.* 1.30c). He offered his own daughter to Constantius and proposed to marry Constantina (Petr. Patr. fr. 16). Constantius refused to negotiate with rivals, and the attempt was unsuccessful. The emperor later took some of Magnentius's ambassadors, including the Roman *princeps senatus* Nunechius, hostage.[61] By late autumn 350, Constantius reached Illyricum and, on 25 December at Naissus (Nish), dispossessed Vetranio of his throne by

---

58. This is the view of Ammianus in Book 14. Paschoud, *Zosime*, 1:250, seems to regard Constantina's marriage to Gallus as a reward for her loyalty in 350. More likely, Constantius hoped that Gallus would prevent his wife, who had once been a queen, from treasonous activity or that his sister would be content, if not happy, as the wife of a Caesar. Barnes, *Athanasius and Constantius*, 101, is more charitable to Constantina in 350.

59. All three, on coinage, advertised themselves as successors of Constans. Each, but Magnentius only in the early period, issued coins in the name of Constantius and himself. Cf. *RIC*, 8, passim.

60. For detailed treatments, cf. J. Šašel, *Živa Antika* 21 (1971): 205–16; and P. Bastien, *Le monnayage de Magnence (350–353)*, 2nd ed. (Wetteren, 1983).

61. Mentioned only by the late source Petrus Patricius, fr. 16; cf. *PLRE*, 1: s.v. Marcellinus 9, Nunechius. Magnentius instead married Justina, possibly a member of the imperial family as a granddaughter of Constantine's eldest son Crispus; cf. Barnes, *New Empire*, 44, 103.

deceit and oratory. The emperor had openly proposed that the joint armies take up arms against Magnentius (Zos. 2.44.2), but, at an assembly where his own men were heavily armed and surrounded the Illyrican army, recalled the loyalty of Vetranio's soldiers to Constantine, inducing them to defect. Vetranio had no choice but to divest himself of the purple and retired to private life. For achieving this bloodless victory, the emperor later received fulsome praise from his panegyrists.

Constantius immediately began preparations for war against Magnentius. To secure the East and to maintain pressure on the Persians, he appointed his cousin Gallus Caesar of the East on 15 March 351. Gallus, whose reputation for indolence is not entirely deserved,[62] married Constantina before he was sent to Antioch. Constantius himself remarried about this time, and it is romantic, though unprovable, to think that he married Eusebia at a double wedding. In the war against Magnentius, minor skirmishes occupied much of 351, until the two sides met in full battle near Mursa on 28 September. The defection to Constantius of a unit led by Silvanus (Am. Mar. 15.5.33) was the turning point and led to the defeat of Magnentius, who fled to Aquileia. By the end of summer 352, Constantius' forces had broken through Magnentius' defense in the Alps and taken Aquileia, which the usurper abandoned for Gaul. The following summer, Constantius advanced. Despairing of rescue, Magnentius committed suicide at Lyons on 10 August 353. Less than a month later, the emperor entered the city and began a purge of Magnentius' most important supporters.

Constantius began the celebration of his *tricennalia* at Arles on 8 November 353, while continuing the pursuit of those guilty of treason by deed or association. By this time, he had become suspicious of Gallus and began a lengthy process of intrigue and negotiation that resulted in the execution of his Caesar in 354 (Am. Mar. 14.5.1–3). Julian, who had probably been summoned to court for the *tricennalia*, remained in the West for some time and seems to have participated in a campaign against the Alamanni in 354 under duress.[63] The emperor kept him in the West to prevent collusion be-

---

62. His reputation stems from Ammianus' account. For a corrective, cf., e.g., E.A. Thompson, *The Historical Work of Ammianus Marcellinus* (Cambridge, 1947), 56–71.

63. This view of Julian's activities during this period (he probably also

tween the two half-brothers, since Julian was regarded with suspicion. A further revolt, this time by Silvanus, began and ended quickly in autumn 355. Not long thereafter, on 6 November 355, Julian was named Caesar and given a sister of Constantius, Helena, as his wife.

Though Themistius was not much involved in public life during this period, he did come to the attention of Constantius, who added him to the Senate in 355. *Orations* 1 and 33 were perhaps responsible, even if the justification is slender. Themistius' acquaintance with Saturninus probably helped. In a speech of gratitude for the consulship of Saturninus in 383, he mentions a debt of more than thirty years standing to the consul, who seems to have introduced Themistius to Theodosius (16.200a). This debt was perhaps for an introduction to Constantius.[64] Saturninus' position is not stated, but, at some point before 361, he held the post of *cura palatii*,[65] an appropriate position for arranging the meeting.

Whatever the occasion and circumstances of introduction, the emperor had immediately been impressed. As a token of his esteem, he attempted to give Themistius a number of gifts, which the philosopher unsuccessfully refused. Since Themistius refers to these in *Oration* 2, they were offered before late autumn 355. He declined what he could, since acceptance was unsuitable for a philosopher (2.25d–26a). From replies to charges that he used his *annonae* as a professor to procure and benefit students, it is clear that Themistius did not collect an official salary as a teacher,[66] but instead accepted only the single *annona* to which many citizens were entitled. Constantius had been willing to provide him with any financial assistance required (2.25d),

---

attended his brother's coronation and wedding) differs from the standard reconstruction. I hope to discuss these matters elsewhere, but on the point that Julian was at the court in 351, cf. Barnes, *CP* 82 (1987): 209.

64. Cf. Seeck, *Briefe*, 269–70, 293–94.

65. Saturninus *ex cura palatii* (Am. Mar. 22.3.7) was exiled after the treason trials at Chalcedon in 361. On his career, cf. *PLRE*, 1:807.

66. Libanius, who attempted to collect a salary from Constantinople long after he had moved to Antioch, chides Gerontius of Apamea (*Ep.* 1391) for insisting on an official salary. On Libanius' salaries, cf. R.A. Kaster, *Chiron* 13 (1983): 37–59.

but Themistius did not accept this either. In 355, he decided again to refuse rewards.[67]

The reason for Themistius' adlection was the emperor's view that his candidate espoused the right kind of philosophy[68] and was concerned for Constantinople. His letter to the Senate, which reads like a panegyric, praises the philosopher on several counts and reveals an acceptance of Themistius' social philosophy. In particular, Constantius was pleased with the concept that philosophers ought to play an important public role, a view largely absent from contemporary philosophy.[69] Themistius held that education in the classics was important and equates educated intelligence to philosophy, holding that this training induces proper moral behavior.[70] There is no room here for withdrawal of philosophy from society. The emperor found Themistius' views easy to accept, as they offered little possibility for discontent and political resistance. Themistius himself was naturally more than merely educated, but his goal was to divert his more specialized knowledge to the public good within the status quo.

The adlection of Themistius was important to Constantius for other reasons. The appointment of a leading pagan intellectual advertised support from some pagans and a willingness to accept diversity of opinion. Themistius' tolerant paganism[71] presented no obstacle. As a philosopher, Themistius possessed *parrhésia* (*licentia*)[72] and could not, strictly speaking, be regarded as a tool used by the emperor for propagandistic purposes. The court gained an influential proponent of imperial wishes, since both the emperors and Themistius were interested in an ordered society.

In return for the honor of adlection to the Senate, Themistius composed *Oration* 2, delivered in the Senate no earlier than the middle of November 355, in the emperor's absence. At several points, Themistius addresses the tardiness of his reply. Constantius' letter to the

---

67. Schemmel, *NeueJbfürPäd* 22 (1908): 156, thinks that Themistius accepted all the gifts offered in conjunction with his adlection to the Senate.

68. See chapter 2 for Constantius' apparent knowledge of *Or.* 32.

69. Cf. Fowden, *JHS* 102 (1982): 33–59; see also chapters 1, 2, and appendix 2.

70. Cf. G. Downey, *TAPA* 86 (1955): 291–307.

71. Evident especially in his panegyric of Jovian; see chapters 1 and 6.

72. See the discussion in chapter 1.

Senate was read, according to a scholion, on 1 September 355, by the proconsul Justinus. Because Themistius refers to the selection of Julian as Caesar, it was not delivered before the middle of November. The delay was not entirely his fault, since his father had died in autumn 355, and Themistius had traveled to Paphlagonia to deliver a funeral speech (*Or.* 20).

The evidence for Eugenius' death comes from the sequence of speeches surrounding the adlection. The emperor's letter to the Senate implies, but does not state, that Eugenius was alive.[73] In his speech of gratitude, Themistius seems to refer to recent acquisition of property (2.28d). Textual variants suggest that he may have written two versions of the passage, one while was his father alive, the other after Eugenius' death.[74] In most manuscripts, Themistius remarks:

> because my wealth is laughable and represents great poverty, and less than a drop of water in the ocean is not only what I possess, but also what my father at one point (ποτε), what my mother and what all the Paphlagonians together possess.

In one manuscript (*Ambrosianus gr. J 22 sup.*), however, the philosopher states:

> because my wealth is laughable and represents great poverty, and less than a drop of water in the ocean is not only what I now (νῦν) possess, but also what my father and all the Paphlagonians together possess.

The first version suggests that Eugenius was dead and that Themistius' mother had inherited some of the property. The second, with the omission of Themistius' mother, appears to indicate that Eugenius was still alive; the philosopher refers to his property before his father's death.[75] The variants are unlikely to be scribal errors or interpolations,[76] and it

---

73. So Scholze, *Temporibus*, 71.

74. Cf. Seeck, *Briefe*, 133.

75. Seeck, *Briefe*, 133, thought that Themistius wrote this version in expectation of an eventual legacy.

76. As Seeck, *Briefe*, 133, thought. Scholze, *Temporibus*, 71, n. 429, citing Schenkl, *WS* 23 (1901): 21, notes that the *Ambrosianus* offers many mistakes in *Or.* 2 and 4 and rejects a double recension, but nevertheless agrees that

appears that Themistius altered his speech.[77] The most reasonable explanation is that the *Ambrosianus* derives from a draft of *Oration* 2 written shortly after 1 September 355. Because this manuscript also refers to
Julian, Themistius perhaps finished an incomplete draft in November
or December of 355, before revising the whole speech.[78]

A letter of Libanius has been thought to indicate that Eugenius was
still alive in 364. Addressing a Eugenius, the sophist remarks that this
individual, in imitation of a god (Asclepius), receives with out-
stretched hands those who come to him from the god (*Ep.* 1192). The
god heals their diseases, while Eugenius, according to report, enables
them to live comfortable lives.[79] Libanius may mean that the philosopher Eugenius can heal minds and attitudes with philosophy,[80] but he
is more likely addressing a different Eugenius. Another letter (*Ep.*
1161), which also dates to 364, mentions a Eugenius in the ointment
business (τὸν μυροπώλην Εὐγένιον)[81] for whom Libanius seeks favors
from Marcellinus. This second Eugenius can easily be equated with
the first, since the application of ointments might well follow divine
healing; neither of them is Eugenius the philosopher. With this obstacle removed, it is certain that Themistius' father died in autumn 355.[82]

In the funeral oration, Themistius praises the learning and wide
interests of his father, and, even if he is ascribing his own views or
some learned from other teachers to Eugenius, it is clear that his own
peculiar combination of philosophy and rhetoric derives in some mea-

---

Eugenius had died when Themistius delivered *Or.* 2, holding that the main
manuscript tradition is correct.

77. There is no evidence that Themistius tampered with speeches once he
had delivered them. According to Scholze, *Temporibus*, 71, n. 429, Themistius
would not alter the text, since he would remember in 357 that his father was
alive in 355 when he wrote what is now in the *Ambrosianus* (if he had written
it, a view Scholze rejects).

78. Interestingly, the *Ambrosianus* does not offer a hypothesis, which may
mean that its text was not the version donated to the new library at Constantinople in 357, on which, see the discussion later in this chapter. Textual con-
tamination would also explain the reference to Julian.

79. The text of the last clause is not certain, with many variants and
conjectures.

80. The influential view of Seeck, *Briefe*, 134. Scholze, *Temporibus*, 71, does
not address the question.

81. Cf. Seeck, *Briefe*, 134.

82. For [Jul.] *Ep.* 193 (to Eugenius), see chapter 2.

sure from his father's instruction. The speech is, however, more than simply a funeral oration. Themistius uses the opportunity afforded by his father's death to justify his own approach to philosophy and rhetoric, and the speech is part of a debate with his contemporaries that escalated at the beginning of his political career. This first debate centered on Themistius' role as a teacher, and he faced accusations of sophistry and ambition. His political involvement is not entirely absent, but the primary concern of his opponents was an approach to philosophy that they found untenable. The debate raged for some time and occasioned several speeches by Themistius (*Or.* 21, 23, 26, 29), but seems to have died at the end of the 350s; it emerged again with a different focus in the 380s.[83]

While in Paphlagonia, Themistius delivered *Oration* 27,[84] which advises a youth not to ignore local schools of rhetoric and promotes the philosopher's own ideals. As a curiosity, it may be possible to conclude that Themistius' children also traveled to Paphlagonia on this occasion. He writes in his *Paraphrase* of Aristotle's *Physica* (pp. 371–72 Spengel = *CAG*, V, 2, p. 185.13–16) that he knew the distances covered by horses and wagons in an hour because he traveled from Nicaea to his native Paphlagonia using the public post while his children took the same road on an ox-cart.[85] A reference to this trip would require a slightly later date for the *Paraphrases* than is usually proposed.[86]

On his return, Themistius delivered *Oration* 2, a speech of gratitude for the beginning of his political career. Like *Oration* 1, it has few points of contact with the standard imperial oration outlined in handbooks of rhetoric. The summary prefixed to the text in the manuscripts addresses this question. Its author notes:

He sets a highly philosophical target for his praise, pointing out that the emperor takes part in philosophy, which he [Themis-

---

83. On *Or.* 20, see chapter 2. On the other speeches and the debates, see the discussion in this chapter, chapter 8, and appendix 2.

84. On the date, Scholze, *Temporibus*, 72. See chapter 2 for discussion.

85. Scholze, *Temporibus*, 71. Presumably, Themistius and his children boarded different vehicles at Nicaea, since he was certainly a resident of Constantinople at this time. As Schemmel, *NeueJbfürPäd* 22 (1908): 153, remarks, the passage is further evidence for Themistius' birth in Paphlagonia.

86. Scholze, *Temporibus*, 84–85, appropriately dates the *Paraphrase* of the *Physica* to the end of 355, citing also 21.256a, a possible reference to this work.

tius] approves. Indeed, he admits none of the things which belong to praise, but leads everything to the rubric which he set
before himself.[87] There are places where he offers general remarks, but in the majority of his effort he starts from the hypothesis before him, attempting everywhere to observe the
proper worth for philosophy. For this is pretty much the goal of
the treatise. (2.24b)

This reading is reasonably accurate. Themistius puts his gratitude to
good use, arguing at some length that Constantius was a philosopher.

The orator begins with a discussion of his debt to the Senate and
especially to Constantius. This debt was difficult to repay, since the
emperor had given him high praise rather than property. To emphasize this, he compares himself to Xenophon, who wrote a long panegyric of Agesilaus when given a small estate. Themistius, who may be
casting himself as Xenophon's equal or superior, could not repay the
debt with material possessions because of his poverty.[88] He instead
delivers a speech that attempts to prove that Constantius' praise of
philosophy in his letter to the Senate was not praise of Themistius,
but of himself, just as Parrhasius had used himself as a model for a
painting of Hermes (2.29c).

In the speech, Themistius attempts to prove Constantius a philosopher. Adopting the procedure of the law-courts, as he does in other
speeches of the 350s, he cites laws and avoids metaphors, since
rhetors are thought to lie when they use the latter (2.31a). The laws
are not those of Draco, Solon, and Cleisthenes, but regulations of
Plato and Aristotle (2.31b). Beginning from statements of Aristotle in
the *Nicomachean Ethics*,[89] Themistius argues that the goal of virtue is
not knowledge, but practice, as Plato shows in the *Republic* and
Laws,[90] and he calls the emperor a philosopher because of his mildness and philanthropy (2.31d–32d). The philosopher and the king, he

87. This complaint is that found in the rubric preceding *Or.* 1 and the
hypothesis to *Or.* 4 (the Φιλόπολις), on which see the discussion later in this
chapter, where authorship is also discussed.

88. Themistius often emphasizes the poverty to which, as a philosopher,
he was entitled. Constantius remarks that the orator had adequate wealth
(*Ep. Const.* 21d–22a).

89. *Eth. Nic.* 1095ab, 1139a27, 1103b27, 1105b1.

90. *Resp.* 364e; *Leges* 655d, 672e.

suggests, have the same attitude about the divine. Kings rule humans as God rules the world and are rightly called "nourished by Zeus," "born from Zeus" and "equal in counsel to Zeus" (2.34d).[91] A true king (i.e., Constantius), rules with virtue and for the good of his subjects; a tyrant does the opposite (2.35c–d).[92]

On the topic of tyranny, Themistius discusses Magnentius briefly, in pursuit of his goal of showing Constantius to be a philosopher-king who entrusts his affairs to reason. The ruled do not fear him, but fear for him (2.36a).[93] He was not chosen by drunken men at a party, an "after-dinner emperor" (2.36a); rather, he is an emperor by nature, born to the role and trained from birth.[94] He was not chosen for size, as Ethiopians choose their kings, nor because of a neighing horse, a bronze helmet or the sight of a Lydian woman,[95] but because of his philosophy. This alone, not the trappings of power that sufficed mad Cambyses and the braggart Xerxes, makes one man stronger than another (2.36a–d). A philosopher-king is successful in his military endeavors: a river overflowed its banks and fought with a descendant of Xerxes (2.37a).[96] Sometimes he needs no weapons: words alone induced one usurper to relinquish the purple (2.37a–b),[97] and Constantius is the foremost philosopher, better than Plato, who could not convince Dionysius of Syracuse to be a philosopher (2.37d). Moreover,

----

91. For Themistius' views on other emperors' similarity to Zeus, cf., e.g., 6.79d, 15.188b–c. Cf. also Dio Chrysos. *Or.* 1.37–41.

92. Cf. the similar remarks about Shapur at 1.10c–12a.

93. So too at 1.10c–d.

94. Cf. 1.12b and Jul. *Or.* 1.10b ff. and *Or.* 2.56c–d, on Magnentius' accession at a party.

95. Examples drawn from Herodotus: 3.20.2: Ethiopian kings; 3.86.1: Darius (the neighing horse); 2.151.2–3: Psammetichus (bronze helmet); 1.10 ff.: Gyges. Cf. also Hdt. 1.133, for the claim that the Persians made decisions while drunk; this may lie behind the remark about the choice of Magnentius at a party.

96. Themistius refers here to the third siege of Nisibis in 350, when the river forced Shapur to withdraw; cf. Theophanes, a.m. 5841. Shapur apparently attempted to use the river to weaken the walls. Xerxes' anger at the Hellespont or the fact that rivers were drunk dry by his armies might lie behind this remark. Cf. Lightfoot, *Historia* 37 (1988): 105–25. Had Themistius written *Or.* 1 as late as 350, he could have inserted this point in his discussion of Shapur.

97. Cf. Jul. *Or.* 1.31c–32a, 2.76d–78c.

he allowed Vetranio to live and kept his hands free from blood, and forced another usurper (Magnentius) to be his own tyrannicide (2.38b).

Further evidence to prove that Constantius was a philosopher is the fact that God gave him success (2.38b). Without wronging his brothers,[98] he became master of the entire empire (2.38b–d). Before noting the strength of the emperor's body and his superiority to Alexander—more typical subjects of panegyric,[99] but mentioned only briefly—Themistius wonders whether he has paid the debt and asks for the cancellation of any balance (2.39a–b). He closes with his final evidence: the choice of a philosopher as coruler, not because of a familial tie, but for similarity in virtue (2.39d–40b).[100]

Oration 2 is clearly Themistius' summary of the first half of the 350s. Just as clearly, the philosopher is putting the best face on what was essentially half a decade of civil unrest. He emphasizes Constantius' ultimate victory and omits the negative completely. This is not surprising; he was, after all, delivering a panegyric. More notable is the complete lack of blame attached to Constantius, to the point that the emperor had not shed any blood whatsoever. This was close enough to the truth in the case of his brothers, Shapur, Vetranio, Magnentius, and Silvanus. But his bloody pursuit of the supporters of usurpers and his removal of Gallus should be placed alongside the positive remarks. Constantius, it seems, wanted to be seen as a congenial ruler whose power always returned to him naturally.

The flurry of activity that began in autumn 355 continued with *Oration* 21, delivered in the Theater of the Muses (21.243a) after Eugenius' death, but while Themistius' mother was still alive (21.243b).[101] Libanius' references to the jealousy and insults that were directed at the philosopher during 355 (*Ep.* 402, 407) help to date the speech to the winter of 355/6,[102] when Themistius first turns his attention specifi-

---

98. Cousins are apparently less relevant, since Themistius is silent on Gallus.

99. Cf., e.g ., Jul. *Or.* 1.41c , 43c; 2.54c.

100. With this, compare praise of Theodosius at 16.203d–204b for preferring virtue to kinship and friendship when he named Saturninus consul for 383.

101. Scholze, *Temporibus*, 73–75. The place is secure, since Themistius refers (21.248a) to the *kallipolis*, a term he frequently uses for Constantinople.

102. Cf., on Libanius' letters, Bouchery, *Themistius*, 36–44, 47–50. Bouchery (48, n. 5) rejects Scholze's date for *Or.* 21 because this speech is close in

cally to opponents in the debate on his role as a philosopher.[103] He had outlined his views previously, but without reference to opponents and charges.[104] The accusations are not detailed in *Oration 21*, but a series of speeches delivered near the end of the 350s indicates that some contemporaries regarded him as a false philosopher. *Oration 21* is a response to such charges, which emerged as Themistius entered the Senate and became a politician. In his reply, the philosopher attempts to silence critics with theory. He was unsuccessful, since the advancement of his political career brought renewed charges, which Themistius answered more specifically later in the reign with *Orations 23, 26,* and *29.*[105]

During the same period, late 355 or 356, Themistius wrote a *protrepticus* to Julian, commending him on his selection as Caesar and urging him to undertake with enthusiasm the tasks he had been given. Citing Aristotle and other philosophers, he outlined for Julian the role of a ruler. The document is not extant,[106] and knowledge of its content derives from Julian's reply, which only reached the East in the early 360s, when Julian sent it as propaganda to undermine Constantius.[107]

Themistius was also involved in a dispute with the praetorian prefect Strategius Musonianus, who wanted him to transfer his residence and school to Antioch; the prefect was probably influenced by Libanius and others.[108] The conflict had its effect, less on Themistius than on Libanius, who complains in 356 that the philosopher had not written for some time and fears that his friend wanted no more to do with him (*Ep.* 508). Themistius was perhaps already on a lecture tour that took him to Antioch and other cities, including Ancyra (23.299a).[109] He was at Antioch in autumn 356 when a Persian delegation seeking peace

---

time to *Or.* 23, which he places in 376 ("Contribution," 196–200). See the discu⁻sion later in this chapter for the view that *Or.* 23 belongs to the 350s, eliminating that objection.

103. As Méridier, *Le philosophe,* 5, correctly notes.

104. Themistius unfortunately never mentions these opponents by name.

105. See the further discussion later in this chapter and appendix 2.

106. See appendix 3 for the view that it was known to Arab scholars.

107. Cf. T.D. Barnes and J. Vanderspoel, *GRBS* 22 (1981): 187–89.

108. Cf. Seeck, *Briefe,* 295, and Bouchery, *Themistius,* 54–68. The attempt to induce Themistius to move to Antioch is known largely from Lib. *Ep.* 402, 434, 447, and 463.

109. So Seeck, *Briefe,* 296; Bouchery, *Themistius,* 73.

arrived (4.57b),[110] and may have undertaken the tour to console some cities for his decision to remain at Constantinople or simply to examine other opportunities after his problems with critics.

In 356, Themistius was given a bronze statue by the emperor. He recalls it in his next panegyric (4.54b) and links it specifically to the delivery of *Oration* 2.[111] Libanius later (359) refers to the statue in a letter to Themistius (*Ep.* 66), remarking that he knew the gist of its verse inscription from a letter of Themistius to their mutual friend Eudaemon. Later, and no doubt in 356 as well, Themistius regarded the statue as a sign of Constantius' esteem (31.353a).

In winter 356/7, the philosopher lost his son Themistius, whose existence and death are known only from a letter (*Ep.* 575) that Libanius sent to Themistius in the first half of 357. Libanius had given the boy some lessons in Isocrates' rhetoric, but the nature of the training is not clear. It is unlikely that the young Themistius enrolled in Libanius' school, either before the sophist left Constantinople or at Antioch. More likely, as Themistius' friend, Libanius taught the boy on an informal basis, in the early 350s or in 356, when Themistius visited Antioch.[112] This leaves the boy's age uncertain, since he was older than seven at some point between 350 and 356.[113]

When Themistius returned from his tour, he was unwilling to undertake the journey to Italy to present a panegyric in Milan on 1 January 357 for the consulship of Constantius and Julian.[114] He nevertheless wrote a speech that was read in the eastern Senate (4.53a–54a) and probably sent to Milan. Themistius focuses on the emperor's relations with Constantinople. The so-called *Philopolis*, once regarded

---

110. See the discussion of the date later in this chapter.

111. Seeck, *Briefe*, 296; Bouchery, *Themistius*, 173. Scholze, *Temporibus*, 17, thinks that the delivery of *Or.* 3 was the reason.

112. So Bouchery, *Themistius*, 103, followed by Dagron, *Thémistios*, 37, n. 9.

113. Themistius' first marriage cannot be dated by normal ages for rhetorical training, as some, e.g., Seeck, *Briefe*, 292, have attempted to do. See chapter 2.

114. Scholze, *Temporibus*, 13–20, places the speech in spring 357, arguing that the remarks on the harshness of winter indicate that it had passed, not that Themistius would have experienced such conditions if he traveled to Italy in winter. Portmann, *Panegyrik*, 149, thinking the speech a plea to avoid selection for the embassy, dates it to the end of 356. If that date is correct, statements about the celebration of the festival already taking place are inexplicable. Wirth, *BF* 6 (1979): 304, dates the speech to 358.

as a summary of a lost panegyric of Julian,[115] has now been identified as the hypothesis of this speech, *Oration* 4.[116]

Themistius begins with a long introduction (4.49a–51b) noting that the festival (the inception of year and consulship) was celebrated throughout the empire, an apology for remaining at Constantinople. He might have used the public post to travel to Italy, since he refers to a journey through Thrace, Illyria, and Italy in a wagon, with frequent changes of drivers and mules (4.49d–50a). He speaks as well of the unpleasantness of the journey, mentioning wind, snow, ice, mud, and the need to dress warmly in felt and sheepskin (4.50a–b),[117] and complains that upon arrival he would lie shivering with disease and require physicians to administer new effective drugs to "drive winter from the limbs" (4.50c).[118] The orator clearly remained at home by personal choice, not because he was ill,[119] but to avoid illness. His choice required an apology; he argues that mental attitude, not physical presence, is the most important part of celebration.

After arguing that he as philosopher is best able to see the nature of kingly beauty (4.51b–52a),[120] Themistius notes that the city and its citi-

---

115. Seeck and Schenkl, *RhM* 61 (1906): 554–66.

116. Philippart, *Serta Leodiensia*, 269–75; Dagron, *Thémistios*, 225–29.

117. Cf. Ael. Arist. *Or.* 48.60–62 Keil, for an earlier description of a winter road journey to Rome.

118. As Seeck, *Briefe*, 296–97, and Gladis, *Themistii*, 9–10, saw, this complaint is the strongest evidence that Themistius wrote *Or.* 4 before *Or.* 3. Constantius spent the winters of 355/6 and 356/7 at Milan and was consul in both years, but *Or.* 4 could hardly have been written in 356: (a) it would follow too closely upon *Or.* 2; (b) Themistius mentions military activity on the Rhine (4.57a–b); Constantius did not fight there in 355 (Am. Mar. 15.4.1); the reference is to 356, on which, Am. Mar. 16.12.15–16, mentioning a campaign of the previous year with events of 357; (c) Themistius refers to the bronze statue (4.54b) for his eloquence (and flattery) in *Or.* 2; (d) Themistius had seen ambassadors from Persia seeking peace (4.57b); negotiations were begun by Musonianus (Am. Mar. 16.9.1–4) in 356.

119. As Scholze, *Temporibus*, 14 suggests: "*Themistius ob valetudinem et hiemis asperitatem domi substitit.*" He must argue that *Or.* 4 was sent to Rome in the spring of 357, while *Or.* 3, delivered in Rome according to a scholiast, was read in Constantinople, thus ignoring clear statements in both texts. Most argue that Themistius was actually ill; cf., e.g., Gladis, *Themistii*, 10, and Baret, *Themistio*, 17. An exception is Seeck, *Briefe*, 296–97, who does not comment on this.

120. Reminiscent of remarks at 1.2c–3a.

zens, especially the senators, mirror the brilliant beauty of the emperor (4.52a–53d). Constantius would approve the gift of a hymn because he thinks skill in speaking (he is called a *philologos*) as important as military prowess (4.54a).[121] This is evident from his response to an earlier speech (*Or.* 2), where the orator "gathered together and wove pure flowers from the meadows of Plato and Aristotle" (4.54b): Constantius granted a statue.[122] The philosopher's hesitation had not left the Senate at a loss: they sent others for the religious occasion (4.54c–d).[123]

The rest of the speech addresses Constantius' concern for the city. The first point is his immediate response to the tyrannies of Vetranio and Magnentius, which had frightened Constantinople more than the rest of the empire, presumably because it was a military target. Constantius quickly arranged matters in the East and soon sent one usurper to Constantinople as a "prisoner of war," an inappropriate term, since Vetranio was captured by oratory (4.55d–56b). The first victory was a premonition of the second and allowed citizens to take heart again (4.56c–d). Soon, the emperor, as the victory bulletins proclaimed,[124] succeeded against other enemies, Germans, Chaonae, Iazyges, and Persians (4.57a–b); recently, Themistius had personally seen Persians treating for peace with the praetorian prefect Musonianus, who began negotiations in 356 (Am. Mar. 16.9.1–4).[125] With a favorable comparison to Alexander the Great, who gave no benefit or increase to Pella (4.58a), Themistius lists the emperor's gifts. His father had walled the city, but Constantius beautified a foundation exactly his own age.[126] He found new sources of water and was building baths.[127] He adorned the city with a covered circuit as if

---

121. Valens receives similar praise at 10.129d.

122. It had a Greek inscription (Lib. *Ep.* 66.5); the location is not stated, but it perhaps stood in the forecourt of the Senate. For the metaphor, cf. Luc. *Pisc.* 6.

123. The ambassadors traveling to Milan were sent "as if to Delos" (4.54c).

124. On these bulletins and the changing concept of victory, cf. M. McCormick, *Eternal Victory: Triumphal Rulership in Late Antiquity, Byzantium and the Early Medieval West* (Cambridge, 1986).

125. *PLRE,* 1:612, citing this speech of Themistius, suggests 357 for the embassy, but elsewhere in the entry on Themistius twice dates the speech to 1 January 357.

126. A reference to the founding ceremonies of Constantinople.

127. Not complete, since Themistius remarks (4.58c) that their size could be seen from their current state. These are apparently the Constantinianae

with a costly girdle and built an imperial forum[128] woven through
with gold and murrhine like a bridal veil.[129] He provided luxury and
added pleasures of other cities (4.58a–d). Themistius does not list
these, but they presumably included monuments removed from
other places.[130] Constantius' choice of Julian, who was not only a
relative, but one conceived, born, raised, and educated in the city,
also proves his concern (4.58d–59b).[131]

Further evidence of the emperor's love for the city is his attempt to
bring to light again the wisdom of the past (4.59d–60c). A reference to
the craft of Cadmus and Palamedes (4.60a) indicates that Constantius
provided funds for the copying of manuscripts and was establishing a
public library.[132] This library, housed in the courtyard of the Theater
and the Hippodrome (4.60d), is more useful than the harbors, where
luxury goods enter the city and nothing except dirt, sand, and refuse[133] leaves. The orator remarks that the inhabitants can now offer
education in the market (i.e., "university" and library) recently established by the emperor. The possibility of a good education would

---

begun in 345 (*Chron. pasch.* s.a. 345 = *Chron. min.* 1:236). *Parastaseis*, 73,
reports that they were built by Constantine, but cf. Cameron and Herrin,
Constantinople in the Eighth Century, 268.

128. Apparently the Forum of Constantine and the Hippodrome, though
both were built by his father. Either Themistius is crediting Constantius with
the buildings or the emperor embellished his father's work. There is, unfortunately, little other evidence for Constantius' building program.

129. Reading μορρίοις for μορίοις; cf. J. Vanderspoel, *Mnemosyne* 40 (1987):
149.

130. Very little specific evidence exists, but *Parastaseis*, 85, mentions a statue
of Perseus and Andromeda brought to the capital from Iconium. Some items
said to have been transferred by Constantine were perhaps moved by his son,
particularly if he completed work begun or intended by his father, as is likely.
For a list of statues at Constantinople, see Cameron and Herrin, *Constantinople
in the Eighth Century*, 48–51. G. Dagron, *Constantinople Imaginaire: Études sur le
recueil des* Patria. Bibliothèque Byzantine, Études 8 (Paris, 1984), 129–31, also
lists the sources of the monuments.

131. The selection of Julian proved Constantius a philosopher in *Or.* 2.

132. The *Philopolis*, a summary of *Or.* 4 (Philippart, *Serta Leodiensia*, 269–
75), refers to τῆς τῶν δημοσίων βιβλίων ἀνανεώσεως, which has been taken to
refer to this public library by Philippart (loc. cit.), but also to the public
accounts by Schenkl, *RhM* 61 (1906): 565–66.

133. An interesting bit of evidence on waste disposal—presumably refuse
was dumped into the sea.

bring to Constantinople the best intellectuals and orators (4.60c–61c). Themistius himself intends to donate his speeches to the library. Given his status in the intellectual life of the capital and a probable commission to appoint or recommend the teachers at the expanded "university,"[134] it would not be surprising if he was associated with the acquisition of library collections and the building itself, probably in a private capacity.[135] His own words, he remarks, had grown feathers and had flown to the emperor and from him to the empire at large.[136] Detractors were already in evidence, Themistius intimates. With an alliterative remark about a "cawing crow croaking" (4.62a: κορώνη λακέρυζα ἐπικρώξειεν) that words designed for philosophy had become mere rhetoric, he, somewhat surprisingly in a panegyric, mentions the troubles that were surrounding him. He adds that the crow had not tasted the muse of Plato, since it failed to recognize Plato's definition of the true king as young, moderate, mindful, courageous, magnificent, and learned (4.61c–62a). He closes with the argument that God had given mankind a living example of the ideal king (4.62b–d).

Themistius clearly devotes much attention to the emperor's relations with a city he had not visited since 350. A prime imperial concern after the defeat of Magnentius was the border in the West, that with the Alamanni in particular. Constantius fought against them each year from 354 to 356, and was to fight a campaign with Julian against various Germanic tribes in 357.[137] If his intended visit to Rome was known, omission of Constantinople from his itinerary no doubt added to a feeling of insecurity in the new city, which naturally sought evidence of its importance. The speech, emphasizing the emperor's goodwill, was designed in part to reassure fellow citizens, in part to influence Constantius to consider the city of greater importance.

---

134. For this interpretation of Lib. *Ep.* 368, cf. Bouchery, *Themistius*, 106–11.

135. For a more detailed discussion of Themistius' association with the library, cf. J. Vanderspoel, *Phoenix* 43 (1989): 162–64. His status depends on whether he was proconsul of the city, on which see the discussion later in this chapter.

136. Compare 31.354d, a remark that Constantius often outlined Themistius' philosophy to his empire.

137. For the chronology, Seeck, *Regesten*, 200–204.

The visit to Rome took place in the spring of 357.[138] Ammianus is less charitable than others, suggesting that the majestic entrance emphasized unearned triumphs won in civil, not external, wars (16.10.1–3).[139] Constantius entered the city on 28 April and left on 29 May (*Chron. min.* 1:239; Am. Mar. 16.10.20).[140] He attended the Senate (Am. Mar. 16.10.13) and toured Rome's antiquities with Hormisdas, the Persian prince who had fled to the Roman Empire (Am. Mar. 16.10.14–17).[141] Revealing a respect for tradition, he allowed state subsidies for the public pagan cults to continue, though he had the Altar of Victory moved out of the Senate chambers.[142]

As might be expected, the Senate of Constantinople sent an embassy. Themistius led the delegation and delivered *Oration 3*, his first official embassy outside the East[143] and his first speech as official representative for his city.[144] The day of the speech is not stated, but it

138. Straub, *Herrscherideal*, 178–80, argues against Mommsen (*Chron. min.* 1:239) that the emperor was celebrating his *vicennalia*, since his *dies imperii* does not fall in May. The *Chron. pasch.* s.a. 357 mentions the *vicennalia*, and Mommsen accordingly changed the *xxxu* of *Cons. Const.* s.a. 357 to *vicennalia*; cf. the most recent edition of the latter in R.W. Burgess, *The Chronicle of Hydatius and the Consularia Constantinopolitana. Two Contemporary Accounts of the Final Years of the Roman Empire* (Oxford, 1993), 215–245. Themistius does not mention the *vicennalia* in his speech, which he almost certainly would have done had the emperor been celebrating it. Burgess, *NC* 148 (1988): 83–84, points out that, on the evidence of coinage, the emperor was celebrating his thirty-fifth year early, by a year and a half. Themistius is silent on this point as well. It may be best simply to suggest that Constantius, intending to visit Rome, found pretexts to celebrate something.

139. Ammianus describes the procession at 16.10.4–12. Cf. Tassi, *Crit. Stor.* 6 (1967): 157–80, and Classen, *RhM* 131 (1988): 177–86.

140. The visit has attracted a large bibliography; works not cited for specific reasons in other notes include J. Češka, *Sborn. prac. filosof. fac. Brněnské Univ.* Ser. E, 10 (1965): 107–15; P. Corsi, *Quad. Med.* (1977): 32–72; Y.M. Duval, *Caesarodunum* 5 (1970): 299–304; R. Klein, *Athenaeum* 57 (1979): 98–115.

141. Cf. R.O. Edbrooke, *Mnemosyne* 28 (1975): 412–17.

142. Symmachus, *Rel.* 3.4, 6–7, provides the evidence, using it in support of his request for similar funding. R.O. Edbrooke, *AJP* 97 (1976): 40–61, argues that the visit had little effect on Constantius' relations with the pagan aristocracy.

143. The title of the speech clearly states that it was an embassy and that it was spoken at Rome. Scholze, *Temporibus*, 13–20, disputes this.

144. This statement can be disputed, if *Or.* 4 is an official speech; Themistius does not state that he is speaking on behalf of others. At 34.13, the

must fall within the limits of the emperor's visit. As often happened, the embassy and speech accompanied crowns of gold, the semiofficial tax that emperors were fond of collecting.[145] Themistius begins by discussing this crown (3.40c–42d). He suggests that no city was able to give a crown equal in honor and value to what it had received from the emperor, but that the eastern city will attempt to make a payment by delivering the crown publicly in the "watchtower of the world" (Rome, as a scholiast remarks), employing a man who speaks the truth (3.41b).[146]

The celebrations, Themistius argues, establish links between the two cities. During a barbarian insurrection (that by Magnentius), a member of the dynasty of Constantine (i.e., Constantius)[147] remained safely in the East and later saved the Romans from the Germans and Iazyges (3.43a–b). This must be the campaign of 356, which Ammianus buries in his account of 357 (16.12.15). The orator praises the emperor for this achievement, perhaps to justify the celebrations, and points out that, while Camillus was the second founder of Rome, Constantius is to be thought a founder superior to Romulus (3.43c–d).[148] Constantine had also been concerned for both cities, since he freed Rome from an almost homonymous tyrant (Maxentius; 3.44b) and founded Constantinople.

Themistius devotes the rest of the speech to discussions of Constantius as the ideal philosopher-king and of his gifts to the city, a reiteration of the major theme of *Oration* 4. He notes that the delivery of the crown of gold, outstanding in itself, was even more

orator dates his *prostasia* (on which see the discussion later in this chapter) to his embassy to Rome in 357; so too Seeck, *Briefe*, 297, citing 31.352d in support. *Or.* 2 is clearly personal, and Themistius delivered *Or.* 1 as part of his public service as a teacher.

145. One title of the Theodosian Code (12.13) is devoted to these "donations." Cf. T. Klauser, in *Gesammelte Arbeiten zur Liturgiegeschichte, Kirchengeschichte und christlichen Archäologie, JAC*, Ergänzungsband 3 (1974): 292–309.

146. I.e., a philosopher; cf. Jul. *Ep. ad Them.* 254a–b. This claim was apparently a sore point with Themistius' detractors.

147. It is tempting to regard this member of the dynasty as Julian, since he remained safely in the East throughout the usurpation of Magnentius and took part in the campaign of 356. But this may give too much to Julian in a panegyric of Constantius. Cf. G.W. Bowersock, *Julian the Apostate* (Cambridge, Mass., 1978), 34–42, on the campaigns.

148. Cf. 13.179c for similar praise of Gratian.

so because a philosopher was leading an embassy to a king who ruled with mildness and moderation, considered education of great value, and pursued philosophy. This had permitted the emperor to achieve a bloodless victory from a rostrum that Themistius himself had seen. Other panegyrists praised the ruler's possessions, but they remained at the entrance to the temple and did not see the statues within.[149] Themistius saw the true emperor, who fulfills Plato's statement that life is happiest when the king is young, moderate, mindful, courageous, magnificent, and intelligent and exercises philanthropy (3.44b–46c).[150] This nature was especially evident in the emperor's gifts to Constantinople, which removed any possibility that the city would die with Constantine, whose city now became even greater.[151] Themistius supports his own view of Constantinople's importance with the rather specious argument that Constantius alone of his brothers was concerned for the eastern city and became master of the entire empire (3.46d–48d).

The theme of *Oration 4* reappears in *Oration 3*, perhaps because the emperor had not changed his mind about visiting Constantinople. After his visit to Rome, Constantius participated with Julian in a joint campaign against various Germanic peoples. Though the subsequent tradition ascribes much of the glory to the Caesar, the forces of the emperor were instrumental in closing off any possibility of escape and drove the Germans directly into Julian's path.[152] Constantius then traveled to Pannonia for his winter quarters and operated until the autumn of 359 in the Balkans, whence he returned to Constantinople after a nine-year absence. He did not stay long, since he was only passing through on his journey to the eastern frontier. The Persians had captured Amida in 359 and posed a threat in 360. While traveling

149. Themistius had begun *Or.* 1 with the same imagery, probably recalling, in a vague sort of way, Alcibiades' description of Socrates in the *Symposium* of Plato.

150. A favorite characterization of Constantius; cf. 4.62a.

151. On Constantius' building program, see the discussion of *Or.* 4 in this chapter. See chapter 3 for the view that Constantinople was at first the personal city of Constantine. As such, it might well have died with him.

152. Bowersock, *Julian the Apostate,* 34–42, unravels the truth behind the attempts of Julian and Ammianus to hide the involvement of Constantius. On the emperor's subsequent movements, Barnes, *Athanasius and Constantius,* 222–24.

to the area in spring 360, Constantius received disturbing news from the West. His cousin Julian had been proclaimed Augustus by his troops at Paris.[153] Unable to turn back because of the Persian situation, Constantius could do little but hope that Julian would act slowly, since negotiations failed. The new emperor, however, occupied the Balkans in a lightning campaign in 361. As soon as he could, Constantius gathered what forces could be spared in the East and traveled toward Constantinople and his cousin. He did not get far. On 3 November 361, at Mopsucrenae in Cilicia, he died after a short illness. On his deathbed, so it was said, the childless monarch named Julian his heir. This succession was undoubtedly a contingency that he had considered for some time. His third wife, Faustina, was pregnant and soon bore a daughter who eventually married Gratian.

Themistius' public activity during the reign was not confined to panegyrics. Each responsibility he undertook can be construed as evidence that Constantius was concerned for Constantinople, either on his own initiative or because he had been influenced by Themistius and others. The philosopher appears to have been associated with the public library established in 356, a position that is perhaps not political, but nevertheless part of a public career. Naturally, his membership in the Senate offered scope for political activity, though the extent of that activity during the first few years is unknown; he never discusses it. Shortly after his adlection, he was given the responsibility of finding suitable new members for the Senate. His office is not easy to define,[154] but he dates one part of his career to the beginning of this task. His own definition (34.13: τῆς γερουσίας προὺνόουν) suggests a censorial function, though hardly the office that had disap-

---

153. Cf. Bowersock, *Julian the Apostate*, 46–54, on the circumstances of Julian's accession. P. Athanassiadi-Fowden, *Julian and Hellenism* (Oxford, 1981), 72–75, implicitly denies Julian's own responsibility. Cf. also Matthews, *Ammianus*, 93–100.

154. Dagron, *Thémistios*, 9: "sans autre titre, probablement, qu'une vague «présidence» du sénat, ..." L.J. Daly, *Byzantion* 53 (1983): 182–84, argues for a presidency and that Themistius was proconsul, since the presidency of the Senate was normally reserved for the proconsul or city prefect. For the view that he never held this office or the urban prefecture during the reign of Constantius, see the discussion later in this chapter.

peared for private individuals centuries earlier.[155] Whatever the precise term, it is not the *prostasia* also mentioned by Themistius in this passage.

In the catalogue of honors recited in 384, Themistius refers to a concern for the general public when he undertook the *sitéresion* (34.13). This role, too, differs from his *prostasia*; he may have arranged a restoration of the corn distribution, halved as punishment for the lynching of Hermogenes in 342,[156] especially since the daily operation of the grain supply was entrusted to the proconsul and, later, the prefect.[157] Libanius (*Ep.* 368.3) refers to a speech, now lost, where Themistius reported his achievements at Rome. Since *Oration 3* does not include a request, any result came from private discussions with the emperor.[158] Possibly, Themistius meant his responsibility to increase the Senate when he outlined his successes in the lost speech. But he specifically refers in *Oration 34* to the entire population of the city and to the grain distribution. The passage progresses from a general honor (*prostasia*) with selection to the embassy, to concern for citizens and the grain distribution, to the search for new senators. The sequence should be chronological; concern for the *sitéresion* belongs to the spring or summer of 357, and the enlargement of the Senate began in the summer of 357 or later.[159]

Themistius' *prostasia* is not the presidency of the Senate, normally held by the prefect,[160] because the orator defines it as a position held continuously from his selection as head of the embassy to Rome in 357 (34.12). Length of tenure is of critical importance for a position that offered primacy, but was not the presidency. It indicates that Themis-

---

155. So Baret, *Themistio,* 19. A. Chastagnol, *AAH* 24 (1976): 350, suggests a position as vice-proconsul.

156. So Seeck, *Briefe,* 297.

157. See chapter 3.

158. Cf. also 23.298b, where Themistius reports that he had brought back an important advantage, either the grain distribution or the new Senate. Even if this speech dates to 377/8, as some think (see the discussion later in this chapter), the reference is hardly his trip to deliver a speech in honor of Gratian.

159. For discussion of the new Senate, see chapter 3.

160. Cf. Dagron, *Thémistios,* 55, n. 124 ("Il ne peut s'agir que de la présidence du sénat, que conférait le titre de préfet de la ville"), and Daly, *Byzantion* 53 (1983): 183, who do not notice a problem with length of tenure.

tius became the equivalent of *princeps senatus* in 357.[161] It was an honor granted by his peers and gave him continued influence without holding a magistracy.[162] Moreover, the orator refers to his own presidency of the Senate as the *prohedria* in *Oration* 31. His terminology is probably precise and indicates a difference between the position as *princeps senatus*, his responsibility to increase the Senate (though these were naturally related), and the presidency he held in 384.

A proconsulship in 358/9 has been postulated.[163] Evidence against this dates to 361, when Constantius listed mandatory attendance at the committee to select praetors.[164] Present, among others, were to be ten former consuls, proconsuls, and prefects and "also the philosopher Themistius, whose knowledge increases his eminence" (*CTh* 6.4.12; 3 May 361: *Themistius quoque philosophus, cuius auget scientia dignitatem*). Themistius is the only individual specifically named. Though *dignitas* can designate high office, it more naturally means "eminence" here and refers to the *prostasia*, rather than high office. The rescript names Themistius quite apart from any office and implies that he had not held one of the positions listed. With no firm evidence to the contrary, it is virtually certain that he was not a proconsul or prefect before May 361.[165]

At *Or.* 23.291d–292d, delivered in 358/9[166] against detractors who

---

161. See chapter 3 for this position at both Constantinople and Rome in the fourth century. Scholze, *Temporibus*, 57, calls Themistius the *princeps senatus* while he was holding the urban prefecture in 384. Dagron, *Thémistios*, 217, n. 29, rejects this honor entirely.

162. Seeck, *Briefe*, 297, n. 1, remarks: "Die προστασία is kein Amt, sondern nur eine Stellung."

163. So Seeck, *Briefe*, 298–99, dating the enlargement of the Senate to the same period: the emperor traveled through the capital on his way to the East in 359/60; cf. also *Regesten*, 297. Daly, *Byzantion* 53 (1983): 164–89, argues for a proconsulship, against Dagron, who suggests that the orator was offered the post, but refused it.

164. S.A. Stertz, *CJ* 71 (1975/76): 352, regards this as a rescript of Julian, but it was issued on the Tigris in May 361.

165. So too Dagron, *Thémistios*, 216. Daly, *Byzantion* 53 (1983): 179, argues that it was the proconsulship whose *dignitas* was increased by the orator's knowledge.

166. The date suggested by Seeck, *Briefe*, 300, accepted by both Dagron and Daly.

accused him of assembling private gain at public expense and being a
sophist rather than a philosopher, Themistius indicates that he rejected grain, oil, and other luxuries to which he was entitled (23.
292b). This is not a rejection of an office or of the perquisites of an
office that he held, that is, the proconsulship.[167] He does not mention
any office, and none should be postulated. Indeed, the debates about
his position in this reign completely bypass the question of office and
focus on legitimacy as a philosopher. For his part, Themistius emphasizes his refusal to accept payments offered to servants of the state
(23. 292d: *tous stratiótas*).[168] The passage concerns perquisites for teachers, who received state or civic salaries when they occupied a chair,[169]
and is not relevant to a proconsulship. Furthermore, Themistius was
away from the city in 358/9, when he is supposed to have been proconsul. Even though he traveled in part to find senators, a task perhaps
not unsuitable for a proconsul,[170] his responsibility for Senate enlargement was not limited to a term in office, since it had begun earlier. A
statement of Libanius that Constantinople had handed its reins to
Themistius (*Ep.* 40.1) merely refers to the honors recently given to
him, not to a proconsulship.[171] Similarly, when the sophist asks
Honoratus, and no longer Themistius, to exempt Olympius from

167. The views, respectively, of Dagron, *Thémistius*, 213–16, and Daly,
Byzantion 53 (1983): 171–76.

168. Daly, 176, translates *stratiótas* as "soldiers." Although Themistius has
just noted that philosophers who changed their cloak, so to speak, were more
burdensome than soldiers bearing arms, he clearly means civil servants here,
because soldiers did not receive the kind of luxury he describes in the passage. On civil servants as soldiers, cf. Jones, *LRE*, 2:566.

169. Cf., among others, Jones, *LRE*, 2:997–1003; R.A. Kaster, *Guardians of
Language: The Grammarian and Society in Late Antiquity* (Berkeley and Los Angeles, 1988), 114–23.

170. Petit, *Ant. Class.* 26 (1957): 349 and passim; and A.F. Norman,
Libanius: Autobiography and Selected Letters, vol. 1 (Cambridge, Mass., 1992),
502, 505, among others, hold that Themistius was proconsul.

171. Contra Daly, 181–82. When Libanius (*Ep.* 68) calls Themistius a φύλαξ
of the city, he merely refers to the philosopher's position as *princeps senatus*
and his role as the leading promoter of Constantinople's interests. Libanius
was at this point (in 359) attempting to convince Themistius to exercise influence on behalf of Cleobulus, and his claims for Themistius' power might be
somewhat exaggerated. On the incident, cf. Bouchery, *Themistius*, 128–36,
154–57; and Kaster, *Guardians of Language*, 213–14, 257–58.

some senatorial requirements,[172] the completion of a term as proconsul need not be the reason. Themistius was responsible for finding candidates; the details of entrance to the Senate perhaps devolved upon the city prefect after the institution of that office, though some exemptions required a vote in the Senate.[173] Or, more simply, enough new senators had perhaps been found by 360; while Libanius occasionally addresses senatorial membership in later years, the issue did not have the importance it did from 357 to 360.

The task of enlarging the Senate, undoubtedly a difficult process, and his disputes with his contemporaries about the role that he was playing in public life occupied Themistius for some time after 357. Unfortunately, little specific evidence on the enlargement of the Senate is available, even the names of senators new and old. Libanius refers to about fifty-five senators of Constantinople; only six can be identified with certainty as appointments made by Themistius.[174] Many were unwilling to serve, and Libanius counseled others to demur. On the whole, Themistius seems to have selected, primarily from the lower ranks of the curial class, men who were willing to serve in hope of higher social standing.[175]

During this same period, the philosopher defended himself on a variety of charges with *Orations* 23, 26, and 29, a closely linked series of speeches in which Themistius attempts to define for his audience the proper role of philosophers in society. *Oration* 21 had not put an end to the debate, and the philosopher's further involvement in politics was at least a pretext for renewed discussions.[176] Possibly, opponents of the new Senate instigated this attack on the institution's leading proponent.

To understand the debate, it is crucial that the speeches be dated accurately.[177] A statement in *Oration* 23 has erroneously suggested a

---

172. See the brief discussion of Olympius in chapter 3.

173. Themistius seems on occasion to have modified some entrance requirements (Lib. *Ep.* 86.5), perhaps to convince candidates to consider membership. For votes on exemptions, cf. Petit, *Ant. Class.* 26 (1957): 368–69.

174. Cf. the catalog offered by Petit, *Ant. Class.* 26 (1957): 380–82.

175. For discussion, see chapter 3.

176. So Dagron, *Thémistios,* 44–48.

177. As Dagron, *Thémistios,* 24–25, remarks, using the early date of the speeches as proof for Themistius' visit to Rome in 357; cf. his discussion at 209–11.

date in the late 370s.[178] At one point, Themistius discusses his travels on behalf of Constantinople, especially a recent trip to Rome. The philosopher visited the West twice, in 357 to deliver *Oration 3* and in 376 to deliver *Oration 13*. He mentions other cities, but explicitly excludes the academic trip to Antioch and Ancyra in 356 (23.298a–299c). Another remark prevents a reference to his visits to Ancyra and Antioch in the reign of Valens: Themistius notes that he had pursued his studies at Constantinople for twenty years (23.298b), a remark suitable in the 350s, but inappropriate in 377.[179]

The title of *Oration 29* indicates a wish to correct a false interpretation of *Oration 23*. The speech refers to an Egyptian poet, perhaps Andronicus, whom Libanius mentions in a letter to Themistius in 359 (*Ep. 77*),[180] but more likely a Harpocration who arrived in 358. Delivered shortly after *Oration 23* (29.344c: τὸν πρῴην λόγον), this speech, like *Oration 23*, belongs to the winter of 358/9.[181] *Oration 26* is not as easily datable on external or internal grounds, but belongs to the group. Its summary notes that a crowd in the Theater had recently (πρῴην) applauded one of his speeches, probably *Oration 23* (26.311c). Addressing selected individuals called the "Areopagus," Themistius mentions that he was reading the charges a second time (26.313c). Since he is attempting to combat misinterpretations of *Oration 23*, *Oration 26* offers to a private audience what he explains publicly in *Oration 29*. It can comfortably be dated between the two public speeches if a private group advised him to make a further public explanation.[182]

The debate to which these speeches bear witness was a bitter battle

---

178. So Scholze, *Temporibus*, 76; Méridier, *Le philosophe*, 14–24; Stegemann, "Themistios," 1663; Bouchery, "Contribution," 196–200; Norman in the Teubner edition, vol. 2, p. 76, apparatus.

179. See the discussion in chapter 2. The statement that he began his studies at the capital when he was young (23.294d) need not mean that he was an old man when he delivered the speech, as Scholze, *Temporibus*, 76, suggests.

180. Suggested by Seeck, *Briefe*, 300–301. A. Cameron, *Historia* 14 (1965): 487–88, urges caution on the identification of any individual as the poet in question.

181. So Seeck, *Briefe*, 300; Dagron, *Thémistios*, 24–25, 209–11.

182. Discussions of the speeches often assume that *Or. 26* was the last of the three speeches, e.g., Méridier, *Le philosophe*, 32.

between two different views of philosophy and its place in society.[183] Themistius' involvement in politics stirred up this debate, and his important role in the Senate was the specific cause, just as his adlection to the Senate had occasioned a debate that he had attempted to silence with *Oration* 21. Neither debate focuses on tenure of office, as happens in the reign of Theodosius, when Themistius was accused of debasing philosophy by accepting the city prefecture.[184] The philosopher continually insists that he has a right to deliver speeches and denies that the practice breaks with tradition. The charges were partly motivated by jealousy, but the clash of views was more important. For philosophers, the charge of sophistry against those with different views lay ready to hand: Plato himself had shown the way. By using Plato and the cumulative weight of philosophical tradition, Themistius is cleverly, with some success perhaps, attempting to hoist his opponents by their own petards. Not surprisingly, his opponents were not pleased. Though it shaped the debate, the philosopher's involvement in politics was only the pretext for a discussion that was taking place in any case. At best, the speeches during the reign of Constantius led to an uneasy truce.

The philosopher's second marriage also belongs to this period. A letter of Libanius, dating to late 359, reveals that Themistius had recently been to Phrygia, where he had married his second wife. Libanius begins his letter as follows (*Ep.* 241):

> May it be your fortune that this womb give birth to heirs, not only of your property, but also of your wisdom, which indeed you have long displayed as more colorful than a meadow, surpassing, if I do not know about those called the same as you [i.e., philosophers], us rhetors at least, who are inferior. And so earlier I was happy for Phrygia, which received you and the wedding, but now for Constantinople, which has regained you and received your bride as well.

According to a scholiast, this was a response to a letter of Themistius. This scholion offers the only extant fragment of the philosopher's correspondence:

---

183. See chapters 1 and 2, and for summaries of the speeches, appendix 3.
184. On this debate, see chapter 8.

When Libanius was asking Themistius for the new speeches that he had begotten in Constantinople during the reign of Julian,[185] he [i.e., Themistius] explained, with reference to his marriage and wife, that "it is not time for me now to give birth to speeches, but to children from a wife whom I have recently married. I hope indeed to be a father of children. For the womb of my wife, which is hastening to give birth, promises this for me. Pray along with us for this." Since Themistius had written this, Libanius prays, "May it be my [sic] fortune that the womb of the wife."

To allow an interchange of letters by late 359, the marriage belongs to early summer 359 at the latest. The speeches requested by Libanius are probably Orations 23, 26, and 29, since he mentions rhetors and philosophers. Themistius left the city after he delivered the speeches, searching for senatorial candidates, but perhaps also to escape until the controversy died down, as he may have done in 356. Nothing more is known about this wife, the outcome of this pregnancy, or the birth of other children.

It remains to consider whether Constantius offered the city prefecture to Themistius. As praefectus urbi in 384, the philosopher explains why he accepted this office, though he had been hesitant earlier.[186] At Oration 34.13, Themistius states that he had been offered the office before, that he had been asked to serve many times and had refused. The remark at Oration 34.14 is qualitatively different. The orator refers to a specific emperor and occasion. While other summonses were requests offered and rejected in private, his refusal on one occasion appears to have been public knowledge and embarrassing. The likely conclusion is that Themistius was designated to the prefecture, but resigned before assuming office.[187] The emperor is Constantius or Julian, and his identity must be determined from the description of

185. A mistake, since the emperor was Constantius, but Libanius did ask Themistius for speeches in the reign of Julian; see chapter 5.

186. Daly, Byzantion 53 (1983): 190–91, correctly argues against Dagron that the city prefecture, not the proconsulship, is the office in question.

187. So A. Mai, accepted by Baret, Themistio, 26, who notes that the Souda, s.v. Θεμίστιος, states that Themistius ὕπαρχος προεβλήθη Κωνσταντινουπόλεως, i.e., designatus est, but during the reign of Julian.

character and the historical allusions. The passage is difficult and may be susceptible to several interpretations;[188] remarks on character seem to describe Julian, while other indications tend to suggest Constantius.[189] The latter are probably more accurate, because it was easier, only about twenty-five years later, to falsify an emperor's character. Themistius writes:

> If someone should ask me why I refused on the earlier occasion, but no longer, I will answer, concealing nothing and without ambiguity. For I reverenced that emperor who is worthy of every laudatory memory. For he did not neglect anything, small or great, of those things that raise philosophy to the heights; indeed, he often made me sit at his side in the philosopher's cloak and at his table and made me a fellow traveler. He bore it mildly when I gave advice and was not distressed when I upbraided. (34.14)

The characterization can be either Julian or Constantius, Julian because he was a philosopher, Constantius because Themistius argued continually that this emperor was a philosopher. If the details are to be taken literally, however, Julian is almost certainly to be excluded, because Themistius and Julian did not eat or travel together. Libanius notes in 359 that Themistius sat at Constantius' table (*Ep.* 66.2), a rare privilege[190] that he perhaps did not enjoy again until the reign of Theodosius, though he was at the court of Valens on occasion. While Themistius' differences from Julian allow the congenial conclusion that he rejected the prefecture because he and Julian were not on the best of terms,[191] it seems more likely that the event occurred during the reign of Constantius.

---

188. On the passage, cf. Daly, *Byzantion* 53 (1983): 189–90, and H. Schneider, *Die 34. Rede des Themistios* (Winterthur, 1966), 124.

189. As Schneider, *Die 34. Rede des Themistios*, 124, points out.

190. Cf. Bouchery, *Themistius*, 171, citing Gothofredus on *CTh* 6.13.1.

191. The view of Daly, *Byzantion* 53 (1983): 199–204. As Daly notes (194), when Themistius, at 34.15, lists philosophers who did not associate with evil rulers, he is not referring to Constantius: the point is that he could accept office from Theodosius. Most recently, T. Brauch, *Byzantion* 63 (1993): 37–78, has attempted to argue that Themistius did serve as city prefect in the reign of Julian and (at 79–115) that the two had very positive relations.

On his failure to hold office, Themistius remarks that "circumstances of human affairs bring it about that many things are believed to have happened in a different way than they in fact did" (34.14). Perhaps Constantius died before Themistius assumed office, with Julian preferring a candidate of his own. However, Domitius Modestus, Julian's first appointee, was not in office until 362.[192] A second possible reason is Julian's usurpation of full imperial power, and the circumstances can be specified. In 360, Julian finished his reply to the *protrepticus* that Themistius had written to him in 356 and sent it as an open letter to pagan intellectuals in the East.[193] Near the end, he states that he had freed himself from charges of inaction and, as their leader, needed the help of all intellectuals (*Ep. ad Them.* 266d–267a). The letter raised questions about the loyalty of Themistius, who had urged the Caesar to action, and was an embarrassment. The emperor was confident, since his rescript on the committee to select praetors was almost certainly written after Julian's letter arrived in the East, but Themistius probably resigned from impending office on principle; contemporaries may have thought that Constantius had requested his resignation.

Beyond responsibilities as senator, *princeps senatus*, and his task of increasing the Senate, Themistius held no public office during the reign of Constantius. He nevertheless became one of the leading figures, as an intellectual and as a politician, of the East. Relations between philosopher and emperor were harmonious, as visits to the palace and dinners at the imperial table (31.353a; cf. Lib. *Ep.* 66) reveal. Not surprisingly, Themistius speaks highly of this emperor for the rest of his life. Constantius had started him on the upward climb and had promoted him to one of two peaks in his career.

---

192. Cf. *PLRE*, 1:606.
193. Cf. Barnes and Vanderspoel, *GRBS* 22 (1981): 187–89.

5

Themistius and Julian

Themistius' panegyric of Julian, Libanius informs its author, was a masterpiece of the genre, deserving of a panegyric in return (*Ep.* 1430.2). The sophist provides an aesthetic appreciation that is enthusiastic, but not very helpful, deriving as it does from his own attitude toward Julian, which has often been discussed and is well known.[1] Themistius and Julian were not on the best of terms,[2] and a panegyric of Julian that excited Libanius would reveal much about Themistius, whose political career did not advance during this reign. Fortunately, the panegyric is extant,[3] at least in a translation, perhaps only in an epitome.[4]

Born probably in the spring of 332, Julian was shattered emotionally in summer 337, when his father, eldest brother, two uncles, and five cousins were eliminated by Constantine's sons in their quest for a secure hold on the throne. He and his surviving half brother, Gallus, were soon entrusted to the care of a relative, Eusebius of Nicomedia, who became bishop of Constantinople in October 337.[5] Four years

1. See, for example, A.F. Norman, *Libanius: Selected Works*, vol. 1, Loeb Classical Library (London and Cambridge, Mass., 1969), xxiii–xxxiv.

2. Estimates of the extent of ill will have varied. In this chapter, I argue that it was for a different reason than L.J. Daly, *BZ* 73 (1980): 1–11, suggests. Most recently, Brauch, *Byzantion* 63 (1993): 37–78, 79–115, has argued that Themistius and Julian were on the best of terms.

3. So F. Dvornik, in *Late Classical and Mediaeval Studies in Honor of Albert Mathias Friend, Jr.*, ed. K. Weitzmann (Princeton, 1955), 77–78. Cf. also his *Early Christian and Byzantine Political Philosophy*, 2:659–69.

4. See chapter 4 for the view that the *Philopolis* is a summary of *Or.* 4 and not of a panegyric of Julian. Daly, *BZ* 73 (1980): 1, with n. 3, ascribes the origin of the view to Dagron, *Thémistios*, 225–28, rather than to Philippart.

5. On Eusebius, cf. T.D. Barnes, *AJAH* 3 (1978): 66. The chronology of Julian's early life adopted here is, in the main, that of Baynes, *JHS* 45 (1925): 251–54. There are differences in detail and justification that require examination elsewhere.

later, in autumn 341, Eusebius died, and Constantius relegated his cousins to Macellum in Cappadocia, undoubtedly when he traveled to Constantinople early in 342. The boys remained at Macellum for six years, under the care of George of Cappadocia, whose library Julian demanded after the bishop's murder at Alexandria. In these years, Constantius visited only once, perhaps in 347,[6] when he was on his way from Antioch to Ancyra and probably to the capital.

In 348 or 349, Gallus was summoned to court and Julian attended school at Constantinople, where the admiration of the citizens forced Constantius to send him to Nicomedia. There, prevented from attending lectures of Libanius by a promise to Hecebolius, he had them taken down. By 351, he began to study philosophy; influenced by students of Iamblichus, he abandoned Christianity for paganism. His activities were not confined to his education, as a later remark about the dangers he faced indicates. He aided fellow pagans in opposition to Constantius and Gallus, who became Caesar at Sirmium on 15 March 351 and was given a sister of the emperor as his wife. Julian was present at the occasion.[7] When Constantius became suspicious of his Caesar, Julian was summoned to the West and was almost certainly at Arles in late 353 for the celebration of his cousin's *tricennalia*. It is equally likely that he took part in a campaign against the Alamanni in spring 354: Julian complains that he had been dragged from place to place for six months by Constantius. After continuing his education briefly, Julian was summoned to court and placed under virtual house arrest at Comum when Constantius was at Milan in winter 354/5. In the summer, he was permitted to return to the East, but, because of a revolt by Silvanus, was ordered to Athens instead.

When the revolt had been put down, Julian was summoned again. On 6 November 355 at Milan, Constantius appointed him Caesar. Then, or at about the same time, he was given Helena, a sister of the emperor, as his wife. Shortly thereafter, he traveled to Vienne until the start of the campaigning season. At some point in late 355 or early 356, he received a *protrepticus* from Themistius. For the next years, Julian was occupied with military campaigns in the West, with Con-

---

6. Or possibly in 343, if the emperor went to Constantinople in that year. For the suggestion of a possible visit, Barnes, *Athanasius and Constantius*, 220.

7. Cf. Barnes, *CP* 82 (1987): 209.

stantius in 356 and 357, on his own thereafter.[8] The successes incurred the emperor's suspicions and undoubtedly induced Julian to consider the possibility of becoming Augustus, though a revolt need not have been his immediate objective. By February 360, Julian and his advisers had made up their minds. Using as a pretext the order to send to the emperor some native legions who had been assured that they would serve near their homes and perhaps capitalizing on discontent created in the West by the attempt to enforce decisions of several councils,[9] his agents fomented enough resentment against Constantius for Julian to be declared emperor.[10] In the aftermath, Julian wanted Constantius to treat him as an Augustus; the emperor refused to consider him anything but a Caesar. In spring 361, when Constantius was preoccupied with the Persians, Julian and his forces quickly moved from Gaul to the Balkans to occupy that strategic region. From Naissus, which he reached in summer 361, Julian sent a series of letters to important cities in a bid for their support.[11] His reply to Themistius' *protrepticus* had reached the East earlier.

Constantius' death on 3 November 361 at Mopsucrenae in Cilicia prevented a civil war. Julian traveled to Constantinople, where he spent the winter of 361/2. While there, he drastically cut down the size of the court and its retinue. In the spring, he journeyed slowly to Antioch, visiting famous sites along the way. Relations with the Antiochenes were disharmonious, in part because of Julian's paganism, in part because of his attempt at economic reform. The addition of a western army created shortages, but a genuine ill will between emperor and city existed.[12] When his preparations for a Persian campaign were complete in spring 363, Julian traveled to Mesopotamia and pursued a campaign deeper into Persia than Roman armies had

---

8. Bowersock, *Julian the Apostate*, 33–45.

9. For this attractive suggestion, cf. Barnes, *Athanasius and Constantius*, 153–54.

10. On the accession, cf. I. Müller-Seidel, *HZ* 180 (1955): 225–44; Bowersock, *Julian the Apostate*, 46–55; Matthews, *Ammianus*, 93–100.

11. On this activity, cf. W.E. Kaegi, *Ant. Class.* 44 (1975): 161–71, and Bowersock, *Julian the Apostate*, 60. J. Szidat, *Historia* 24 (1975): 375–78, argues that Julian reached Sirmium and Naissus earlier than is usually thought, i.e., by the summer of 361.

12. For a recent discussion, Matthews, *Ammianus*, 406–9, with 540, n. 6.

been for some generations.[13] He died on 26 June 363, in the heart of Persian territory.

Julian's first association with Themistius cannot be dated precisely, but that he encountered the philosopher during his education is clear from his letter to Themistius and arguable from the fact that the philosopher sent Julian a *protrepticus* after his appointment as Caesar. Objecting to a point raised by Themistius, Julian quotes from the *Laws* of Plato, observing, "You know it well and indeed taught it to me" (*Ep. ad Them.* 257d; trans. Wright). Julian did not find these words of Plato in a speech of Themistius, who does cite the *Laws*, but not this passage.[14] Themistius may have mentioned the passage in an earlier letter to Julian, but this leaves the beginning of the correspondence, attested at *Ep. ad Them.* 260a, unexplained.[15] More likely, the text (*Ep. ad Them.* 259b–c) is to be taken literally. Later, Julian again notes that he studied with Themistius and other philosophers:[16] Themistius was aware of his activities and the dangers "when I was beginning my studies with you."[17] The first opportunity for Julian to encounter Themistius as a teacher, formally or informally,[18] was 348/9, when he lived in the capital briefly before he was forced to move to Nicomedia. Early in the 350s, Julian was perhaps again in Constantinople for a

13. Cf. Matthews, *Ammianus*, 138–83, for a full account of the campaign; Dodgeon and Lieu, *Roman Eastern Frontier*, 231–74, for the sources.

14. C. Prato and A. Fornaro, *Giuliano Imperatore: Epistola a Temistio*. Studi e Testi Latini e Greci 2 (Lecce, 1984), 44, cite 33.365c, where Themistius uses Plato's *Laws* (cf. Norman's source apparatus ad loc.) without mentioning Plato. If he had heard or read the speech, Julian would have needed prior knowledge of the *Laws* to understand the allusion. On the treatise, cf. also Bradbury, *Innovation and Reaction*, chap. 1.

15. Prato and Fornaro, *Giuliano Imperatore*, 49, note that the passage reveals an established friendship.

16. If (cf. Vanderspoel, *AHB* 1 [1987]: 71–74) a Maximus with whom Julian agreed against Themistius is Maximus of Byzantium, he may also have been one of his teachers.

17. Prato and Fornaro, *Giuliano Imperatore*, 47, argue that Julian was never Themistius' pupil and that he means "*presso di voi, filosofi.*" He might, but the other statement requires explanation.

18. Both were at Constantinople in the late 330s and early 340s, but Julian was then too young to be a pupil of Themistius. On Julian as a student of Themistius, cf. also S. Bradbury, *GRBS* 28 (1987): 236; Brauch, *Byzantion* 63 (1993): 81–82.

short time, spending his summers on a small estate in Bithynia inherited from his grandmother.

Julian's reply offers the only extant fragments of Themistius' *protrepticus*.[19] Primarily a private letter replying to philosophical positions advanced by Themistius, the response had no political purpose in the original form written in 356. When it finally reached its addressee some years later in 360, Julian's letter, with an ending added, was part of an attempt to explain his actions, in particular the revolt against Constantius. The letter is therefore the earliest of a group that includes letters to Athenians, Corinthians, and others and is propaganda designed to attract public sympathy. Like these, it was an open letter, with one important difference. Because of the nature and date of its composition, this letter offers a candid account of Julian's actions and attitudes, not propaganda. Only the final paragraphs reflect the situation of 360.[20]

The *Letter to Themistius* reveals philosophical differences between Julian and Themistius, and a respectful animosity familiar enough to academics.[21] Julian begins pleasantly by stating that he hoped to fulfill the philosopher's expectations. He notes that he had given up his earlier goal to rival distinguished men, such as Alexander and Marcus Aurelius,[22] in favor of a life of leisure. Here the discussion of

19. Stertz, *CJ* 71 (1975/76): 352, thinks that Julian's letter is a response to Themistius' panegyric rather than to the *protrepticus*. On the relation between Julian's letter and the panegyric, see the discussion later in this chapter. See appendix 3 for the suggestion that the *protrepticus* or at least its existence was known to Arab scholars.

20. Cf. Barnes and Vanderspoel, *GRBS* 22 (1981): 187–89; see also chapter 4. U. Criscuolo, *Koinonia* 7 (1983): 91, with n. 10, and Prato and Fornaro, *Giuliano Imperatore*, vii–x, reject this. Prato and Fornara put the letter after Julian's arrival at Constantinople. Bradbury, *GRBS* 28 (1987): 235–51, places the entire letter in 356, while Brauch, *Byzantion* 63 (1993): 83–85, and esp. n. 18, proposes a reediting of an earlier letter in late 361. But Julian's remark that Themistius would respond soon (*Ep. ad Them.* 263b) need not mean a response in person at Constantinople.

21. Cf. Bowersock, *Greek Sophists*, 89, on the quarrels of sophists in the second century A.D.: "Throughout all the accounts of sophistic animosity there is a strongly academic odour. One recognises that exquisite polemic which arises so naturally in communities of the highly educated."

22. On Julian's attitude to these rulers and for a list of passages, cf. Prato and Fornaro, *Giuliano Imperatore*, 36–37. On Marcus Aurelius specifically, Lacombrade, *Pallas* 14 (1967): 9–22.

disagreements begins. The *protrepticus*, Julian avers, increased his fears by placing a greater burden on the Caesar than he could carry. Themistius had written that God put Julian in the position of Heracles and Dionysus[23] (called philosophers and kings by Themistius), who had purged the earth of evils. Julian was to give up leisure to be worthy of this role and to become greater than Solon, Pittacus, and Lycurgus (*Ep. ad Them.* 253c–254a). Julian complains about Themistius' unfairness on two counts: first, as a philosopher, Themistius ought not to flatter or deceive; second, Julian mentions his own deficiencies, even as a philosopher.[24] He had misunderstood Themistius' point until he recognized a reference to the difficulties that statesmen face continually (*Ep. ad Them.* 254a–c)[25] and which discourage men from entering public life. Julian also signals his disagreement with the Stoic view that wisdom and virtue are more important than Fortune in public life,[26] citing Plato's *Laws* as proof that Fortune is more important in practical matters and that his own attitude was not induced by sloth. With a lengthy quote from *Laws* 713–714 to indicate that God set divinities over the human race because it could not manage its own affairs properly, Julian concludes that the expectation of semidivinity for a ruler might well lead to inaction (*Ep. ad Them.* 254c–259b).

With this established, Julian defends himself against the charge of inaction, pointing out that acceptance of the previous argument does not necessarily result in an Epicurean approach. He lists some of his own actions performed on behalf of others in the early 350s, at considerable danger to himself and done without complaint.[27] To the philoso-

---

23. The examples reflect Stoic ideals; cf. Prato and Fornaro, *Giuliano Imperatore*, 38–39. They are a normal part of panegyric; cf. Men. Rhet. 2:380 (p. 99 Russell and Wilson).

24. Cf. *Ep. ad Them.* 266d, where Julian repeats his remark; other passages cited by Prato and Fornara, *Giuliano Imperatore*, 39–40. On the other hand, the *Epit. de Caes.* remarks (43.5): *aequauerat philosophos et Graecorum sapientissimos.*

25. Prato and Fornara, *Giuliano Imperatore*, 39, consider the possibility that Themistius had offered to be Julian's adviser, an offer that, they argue (41), the emperor refused. This is predicated on their view that the treatise was written in 361, and the suggestion is impossible at an earlier date.

26. For brief discussion, Athanassiadi-Fowden, *Julian and Hellenism*, 90–91, 95.

27. On these actions and individuals, Prato and Fornara, *Giuliano Imperatore*, 47–48.

pher's possible objection that Julian was able to lead an active life, but preferred to avoid the work that this entailed, the Caesar replies that Themistius was considering the wrong question. As a basis for judgment of Julian, he ought to apply the precept "Know thyself" and the proverb "Let every man practice the craft which he knows" (*Ep. ad Them.* 259b–260c; trans. Wright). Julian thinks, with Plato, that the task of a ruler is beyond human ability and quotes several passages from Aristotle's *Politics* that support his argument and harmonize with Plato. Subtly, Julian is suggesting that Themistius had not read Aristotle carefully.[28] After remarking that Themistius' statements made him nervous, Julian admits that his interpretation may be wrong and indicates a willingness to be corrected (*Ep. ad Them.* 260c–263b).

The rest of Julian's letter is mostly a philosophical reply to points that confused him in the *protrepticus* and is less personal, though not entirely. Julian begins innocuously enough, referring to a genuine eagerness for clarification and addressing Themistius as friend and master (*Ep. ad Them.* 263c). To support his statement that he preferred a life of action to a philosophical life, Themistius had cited Aristotle, who defined happiness as virtuous activity and approved architects of noble actions. Julian replies, "But it is you who assert that these are kings, whereas Aristotle does not speak in the sense of the words you have introduced: and from what you have quoted one would rather infer the contrary" (*Ep. ad Them.* 263d; trans. Wright). Julian interprets Aristotle's definition of action as a reference to lawgivers and philosophers, that is, those whose activity lies in their use of intelligence and reason, not in the business of politics.[29] They naturally do more than prescribe and instruct, but the performance of deeds alone does not entitle anyone to be called an architect of noble actions (*Ep. ad Them.* 263c–264a). Socrates was responsible for the wisdom of Plato, the generalship of Xenophon, the fortitude of Antisthenes, the schools of philosophy, and philosophy itself. As support for his inclination toward a contemplative life, Julian offers the very examples used by Themistius: Arius, Nicolaus, Thrasyllus, and Musonius, famous not

---

28. Athanassiadi-Fowden, *Julian and Hellenism*, 93, remarks that Julian wrote "with conscious polemic intent."

29. Probably criticism of Themistius' role as senator and other political activity.

for deeds, but for writings or endurance under tyrants.[30] Themistius himself is not inactive because he was not a general, a politician, or a governor of a nation or city.[31] By training even a few philosophers, he could confer great benefits on the lives of men.[32] A philosopher was to be active in society, but only to increase his effectiveness as a philosopher, and was to avoid politics (*Ep. ad Them.* 264b–266c).

Julian's letter reveals some important differences between the views of author and addressee.[33] It also serves as a basis for understanding the relations between them, both before and after Julian's accession. Julian criticizes the methods of Themistius in his *protrepticus* and critiques the philosopher's interpretation of Aristotle. His response thus falls into two parts, emotional and intellectual, an important consideration for any interpretation. The most acrimonious point is a remark that Themistius had not accurately understood Aristotle,[34] but this criticism is only one part of the intellectual response and should not be too much emphasized in the first instance. A difference in philosophical views could lead to disharmonious relations, but does not rule out mutual respect.

Themistius was not pleased with Julian's tardy reply. As an open letter to intellectuals, it placed him in a difficult position. Linked politically to Constantius for more than a decade, he could now be labeled, rightly or wrongly, an adherent of Julian. The usurper's fre-

---

30. Some of these examples appear elsewhere in Themistius' works; see chapter 2. Prato and Fornara, *Giuliano Imperatore*, 56–57, discuss them briefly.

31. This remark has needlessly caused problems for those who believe that Themistius held office under Constantius, on which see chapter 4. On any date for the letter, Themistius was a senator. Cf. also Bradbury, *GRBS* 28 (1987): 240–42.

32. Athanassiadi-Fowden, *Julian and Hellenism*, 93, who suggests that Julian is here declining Themistius' offer of aid, has apparently misunderstood the text. Julian is stating that philosophers are more valuable than kings. Two paragraphs later, Julian asks philosophers for support (266d–267a).

33. Athanassiadi-Fowden, *Julian and Hellenism*, 94, finds a conflict with Julian's own ideas, remarking that the treatise "appears as a momentary aberration," since it rejects ideas that began in 358 with his dream of the Genius Publicus: not a problem if the letter is dated to 356.

34. The dispute between Maximus and Themistius that Julian arbitrated in favor of Maximus (Ammon. *In anal. prior.* 1.1.24b.18 = *CAG* IV, 6, p. 31.17) involved the interpretation of a point in Aristotle. For brief discussion, cf. Vanderspoel, *AHB* 1 (1987): 73.

quent references to Themistius' incitements to action could support a view that the philosopher was partly responsible for Julian's assumption of full imperial power. The statement that he had cleared himself of Themistius' charges and his request for aid from philosophers, because he had become their leader and had taken the first risks, would confirm the impression. A combination of Julian's unwillingness early in the letter and his espousal of his cause at the end would make this conclusion almost inescapable for a casual reader unaware of the circumstances of composition.

Almost certainly, Julian used his reply as an instrument to undermine Themistius' influence in the East. He was unsuccessful, since Themistius appears as an important figure in a rescript of 3 May 361 (*CTh* 12.6.3). Possibly, supporters of neither Constantius nor Julian trusted him completely, the former because of the clear implication of the letter, the latter because of his adherence to Constantius. His resignation from an impending term as city prefect, which resulted in something of a political impotence, may be a tangible result of this distrust.[35]

The death of Constantius on 3 November 361 and Julian's assumption of power in the East as well as the West profited Themistius very little, if at all. He appears rarely in the sources for the first part of Julian's reign, and he was silent,[36] if not necessarily silenced, while retaining his prominent position in the Senate. Defending himself against various charges in 384, Themistius refers to his *prostasia*, that is, his position as *princeps senatus*, from 357 on (34.13) and gives no evidence of a period of decline.[37] Naturally, he would not mention this in a speech of defense, but the evidence as a whole points unambiguously to the conclusion that Themistius did not lose official status while Julian was on the throne. Equally clearly, his career did not advance.[38] An important distinction must be made between official position and personal influence. Without any change in official status, Themistius

---

35. This possibility is argued more fully in chapter 4.

36. So Criscuolo, *Koinonia* 7 (1983): 94. No extant evidence compels the hypothesis of a *gratulatio* to Julian after Constantius' death. The normal statement that he did (cf., e.g., Athanassiadi-Fowden, *Julian and Hellenism*, 90, n. 7; Brauch, *Byzantion* 63 [1993]: 85) depends solely on the view that the *Letter to Themistius* was written in 361 as a response.

37. See chapter 4 for extended discussion.

38. Cf. Dagron, *Thémistios*, 232–35.

lost influence: Julian relied on him less than Constantius had done and later emperors were to do. Some officials who lost their positions were his friends,[39] but this did not result from acrimony toward Themistius: Julian reestablished a single court, and some officials, like the *cura palatii* Saturninus, who was cashiered (Am. Mar. 22.3.7), were simply superfluous. Wholesale changes in the upper levels of the civil service are not uncommon after a change of regime,[40] and friendship with Themistius was not an important consideration.

This interpretation of Julian's motives in releasing his letter to the philosopher provides a good reason for any reluctance on the part of Themistius to join Julian's cause with enthusiasm. Later in Julian's reign, the philosopher reveals a resilience and flexibility. He may have had little choice: his panegyric, possibly for the consulship of Julian in 363, was almost certainly an obligation mandated by his position and his status as the city's representative. The Senate cannot have allowed the occasion to pass entirely unnoticed, and Themistius rarely, if ever, shirked his civic duty. Surrounded by advisers whose views differed from those of Themistius and were closer to his own, Julian may have regarded the political support of the philosopher as expendable. He continued to respect Themistius as an intellectual.[41]

Different approaches to kingship and legitimacy were not the main reasons for a rift between Themistius and Julian.[42] The philosopher had adopted the position that an emperor was semidivine. In practical terms, this allowed an emperor the freedom to act as he wished. To moderate the implications of this, Themistius advised emperors to emphasize the good divine qualities. In contrast, Julian's acceptance of Plato forced the view that the best ruler is a philosopher who did not want to rule. This is the reason for his protest in the *Letter to Themistius* that he was neither a philosopher nor an experienced administrator. He was unable to accept the view that he was semidivine by virtue of his position. The dismantling of the court apparatus is evidence for Julian's philosophical standpoint. In the belief that he

---

39. Cf. Dagron, *Thémistios*, 234, n. 26; Stertz, *CJ* 71 (1975/76): 352; Prato and Fornara, *Giuliano Imperatore*, 41.

40. Cf. Bowersock, *Julian the Apostate*, 66–78, on Julian's changes and reforms.

41. So Dagron, *Thémistios*, 234–35.

42. Cf. esp. Daly, *BZ* 73 (1980): 1–11, for the view here denied, and Brauch, *Byzantion* 63 (1993): 85–88, for a similar one.

was no more than first among equals, Julian attempted to strip the
court of the retinue and ceremonial that elevated the court beyond the
merely human.[43] Ultimately, he was unsuccessful. His successors did
not accept this, and his actions did not long survive him.

Julian's view led him to emphasize deeds and virtues, not the
dynastic policy of his predecessors, as a foundation of legitimacy.[44]
The contrast appears in his work. In panegyrics of Constantius, Julian
discusses dynastic history,[45] while his own legitimacy in the *Letter to
the Athenians* rests on his accomplishments. In contrast, Themistius'
position was at its core an acceptance of the status quo. The foundation of imperial legitimacy was successful accession.[46] Yet he regarded
usurpers as usurpers, on the basis of opposition to legitimately constituted authority. Consequently, he may have had difficulties with Julian's assumption of full imperial power in 360. Constantius' death,
and his deathbed proclamation (Am. Mar. 21.15.2), resolved the difficulty, and Julian became, for Themistius, the legitimate emperor.[47]

This difference was primarily an academic debate, naturally not
devoid of practical considerations. The dispute, if that term is appropriate, lay elsewhere, in the issue of religion. Themistius held that
religious plurality was acceptable and desirable. Evident in his panegyric of Jovian, it is implicit in his attempt to urge Valens to this view,
in an oration of which only summaries survive.[48] At the beginning of
his reign, Julian displayed tolerance, allowing bishops exiled by Constantius to return. His goal, as he later stated to pagan friends, was to
provide fertile ground for factional strife within Christianity, but at
first the pronouncement seems to permit plurality. Later, he initiated
measures against Christianity. At this point, Julian and Themistius

---

43. On Julian's actions, Lib. *Or.* 18.130–145. On the idea behind ostentation, cf. Soc. *HE* 3.1.53: οἱ πλείους δὲ ψέγουσιν, ὅτι παυομένη ἡ ἐκ τοῦ
βασιλικοῦ πλούτου τοῖς πολλοῖς ἐγγινομένη κατάπληξις εὐκαταφρόνητον
ἐποίει τὴν βασιλείαν.

44. His panegyrists naturally followed him in this. Cf. MacCormack, *Art
and Ceremony*, 192–96.

45. E.g., *Or.* 1.6c–9b; 2.51c–52d. In both passages, Julian trots out the
unhistorical dynastic link to Claudius Gothicus.

46. Cf. Straub, *Herrscherideal*, 160–74, on Themistius; see also chapter 4.

47. Clear from later references to Julian, e.g., *Or.* 5.65b, where Jovian is
praised for not rising against a legitimate emperor, even though (in Themistius'
view) he deserved to be emperor earlier. See chapter 6.

48. See chapters 6 and 7 for discussions of these speeches.

parted company;[49] the rift arose from different responses to the new reality. Julian wanted a return to an earlier period; Themistius accepted the need for moderation.[50]

In essence, Julian and Themistius held differing views on the meaning and parameters of Hellenism in the fourth century. Julian, influenced by "extreme Neoplatonists, the so-called theurgists, or wonder-workers," adopted a strong stance, equating Hellenism not only with the knowledge and assimilation of Greek cultural antiquity and traditions, but also with the performance of religion. In this, he differed from many pagan contemporaries, who used the term *Hellenism* for Greek culture generally, as "language, thought, mythology, and images that constituted an extraordinarily flexible medium of both cultural and religious expression."[51] Interestingly, the definition used by Julian became or was already operative among Christians of his generation.[52] Like the emperor, they were perhaps incapable of visualizing anything but a hard line between Christians and non-Christians; the intellectual position thus adopted is a militant one. The other group, more numerous,[53] but with less influence on scholarly tradition (ancient and modern), included thinkers like Themistius who limited Hellenism largely to education and moral, not religious, consequences of a thorough grounding in the ideals of the Greek cultural past.[54] They foresaw the outcome of a hard-line position: with continuing Christianization, militant paganism was bound to fail, unable to survive a struggle to the death. For them, elimination of religion as an issue (and the resulting toleration) offered a stronger guarantee for survival of the essentials of Greek *paideia*.

Julian and Themistius thus held mutually exclusive positions in their approaches to Hellenism, but this did not prevent further relations between them. Though Julian relied more heavily on other advisers, statements by medieval Arab scholars refer to frequent correspon-

49. So too Baret, *Themistio*, 22, who adds Julian's preference for the philosophy of Iamblichus.

50. On these differing views, see chapter 1.

51. G.W. Bowersock, *Hellenism in Late Antiquity* (Ann Arbor, 1990), 13 and 7, respectively; his first chapter delineates the issues involved in the concept of Hellenism.

52. Cf. Bowersock, *Hellenism*, 10 ff.; A. Cameron, *Anc. World* 24 (1993): 25.

53. As Cameron, *Anc. World* 24 (1993): 25–29, points out.

54. See chapter 1 for some additional remarks.

dence between them on philosophical and practical topics, and Libanius refers to a panegyric of Julian written by Themistius. The extant speeches of Themistius include an item, called a *Risâlat*, preserved in two Arabic copies that are similar but not precisely the same.[55] Despite doubts about authenticity, the treatise, which Greek sources do not mention, is clearly a work by Themistius.[56] His name is given in both Arabic copies, Arab scholars refer to a work of this nature, and an analysis of its content reveals an affinity to his other orations. For the most part, views on kingship and the royal task reflect those expressed to other emperors. Some differences do occur,[57] and these permit the conclusion that the addressee was Julian.[58]

The *Risâlat* is neither Themistius' *protrepticus* nor a response to Julian's *Letter to Themistius*.[59] The *Risâlat* offers none of the direct quotations that Julian cites, and the central themes do not harmonize closely; the protreptic letter exhorted Julian to activity, while the *Risâlat* suggests specific directions for practical activity after a discussion of the theoretical basis for kingship. Themistius need not have sent his treatise to Julian as private correspondence. Julian himself sent his *Letter to Themistius* to the East as an open letter, and Themistius may have done the same,[60] sending it to Julian when he

55. See appendix 3.

56. J. Bidez, *La tradition manuscrite et les éditions des Discours de l'Empereur Julien* (Gand, 1929), 141–47, and Stertz, *CJ* 71 (1975/76): 352–53, have reservations about the authenticity of the work.

57. J. Croissant, *Serta Leodiensia*, Bibliothèque de la Faculté de Philosophie et Lettres de l'Université de Liége 44 (1930): 7–30, discusses the affinity of this work to Themistius' other imperial speeches, as well as the differences. She bases her conclusions on the summary of the text provided by Bouyges, *Archives de Philosophie*, 2.3 (1924): 21–23. I recognize the danger of reaching conclusions on the basis of a Latin translation of an Arabic document that is itself several stages from the original.

58. The argument is complex and protracted; it can be found in Appendix 4.

59. Croissant, *Serta Leodiensia*, 28–30, inclines to the view that the *Risâlat* is Themistius' reply to Julian's request for aid from philosophers at the end of his *Letter to Themistius*, a view somewhat different from, but not entirely incompatible with, the view here suggested. Her view is accepted by Dvornik, in *Late Classical and Mediaeval Studies*, 77.

60. The open letter sent to the citizens of Medina by Mohammed before he traveled to that city is called a *Risâlat*. I owe this information to Professor Andrew Rippin.

himself was unable to be present. Since Julian is directly addressed as sole emperor,[61] the treatise should postdate Julian's visit to Constantinople and might then be the panegyric of Julian mentioned by Libanius.[62] That Julian and Themistius were engaged in public discussion of some philosophical issues can explain the greater divergence from the standard for imperial panegyric. The circumstance of delivery is not unique for Themistius. In 357, he was unwilling to undertake the journey to deliver *Oration* 4 at Milan personally.[63] He nevertheless sent a speech, which is clearly a panegyric and was doubtless delivered for the emperor's gratification.

In spring 363, Libanius wrote to Themistius, requesting a copy of the latter's panegyric of Julian (*Ep.* 818.3). He and Themistius were not on the best terms at this point:[64] Themistius had sent copies to friends at Antioch, but had not included Libanius. Having learned it was in circulation, Libanius, with typical petulance, asked for a personal copy. Themistius yielded. A second letter, dated to the autumn of 363, reports the sophist's reaction (*Ep.* 1430): he had been about to respond when he heard of Julian's death deep in Persian territory.[65] For the most part, his remarks about the panegyric are an aesthetic appreciation, and he has little to say about the content. Nevertheless, an examination is useful. Apart from a general statement that the speech was a noble effort about a noble man (*Ep.* 1430.1), Libanius specifies some items worthy of praise. Most of these are favorable or flattering assessments of the rhetorical qualities of the panegyric and may be cast aside. But a reference to the "well-yoked three-horse chariot of divinities and the necessities which bound them together" (1430.2) perhaps reflects the content of the panegyric in some way.

61. Cf. the Teubner edition, vol. 3, pp. 98–99, for I. Shahîd's text and Latin translation; all subsequent references to the *Risâlat* are to this volume. It is possible, but unlikely, that Themistius sent the treatise between the death of Constantius and Julian's arrival at Constantinople.

62. Dvornik, in *Late Classical and Mediaeval Studies,* 77, suggests that the *Risâlat* is a "laudatory treatise addressed to Julian but for public circulation," without discussion of the circumstances and date. Croissant, *Serta Leodiensia,* 9, denies this: "Notre *Risâlat* n'est pas, comme la plupart des discours de Thémistius, une œuvre de circonstance . . . ."

63. For discussion, see chapter 4.

64. For discussion, Bouchery, *Themistius,* 204–9.

65. Cf. Ballériaux, *Byzantion* 58 (1988): 34. *Ep.* 1430 is now accessible in Norman, *Libanius: Autobiography and Selected Letters,* vol. 2, no. 116.

Part of this statement is a quotation of Euripides, *Andromache* 277–278, where the subject is the three goddesses judged by Paris: Hera, Aphrodite, and Athena. The second part prevents the conclusion that Themistius referred to the judgment in his speech. To retain association with the goddesses, H.F. Bouchery has suggested that the necessities are to be regarded as bound to their manifestations: dignity, grace, and clarity, respectively.[66] Jeanne Croissant has quite reasonably taken Libanius' remark as a reference to the chariot myth of the *Phaedrus*, though the image does not occur in the *Risâlat*. She recognized problems with this interpretation, the most important being the myth itself. Plato refers to two horses guided by a charioteer, while Libanius (like Euripides) mentions a triad. Croissant suggests that Libanius' words are an adaptation of Plato's psychology to the political life of the empire, referring to the three classes of the state.[67]

Libanius' citation of the divinities need not be taken literally, since he employed a ready and recognizable phrase to enliven his remarks, but Themistius clearly included a triple manifestation linked by necessities. Human psychology may yet be apposite. The two horses drawing the chariot (*thymos*, *epithymia*) are, in the *Phaedrus*, directed by a charioteer (*nous*), the third element of human psychology. Themistius does not often outline his view fully in his speeches, but a tripartite division similar to the *Phaedrus* appears at *Oration* 32.360a–c. While the chariot is missing, two elements are directed by a third.

Before its examination of how an emperor is to rule an empire, the *Risâlat* gives an account of Themistius' psychology. The philosopher begins by noting that God inserted three faculties in man: *appetitiva*, *animalis*, and *rationalis*. These three elements, which might well be called *daimones* because of their origin and are not entirely coordinate with the Platonic Greek terms, have different roles in human experience. The first is responsible for the intake and transformation of food for the nourishment of the human body and is shared with plants. The second directs the emotions, a faculty shared with animals. The third occurs in man, allows him to think, raises him above animals,

---

66. *Themistius*, 227, n. 10 (on 228), where Bouchery proposes that the second part of the statement is a quotation from Themistius' speech, accepted by Dagron, *Thémistios*, 225, and Norman, *Libanius: Autobiography and Selected Letters*, 2:209.

67. *Serta Leodiensia*, 28, n. 1.

and makes him similar to God. In this first summary, the third element is not closely involved in the acquisition of necessities for continued existence. Later in the speech, Themistius develops his views on the nature of man in a different direction, and the third element, reason, is arguably involved in the process of acquiring the necessities (p. 93): it computes the amounts required. Not confined to controlling the other elements, reason is active in the nutritive and regenerative processes, a view that Plato seems occasionally to have held.[68] With remarks intended as praise, Libanius appears to refer to this rather lengthy portion of the Risâlat,[69] pointing out that Themistius has adopted the psychology of Plato in his panegyric of Julian.

The evidence of Libanius (and a desire for economy) suggest that the Risâlat and the panegyric of Julian are to be equated, and the Risâlat then provides hitherto unexploited evidence on the relations between Julian and Themistius. The very fact that the philosopher wrote a panegyric at all should do much to reduce suspicions that the two were mutually and continually on bad terms, even if Themistius wrote the panegyric from a sense of obligation. Libanius' words indicate that at least he was happy with the speech.[70] Given the sophist's attitude toward Julian, the speech must have been laudatory. Its sincerity is an open question.

To allow for Libanius' discovery that the panegyric had been sent to some individuals in Antioch, for his complaint that he had not received a copy personally, for Themistius to send a copy, and for the sophist's remark that he received the panegyric before he received news of Julian's death, the speech cannot be dated much later than the beginning of 363. On this argumentation, the most suitable occasion is 1 January 363, when Julian inaugurated his final consulship at Antioch,[71] the only realistic excuse for a panegyric at this point of the reign, but not indicated in the text in accord with Themistius' normal practice. It is equally possible, and perhaps better, to argue that the panegyric was written for no specific reason, but during the winter of

68. Cf. D.A. Rees, JHS 77 (1957): 112–18.
69. More than a third of the Risâlat (pp. 83–97) is given to a study of human psychology, and a few more pages discuss the philosophy of human society.
70. So too Ballériaux, Byzantion 58 (1988): 34, n. 45.
71. So Seeck, in Seeck and Schenkl, RhM 61 (1906): 559; Bouchery, Themistius, 219; Dagron, Thémistios, 224.

362/3. The probable allusion to *CTh* 6.26.1, where Julian announced the primacy of the military (see the discussion later in this chapter), may give a *terminus post quem*.

The document itself is typical of Themistius. Rather than rehearsing standard items and praising the emperor for deeds,[72] he draws a picture of an ideal ruler, detailing the performance of this fictitious emperor in various spheres of activity. By choosing areas where the reigning emperor had been active, Themistius, whether he states this explicitly or not, leads his audience to the conclusion that the subject of his panegyric was a manifestation of the ideal ruler. The *Risâlat* is no different in this regard; Themistius, in fact, mentions the practice directly (p. 105).[73] He takes great pains to point out that the best state is one under a single ruler, in terms that can refer to an emperor other than Julian only with great difficulty; he implies that the emperor had known the discord and disharmony of a plurality of leaders before becoming sole emperor (p. 99). The dispute between Constantius and Julian and the sudden death of the former fit the circumstances perfectly.

According to Themistius, the emperor presided over a happy age because he had the necessary character and virtues and was able to display these in himself and inculcate them in his subjects (p. 103). The philosopher continues with a list of the features of this age (pp. 103–5). The statements are generic and could apply to more than one emperor, but appear to refer to activities of Julian. The accession of a good emperor allowed all citizens to live normal lives, in great security. A simple statement that the new political climate allowed commerce to proceed in normal fashion and grain to become cheaper may be no more than an example of the present security in the empire,[74] but it is tempting to regard Julian's actions on the grain supply at Antioch as background.[75] Finally, remarks about a new harmony, with

---

72. As Libanius does in *Or.* 12, his own speech for the consulship of 363.

73. Claudius Mamertinus, in his panegyric on Julian, is much more inclined to contrast Julian to Constantius, to the latter's detriment; cf. on this, R.C. Blockley, *AJP* 93 (1972): 437–50. A translation of this panegyric can be found in S.N.C. Lieu, ed., *The Emperor Julian: Panegyric and Polemic* (Liverpool, 1986).

74. Cf. 14.180c–d, 15.189b–c.

75. Cf. P. Petit, *Libanius et la vie municipale à Antioche au IVe siècle apres J.-C.* (Paris, 1955), 108–18; G. Downey, *A History of Antioch in Syria from Seleucus to the*

soldiers remaining in their places, suggest that a civil war had been or was a threat.

Themistius proceeds to the characteristics required by a good ruler, noting that an emperor should not be greedy for wealth and ostentatious display. While allowing distinction, he points out that an emperor must behave correctly (pp. 107–9). He is describing an ideal emperor, but specific proposals ground the speech firmly in historical reality.[76] The ideal emperor prohibits his adherents from the use of precious metals, perhaps a response to Julian's attempt to remove ostentation from the court.[77] The final words of the paragraph may refer to the buying and selling of offices, an abuse that Julian attempted to correct.[78]

Themistius next addresses the issue of officials, imperial advisers, and personal servants.[79] The primary consideration is the suitability of these individuals for their tasks (pp. 109–11). The remarks reflect Julian's actual practice or the situation at his court, since he surrounded himself with individuals he had met during his education and upbringing. Themistius' suggestions may also take their origin in part from Julian's own lengthy remarks on this theme in his panegyrics of Constantius (*Or.* 2.90c–91d).

After remarking that an army should be composed of soldiers able to withstand severe climates and other hardships of their position, referring perhaps to Julian's emphasis on army discipline and the fact that his legions had experienced European winters,[80] Themistius discusses the proper attitude toward peoples on the borders. His suggestions, or rather vague generalizations,[81] may seem point-

---

Arab Conquest (Princeton, 1961), 388–91; J.H.W.G. Liebeschuetz, *Antioch: City and Imperial Administration in the Later Roman Empire* (Oxford, 1972), 130–31.

76. Cf. similar remarks by Claud. Mamer. *Pan. Lat.* 3[11].11.1–4.

77. Cf. Bowersock, *Julian the Apostate,* 71–73. S. Mazzarino, *Aspetti sociale del quarto secolo* (Rome, 1951), 186–87, and Athanassiadi-Fowden, *Julian and Hellenism,* 97–98, point to an attempt to restore the curial class with this measure.

78. *CTh* 2.29.1; Claud. Mamer. *Pan. Lat.* 3[11].21; Am. Mar. 20.5.7, 22.6.5. Cf. W. Goffart, *CP* 65 (1970): 145–51; T.D. Barnes, *CP* 69 (1974): 288–91.

79. Claud. Mamer. *Pan. Lat.* 3[11].25, similarly devotes a section of his panegyric to this theme.

80. Cf. W.E. Kaegi, *BF* 2 (1967): 256–58.

81. Not much more general than some prescriptions in the *de rebus bellicis,* also addressed to an emperor.

less or insulting, but perhaps reflect Julian's procedure. He states that the emperor ought to place a suitable number of soldiers on the borders, make certain that the enemy remains unaware of his plans,[82] and take care less any ambassador from the enemy court engage in espionage (pp. 113–15). Worth noting here is Julian's rejection of a Persian offer to send an embassy to negotiate peace (Lib. *Or.* 12.76– 77, 17.19, 18.164–166).

Advice on military matters is followed by a prescription for the arts. The emperor must ensure that they prosper.[83] According to Themistius, they divide into three kinds, contemplative arts, like philosophy, oratory and grammar, craftsmanship (*usu*), such as carpentry and iron-working, and a combination of the other two, like medicine and music (p. 115). The practitioners ought to be intellectually or physically suited, because then the empire will prosper (pp. 115–19). The sequence of Themistius' last two topics, military and then arts, may be significant, since Julian opined in a rescript of 9 November 362 that military service was of prime importance, followed by the protection of letters as an adornment of peace (*CTh* 6.26.1). If the words of Themistius postdate this rescript, the earliest possible date for the *Risâlat* is November 362. Themistius closes with the view that an emperor ought to leave behind an empire more prosperous than the one he had received from his predecessor; in consequence, he would win an appropriate reward from God and lasting memory among men. For his last word, the philosopher applies his injunctions not only to the emperor, but also to his chief adviser (*ministrum*), almost certainly Julian's praetorian prefect Salutius.

The *Risâlat* is, in the final analysis, neither very enlightening nor particularly interesting. Themistius seems to take refuge in a simple account of Julian's activities, expressed more in terms of the emperor's philosophy than of his own.[84] He was intelligent enough to find elements that were common to the different views on Hellenism espoused by the two principals. He does not use the opportunity to promote his own views or the attitudes of those he represented on political or other issues, and he makes no request. Julian had strong

---

82. Cf. W.E. Kaegi, *Athenaeum* 69 (1981): 209–13.
83. Cf. Claud. Mamer. *Pan. Lat.* 3[11].23.4.
84. Cf. Brauch, *Byzantion* 63 (1993): 92.

views of his own and was perhaps not amenable to suggestions, despite his willingness for philosophical debate. Under the circumstances, harmony rested in the ability to appease an emperor who was himself quite aware of the strictures imposed by a shared sense of the cultural heritage. He did not need stiff reminders as, for example, Valens did. Nevertheless, Themistius must have been disappointed in some aspects of the reign.

During this reign, the philosopher was not as involved in politics as he had been. His public activity, beyond his work as senator, is apparently limited to one panegyric, which was in part a duty by virtue of his *prostasia*. So too were any discussions on policy with Julian: as *princeps senatus*, he bore the responsibility of providing a link between emperor and Senate. Different views on kingship and especially on the appropriate attitude toward the new reality of the Christian empire restricted Julian's reliance on Themistius, who discovered, in the reign of this pagan emperor, a relationship between philosophy and politics rather different from his experience under the Christian Constantius. Since Julian had Maximus of Ephesus and Priscus at his court, he did not need the adornment of philosophy that Themistius could provide, though he did respect his former teacher's skill as a philosopher (31.354d). Themistius' panegyric, which reveals a willingness to adapt to political reality, indicates that Julian must bear some responsibility for the interruption of the philosopher's political career. But Themistius himself withdrew to some extent from what he saw as excesses and from those who were opponents in the larger debates of his generation.

6

Themistius and Jovian

The death of Julian on 26 June 363 deep in Persian territory left the Roman army in a precarious position. Leaderless, and in danger of their lives, the Roman forces needed a new commander quickly. With the army council unable to agree on a candidate, an attempt at compromise failed when Salutius, Julian's praetorian prefect and de facto head of state upon the emperor's death, refused to serve. In consequence, the army and council accepted the Christian Jovian as the new emperor.

Jovian was born in 331 to Varronianus, a Pannonian military officer who became tribune of the Joviani before retiring as *comes*[1] and was no doubt instrumental in the enrollment of his son among the protectores et domestici.[2] Jovian is first attested as *protector* late in 361, when he accompanied the funeral cortege of Constantius to Constantinople (Am. Mar. 21.16.20). In 363, according to Ammianus, he was *domesticorum ordinis primus* and *adhuc protector* (25.5.4, 8). Eutropius, a participant in the campaign (10.16.1), records that Jovian *tunc domesticus* (10.17.1) succeeded Julian. John of Antioch (fr. 179) implies the same post. Jerome states that Jovian became emperor *ex primicerio domesticorum* (*Chron.* s.a 363), and Jordanes notes that he was *primericerius domesticorum* (*Rom.* 305). These differences are not problematic: Jovian was still attached to the *domestici* because he had not yet been graduated from the corps, but had reached the highest position within it.[3]

---

1. Cf. *PLRE*, 1:461, 946 for the details. Zos. 3.30.1, is alone in making Varronianus the *comes domesticorum*, and not all have accepted this; cf. Paschoud, *Zosime*, 2, 1:211–12, for brief discussion. It is possible that Varronianus was given an honorary rank when he retired as tribune.

2. Cf. Jones, *LRE*, 2:637–40, on the corps as a training ground for future officers drawn from army veterans and sons of high-ranking officials.

3. Some Christian sources (Soc. *HE* 3.22.2; *Souda*, s.v Ἰοβιανός; Joh. Ant. fr. 179, 181; Zon. 13.14) falsely report that Jovian had preferred to retire from the military rather than sacrifice to pagan gods on Julian's demand. On the incident, cf. Bowersock, *Julian the Apostate*, 107, with n. 3.

The new emperor was immediately faced with the problem of extirpation. Perhaps to appease pagan elements in the court and army he had inherited, he consulted haruspices before deciding on a course of action.[4] They suggested that the only hope of escape was immediate departure for safer confines, a view as obvious from the military situation as from the entrails. Because the Persians continually harassed the Roman army in retreat, Jovian, whose hold on power had yet to be consolidated, quickly agreed to peace. Terms included the transfer of Nisibis and other territory to Persian control. By 22 October 363 (CTh 10.19.2) at the latest, Jovian had reached Antioch. He did not stay long, since he was at Ancyra when he inaugurated his consulship on 1 January 364. Less than two months later, he was dead.

On his return from the Persian front, an embassy from Constantinople met Jovian at Antioch to congratulate him (Lib. Ep. 1430, 1436, 1439, 1444). Libanius complains that Themistius had not joined.[5] He regards this as a personal insult, suggesting that Themistius was avoiding him (Ep. 1430.4).[6] Libanius' assessment may be valid. He spent his life after 363 mourning the death of Julian. In a letter to Themistius, he notes that his only solace at the news of Julian's death was to weep (Ep. 1430.3), complains that he could not speak or write (1430.4), and in despair adds that only God knew if time would heal the grief (1430.4).[7] During the summer of 363, Themistius had perhaps learned of

---

4. Ammianus (25.6.1) alone reports this action and may be attempting to discredit Jovian. More likely, the emperor was treading carefully in a pagan court; so too Seeck, Geschichte des Untergangs der antiken Welt (Berlin, 1911), 4:366, and A. Solari, Klio 26 (1933): 333, 335. This does not mean that he was not a Christian. Compare Julian, who acted like a Christian while he was Caesar. Matthews, Ammianus, 185, suggests that the death of Julian did not change normal procedure and that Jovian, "though a Christian, concurred."

5. Seeck, Briefe, 301, 414, held that Themistius refused to meet Jovian until he had proclaimed an edict of toleration, a view explicitly designed to explain the delivery of a panegyric only three months later (Geschichte, 4:368–70) and widely accepted.

6. This suggestion is the only evidence that Themistius was to join the delegation. It might, however, merely reflect a reasonable expectation by Libanius: Themistius was, after all, the Senate's chosen leader and representative.

7. For a good brief discussion of Libanius' grief, see Norman, Libanius: Selected Works, xxxiii–xxxviii.

Libanius' reaction. He himself was not emotionally attached to Julian, as the sophist clearly was, and no doubt did not wish to hear the inexhaustible complaints of Libanius.[8] A more potent argument suggests that Themistius purposely avoided the delegation. A visit to Antioch would involve contact with Libanius, who was regarded with suspicion by some elements at the court (*Or.* 1.138). A barbarian, probably an officer,[9] accused Libanius of incessantly mourning Julian, a charge certainly true and apparently dangerous: a former fellow student saved the sophist from execution (*Or.* 1.138).[10] Themistius was perhaps unwilling to risk negative relations with a new emperor by allying with an emotional devotee of the old.

Reference to a speech has induced the view that Themistius wrote a *gratulatio* instead,[11] but the oration is his panegyric of Julian (1430.1–2).[12] Clearchus, who traveled to Antioch about this time, had not necessarily joined the delegation as a replacement when the philosopher declined to make the journey; though his presence in Antioch may owe its impetus to Themistius' refusal, he may also have been selected on his own merits. Alternatively, since Clearchus seems to have become *vicarius Asiae* in 363, Jovian had perhaps summoned him to Antioch for his investiture in that office.[13] Libanius (*Ep.* 1430.5) states only that Clearchus visited him at Antioch,[14] perhaps at Themistius' request. The philosopher's relations with Jovian thus begin and end with the panegyric delivered on 1 January 364 at Ancyra, where Jovian and his infant son Varronianus inaugurated

---

8. Libanius and Themistius were not always close friends. The subject bears reinvestigation; for the moment, see Bouchery, *Themistius*, passim.

9. A.F. Norman, *Libanius' Autobiography* (Oxford, 1965), 188–89. I. Shahîd, *Byzantium and the Arabs in the Fourth Century* (Washington, D.C., 1984), 134–37, suggests the commander of Arab *foederati*, possibly the husband of Queen Mavia.

10. Norman, *Libanius' Autobiography*, 189. Libanius may exaggerate the danger.

11. Scholze, *Temporibus*, 23. Only a few reject this suggestion, e.g., H. Schenkl, *SitzAkadWissWien* 192 (1919), Abh. 1, 79, and Bouchery, *Themistius*, 221, n. 3.

12. Bouchery, *Themistius*, 227. See chapter 5.

13. As Scholze, *Temporibus*, 23, suggested. Seeck, *Briefe*, 108, places him on the embassy, but not as a replacement for Themistius. On Clearchus' career, cf. *PLRE*, 1, s.v. Clearchus 1.

14. Bouchery, *Themistius*, 224, n. 1.

their consulship (Am. Mar. 25.10.11).[15] He delivered the speech at
the head of a delegation from the Senate (Soc. *HE* 3.26).

This panegyric of Jovian is the clearest example of a method often
adopted by Themistius. He devotes considerable space to Jovian's
accession and his virtue as emperor and discusses the treaty with the
Persians. Unlike other writers, he is favorable on these points, in an
attempt to capture the emperor's attention for a request. He asks
Jovian to extend religious toleration to every variety of religion, on the
grounds that God created diversity in the world and wanted to be
worshiped in different ways. The philosopher hoped that his favorable treatment in the early part of the panegyric would result in a
positive response.

The proportions devoted to the various topics indicate his preoccupations. The orator acknowledges that Jovian was elected emperor in
circumstances not ideal for the consideration that the selection of an
emperor deserved:

> They [electors and soldiers] did this not in leisure, not in peace,
> not permitting opportunity for the paying of court, the bringing
> of news and bribery, but as though in the critical point of Enyo,
> in swords and spears, they cast their votes, a judgment that
> was not sought, an unorchestrated election that the time de-
> creed, for which utility was the guiding hand. And this is
> indeed even more astonishing in an assembly beyond the bor-
> der, outside Roman territory, on behalf of the Roman Empire.
> (5.65c–d)[16]

Earlier in the speech, Themistius had noted that Jovian deserved the
throne because of his virtue:

---

15. Scholze, *Temporibus*, 24. Soc. *HE* 3.26.3, states that the speech was
delivered in Dadastana, where the emperor soon met his death. Baret,
Themistio, 27, accepts the statement of Socrates. *PLRE*, 1:891, manages to
accept both: Themistius met Jovian at Dadastana late in 363, then delivered
the oration at Ancyra on 1 January 364! L.J. Daly, *GRBS* 12 (1971): 71, places
delivery at Antioch.

16. In contrast, cf. remarks by Symmachus at *Or.* 1.8–10, on the leisurely
accession of Valentinian. He notes as well the preference for a ruler reluctant
to take the throne.

... the empire was owed to you even earlier because of your ancestral virtue,[17] but when the elder [Constantius] of the two previous rulers died, you hesitated to recover the debt, so that you might not seem to attack the survivor of the dynasty of Constantine. You watched for the present opportune moment, so as to recover the debt owed to your father without harming anyone. (5.65b)[18]

By citing ancestral virtue, Themistius is yielding to the popular opinion, evident in the accounts of the historians, that Jovian owed his throne to the influence and popularity of his father, though he may also be conceding to the prescription for imperial panegyric, which dictated accounts of the characters of ancestors.[19] After a comparison with events following the death of Alexander, Themistius claims that the army council carefully considered and accepted the candidacy of Jovian before his proclamation:

But our voters [i.e., the army council] and the soldiers preferred inheritance of the mind to that of the body and declared as heir of the purple the heir of virtue. (5.65c)

Other sources offer different versions. Eutropius writes, without elaboration, that Jovian "was chosen by the consent of the army" (10.17.1). Ammianus is more detailed. Two groups of high-ranking officers meeting in council, adherents of Constantius and Julian, respectively, could not agree. Eventually, they approached Salutius, who refused on grounds of poor health and old age.[20] At some point,

17. For the suggestion that this and other parts of *Or.* 5 are based on Ael. Arist. *Or.* 35 Keil, see chapter 1.

18. Themistius adds that Jovian had been content with an emperor "unpleasant as regards dignity" (5.65c), suggesting that Jovian had been passed over for promotion.

19. Cf. Menander Rhetor, p. 370.

20. R. von Haehling, in *Bonner Festgabe Johannes Straub zum 65 Geburtstag am 18 Oktober 1977*, ed. A. Lippold and N. Himmelmann (Bonn, 1977), 352–53, notes that this refusal is a topos, even given the fact that Salutius' illness is known from Lib. *Ep.* 1298.2, 1429.1. On the career of Salutius, cf. *PLRE*, 1:814–17.

a few soldiers proclaimed Jovian (25.5.1–4).[21] Zosimus reports only that Jovian was elected "by common consent" (3.30.1), while Socrates implies the same, but adds that Jovian refused to serve until the army declared its Christianity (*HE* 3.22.4). The last claim is false,[22] and a suggestion that Jovian was not the first candidate is susceptible to varying interpretation. Adding to the confusion is a report of Zosimus that, after the death of Jovian, the throne was offered to Salutius, and then to his son, before Valentinian gained general acceptance (3.36.1–2). No other source, except Zonaras (13.14), offers the story.

The accounts of Salutius' candidacies are sufficiently divergent to suggest two attempts to make him emperor.[23] Ammianus does not mention an attempt to crown his son, though he does note that several candidates were proposed before Valentinian was chosen in 364 (26.1.4–5). He includes under 363 the remarks of a "certain soldier of higher rank" (*honoratior aliquis miles*),[24] who suggested that the prefect lead the army to Roman territory, where the troops, with the forces of Procopius, could elect a new emperor (25.5.3). This conversation cannot have taken place in 364.

---

21. Matthews, *Ammianus*, 184, suggests that they were junior officers excluded from the council's deliberations, but otherwise his view is similar to that proposed here. He also points out that Jovian had a higher profile than is usually thought.

22. Scholars do not consider it seriously, because it is too schematic in the context of Julian's paganism. However, R. Soraci, *L'Imperatore Gioviano* (Catania, 1968), 19–21, finds it more acceptable than the story of the retirement from a putative tribunate.

23. For a list of those who accept both candidacies or reject one or the other, cf. Paschoud, *Zosime*, 2, 1:238–39. Von Haehling, in *Bonner Festgabe Johannes Straub*, 351, 353, thinks that Salutius was not a candidate in 363, explaining Ammianus' account as an attempt to discredit Jovian. Cf. H. Gärtner, *AkadWissLitMainz. Abh. geist. und sozialwiss. Kl.* (1968), Abh. 10, 525–29, for the view that Ammianus regards Jovian as an appendix to his treatment of Julian.

24. This soldier, sometimes thought to be Ammianus himself, is rather a friend whom the historian is shielding; cf. Thompson, *Historical Work of Ammianus Marcellinus*, 12. Matthews, *Ammianus*, 183–84, notes that the historian never stood so close to the center of power. The statement may represent an attempt to put Procopius on the throne, with Salutius holding the position open; cf. Solari, *Klio* 26 (1933): 331; Soraci, *L'Imperatore Gioviano*, 17–18. Von Haehling, in *Bonner Festgabe Johannes Straub*, 354, finds entire suggestion absurd.

The confidence in Salutius on both occasions indicates his importance and the nature of his position. Though Constantine and his sons had begun to develop a system of regional prefectures, Salutius was not a prefect of this type. Ammianus calls him *praefectus Salutius praesens* (23.5.6), a prefect of the old style who remained at court.[25] Since Julian was sole emperor without a designated heir, a prefect of this description, who would be the second man in the state, was almost a necessity. In an emergency, he would become interim head of state. Though this does not explain his candidacies for the throne, it does clarify the remark of the unnamed soldier and an item reported by Ammianus for 364. In the soldier's view, Salutius, as acting ruler, could best ensure a smooth succession by ruling in his constitutional capacity until time and place were suitable for deliberation. Salutius' interest in smooth successions is evident in 364. On the eve of Valentinian's accession, he proposed, and other officials agreed, that incumbents of high office and those suspected of attempting revolution were not to appear in public on the following morning under penalty of death (Am. Mar. 26.2.1). His continued tenure of the prefecture under Jovian and Valentinian, and a second tenure after a brief interlude in 365,[26] indicates popularity with pagan and Christian emperors and court officials alike.

While discussions with Salutius were in progress, so Ammianus states (25.5.4), Jovian was acclaimed emperor by some soldiers. Presumably, the deliberation ended at this point. All sources record that Jovian was chosen by the army, and the majority suggest that the vote was unanimous. Ammianus alone credits only part of the army for the original acclamation,[27] possibly Illyrian soldiers.[28] This may be part of an attempt to discredit Jovian, or most sources may simply reflect the reality that Jovian's support came from the army, not the army council.[29]

---

25. Cf. T.D. Barnes, in *Bonner Historia-Augusta-Colloquium 1984/85* (1987): 15.

26. Cf. *PLRE*, 1:816.

27. Accepted by Solari, *Klio* 26 (1933): 331–32, and von Haehling, in *Bonner Festgabe Johannes Straub*, 355–56.

28. Soraci, *L'Imperatore Gioviano*, 23.

29. Some scholars nevertheless think that the council was responsible for the accession; cf. e.g., G. Wirth, in *Vivarium: Festschrift Theodor Klauser zum 90. Geburtstag. JAC*, Erganzungsband 11 (1984): 357.

Stories of Jovian's refusal to assume power until the army declared its Christianity may have a valid basis.[30] Combined with remarks that Jovian owed his throne to the influence of his father (Am. Mar. 25.5.4; Zos. 3.30.1; Eutrop. 10.17.1; Joh. Ant. fr. 181; *Souda*, s.v. Ἰοβιανός), these reports allow the conjecture that he was selected by a legion that was largely Christian. His father, Varronianus, had for a time been tribune of the Joviani (Am. Mar. 25.5.8), a unit whose standard-bearers had refused to remove the labarum at Julian's command and were executed for treason. This legion was perhaps the first part of the army to acclaim Jovian, who was then quickly accepted by the rest.[31] On this suggestion,[32] Ammianus emphasizes a somewhat limited first acclamation of Jovian. The defection of a standard-bearer of the Joviani, perhaps a pagan replacement for an executed Christian, may support this. He had previously been at odds with Varronianus and Jovian (Am. Mar. 25.5.8) and possibly opposed the proclamation of Jovian. Ammianus notes that he fled to the Persians in fear, quite possibly legitimate: elsewhere, he records the fate of a *notarius* Jovianus who had been put forward as a candidate and was executed for acting immoderately after Jovian's accession (25.8.18).

This interpretation, relying heavily on a hostile Ammianus, ascribes considerable initiative to Jovian or to a legion, perhaps to both. It also permits an understanding of that historian's view that the accession was not fully legitimate. While acclamation by the army was an acceptable procedure for electing an emperor when no ruler survived to make an appointment,[33] initial promotion by part of the

30. Greg. Naz. *Or.* 5.15, does not note this refusal which first appears at the end of the fourth century; cf. von Haehling, in *Bonner Festgabe Johannes Straub*, 348, 356–57. Refusals are, of course, a standard feature of accessions. For discussion, cf. J. Béranger, *Recherches sur l'Aspect Idéologique du Principat.* Schweiz. Beiträge zur Altertumswiss. 6 (Basel, 1953), 137–69: "Le Refus du Pouvoir"; at 139–40, Béranger lists emperors who refused to serve.

31. Soraci, *L'Imperatore Gioviano*, 21–22, points out that proclamation by a minority does not necessarily imply that Christians were seizing an opportunity and puts greater emphasis on the view that Jovian was a compromise candidate.

32. Vegetius (1.17) indicates that the Joviani and Herculiani were Illyrian. Soraci, *L'Imperatore Gioviano*, 23, suggests that Illyrian soldiers first proclaimed Jovian, but goes no further.

33. Cf. Straub, *Herrscherideal* 11–17; MacCormack, *Art and Ceremony*, 161–64, 165–205.

army, if an individual engineered this, could be considered usurpation. Ammianus clearly wants to convey this impression, without
stating it unambiguously, and Themistius' suggestion that the accession was "unorchestrated" may be an attempt to counter such claims.
The evidence does not permit certainty about Jovian's own role, and it
is perhaps best to register a possibility that the accession was not
entirely legitimate because machinations behind the scenes were a
contributing factor.[34]

Other elements of the orator's thoughts on the accession also differ
from Ammianus. According to Themistius, all men, friends and enemies, as arbiters and witnesses, respectively, were present at Jovian's
election. He explains the Persian presence as follows:

> For the fact that the Persians elected you, not less than the
> Romans, they revealed by throwing away their weapons when
> they heard the proclamation and by quickly regarding with cau-
> tion the very men over whom they had earlier exulted. (5.66a)

In contrast, Ammianus reports that the Persians immediately attacked
the Roman army when informed, by the standard-bearer who had
defected, that Jovian had become emperor (25.6.8–9). Similarly, Themistius suggests that the entire Roman Empire voted for the accession
of Jovian:

> Moreover, both the East and the West concurred [in the election],
> as it was reasonable that the one about to rule the entire world
> hold no part whatsoever that did not share in the vote. (5.66b)[35]

While this statement could simply indicate that Jovian was a compromise candidate,[36] Ammianus records incidents that reveal resistance
to the new emperor in the West, even after the army and the army

---

34. Cf. Alföldi, *Conflict of Ideas*, 13: "And so it is likely enough that the
small group that by a bold stroke forced through the proclamation of Jovian
also consisted of his countrymen."

35. As Dagron, *Thémistios*, 123–24, notes, Themistius offers divine selection, acclamation by the army, and the consent of the governed as bases for
Jovian's legitimacy.

36. As. e.g., Piganiol, *L' Empire chrétien*, 2nd ed., 163; and Daly, *GRBS* 12
(1971): 71, think.

council in the East, composed of eastern and western elements, had accepted the proclamation. Some agents sent to the West to announce the accession, including Lucillianus, the emperor's father-in-law, were murdered because of a false rumor that Jovian had rebelled against Julian (25.10.6–8).

Themistius reports the outcome of the events surrounding the accession, not the events themselves. He ignores, as is to be expected of a panegyrist, any negative aspects of the original proclamation and acceptance of the new emperor. Noting that the proclamation occurred in a difficult situation, he emphasizes the correctness of the decision despite circumstances and the view that the emperor was a legitimate and worthy successor to Constantine and his dynasty. The suggestion that Jovian belatedly collected a debt owed to him because of his ancestral virtue is an attempt to influence popular opinion to the view that the aftermath of Julian's death resulted in a suitable outcome. Combined with the statement that Jovian was a new Constantine (5.70d), the view espoused by the orator reveals that he was able and willing to accept and to promote political realities as they occurred. It is evident from the second part of the speech that he nevertheless attempted to change the emperor's perspective on one of the main religious issues of the generation.

Themistius does not discuss Jovian's treaty with the Persians at length.[37] In a passage already quoted (5.66a), he notes that the accession induced fear among the Persians, though they were confident earlier. Other sources report that the Persians harassed Jovian's forces, to the point that circumstances compelled him to conclude a treaty. Under this agreement, the Persians received undisputed rights to considerable territory regarded by Romans as their own, as well as a number of cities and fortresses, including the strategically and psychologically important Nisibis (Am. Mar. 25.7.9–12).[38] Unlike Themistius, most sources treat the agreement as shameful in varying degrees,[39] though Christian writers attempt to mitigate the dishonor

37. On its background and importance, Wirth, in *Vivarium*, 360–66.

38. Cf. R. Turcan, *Mélanges A. Piganiol* (Paris, 1966), 2: 875–90; Soraci, *L'Imperatore Gioviano*, chap. 2: "La pace con i Persiani e l'abbandono della città di Nisibi."

39. Handbills denouncing Jovian littered the streets of Antioch after his arrival, according to the *Souda*, s.v. Ἰοβιανός, probably a fragment of

by calling the treaty the necessity it was.[40] After the transfer of Nisibis, described by Ammianus in a passage laden with emotion (25 9.1–11),[41] Jovian journeyed to Antioch (25.10.1). Later in the panegyric, Themistius again mentions the treaty positively, when he notes that the action of the new emperor meant peace for the Empire (5.69b–c). Libanius, no doubt deliberately, expounded an opposite view.[42] In a funeral oration for Julian, written soon after Themistius' speech,[43] he suggests that the Persians were about to seek peace from Julian (*Or.* 18.268; cf. *Or.* 1.133), but at his death forced Jovian to sue for peace (*Or.* 18.277–280).[44]

Neither view is entirely correct. The Persians were at no time forced to seek peace from either emperor. From a position of strength, they offered peace to both Julian and Jovian (Am. Mar. 25.7.5 ff.). With legends like *RESTITVTOR REIPVBLICAE, VICTORIA AVGVSTI,* and *VICTORIA ROMANORVM* on his coins[45] and in other ways, Jovian spread propaganda designed to lessen the negative impact of his treaty (Am. Mar. 25.8.12).[46] The attempt was not without success. Themistius concurs and promotes the view, and Festus (*Brev.* 29), who finds the treaty shameful, writes of Persian respect for the Romans.[47] Except in the statement that the Persians threw away their weapons (5.66a), Themistius does not address the sequence of embassies, nor does he intimate that Jovian's motive for a hasty treaty was a

---

Eunapius (fr. 29 Blockley); cf. R.C. Blockley, *The Fragmentary Classicising Historians of the Later Roman Empire,* vol. 1 (Liverpool, 1981), 156, n. 3; vol. 2 (Liverpool, 1983), 44–47. An example: "You came back from the war. You should have perished there."

40. As does Eutrop. 10.17.1: *necessariam quidem, sed ignobilem.* For a complete list of sources (quoted), cf. Soraci, *L'Imperatore Gioviano,* 42–44, with nn. 43–57. *Chron. Pasch.* s.a. 363 (p. 553 Bonn) is non-committal.

41. Ammianus was perhaps on the staff of the governor of Mesopotamia before joining the Persian expedition of Julian. This position, and his presence in the city earlier (14.9.1), would explain his emotion.

42. Dagron, *Thémistios, passim,* points to differences between Themistius and Libanius on many points.

43. On the date of Lib. *Or.* 18, Norman, *Libanius: Selected Works,* 1:xxxiv.

44. Cf. Turcan, *Mélanges A. Piganiol,* 2:882; and Petit, *Libanius,* 185–86.

45. Cf. *RIC,* 8:230–31, 281, 424, 438, 464–65, 533.

46. For discussion, cf. Soraci, *L'Imperatore Gioviano,* 37–38.

47. This does not mean that the Persians were *compelled* to seek peace.

wish to consolidate his throne.[48] He emphasizes only the benefits of peace.[49] His view, like his view of the accession, reflects the reality of the situation six months later. The treaty had been signed and the territory lost, but the positive benefits of peace, with the vision of hindsight, outweighed possible criticisms.

Themistius proceeds to a brief discussion, in philosophical terms, of Jovian's character, comparing him to the Platonic ideal:

> Having received the empire suddenly and all at once,[50] you kept it more bloodless[51] than those who receive it from their family. The reason is that you neither suspected anyone of disloyalty nor feared anyone as more worthy, and you proved the truth of the second of the pronouncements of Plato, that governments would be free from strife at the moment when those fit to rule, but least eager to do so, rule. (5. 66d)

After stating that Jovian's earlier character, particularly his attitude toward associates (5.66d–67a), was worthy of praise, he notes that this had not changed with his new position:

> But having by your good fortune surpassed all to such an extent, you held to your earlier disposition toward all, as if you knew very well that kingship must be thought preeminent in virtue,

48. Essentially the view of Ammianus (25.7.10; cf. Festus, *Brev.* 29: *cupidior regni quam gloriae*), accepted by many scholars, e.g., Seeck, *Geschichte*, 4:364 ff.; others cited and quoted by Soraci, *L'Imperatore Gioviano*, 46, nn. 62–65. Soraci himself disagrees, suggesting (35, 46–47) that Jovian already had the intention, more obvious in his successors, of directing his greatest attention toward the border problems of the West.

49. As he does during later reigns; see chapters 7 and 8.

50. I.e., he had not been Caesar or in any way associated with governing the empire. This is significant praise, since no emperor had become an Augustus without challenging opponents militarily, or having first been Caesar, for a very long time.

51. A standard-bearer of the Joviani had in anticipation defected to the Persians, while Themistius has forgotten the fate of the *notarius* Jovianus; cf. Am. Mar. 25.8.8, 18. The reference may be to the blood-letting of relatives after the death of Constantine or to Persian customs. Note the reference to Darius at 5.67a.

not in fortune; you showed Darius, son of Hystaspes, to be petty in respect to generosity of compensation. (5.67a)

As proof, Themistius praises Jovian's choice of advisers:

Perceiving that the foundation of safety for a king is the justice of his associates, from the best men everywhere you restored some, made some your associates and discharged others, and the good counsel of Nestor[52] now keeps guard over your palace. (5.67a–b)[53]

In his character sketch of Jovian, Ammianus agrees with this assessment. The emperor chose carefully the officials he appointed (25.10.15), but made few changes. The military high command remained much the same, as is clear from the division of empire and generals by Valentinian and Valens in 365 (Am. Mar. 26.5.2–3). Salutius and Mamertinus remained praetorian prefects, though Germanianus seems to have replaced Sallustius (26.5.5).[54] Jovian may have recalled some officials of Constantius,[55] but insufficient evidence survives to substantiate this.[56] In any case, many of Constantius' advisers had been tried at Chalcedon in 361 and had been banished or put to death.[57] Of those mentioned by Ammianus (22.3.3–12), none appears in office during the reign of Jovian, and only a few ever reappear in the extant evidence.[58] At best, Jovian relied less on friends and advisers of Julian, though Maximus and Priscus remained with the court (Eunap. *VS*, p. 478). Nestor, in the passage quoted earlier, is clearly Salutius, the aging prefect who

52. Cf. Lib. *Ep.* 114, where Datianus is called a Nestor to Constantius.

53. For the similarity of this passage to Ael. Arist. *Or.* 35 Keil, see chapter 1.

54. Seeck, *Regesten*, 80.

55. Piganiol, *L'Empire chrétien*, 2nd. ed., 164.

56. Ammianus' statement (25.10.14) that Jovian imitated Constantius does not prove or, in fact, suggest this, as Soraci, *L'Imperatore Gioviano*, 50, thinks.

57. On the trials, W. Ensslin, *Klio* 18 (1922): 111–18; Kaegi, *BF* 2 (1967): 251–53.

58. Cf. the following entries in *PLRE*, 1: Apodemius 1; Cyrinus; Evagrius 5; Eusebius 11; Florentius 3; Flavius Florentius 10; Palladius 4; Paulus "Catena" 4; Pentadius 2; Flavius Saturninus 10; Flavius Taurus 3; Vrsulus 1.

retained his office and was accepted by Christians and praised by Christian authors.[59] A statement that Jovian had elevated philosophy into the palace again (5.63c) does not constitute evidence that Julian's friends were removed. Rather, the orator means that his own brand of philosophy, little more than proper training in the classics and respect for its traditions, had become the court philosophy in place of the esoteric philosophy espoused by Julian and his friends.

Themistius next addresses religion, attempting to persuade Jovian to allow diversity in religious practice. He praises him for toleration, which has led to a suggestion that an edict was in place,[60] though a plea should not follow promulgation.[61] Two passages reveal that Themistius' words are a plea, not praise of an edict:

> Just as all the runners go to the same awarder of prizes, not indeed all for the same race, but some for this, others for that, and the loser is not wholly unrewarded, you understand that there is one great and true awarder and that the road that leads to him is not a single road.[62] There is the one quite difficult to travel, another is more direct; one is a rough road and another smooth. Nevertheless, they all stretch toward that one same resting place, and our rivalry and zeal stem from anything but the fact that all do not take the same road. If you allow a single road and wall off the remainder, you will block up the free space of the contest. (5.68d–69a)[63]
> We were worse to one another than the Persians [to us], worse than their attacks were the indictments coming from the capital

---

59. Cf. *PLRE*, 1:816, for the identification and references.

60. Seeck, *Briefe*, 301, and *Geschichte*, 4:368; Bouchery, *Themistius*, 222.

61. Geffcken, *Last Days*, 159, 208, n. 8, dissents from Seeck's view, but fails to notice the logical fallacy.

62. With this statement, compare Symmachus, *Rel.* 3. 10: "It is reasonable that whatever each of us worships is really to be considered one and the same. We gaze up at the same stars, the sky covers us all, the same universe compasses us. What does it matter what practical system we adopt in our search for truth? Not by one avenue only can we arrive at so tremendous a secret" (trans. Barrow).

63. See Daly, *GRBS* 12 (1971): 75, for brief discussion of the reasonable view that Themistius is here influenced by Heraclitus' concept of unified plurality. At 5.69b, Heraclitus is cited by name.

from each of the two religions, Emperor most loved of God; of this the past gave plain examples for you. Allow the balance to remain level; do not drag the beam down to one side or the other; allow supplication on behalf of your scepter to go to heaven from all sides. (5.69c)

Despite these clear statements, Themistius also pays tribute to some imperial pronouncement on religious matters in terms that suggest an edict of toleration:

> . . . the legislation (*nomothesia*) concerning the divine was the beginning of your care for men. (5.67b)
> . . . you ordain by law (*nomotheteis*) that the heritage of the rites is available to all, and in this rival God, who made the capability for piety common to human nature, but left the manner of service to personal choice. He who applies compulsion takes away the personal authority conceded by God. (5.68a)[64]

Elsewhere, Themistius again uses *nomos* for this activity of Jovian (5.68b, 69b, 69c).

Jovian did not officially proclaim religious toleration before 1 January 364. While his religious inclination was undoubtedly known, legislation on the subject does not appear until 364, though he did not enforce Julian's anti-Christian measures. Even then, the single treatment of religion is a rescript forbidding solicitation of consecrated virgins and widows (*CTh* 9.25.2), dated 19 February 364, two days after his death, but representing his wishes and not a rescript of Valentinian.[65] Though Christians destroyed temples during the brief reign, Jovian did not order them closed.[66] The earliest evidence that Julian's gifts to temples were returned to the imperial treasury dates to 23 December 364. Valentinian, who had been emperor for ten months, issued to the praetorian prefect Mamertinus a rescript to this

---

64. G. Richard, *REA* 42 (1940): 499, neatly juxtaposes this passage to Lact. *Div. Inst.* 5.20 (*religio cogi non potest* . . .) and *Epit. Div. Inst.* 14 (*religio sola est in qua libertas domicilium collocauit* . . .).

65. As Solari, *Klio* 26 (1933): 334, suggests. Solari's view, loc. cit., that all laws dated to the reign of Jovian are Julian's, except *CTh* 9.25.2, has gained no following.

66. So too Geffcken, *Last Days*, 159.

effect (CTh 5.13.3). Another rescript on the same topic (CTh 10.1.8) was addressed to Caesarius comes rei priuatae on 4 February 365.[67]

Even if CTh 10.1.8 is a rescript of Jovian, it was issued after the delivery of the panegyric. Another measure, which may represent the emperor's wish for Christian educators to return to their tasks, similarly dates to 364, after Themistius had made his plea (CTh 13.3.6: 11 January 364).[68] Moreover, Jovian had not yet officially promoted Christianity, whatever he may have done unofficially. The rescript on educators announces that anyone who was "equally suitable in eloquence and life(style) for teaching the young" was to found a new school or take a position in an established one; it applied to pagans and Christians alike. The measure reveals its religious intent only against the background of Julian's attempt to prevent Christians from teaching the classics.[69] Similarly, the rescript on consecrated women dates to 364, more than a month after the delivery of the panegyric, and protects these women from adherents of all beliefs. The implication is that Jovian began to promote Christianity and attack paganism only after he had held the throne for six months. He began slowly, with measures that were relatively innocuous.[70]

Nevertheless, Themistius was able to praise an attitude of toleration, and something must be made of his statements. Earlier, he had

---

67. CTh 10.1.8 has been dated to 4 February 364 by emendation of the place of issue from MEDIOLANO to MNIZO. Cf. Seeck, Regesten, 111. But this measure has the same date and place as two others (CTh 11.30.32, 11.36.15); cf. Seeck, Regesten, 70–71. Since no emperor was at Milan on the transmitted date, 4 February 364, emendation of either place or date is necessary. CTh 11.30.32 and 11.36.15 have correctly been redated to 4 February 365, when Valentinian was at Milan. Emendation of CTh 5.13.3 to the same date seems more suitable than emendation of the place of issue.

68. Seeck, Regesten, 214, following Mommsen. Either the date or the imperial college named in the superscription is wrong, since Valentinian and Valens are listed as the emperors who issued the rescript.

69. Daly, GRBS 12 (1971): 71, implies that Themistius' praise of Jovian for restoring philosophy to the palace (5.63c) indicates a repeal of Julian's law on educators. Given the cautious wording of CTh 13.3.6, I cannot accept this, though Themistius may be referring to Jovian's unofficial attitude or speaking in expectation of a repeal.

70. Wirth, in Vivarium, 370 ff., ascribes political and religious caution to Jovian and argues that he could not act until his control over the empire was secure and the shock of the sudden transition had died down.

noted that philosophy regarded the emperor as "living law" (5.64b: *nomos empsychos*).[71] This view has its origins, though not its developed form, in the writings of Aristotle, who (*Pol.* 1284a11–15) allows the most virtuous men to be regarded as law. When they are also kings, the government is naturally ideal, but this happens rarely, and, in general, law should have the upper hand while remaining flexible. Themistius promotes this last element when praising emperors for moderating written laws.[72] Aristotle's concept, if misunderstood or misapplied, could lead to the justification by a king or his advisers of any activity whatsoever, and the idea of a king as law incarnate was no doubt used at times to give rulers a greater status than Aristotle would have approved.

Since the emperor was living law, any imperial pronouncement was equivalent to *nomos*. According to Themistius, Jovian declared that the heritage of the rites was open to all (5.68a). Only one known incident provides a possible occasion. Besieged by various factions of bishops, Jovian stated his own views and announced his intention to persecute no sect (Soc. *HE* 3.25.1–19). Themistius, cited as evidence by Socrates (*HE* 3.25.20–21), undoubtedly had this statement in mind when he praises Jovian's tolerance.[73] The emperor, he argues, knew the benefits of strife:[74]

> For the mind is ever easily kindled by love of quarrel to love
> of labor. For this reason, you do not prevent the good strife
> of piety; for this reason, you do not blunt the sting of zeal

---

71. Themistius mentions this frequently; cf., e.g., 16.212d, 19.227d. The classic treatment is E.R. Goodenough, *YCS* 1 (1928): 55–102. Cf. also V. Valdenberg, *Byzantion* 1 (1924): 573–74; and G.J.D. Aalders, in *Politeia und Res Publica*. Palingenesia, Monographie und Texte zur klassische Altertumswissenschaft 4 (1969): 315–29. For the different fourth century views, Dagron, *Thémistios*, 127–34.

72. Cf., e.g., 15.190b–c.

73. Daly, *GRBS* 12 (1971): 72, with n. 26, makes a similar suggestion, but does not notice that Jovian's statement, that he preferred those who worked toward harmony, ought to apply to all groups.

74. Daly, *GRBS* 12 (1971): 75, with n. 35, reasonably finds an echo of Heraclitus, fr. 80 (καὶ δίκην ἔριν) and perhaps Hes. *Op.* 24 (ἀγαθὴ δ' Ἔρις ἥδε Βροτοῖσιν). In *Or.* 30, Themistius has much praise for this work of Hesiod (not noted by Daly).

concerning piety, the rivalry and love of honor toward one another. (5.68c–d)

Based on the inclination to allow variety of religious practices and beliefs within Christianity, Themistius pleads to have the "good strife of piety" applied to pagans as well. Just as Jovian had not forced his views on Christians by appropriation of property, imprisonment, or execution (5.68b), a logical extension of the principle led to the conclusion that pagans should be free from fear of reprisal. The argument implies knowledge or expectation that Jovian intended to act against paganism. Themistius may have known of actions by some Christians;[75] on Corfu, for example, a temple was overturned and a church erected. The accompanying inscription (IG ix 1.721) credits Jovian, who did not instigate the event, though he allowed it to occur. Socrates (HE 3.24.5) mentions the closure of temples, but cites no law.

The portion of the speech devoted to religious matters is designed to broaden the perspective of Jovian, and Themistius supports his plea with several arguments. Of these, the variety of human nature is the most prominent. Just as the emperor's armies consisted of individuals performing different services and his subjects engaged in various occupations, God too takes delight in variety (5.70a). Symmachus uses the same argument, whose source may be Porphyry, in his plea for restitution of the Altar of Victory. In comparisons of the two, Symmachus has fared badly. Themistius has been praised for expressing his ideas with clarity, vividness, and originality,[76] and for stating the philosophic merits and bases of his view.[77] Symmachus has been castigated for relying on tradition without argument of fundamental issues,[78] though he simply took the essentials and added some argu-

---

75. Geffcken, Last Days, 159, and Piganiol, L'Empire chrétien, 2nd ed., 165, n. 5.

76. Valdenberg, Byzantion 1 (1924): 579–80, from Leningrad: "Ici Thémistius, à strictement parler, n'a pas eu de prédécesseurs. Il expose cette idée avec une telle clarté, une telle netteté, que dans la littérature antérieure nous chercherions vainement quelque chose de pareil. . . . Il n'a d'obligation qu'envers lui-même, et les faits historiques qu'il a considérés avec attention."

77. Daly, GRBS 12 (1971): 76–77.

78. H. Bloch, HTR 38 (1945): 209. Daly, GRBS 12 (1971): 77, quotes N.Q. King, The Modern Churchman, n.s., 4 (1961): 113: "The well-known plea of the pagan Symmachus is really only for the remnants of Roman paganism to be

ments on the cumulative weight of tradition.[79] Themistius calls the constant change of religion at the capital a disgrace (5.67d). He does not ask Jovian to relinquish all control over religion, since legislation is necessary to prevent imposters and sorcerors (5.70b), and gives no indication that Jovian closed temples,[80] but describes the situation when tolerance exists under an ideal emperor.

With its focus on a religious theme, the panegyric contains little evidence that it was written for a consulship. It appears briefly at the beginning (5.64d–65a) and at the end, where Themistius praises the infant consul Varronianus:

> Meanwhile, array for me the Morning star, the consul in arms, the one emulating his father already from the breast; how courageous, how undaunted, how similar to one who will address the people. And may God who made him a partaker of this eponymous rule proclaim him also as a partaker of the purple. (5.71b)

Twenty years later, Themistius had reservations about children as consuls, including Varronianus and Valentinianus Galates (*cos.* 369). Thanking Theodosius for the consulship of Saturninus when the emperor was expected to hold it himself, he praises him for not giving the office to his son Arcadius (16.204c). While the orator emphasizes the acceptability of this practice, he adapts his thoughts to the situation of the moment. Ammianus, with Jovian not in his audience, is less generous: the young Varronianus destroyed the ceremony by his plaintive howling and his obstinate refusal to be carried in the curule chair (25.10.11).

Socrates reports that Themistius delivered the speech again at Constantinople (*HE* 3.26.3).[81] The philosopher would not have complained

---

allowed to co-exist with Christianity. The old man's thinking does not reach fundamentals."

79. For the view that Porphyry is a common source and that Themistius has adopted the anti-Christian stance of Porphyry in this part of the speech, see chapter 1. Cf. also Dagron, *Thémistios*, 154–59.

80. As Geffcken, *Last Days*, 159, saw; contra Seeck, *Geschichte*, 4:366–68. Soraci, *L'Imperatore Gioviano*, 65, with n. 18, cites this passage as evidence that Jovian banned certain practices, without postulating a law to this effect.

81. Accepted by Seeck, *Briefe*, 301; Scholze, *Temporibus*, 24; and Bouchery, *Themistius*, 249–50.

there that the citizens of the capital were not present (5.70c–d). Libanius, who asked for a copy of the speech at Ancyra (*Ep.* 1193.5), does not mention a repeat performance, but there is no reason to distrust Socrates. A second delivery is a clear indication that Themistius delivered the speech as official delegate of his city.[82] Since evidence is entirely lacking for similar occurrences, there may have been some point to a second performance on this occasion. Some members of the senatorial delegation were no doubt pleased with Themistius' eloquence on behalf of religious toleration and his implicit attack on Christian claims to exclusivity. In their view, the Christians of the capital, especially Christian senators, could benefit from hearing what their chosen representative had said. The second delivery of the panegyric might then be seen in part as an attempt by Themistius and his supporters to stem the tide of increasing Christianization and hostility toward tradition. Possibly, Julian's reign made enough of an impact on the philosopher to induce him to adopt a stronger anti-Christian stance in the reign of Jovian than he did at any other point in his life.

Themistius' plea for religious tolerance had little effect on Jovian. The emperor died soon after the delivery, before he could have effected any major policy. Rescripts on religious matters dating to the interregnum before Valentinian's accession may be an attempt by the new emperor to enact legislation in the name of Jovian to avoid criticism. As for Themistius' political career, it did not advance during the reign, which was too short to allow this. He nevertheless emerged from the relative seclusion he had adopted in the previous reign. He attempted to place his own stamp on imperial politics as a public dissident for the first time, revealing maturity as both a philosopher and a politician.

---

82. MacCormack, *Art and Ceremony*, 353, n. 176.

7

Themistius and Valens

During the reign of Valens, Themistius held no office. He neverthe-less engaged in activities that reveal his continued and possibly greater political importance. For the first time, he exercised the inde-pendence from the court demanded by philosophy, while maintain-ing an active role in politics. He continued to lavish praise, but on occasion opposed imperial policy and attempted to change it, with some success.[1] Themistius' maturity and his security as a philoso-pher and politician allowed him this luxury, but the new approach kept him from office until the reign of Theodosius. When proper weight is given to his relations with Valens, it is considerably more difficult to regard him as simply a tool of the court;[2] his favorable attitude toward Constantius and Theodosius derived from agree-ment with their policies. No great dislike of Valens, but rather disap-proval of the emperor's approach to some issues drove Themistius to oppose imperial policy. Contemporaries noticed the greater distance from the court: there is less trace of any dispute on Themistius' role in this reign.[3]

Themistius' first panegyric of the reign concentrates on the rela-tions between Valens and his brother Valentinian. On 28 March 364, Valens was added to the imperial college, by his brother, who had himself been emperor for only a month. There is no doubt about Valens' legitimacy: selection by a reigning emperor was a preferred method of creating a new Augustus. Valentinian's own accession, too, was legitimate. A council of leading civic and military officials met during the interregnum after Jovian's sudden death on 17 Febru-ary 364 to discuss the succession. After some discussion of other

---

1. 31.354d: ἀρκεῖ Οὐάλης, ἡττηθεὶς ὑπὸ τῶν ἐμῶν λόγων πολλάκις.

2. For attacks by contemporaries, see chapter 4, and on modern views, chapter 1.

3. On the view that Or. 23, 26, and 29 belong to the reign of Constantius, see chapter 4.

candidates, Valentinian became the council's choice (Am. Mar. 26.1.4–5).[4]

Salutius' actions make it clear that his position had not changed during the short reign of Jovian. *Praefectus praetorio praesens* under Julian,[5] he was second in command and de facto head of state at Julian's death. The circumstances were similar in 364. Salutius was offered the throne again. He refused the throne for himself and for his son.[6] He was clearly in charge, as events of the evening before Valentinian's accession reveal. To ensure an orderly transfer of power, Salutius suggested, and the rest of the council agreed, that all who held high positions or were suspected of desiring the throne be forbidden to appear on the following morning, on penalty of death (Am. Mar. 26.2.1). Salutius and his colleagues thus maintained order, and the accession occurred without incident.

As was customary, Valentinian was acclaimed by the assembled army. The single difficulty was the soldiers' wish that he select a colleague immediately, to prevent a recurrence of a leaderless empire (Am. Mar. 26 2.4). In his speech to the troops, Valentinian addressed this issue and promised to search for the man most suited to the task (Am. Mar. 26.2.9). When he later asked the council for advice, he was told by Dagalaifus to choose his brother if he loved his relatives, but to select another if he loved the state (Am. Mar. 26.4.1). Displeased, Valentinian did not press the matter. On 1 March 364 at Nicomedia, he promoted Valens to *tribunus stabuli*, and on 28 March, in a suburb of Constantinople, he named his brother coemperor (Am. Mar. 26.4.2, 3). Pannonians from Cibalae and sons of Gratianus,[7] neither

---

4. Cf. also Symm. *Or.* 1.7–9, who emphasizes the smoothness of the accession.

5. See chapter 6 for discussion of Salutius and his position.

6. For discussion with references to other views, see chapter 6. Cf. also V. Neri, *Riv. stor. Ant.* 15 (1985): 153–82.

7. Gratianus' career is known almost entirely from Am. Mar. 30.7. 2–3, and a brief treatment in *Epit.* 45.2. Elsewhere, Symm. *Or.* 1.1–3, mentions him briefly, Themistius notes that a bronze statue was erected in his honor (6.81d), and he is honored on *ILS* 758. According to *Epit.* 45.3, he reached the rank of praetorian prefect. This is dismissed as a mistake by *PLRE*, 1:401, but that may be premature. If *CIL*, 3:12900 refers to this Gratianus (*Gr]atiani pr[otectoris d]omestici . . . [prae]fecti*), he was a prefect, but not of the *domestici*, who were governed by a *comes*. Ammianus' omission of this office may indicate that he held it, if at all, under a usurper, perhaps Magnentius. While

Valentinian nor Valens had had an illustrious career. Valentinian was a competent officer, but experienced difficulties under Julian, because of his Christianity.[8] Valens had almost no experience; this was the point of Dagalaifus' remark.

In spring 364, the emperors left Constantinople for the Danubian provinces. There they divided the empire between them, separating the armies and generals into two forces. By early September, Valentinian was at Aquileia, while Valens remained near the Danube frontier through the autumn. On 16 December, Valens is again attested at the eastern capital.[9]

The precise date of Themistius' first panegyric of the reign cannot be determined, but Valens was clearly present in the Senate chambers at Constantinople when it was delivered. At the outset, Themistius remarks that he was unable to speak Latin, hardly a major obstacle in a Senate that spoke Greek, but of concern to Valens.[10] The orator sometimes refers to a pair of emperors, but he mentions Valens alone too frequently to suggest that Valentinian was present. This may indicate a date in the winter of 364/5.[11] If Valentinian was merely otherwise occupied, delivery in the spring of 364[12] cannot be ruled out.

The text offers no specific evidence to support either view. The statement that Valens had called the city the "mother of his empire"

---

comes in Africa, he incurred suspicion of theft, left the region, and did not return to office as *comes*, in Britain, until much later. He retired to his estates, where Magnentius visited him before 351, and perhaps became the usurper's praetorian prefect.

8. Cf. *PLRE*, 1:933–34, for a list of sources on this point. For brief discussion of Valentinian's early life and career, cf. Alföldi, *Conflict of Ideas*, 9–12.

9. Cf. Seeck, *Regesten*, 216–19, for their movements. For the accession and division of empire, Matthews, *Ammianus*, 189–91.

10. Because Themistius is said in a scholion (cf. Norman's apparatus) to have turned Constantius' letter to the Senate at Constantinople into Greek from Latin himself, G. Sotiroff, *CW* 65 (1972): 231–32, thinks that he knew Latin and is here complaining about his inability to speak Illyrian, which can hardly be called the language of rule. A scholiast correctly points out that Themistius means the language of the court. The point is that Valens was not proficient in Greek, even if he had high esteem for its speakers; cf. 10.129c. Valentinian did know Greek; cf. 9.126b.

11. So Scholze, *Temporibus*, 25–27. Harduin (p. 493 Dindorf) had suggested December 364.

12. Seeck, *Briefe*, 302; Stegemann, "Themistios," 1659. Dagron, *Thémistios*, 21, proposes April 364, followed by Portmann, *Panegyrik*, 160.

(6.82d) is appropriate at any time. Themistius notes, however (6.75a–d), that Valentinian had gained a second set of eyes to help him to oversee the empire.[13] This comment, as well as frequent remarks about the need for harmony, implies that Valens and Valentinian were responsible for different parts of the empire and maintained separate courts, a division that was not immediate (cf. Am. Mar. 26.5.1–5). Because Themistius pleads for harmony, Valens had perhaps begun to resent his brother's seniority, though such sentiment is unlikely in the context of the accession; possibly, the orator simply remembered the various periods of discord since the death of Constantine. Most likely, Themistius waited until Valens returned to the capital for the winter. The oration is then not a *gratulatio* on Valens' accession, but a speech written after reflection.[14] It was delivered late in 364, since Themistius does not refer to the joint consulship of 365. The only solid evidence is a letter of Libanius, who refers to a speech at the beginning of winter 364/5, probably *Oration 6*,[15] and another delivered not much later (*Ep.* 1495) to celebrate the consulships.[16]

The extant speech, "The Loving Brothers or Philanthropy," praises Valentinian's selection of his brother as coruler and pleads for harmony. Themistius begins by turning his inability to speak the language of rule, that is, Latin, to advantage, remarking that many panegyrists, not intending to be useful, prefer the absence of an interpreter. For a philosopher, words are less important than thought, and the actual language is of little consequence (6.71c–72a). Themistius immediately establishes the emperors' esteem of philosophy and philosophers, despite false practitioners, by noting that they had not banished philoso-

---

13. On this theme, cf. Dio Chrysos. *Or.* 3.104–107; Ael. Arist. *Or.* 27.29–30 Keil.

14. No extant speech of Themistius is a *gratulatio* directly upon accession, and there is no evidence to suggest that he ever delivered one. He seems to have preferred a delay of several months (though he apologizes to Theodosius for the illness that prevented participation in an earlier senatorial delegation [14.180b–c]).

15. As Scholze, *Temporibus*, 27, notes.

16. Known only from this letter of Libanius. Scholze, *Temporibus*, 27, cites 9.128b as additional evidence, but Bouchery, *Themistius*, 270, n. 12, correctly points out that, when Themistius notes that "we were the first to herald you as the emperor of all men, as consul," ἡμεῖς means "we citizens of the capital." Scholze's view (loc. cit.) that Themistius delivered the speech a second time for the benefit of Valentinian is almost certainly wrong.

phers from the court.[17] Valentinian and Valens, unlike one dramatist who linked philosophy and tyranny,[18] recognize kinship between throne and God-given philosophy. Themistius then links philosophy to brotherly love, noting that Dionysius, Nero, and Domitian, who mistreated Plato, Musonius, and Apollonius, respectively, dealt harshly with brothers as well (6.72a–73a).

In his discussion of Valens' accession, Themistius claims that it was not the result of soldiers' desires, but the wish of God, who used humans as agents. Valens[19] has the legitimacy of both popular acclamation and selection by a reigning emperor (6.73b–74a).[20] Adopting the (convenient) position that divine intervention in accession is evident only after the fact, Themistius announces that virtuous rule proclaims divine selection. He points to harmony between brothers as proof of virtue, since kinship to a ruler normally arouses hatred. As examples, he cites Cambyses, Nero, Domitian, Caracalla, and others, in contrast to Darius, Seleucus, and Eumenes (6.74c).

Reflecting Aelius Aristides' remarks on Marcus Aurelius and Lucius Verus,[21] Themistius lists some benefits of joint rule. Valentinian received the empire, but the selection of Valens made him greater and did not reduce his empire. When Valens took the purple, he gave his brother another mind, another watchful eye to govern the furthest reaches of a large empire now ruled by two emperors as if they were one (6.74a–75d). The partnership is equal, in name and division of labor. Valentinian not only takes honor and advantage from the adlection of his brother, as often happened in the past, but retains control of the whole empire because of his brother's obedience. As a result, the empire is harmonious (6.76a–b), with benefits

---

17. A reference, perhaps, to the continued presence of Salutius.

18. 6.72c: Εὐριπίδης μὲν γὰρ ἢ ὅστις δήποτέ ἐστιν ὁ ποιήσας, Σοφοὶ τύραννοι τῶν σοφῶν συνουσίᾳ. Plato, *Resp.* 56a and *Theages* 125b, ascribes the line to Euripides, but it is also ascribed to Sophocles; cf. Aul. Gell. 13.19. Themistius' hesitation may indicate that he recognized a problem. He also notes that Euripides was wrong (*Phoen.* 506, *Troad.* 1169) to make tyranny a god.

19. Here, among other passages, Valens alone is addressed, indicating that Valentinian was not present.

20. On contemporary theories of legitimacy as relevant to the accessions of Valentinian and Valens, cf. MacCormack, *Art and Ceremony*, 197–99.

21. Ael. Arist. 27.25–39 Keil. See chapter 1 for Themistius' use of Aristides.

for the entire population. Justice and recourse to arms are nearer to hand than under a single ruler. Brotherly love, Themistius states, indicates the presence of philanthropy, a main theme of the speech, as the title indicates. Humanity generally circumscribes the application of philanthropy within closely defined limits, but the emperors disagree with this precept, treating each other and their subjects in divine fashion (6.76b–78d). Of God's powers, only philanthropy is possible for man, and it enables an emperor to be like God (6.78d–79b). Like God, Valentinian and Valens have epithets suitable to philanthropy, such as "the gracious," "the friendly one," "the hospitable one," "hearer of suppliants," "the guardian of the city," and "the savior." These are more divine than victory titles like "Germanicus" and "Parthicus," are useful in both war and peace, and allow emperors, like Titus,[22] to benefit their subjects. The orator reminds Valens that Constantius permitted even a usurper (Vetranio) to repent (6.79c–81a).[23]

Themistius then turns to a statement of Valens. What Valens said in the Senate is unknown, but he remarked the preeminence of Constantinople,[24] if the last portion of the speech is an accurate indication. He also mentioned his father, perhaps when dedicating a bronze image noted in the panegyric (6.81d). After some further remarks about the harmony between brothers (6.82a–b), Themistius requests that the capital, which first witnessed the accession of Valens and fraternal accord, receive extra attention from Valens. On the previous day, Valens had not hesitated to call the city the mother of his empire, which even Constantine could not do. In response, the city asks for the goodwill of the emperor, to be expressed by means of public works (6.82b–83c).

Beyond the typical request that the emperor esteem an eastern capital, which Valens may have called a "metropolis," the reason for the delivery of a speech of this content is obvious. Only a few years previously, an empire shared by relatives had narrowly escaped a civil war by the sudden death of one combatant. The desire for harmony and order is an important theme for Themistius, recurring in the reign

22. A favorite theme of Themistius; cf. 8.10a, 13.174c, 18.225a.

23. See chapter 4 for praise of Constantius on this point.

24. Relations between emperor and city soon deteriorated. By the end of his reign, Valens threatened to destroy it (Soc. HE 4.38.5).

of Theodosius when he pleads for harmony with Gratian.[25] On both occasions, the orator reminds his subject that a fellow emperor had chosen him and deserved preeminence. Though Themistius does not state this directly, he seems to have had Julian's behavior and actions in mind. He also implies a belief that the empire was best with a single emperor at its head, a view he had stated directly in the *Risâlat*, when, however, that situation obtained.

Other than a speech for the joint consulship of Valentinian and Valens in 365, undoubtedly delivered on 1 January, Themistius' activities for the next two years are unknown. From 28 September 365 to 27 May 366, a civil war raged in the East. Procopius had been given a command in the Persian campaign of his relative Julian. Unlike the emperor, who struck deep into the heart of enemy territory, Procopius was to guard the north and had perhaps been instructed to proceed toward Julian's forces in a pincer campaign modeled on the joint attack by Julian and Constantius in Gaul in 357. For some reason, he never came to his emperor's aid; he may have been waiting for Julian to drive the Persian forces to the north. After Julian's death, Procopius went into hiding and began to intrigue for the throne.[26] Not surprisingly, he focused on Constantinople, before and after his proclamation as emperor; that the dynasty appealed to the city's citizens is sufficiently clear in Themistius' panegyrics of Constantius. The usurper used his blood relationship to Julian to great advantage and appeared in public with the posthumously born daughter of Constantius and her mother as further advertisement of his links to the previous regime (Am. Mar. 26.7. 10; 9.3).[27]

For some time in the first period of the usurpation, the situation was in doubt, to the point that Valens contemplated abdication (Am. Mar. 26.7.13). At an early military engagement, Procopius convinced two legions sent against him to defect (26. 7.13–17) and gained the support of others by ruse or appeal. For a short time thereafter, he enjoyed moderate success, taking Bithynia and defeating the

---

25. See chapter 8.

26. Cf. Am. Mar. 26.6, for an account of Procopius' activity.

27. Cf. N.J.E. Austin, *Riv. Stor. dell' Ant* 2 (1972): 187–94. I. Hahn, *AAH* 6 (1958): 199–210 (in Russian, with German summary, p. 211), argues that Procopius was not attempting to reestablish the dynasty of Constantine. For a recent modern account, cf. Matthews, *Ammianus*, 191–203.

emperor's forces elsewhere, but eventually Procopius' soldiers deserted him (Am. Mar. 26.8–9). Not long thereafter, in May 366, the civil war came to an end.

Themistius' response to the usurpation does not appear until *Oration* 7, "To Valens, Concerning the Unfortunates," when his attitude after Procopius' death is abundantly clear. Whether he held the same view throughout the conspiracy cannot be determined, but his desire for legitimate rulers suggests an affirmative answer. As he often did, Themistius delivered his response after a period of reflection. He excuses this on the grounds that an accurate assessment of events requires time, especially when a philosopher, not a flatterer, is offering his interpretation (7.84b–86b). While the exact length of time is not specified, the orator refers to "months" (7.84c). The speech therefore dates to the winter of 366/7.[28]

Themistius devotes *Oration* 7 to the two themes of clemency and the evil character of Procopius. The topics were extremely relevant: Constantinople supported the rebellion from the outset, and its mint struck coins for Procopius.[29] By painting the harshest picture of Procopius in any extant source, Themistius intended to show Valens that the citizens were not responsible for their actions and deserved forgiveness. As might be expected, he pays little tribute to the success enjoyed by Procopius, emphasizing instead Valens' ultimate victory. Delivered in the context of the emperor's continuing attempts to punish supporters of Procopius, the panegyric is one occasion when Themistius attempted to change imperial policy. True to his remarks in an early private speech, the orator mingled the bitter draught of rebuke with the honey of rhetoric.[30] In this speech, he also directly cites Christian Scripture for the first time, to show that the heart of the emperor is guarded in the hand of God (7. 89d), as if to point out that God had supported Valens from the beginning. Themistius perhaps felt a need to pay tribute to Valens' religion, or, more subtly, he perhaps intended to remind the emperor of Christian forgiveness.

---

28. So Seeck, *Briefe,* 302; Scholze, *Temporibus,* 28–29; Stegemann, "Themistios," 1659; Dagron, *Thémistios,* 21. Harduin (p. 493 Dindorf) placed the speech in 367.

29. Procopius also minted at Heraclea, Nicomedia and Cyzicus; cf. *RIC,* 9:192–93, 209–15, 251, 239–40. Cf. V. Grumel, *REB* 12 (1954): 11.

30. See chapter 2 for this attitude, expressed most clearly at 24.302b.

Themistius addresses each theme more than once. After his introduction, he discusses Procopius and Valens' victory, praises Valens' forgiveness of some supporters of Procopius (cf. Am. Mar. 26.10.7–8) while pleading for continued mildness, returns to the conspiracy, and closes with further discussion of mildness and clemency. The themes are thus interrelated, concentrating on clemency, while emphasizing, as a good reason for it, the deceitfulness of Procopius. Themistius clearly wanted Valens to extend forgiveness to all. He praises one action as a starting point for a plea for continued action.[31]

This speech is one of the few occasions when Themistius indulges in standard panegyrical practice, or rather invective. While he does not offer a full discussion of Valens' response to Procopius, the orator does treat the subject and denigrates the usurper with satirical references to his person and the social status of his supporters. Though he had called Magnentius an "after-dinner emperor" (2.36a), Themistius rarely sinks to this level of ridicule. The strength of the threat caused this departure from his usual procedure:[32] Procopius had widespread support, and the capital had committed itself early in the revolt.

Themistius characterizes Procopius as an enemy of the gods, a clerk (7.86b) who made a living with pen and ink, but dared, in complete blindness, to hope for the throne. Ammianus, writing some years later, notes that Procopius had been tribune and had reached the rank of *comes* (26.6.1), but is no less willing to note negative aspects of the usurper's character and goals.[33] Both Themistius and Ammianus remark the low status of many of Procopius' supporters, but the historian also refers to support by ranking officers and others.[34] According to Themistius, Procopius was initially supported by

---

31. See chapter 6 for Themistius' use of this method in the reign of Jovian.

32. Ammianus, too, is unkind to usurpers; cf. e.g., 16.5.15–16, on Silvanus.

33. Cf. R.C. Blockley, *Ammianus Marcellinus: A Study of His Historiography and Political Thought.* Collection Latomus 141 (Brussels, 1975), 55–61, for discussion of Ammianus' attitude toward Procopius and toward usurpers generally; cf. also the remarks of Matthews, *Ammianus,* 201–3. pointing out that even Ammianus' dislike of Valens did not prevent him from regarding Procopius as an illegitimate ruler.

34. Blockley, *Ammianus Marcellinus,* 56, n. 10, and 60, with n. 32, provides a list of the most important individuals. Cf. Austin, *Riv. Stor. dell' Ant* 2 (1972): 191–92. I. Hahn, *AAH* 6 (1958): 211, shows that most of Constantius' important officers remained loyal to Valens.

the lower classes, armed with kitchen knives and confiscated and gladiatorial weapons, and worthy of ridicule. They soon forced others to join against their will (7.86c–87a). The circumstances allow Themistius to compare Procopius, unfavorably because Procopius' daring was more outrageous, with Crixus and Spartacus (7.87c). Ammianus describes the first supporters as former and current palace servants and merchants in cheap dainties (26.7.1), joined not much later by a band of deserters (26.7.14).[35]

Later, Themistius discusses the beginning of the revolt in more detail. During the night before the acclamation, some citizens were taken from their beds to prison; the beds of others were used as clubs against them (7.91b). Valens' officials were treated like criminals.[36] In the morning, Procopius emerged from the Anastasian Baths (cf. Am. Mar. 26.6.14–15),

> a counterfeit emperor, grinning, calling all to himself, smiling a deceitful smile, a smile full of laments, a smile that was the origin of many tears. (7.91c)

The guards of the treasury opened the gates, resulting in a siege within the walls of Constantinople, while Procopius set in motion a variety of schemes to win support, arranging false messengers to report that various parts of the empire—Illyria, Italy, and Gaul—had defected to him. Ammianus adds the information that Procopius devised similar news from the East and the report that Valentinian had died (26.7.3). Procopius acted as if the entire world supported him, forcing belief in his widespread popularity on penalty of death, with spies everywhere to record and report disbelief (7.90d–92a). He exacted tribute from senators for more than a winter, and his policies affected all citizens, rich, poor, and upright, who believed that the dead ruler (Procopius: ὁ μὲν τεθνηκὼς ἠπιστεῖτο) was alive and that the living emperor (Valens: ὁ δὲ οὐ τεθνηκὼς ἐπιστεύθη τεθνάναι) had died (7.92a–c). This last statement is significant: the point of the passage is that the people, after all the disinformation they had heard,

---

35. Hahn, *AAH* 6 (1958): 211, argues that supporters of this type indicate a social and political program on the part of Procopius.

36. Ammianus retails none of this for the night before the proclamation, though he does note that some officials were imprisoned later (26.7.4–7).

did not believe that Procopius had died and Valens had not. It is an attempt to explain continued resistance after Procopius' death and may indicate some ambivalence on Themistius' part during the conspiracy. His plea for clemency is then personal as well as civic.

The philosopher blames the character of Procopius, who intended to drag down with himself as many people as possible. He includes an impressive string of adjectives:

> He was never regarded as a useful servant, but malicious, sinful, always bowed down, always gloomy, frowning, pursuing silence as if it were something solemn, unsociable, ill-omened, full of disgust, boasting about his hatred toward all and the hatred of all toward him. Even Phalaris, Aristomachus, Apollodorus, and Dionysius each used to have near themselves some individual who both loved and was loved. For nature has made neither adders nor scorpions completely incapable of giving or receiving love, but even if they are equipped for hostility toward men, they are not excluded from friendship toward their own species. (7.90b–c)

This depiction of the usurper's character agrees in parts with Ammianus' report. The first remarks, however, ring false. The historian notes that Procopius was a highly regarded civil servant until he aspired to loftier positions. His early success was due in part to his silent reserve and his strict life and character (26.6.1). In a final assessment, Ammianus states that Procopius walked with his gaze fixed on the ground and was gloomy and secretive (26.9.11); Themistius' exaggerations were based on fact.

The philosopher bases his plea for clemency on this characterization, beginning with the remark that Valens treated conspirators differently from their supporters (7.92c–93c). This statement cannot be entirely false, since Libanius (*Or.* 1.171) mentions the different treatment as well. Brief reflection reveals Themistius' purpose in the second part of the speech. His emphasis had been the deceit and force that drew many followers to Procopius unwittingly and involuntarily. These individuals, in the view of Themistius, ought not to be held responsible and punished, since they had little choice. In particular, citizens of the capital, where the proclamation had taken place, should be spared. The orator's insistence on this point belies the level of support for Procopius at Constantinople, and his speech is at points little more than a plea for clemency toward the city.

He begins his final plea by discussing the superiority of mildness and notes that it, like its opposite, creates a lasting memory: Alexander's murder of Callisthenes still arouses anger (7.93c–94a).[37] By the mildness already shown, Valens won a double victory, over his enemies as well as his allies. He conquered some with courage and others with mildness, preventing a civil war that would tear the whole empire in two. In the past, the Romans allowed Massinissa to live, despite the harm he had done.[38] Socrates too was aware of the need for mildness, when he corrected the typical view that one was to treat friends well and enemies badly (7.94b–95b). Finally, Themistius suggests that clemency has its rewards. Forgiveness creates support for the forgiver and is as suitable for emperors as for philosophers. Examples include Philip of Macedon, who refused to punish Nicanor for denigrating him, and instead investigated the reason for his behavior. When he discovered that Nicanor was living in poverty, the king gave him a gift and received Nicanor's continual praises.[39] Near the end of the speech, he discusses Salutius, a philosopher who had acted in opposition to the "most philosophical of emperors," a reference to the trials at Chalcedon in 361 whose consequences Julian disavowed (7.99d–100b). After the usurpation, Clearchus, an associate of Themistius, began to rehabilitate Maximus and to intrigue, successfully, against Salutius.[40]

---

37. On the basis of Valens' mildness after the clemency, Portmann, *Panegyrik*, 164, argues that Themistius' exempla are justifications of Valens' behavior. If Ammianus correctly states that the emperor revealed no mildness, the exempla are meant to deflect Valens' anger.

38. Themistius uses this example at 16.212a in the context of peace with the Goths. As Portmann, *Panegyrik*, 167, 273, n. 14, points out, Massinissa is not otherwise known to have been captured alive.

39. Cf. Plut. *Apoph.* 177d–e, for a more complete version of the story and the name. Frontin. *Strateg.* 4.7.37, offers a similar story, but enough details are different (e.g., the name of the man is Pythias, a warrior) to identify it as a second incident.

40. The passage is usually thought to refer to Julian's theurgist Maximus; cf., e.g., Seeck, *Briefe*, 209; Dagron, *Thémistios*, 37, n. 4; *PLRE*, 1:584. But the remarks are negative, implying that the philosopher in question was not a true practitioner. Themistius would be incredibly naive to refer negatively to a

Themistius never indicates that the methods of taxation employed by Valens and his agents were largely responsible for the discontent that made the usurpation extremely dangerous. Throughout his account, Ammianus blames the actions of Valens' father-in-law Probus as a direct cause (26.6.7–9).[41] The philosopher was not likely to emphasize civil discontent when asking for clemency from a financially desperate regime, though his reference to Procopius' exactions may well have been a warning to Valens. Instead, he moves directly from his description of the rabble to Valens' victory over Procopius and omits completely any indication of the usurper's success. This is true even when he later discusses the usurper's actions, since he there concentrates on Procopius' goals and the deceit used to achieve them. He emphasizes the emperor's absence from the final fight, noting that the army threw down their weapons as soon as the imperial army and Valens came into sight at a distance of thirty stades (7.87a–c). The orator has conveniently forgotten that, earlier in the conspiracy, armies of Valens defected to Procopius just before a battle (Am. Mar. 26.7.13–17).

For the only time in his career, Themistius does more than simply give a favorable interpretation. He omits items of importance and grossly exaggerates Procopius' character. The reasons are twofold. First, the conspiracy was more successful and dangerous than either Themistius or Valens was willing to admit. Second, Valens instituted a reign of terror after his victory. Themistius was able to bury the first point, but the evidence of Ammianus permits its exhumation; the philosopher was unable to hide Valens' vindictiveness. Clearly, the East remained in crisis after the death of Procopius.

In spring 367, Valens traveled to the Danubian frontier to punish the Goths, who had supported Procopius. A detailed chronology of the three years he spent in the region is difficult to establish: Ammianus discusses the Gothic wars in a very short account, culminating in the emperor's success in the winter of 369/70 (27.5.1–10). A peace treaty

recently rehabilitated Maximus. Though he had been positive about Salutius in earlier speeches, he is here responding to the current situation. I am grateful to Ted Nixon, whose innocent question induced me to reconsider the passage, and hope to discuss Salutius more thoroughly elsewhere.

41. On his career, cf. *PLRE*, 1:690–91.

was signed with Athanaric on a boat in the middle of the Danube in winter 369/70.[42]

During this period, Themistius went to Marcianopolis near the Danube frontier to deliver *Oration* 8 for the quinquennial celebrations of Valentinian and Valens. He refers to the rate of taxation for the first three years of the emperor's reign (365, 366, 367, since the rate for 364 had presumably been announced before the death of Jovian) and proclaims that the rate for the fourth (368) had been reduced. The speech, which does not refer to the consulship of Valens's son in 369, thus dates to 368, more likely toward the beginning of the year.[43] It was probably delivered on 28 March, with Valens still in winter quarters.[44]

Themistius first remarks that he has some knowledge of the nature of kingship, but he moves quickly to a discussion of time, focusing on the relation between time and human happiness. He concludes that tyranny seems longer than it is because of the constant pain;[45] a long period of good rule is an occasion for celebration and festival. Without much further ado, he leaves discussion of these matters to others, remarking on his preference for philosophical topics. He notes with some distaste the dispute about speeches by philosophers, who are treated worse than pedagogues (8.101b–103d).[46]

A discussion of philosophy and the emperor's attitude follows. Philosophy is different from other pursuits because it is not influenced by flattery, and a philosopher benefits humanity more than

---

42. Cf. Seeck, *Regesten*, 229–39, for chronology; he dates the peace to March 370, but this is probably too late. P.J. Heather, *Goths and Romans 332–489* (Oxford, 1992), 116–21, discusses these wars briefly. Heather, here and elsewhere, ascribes less independence to Themistius than I do, arguing that the philosopher was simply a "mouthpiece" for Valens.

43. The precise date that the indiction for 368 was announced (probably autumn 367) is irrelevant, since it would still be the fourth set by Valentinian and Valens.

44. Marcianopolis is named in the title in one manuscript. O. Seeck, *Hermes* 18 (1883): 150–53, and *Briefe*, 302, argues for 369, correctly rejected by Scholze, *Temporibus*, 29; Stegemann, "Themistios," 1659; and Dagron, *Thémistios*, 21.

45. Themistius continues to remind the emperor that the usurpation of Procopius had not been pleasant for his subjects and is perhaps still pleading for mercy.

46. A reference to debates which are much more clearly in evidence during the reign of Constantius; see chapter 4 for discussion. Obviously, Themistius had not completely silenced his critics.

himself.[47] Valens puts an end to the search for an ideal ruler,[48] the orator informs Plato, who is addressed directly. The emperor, who does not know Greek,[49] is more attentive to Themistius than Alexander was to Aristotle and has in mind the statement of the emperor Titus (8.103d–107c). Themistius moves to a lengthy discussion of Valens' reflection of the Platonic ideal, but disputes Plato's view that evil would cease to exist when philosophers became kings, preferring Aristotle's emphasis on deeds. He points out that an emperor need not study philosophy, as long as he takes advice from a philosopher— a somewhat self-serving remark. Valens had done this after the recent insurrection, because his anger was not deeply rooted. His mildness reminds Themistius of the emperor's magnificence and generosity, true marks of the good emperor, especially if he is fiscally responsible (8.107c–112d).

This leads Themistius to his main point: the emperor is giving more by taking less.[50] For the first three years of his reign, Valens did not raise taxes, which had doubled in the forty previous years from Constantine's victory over Licinius to the reign of Jovian.[51] In the fourth year, during a campaign against the Goths, when a doubling might be expected, the rate of taxation was to be cut in half. The orator adds the cautionary remark that the reduction would occur if the calculations were correct, indicating that the announcement was recent (8.113a–c).[52] The effect of the reform was to bring the level of

47. The remarks are highly reminiscent of 26.327a–b.

48. Less than a decade later, Themistius discovered that Gratian represented the end of his search; see the discussion later in this chapter.

49. Cf. n. 10 in this chapter.

50. The portion of the speech from 8.113a to the end is translated (by D. Moncur) and annotated in P. Heather and J. Matthews, *The Goths in the Fourth Century* (Liverpool, 1991), 26–36.

51. So A. Cameron, in *De Rebus Bellicis*. BAR International Series 63 (Oxford, 1969), 5, and the revised version in A. Cameron, *Literature and Society in the Early Byzantine World* (London, 1985), IX:10.

52. This differs from the view offered by Heather and Matthews, *The Goths*, 27, nn. 38, 41, who see two consecutive 25 percent reductions. Themistius refers to decrees such as "The measures of grain and wine you shall pay in taxes shall be reduced by such and such an amount, and for the future also shall fall short of what is customary by equal quantities" (trans. Moncur). The reduction "by such and such an amount" is the indiction set for the fourth year, and "fall short of what is customary by equal quantities"

taxation back that of to Licinius' time, and the emphasis on the proposal perhaps represents a disavowal of Constantine's dynasty by Themistius, who had compared Valens favorably with Constantine in *Oration* 6 (83b). The reason is almost certainly the revolt of Procopius and Constantinople's espousal of the usurper's cause.

After a discussion of Valens' desire to distribute the tax burden equitably, based on the emperor's knowledge of what the land could bear, Themistius compares him to Aristides (the Athenian), noting that he would have the eternal gratitude of his subjects and make defection to the barbarians less attractive (8.113d–115d).[53] The lower rate was possible because of reduced military spending. Themistius mentions some of the measures, praising Valens in the process. The lists of soldiers were examined carefully to ensure that only those in service were registered, with a decrease in the payroll. The officer corps was reduced, with some generals forced into retirement. At the same time, corrupt officials were eliminated to restore justice and remove the graft that caused an extra burden on taxpayers. While earlier emperors were more concerned with horse races than the state of the empire, Valens cared about the government of his subjects and chose their governors with care (8.115d–119a).

Themistius concludes with a reiteration of his view that Valens was the ideal king, as peace within the empire would indicate.[54] When he became emperor, trouble abounded. Since then, the Persians in the east had bought by a treaty what they could not obtain with arms. The Germanic peoples in the west had been cut down and were less troublesome. At the center of the empire, the Goths had paid for their intentions. At the very end of the speech, Themistius notes that Valens was at the peak of his age and had a young son who might

---

means that, in the fifth and subsequent years, the reduction would continue to be applied. The phrase "what is customary" must refer to rate of taxation before the reduction; otherwise, as it must do in the interpretation of Heather and Matthews, it refers to a single year, i.e., the fourth.

53. There is little evidence that defection was rampant. Cf., for brief discussion, Jones, *LRE*, 2:1059–62 (primarily on the fifth century). At 8.115c–d, Themistius again disparages the dynasty of Constantine, especially Julian; cf. Heather and Matthews, *Goths*, 30, n. 53.

54. Themistius also refers to the coming of Bacurius to the Romans (8.116c) and the outbreak of the revolt of Queen Mavia (8.117a); cf., on these, Heather and Matthews, *Goths*, 31, n. 56, and 32, n. 59.

become a new Alexander under Themistius' tutelage and was not impressed by a miracle worker (8. 119a–120b).[55]

The remarks on peace may indicate that Themistius is opposing the military and financial policy of Valens, implying that peace would reduce military expenditure.[56] Despite his promotion of peace, however,[57] the intensity of any attack on imperial policy should not be overestimated. The contemporary anonymous treatise *de rebus bellicis* offers proposals for reduction in military spending to permit a halving of taxes. Tax reduction was thus a current issue in 368, and Themistius reveals specific policies on items that appear as possibilities in *de rebus bellicis*.[58] The main difference lies in emphasis. As a man interested in the military, the author of *de rebus bellicis* is concerned with increasing the efficiency of the army, with fewer men and better equipment. Themistius thinks that peace would permit the same reductions. Though Valens was perhaps more inclined to continue his campaigns than the philosopher wished, the praise of current financial policies of Valens indicates that these were reality and not merely wishes. Ammianus notes that both Valentinian and Valens reduced taxes (30.9.1; 31.14.2, including a remark that the East had never had an emperor who eliminated corruption as thoroughly).

At the beginning of the next year, Themistius delivered a panegyric in honor of Valentinianus Galates, the infant son of Valens who entered the consulship on 1 January 369 with the general Victor as colleague. Valens, and presumably his son, were at Marcianopolis, once again in winter quarters. The philosopher was either with the

55. Not surprisingly: the son was probably not yet two years old. The miracle worker is Maximus, on whom Themistius has apparently changed his view.

56. Dagron, *Thémistios*, 95–112, including discussion of Themistius' attitude during the reign of Theodosius.

57. On Themistius' desire for peace, cf. L.J. Daly, *Historia* 21 (1972): 351–79.

58. For this reason, *Or.* 8 probably postdates the treatise. If so, the treatise should date to the winter of 367/8, rather than 368/9 as Cameron has proposed in *De Rebus Bellicis*, 1–10, and in the revised version (1985). Cameron, who accepts a March 368 date for *Or.* 8, suggests that Themistius is stretching the truth about Valens' financial measures to account for his date for the *de rebus bellicis*. But the difference between proposals (*de rebus bellicis*) and actions (Themistius) is critical. A date in 368/9 is possible if a writer intended to propose that Valentinian adopt the actions taken by Valens in the East.

court or pretends to be, with the oration sent to Marcianopolis. The latter is perhaps more likely.[59] Themistius elsewhere refers to periods spent with the court on the Danube during this reign, but probably means nothing more than the journey to deliver *Oration* 8 and the embassy later in 369.

After brief remarks on the boy's birth at the Danube and his acquaintance with war (9.120c–121d), the speech is largely a treatment of the Platonic ideal for kingship that Valentinianus was to learn from his father, his uncle, and his cousin Gratian. Themistius emphasizes the education suitable to an emperor, promising a good reign as a result (9.121d–123c), and offers himself as the Apollo to the infant's Achilles, to aid him in learning the philosophy of Plato and Aristotle (9.123c–124b).[60] The child is encouraged to emulate Gratian, who heeds his teachers (9.125b–c),[61] and to remember that the greatness of his father, uncle, and cousin lies in their deeds (9.125d–127a). Themistius notes that the members of the imperial college support each other in every way, before he passes to a request that Valentinianus Galates join the college and be established as emperor at Constantinople (9.127a–128d).

Given the likelihood that the young boy understood little of Themistius' speech, the philosopher used the occasion to deliver another panegyric of Valens and Valentinian. A primary motive was almost certainly the request at the end. With the addition of Gratian as Augustus in 367,[62] the West had two emperors and the East only one. Themistius attempts to redress the balance, by asking for an imperial presence at Constantinople, as he himself remarks (9.128b–d). Once again, Themistius, acting on behalf of the Senate, is reminding an emperor to take thought for Constantinople and to make the city and the empire it governed as much like Rome as possible. The request was apparently never granted, and Themistius did not be-

---

59. So too Scholze, *Temporibus*, 36–37.

60. Lib. *Ep.* 151, makes the same claim for Cleobulus and Bassianus, and at *Ep.* 1492 for Nicocles and Clearchus, to indicate a teacher-student relationship; cf. Kaster, *Guardians of Language*, 256, 318.

61. Themistius repeats this in his panegyric of Gratian at 13.173d–174c, where he also mentions the relationship of Apollo and Achilles.

62. Shortly after his eighth birthday, on 24 August 367 (*Cons. Const.* s.a. 367; *Chron. Pasch.* s.a. 367), when his father had not yet recovered fully from a serious illness (Am. Mar. 27.6.4).

come the boy's tutor: Valentinianus Galates did not long survive the delivery of this speech.

In the summer or autumn of 369, Themistius traveled to the Danube at the head of a delegation from the Senate that attempted to persuade Valens to conclude peace. No speech from the embassy, known only from later statements by the philosopher, is extant, but he seems to have delivered more than one; he may, however, be referring to discussions only.[63] In *Oration* 10, his treatment of the peace concluded with Athanaric in winter 369/70,[64] Themistius mentions discussions of philanthropy and his emphasis on saviors of men as closer to the divine than destroyers (10.133a–b). Later, in *Oration* 11, delivered to celebrate the emperor's *decennalia*, he refers again to speeches on peace, some delivered at the Danube, others at the capital (11.144a).

With some difficulty, the philosopher avers, he and his fellow delegates convinced the emperor to seek peace with the Goths, who had been asking for terms (10.133b; cf. Am. Mar. 27.5.7–8). After his agents Arintheus and Victor investigated the sincerity of the Goths, the emperor was successful in this endeavor. Since neither side, especially not Athanaric, was prepared to set foot in the other's territory, Valens and Athanaric concluded peace on a boat in the middle of the river (Am. Mar. 27.5.9).[65] Early in 370, Valens returned to Constantinople, where Themistius congratulated him with *Oration* 10 shortly after the emperor's arrival (10.129a–b).[66]

Themistius begins *Oration* 10 with the now familiar theme of Valens'

---

63. Cf. Scholze, *Temporibus*, 37–38, for the journey and its date.

64. The evidence for the date is the chronologically imprecise account of Amm. Mar. 27.5.1–10. Valens had returned to winter quarters before the treaty was concluded. Cf. Seeck, *Regesten*, 239. E.A. Thompson, *The Visigoths in the Time of Ulfila* (Oxford, 1966), 18–20, and Heather, *Goths and Romans*, 119, place the entire affair (campaign and peace) in 369, perhaps correctly, while T.S. Burns, *The Ostrogoths: Kingship and Society. Historia* Einzelschriften 36 (Wiesbaden, 1980), 44, places the whole campaign in 367.

65. Cf. Thompson, *Visigoths*, 18. Heather, *Goths and Romans*, 119–20, points out that this reveals Valens' lack of success in the campaign and argues that Valens was forced to negotiate, not induced to do so by Themistius and others.

66. So Scholze, *Temporibus*, 38–39, dating it to late January or February. Seeck, *Briefe*, 302–3, dates the speech to 369, but Valens is attested at Marcianopolis as late as 31 January 370 (*CTh* 7.13.2; cf. Seeck *Regesten*, 238). The speech is translated (by D. Moncur) and annotated in Heather and Matthews, *Goths*, 36–50.

greater interest in philosophy than rhetoric. He hates flatterers, but gives philosophers equal status with generals.[67] As evidence, Themistius notes that, unlike Alexander, Augustus, and Marcus Aurelius, Valens sought honor in peace rather than trophies. The philosopher here follows Plato, who states that kings who can make war can also make peace. War, in fact, is necessary only to establish peace. To Plato's remark that the seeds of war and peace exist in each individual,[68] Themistius adds the suggestion that the barbarian element, which causes disorder, exists in everyone as well. For rulers, it is better to defeat the daring of the barbarians and incorporate them into the empire. In the philosopher's view, an emperor who destroys the barbarians is emperor of the Romans alone, but one who conquers and spares is ruler of all men and rivals Zeus, who is the father of all (10.129a–132c).

The rest of the speech focuses on a treatment of the negotiations and the benefits of peace, as is suitable given the title, "To Valens, On Peace."[69] The orator claims that the emperor's activity at the Danube was necessary and performed with distinction. He had personally witnessed Valens' mildness and boasts that the ship on which the emperor had concluded peace with the Goths was better than the entire fleet of Xerxes. The philosopher, who was apparently present when peace was accomplished, had seen the Goths not drawn up in battle lines, but assembled in fear, with Roman generals giving orders to the kings of the Goths (10.132c–133a).[70] He discusses the kindness of the emperor toward the barbarians, including a willingness to provide them with land and opportunities for commerce.[71] He mentions

---

67. Cf. the similar praise of Constantius at 4.54a.

68. *Leg.* 626e, 628d–e.

69. On the speech, I. Barnea, *SCIV* 18 (1967): 563–73 (in Romanian, with French summary on pp. 573–74).

70. Heather and Matthews, *Goths,* 18–26, suggest that Valens' "victory" was at best a compromise. This is undoubtedly correct, but does not necessarily transform Themistius into an abject flatterer. The philosopher genuinely believed in the benefits of peace, and he calls the compromise a victory to prevent further war on this front. Ammianus (27.5.8–9) and Zosimus (4.11.4) regard the compromise as a suitable solution. Heather and Matthews, *Goths,* 49, n. 112, think that they were influenced by imperial propaganda, but there is no reason to deny these writers some independence of thought.

71. During the campaign of 369, Valens had not allowed the Goths to trade with the Romans (Am. Mar. 27.5.7). Cf. Thompson, *Visigoths,* 19–20. Burns, *Ostrogoths,* 29–30, dates the interruption of commerce to 367.

fortifications on the Danube,[72] Valens' military reforms,[73] and the benefits of peace to the Empire. As a result, the region was again secure for its inhabitants, and the barbarians became useful servants of the empire (10.133b–139c).

Themistius has here obviously extended his definition of philanthropy, since peoples outside the empire are now included. Because of peace, it was possible to count not the dead but the living, who are barbarians, but nevertheless men (10.139c–140a). For this, Valens deserved special praise. Unlike earlier Romans, who took victory titles for destroying peoples, Valens should be called "Gothicus" from the name of the people he saved. Valens, Themistius intimates, had chosen peace, and the happiness of his subjects, not destruction of peoples, makes him a true ruler (10.140a–141c).

This speech is the main evidence that Themistius and his colleagues opposed Valens' military policy.[74] Their solution to the Gothic problem was the conclusion of peace; another group, including, at first, the emperor, preferred thorough destruction. This difference of opinion does not, however, indicate a serious split along "party lines" in the East, nor does it necessarily indicate opposition. While Libanius and others may have argued that the strength of the empire lay in its army, Themistius does not deny the military its position of importance. Rather, he emphasizes different solutions, for financial and other reasons. In any case, Themistius refers to discussions with the emperor over a period of time in 369, and, while he emphasizes his own role, it is likely that a senatorial delegation, perhaps by showing Valens how a treaty could be interpreted as a victory and how peace itself could be portrayed as such, had some influence on the emperor. The effect was not immediate, since the emperor probably continued his attempt to defeat the Goths after these discussions; his lack of success in the campaign may have convinced him that the senators were correct.[75] That Valens did not see the hypothetical opposition,

---

72. On these, cf. H. von Petrikovits, *JRS* 61 (1971): 184–87, who attributes them to Valentinian.

73. Cf. Cameron, *Literature and Society in the Early Byzantine World*, IX:18, who suggests that 10.136a on the weaponry placed on the Danube by Valens may indicate that some of the Anonymous' inventions had come into use.

74. The view of Dagron, *Thémistios*, 95–112.

75. On the need for victories, cf. McCormick, *Eternal Victory*, esp. 35–46. The senatorial delegation perhaps met Valens during the campaign of 369 to

which is rather to be seen as the formation of policy, as a problem, is evident from the continued influence of Themistius, who was able to deflect Valens' persecution of non-Arian Christians only a few years later. Themistius' praise of peace in *Oration* 10 is thus not an attack on policy, but an example of his lifelong commitment to peace.[76]

Not unreasonably for a panegyric, *Oration* 10 thus presents the new imperial policy in the best light possible. It was naturally in Valens' best interests that his treaty be considered a victory, but the speech is as much propaganda for peace as for the emperor. Themistius' view has its origin in the philosophy of Aristotle, who proposes that one purpose of the state is the achievement of peace (*Eth. Nic.* 1333a41–b 2). Plato, not uninterested in peace, places more emphasis on the military. He holds that humanitarianism should be a guiding force in war between Greeks, but more or less excludes barbarians from this principle. Aristotle, in contrast, argues that the concept of humanity was to be operative in all wars against all opponents.[77] On this point, which is primarily a question of emphasis, Themistius adopted the perspective of Aristotle, and he is at his most eloquent when rehearsing the benefits of peace.

Valens did not stay long at the capital after his celebration of peace. By 30 April 370, he is attested at Antioch (*CTh* 10.19.5). Though he returned to Constantinople for winter and spring 370/1, he resided at Antioch for most of the rest of his reign, with frequent journeys and campaigns at least as far as Hierapolis in the summers.[78] In 371/2, after he discovered an attempt at Antioch to divine the name of his successor by the use of magic arts, Valens unleashed a reign of terror which caused many to burn their books and "creep about as if in Cimmerian darkness" (Am. Mar. 29.2.4).[79] Nothing is known of the effect on Themistius, but his continued political activity suggests a minimal

inform him that enough had been achieved to allow him to extricate himself from a difficult position.

76. Cf. Daly, *Historia* 21 (1972): 351–79.

77. For some remarks, cf. M. Defourny, in *Articles on Aristotle.* vol. 2, *Ethics and Politics,* ed. J. Barnes, M. Schofield, and R. Sorabji (London, 1977), 195–201.

78. For the chronology, Seeck, *Regesten,* 239–51.

79. On the incident and its aftermath, cf. Am. Mar. 29.1.5–2.28. Cf. Blockley, *Ammianus Marcellinus,* 108–13, and Matthews, *Ammianus,* 219–25.

impact on him personally. At Antioch, Valens also began or intensified his effort to destroy non-Arian Christianity, a policy that did not endear him to Constantinople. Later, when he passed through the capital on his way to the lower Danube in 378, the citizens questioned his concern for the city. The emperor responded with a threat to overturn the city and plough the site on his return from campaign (Soc. *HE* 4.38). The citizens of the capital were not overly distraught when he did not return.

Almost certainly at Antioch, Themistius addressed Valens with a decennial speech, *Oration* 11.[80] As with the quinquennial speech, there is a dispute about date, either 28 March 373 or 29 March 374, but the former is more likely.[81] Themistius' first task during his visit to Antioch was the delivery of *Oration* 25 in response to the emperor's request that he speak ex tempore. The short speech is an apology for his inability. He notes that Phidias could not complete a sculpture in a single day despite his skill and would have sent a person who requested this to admire a completed statue. The philosopher will do the same, since he cannot compose an instant speech, as sophists could, but needs time to construct a suitable portrait. He closes with a few words about his intended creation, requesting a period of time for composition (25.309d–311a). The philosopher's discussion of a statue here and in *Oration* 11 may constitute evidence that Valens had granted Themistius a bronze statue. In his defense against opponents in the next reign, Themistius mentions a second statue, but does not name the emperor who granted it (31.353a; 17.214b). Constantius is out of the question, because the statues were offered by different emperors (34.13).[82] Julian and Jovian are not likely candidates, and Themistius nowhere credits Theodosius, leaving Valens.[83] *Oration* 10 was perhaps the pretext.

The promised portrait appears in *Oration* 11, composed, supposedly, after Themistius was refused the time he had requested (11.143b–c).[84] That is fiction, since the philosopher is unlikely to have

80. So Scholze, *Temporibus*, 41. Harduin (p. 594 Dindorf) had placed delivery at Constantinople.

81. So Scholze, *Temporibus*, 41. Seeck, *Briefe*, 303, proposed the later date.

82. See chapter 4 on the first statue.

83. So Baret, *Themistio*, 37. Seeck, *Briefe*, 296, suggests Julian.

84. On the dates of the two speeches and their interrelation, cf. Scholze, *Temporibus*, 40–42.

traveled to Antioch completely oblivious to the fact that he was to deliver a speech. Arguing from the premise that only the emperor was permitted to wear a crown and imperial dress, the orator notes the suitable character for an emperor and points out that the statue most like the divine is the most imperial.[85] Naturally, this is Valens, who was attentive to a philosopher, following the example of Philip and Aristotle and others (11.141a–145c).[86] Themistius soon begins a discussion of philanthropy, the most kingly and divine of the virtues. In that discussion, he cites Christian Scripture for the second time during the reign of Valens. He cites Homer as well, to show the special relationship between king and God. Peace in the empire and prosperity in cities are results of Valens' philanthropy (11.146c–150d). Constantinople especially benefited, and Themistius describes the building program in the city (11.151a–152c). After briefly comparing Valens to Alexander, the philosopher asks God to increase the emperor's philanthropy and to provide him with children and successors, as replacements for Valentinianus Galates, who had recently died (11.152d–154b).

The emphasis on philanthropy may in part be an attempt to convince Valens that continued anger and persecution were not necessary. The obvious context is the reign of terror unleashed in 371/2, and Themistius here adopts his standard procedure, praising an attitude of the emperor in an effort to obtain further expression of that attitude. No positive results of the speech are known, but Themistius, who later mentions his effect on Valens, perhaps succeeded in mollifying the emperor to a small degree.

Themistius addressed Valens once more, with a speech designed to turn Valens away from persecution of non-Arian Christians. The text is not extant, and the Latin version found in some editions is a Renais-

---

85. The imagery in some ways recalls the metaphor used at the beginning of *Oration* 1, where only some can see the true divinity within the emperor, but most see only externals; cf. esp. 1.2b–3a. Philanthropy is the main subject of both speeches.

86. Including, probably, Diocletian's treatment of Themistius' grandfather. Cf. 11.145b: "the deeds of the eponym of Zeus to the philosopher practicing in Byzantium at the time." A scholiast suggests that Zeno is meant, apparently thinking of the use of ὁ Ζήν for Zeus, with a transfer of eponym from the ruler to the philosopher, but this is impossible. On Themistius' grandfather, see chapter 2.

sance forgery.[87] Socrates mentions the speech and its circumstances, briefly reports its content, and notes that Themistius enjoyed some success in his endeavor (*HE* 4.32). The oration required a visit to Antioch, where the emperor was resting from his campaigns, with the borders of the empire relatively secure. Because Socrates places the speech between his accounts of the death of Valentinian in the West on 17 November 375 and the crossing of the Danube by the Goths in 376, it probably dates to the winter of 375/6. Themistius perhaps went to the court at the request of the Senate to offer condolences to Valens.[88] A key argument was the suggestion that Christian views differed less from each other than they did from paganism. Some arguments of *Oration* 5, including the desirability of religious diversity, were repeated as well.

Before the end of Valens' reign, Themistius delivered a panegyric of Gratian in Rome. The orator's direct relations with Gratian, whom he perhaps never met, are limited to this single speech in his honor. Gratian is important in Themistius' panegyrics of Theodosius, but only as the emperor responsible for Theodosius' accession.[89] The speech on Gratian celebrated an important occasion in either 376[90] or 377.[91] The philosopher remarks that he had made a journey in haste from the East to the West for this speech:

> There was a course, almost equal to the course of the sun, from the Tigris to Ocean, an intense journey, an earthbound flight of the sort that you [Socrates] say Eros once made, with days as well as nights unrestful. (13.163c)

At several other points, he refers to a journey from "boundary to boundary" or from East to West (13.165d, 168c, 171b). Before he

---

87. Dvornik, *Early Christian and Byzantine Political Philosophy*, 2;764, n. 165, is not convinced of this.

88. A suggestion of Seeck, *Briefe*, 303, accepted by Scholze, *Temporibus*, 43.

89. See chapter 8.

90. Seeck, *Briefe*, 303, proposes the summer of 376.

91. Scholze, *Temporibus*, 48, suggests July or August 377, accepted by Stegemann, "Themistius," 1660–61. Both he and Seeck link the speech to the *decennalia*. Harduin, without connecting the speech to the *decennalia*, dated it to April or May 377.

undertook this visit, the philosopher had been at Valens' court, possibly moving with the emperor on campaign, since he remarks, in exaggeration perhaps, that he was near the Tigris and Euphrates.

His brief for this embassy came from Valens himself, not the eastern Senate.[92] Themistius delivered the speech in the Senate chambers: he refers to the city, the Roman Senate, and the senators who accompanied him on the last part of his journey (13.162c, 177d–180b).[93] The young emperor was not present. He is addressed in the second person and discussed in the third, but the crucial consideration is an invitation to Gratian (and Valens) to come to Rome (13.179b, d).[94] Whether Valens intended to make the journey is unknown.[95] Gratian probably did: one source mentions a visit to Rome at some unspecified date after his marriage, when he set up silver statues of himself and his wife (*Brev. Ennar. Chron.* 50).[96]

The panegyric almost certainly dates to 376.[97] Gratian is attested at Trier on 17 May 376 (*CTh* 16.2.23) and, on the basis of a reasonable emendation,[98] reappears there on 15 August (*CTh* 8.5.31; 11.10.2). Three months are available for a visit to Rome.[99] The situation is similar in 377. Gratian is last attested at Trier on 29 March (*CTh* 1.32.3)

92. Even though the philosopher mentions the attitude of Constantinople to Gratian (13.167c–168c). He was not asked to deliver a private message from Valens to Gratian in Gaul, as Seeck, *Briefe*, 303, thinks.

93. For the location, cf. Scholze, *Temporibus*, 45–46; and T.D. Barnes, *HSCP* 79 (1975): 329.

94. Cf. Baret, *Themistio*, 39; Scholze, *Temporibus*, 46–47; and Barnes, *HSCP* 79 (1975): 329.

95. Scholze, *Temporibus*, 47, has Themistius suggest that Valens did and notes that this was pretense because relations between the two emperors were bad.

96. So Barnes, *HSCP* 79 (1975): 328, with n. 25. Cameron and Herrin, *Constantinople in the Eighth Century* 239, point out that this is the only record of the statues.

97. Seeck, *Briefe*, 303; *Regesten*, 248; Barnes, *HSCP* 79 (1975): 329–30.

98. Seeck, *Regesten*, 35, 248.

99. If Seeck's emendation is rejected, Gratian is not attested at Trier until 17 September (*CTh* 9.35.2), and this would allow him to be at Rome for the celebration. Bouchery, "Contribution," 197, accepts the emendation, and suggests that Themistius delivered the speech on 24 August 376, while Gratian was on his way to Rome. That date allows the emperor only one month (15 August–17 September) to make the journey to Rome and back to Trier.

and returned there by 8 July (*CTh* 1.32.2). Once again, a visit to Rome could be dated to the interval.

The speech offers evidence of celebration and the suggestion that Gratian was bringing to Rome a crowd of people who had been rescued and redeemed from slavery (13.169b, 171c, 179b). The orator refers to a triumph (13.179b), and it is apparent that the intended visit to Rome was meant to be a triumphal entry,[100] with the empire at peace (13.176b–d, 179b–180a). Gratian, it appears, did not engage the barbarians in 376, and Valens annexed Armenia without a fight.[101] In 377, the Goths, who had crossed the Danube in 376,[102] began to cause severe problems, ravaging Thrace and besieging Marcianopolis and Hadrianople. Ammianus dates this to 377, at the end of summer (31.8.2: *anno in autumnum vergente*), though it must have begun earlier.[103] Valens was forced to send two generals, Trajan and Profuturus, and an army to Thrace, and he demanded and received from Gratian a second army, under the leadership of Richomeres. By 6 July, Valens was at Hierapolis and himself on campaign; the empire was no longer at peace. From autumn 376 to early spring 377, Gratian is too often attested at Trier to support a visit to Rome.

Realistically, only early summer 376 and late spring 377 are possible dates for the panegyric. Since a speech in the decennial year would hardly fail to mention that occasion,[104] the later date is next to impossible; the panegryic was thus delivered in spring or summer 376, shortly before Gratian's arrival at Rome. The festive occasion that Themistius mentions is the *aduentus* of the emperor. The philosopher beseeches Rome to "put on, much honored shoot of Romulus, white clothing for a

---

100. So Harduin (p. 608 Dindorf); Scholze, *Temporibus*, 46; Bouchery, "Contribution," 199; and Barnes, *HSCP* 79 (1975): 329.

101. So Bouchery, "Contribution," 198.

102. For the date, *Cons. Const.* s.a. 376. For discussion, Thompson, *Visigoths*, 21–23.

103. The chronology of this period is difficult to determine, since adequate specific source material is lacking. According to *Cons. Const.* s.a. 377, the Goths did not revolt until 377. Bouchery, "Contribution," 198, places it in 376.

104. *Orations* 8 and 11, to Valens (and Valentinian), refer to quinquennial and decennial anniversaries, while this speech does not. Bouchery, "Contribution," 196–200, proposes 24 August 376, accepted by Dagron, *Thémistios*, 23. Alföldi, *Conflict of Ideas*, 90, suggests that Gratian and Themistius were both at Rome to celebrate the *decennalia* in the summer of 376, the philosopher having been invited by Gratian.

white reign and white days" (13.178d). It may seem unlikely that Valens would send Themistius to Rome simply to celebrate an *aduentus*, even a triumphal entry, but this is apparently what happened. The dynasty's relations with the Roman Senate had been strained even before the death of Valentinian in November 375.[105] The executions of Theodosius and Maximinus had created tension,[106] and the young emperor visited the capital to repair the damage.[107] Much of the speech is devoted to the youth of Gratian, his physical appearance, and his wisdom, which rivaled the wisdom of old age.[108] It represents an attempt to inculcate positive regard for the young emperor, whose rule had already shown a direction somewhat different from that of his father.[109]

Themistius commences with Socrates' views on Eros as recorded in the *Symposium* of Plato, concentrating on his own search for a youth of true beauty and virtue, unsuccessful until he encountered the beauty of Gratian, which was so great that it made the barbarians good, the Goths mild, the Persians reasonable, the Armenians Roman, the Iberians Greek, and the nomad a house-dweller, changing each of these from its earlier shame to its opposite beauty (13.161c–166c).[110] The rest of the speech continues to praise Gratian for his beauty, his wisdom, and the resulting benefits. For example, when Gratian's uncle[111] foresaw that the young emperor would make a (marriage) connection with the East,[112] he made an effort to inscribe the name of Constantinople on an adamantine stele, regarding the city as the mother of the

---

105. For the political context, cf. Matthews, *Western Aristocracies*, 65–68.

106. The bibliography on this topic is extensive, much of it devoted to Theodosius and cited in chapter 8. Thompson, *Historical Work of Ammianus Marcellinus*, 87–107, suggests a conspiracy against Valentinian. Others reject this. Cf. P. Hamblenne, *Byzantion* 50 (1980): 198–225, with bibliography in the notes.

107. Barnes, *HSCP* 79 (1975): 329–30.

108. This last theme recurs in panegyrics of Theodosius when Gratian is mentioned; cf. e.g. 14.182b.

109. Cf. Alföldi, *Conflict of Ideas*, 85–94, for discussion.

110. This remark about the Goths could not have been made in the summer of 377, but is perhaps suitable enough in the summer of 376, when they were asking for permission to cross the Danube.

111. πάτρων. Harduin conjectured πάτρως, but this may be unnecessary, since πάτρων is attested in the sense of "uncle" in one inscription; cf. *LSJ* s.v.

112. Reference to Gratian's marriage in 374 to Constantia, the daughter of Constantius.

purple and giving gifts to increase its beauty (13.168a–c).[113] Gratian is thus credited with Valens' treatment of Constantinople.

The topic of philosophers as advisers also appears. After a list of emperors counseled by philosophers,[114] Themistius notes that Gratian's obedience to his teachers goes far beyond his lessons with them, since his conduct as ruler reveals his training.[115] Gratian has raised the "dead" nations of the West back to life, while gold is going out of, not into, the treasury. Moreover, Gratian has the famous statement of Titus firmly in mind, ever looking for ways to do good.[116] As a result, the entire empire is secure (13.171a–175a). Even barbarians love Gratian's beauty. They have crossed the Rhine in great numbers and fight on the Roman side, with their independent spirit gone (13.176a–d).

The orator also praises Rome, its laws established by Numa, and its Senate as a guardian of tradition against the incursions of Empedocles,[117] and mentions that some Romans accompanied him on the last stages of his journey to the West. He praises Gratian as well, for providing favorable conditions, such as winds,[118] for his journey. After mentioning earlier Romans and triumphs, Themistius remarks that the emperor will be leading into Rome a crowd of people released from their cares and saved from destruction, which is a better triumph than showing spoils of war (13.177d–179b). He mentions the deeds of Gratian and Valens again before closing the speech, comparing them with Camillus, regarded as a second founder of Rome because he defeated the Gauls.[119] The empire is now com-

---

113. Cf. 6.82d on the "mother of the empire." Gratian was born at Sirmium (*Epit.* 47.1) on 18 April 359 (Jer. *Chron.* a. 359; *Cons. Const.* s.a. 359), to Valentinian and Marina Severa, and was thus five years old when Valens made his remark about the importance of Constantinople.

114. E.g., Augustus and Arius, Titus and Musonius, and, negatively, Nero, who did not heed Seneca.

115. The philosopher asks Valentinianus Galates to emulate Gratian in this at 9.125b–c. Cf. also Auson. *Epig.* 26, *grat. act.* 8.39–40, and, on Gratian's education and literary accomplishments, Symm. *Or.* 3.7.

116. Few emperors escape praise for this; cf. 6.80a, 8.107a, 15.193a, etc.

117. For the meaning of this remark, see chapter 1.

118. As often, under a good emperor (i.e., the subject of a given panegyric), all humanity prospers under favorable conditions; cf., e.g., *Risâlat*, pp. 103–5.

119. For a similar comparison of Constantius with Camillus, cf. 3.43c. Compare also Claud. *Cons. Stil.* 2.390, for Stilicho as a second Camillus.

pletely at peace, and the Germans, Persians, Goths, and Sarmatians are at rest.[120] With an invocation to Zeus, Themistius closes by asking for mutual love between the emperors and Rome (13.179c–180b).

The last part of this speech, with its praise of Rome and the prayer that the emperors and Rome show each other mutual love, suggests that the opposite was true at the time and lends support to the view that Gratian visited Rome to repair relations with the city. His constant emphasis on the beauty of Gratian is not simply praise, but designed to engender in the audience a feeling of admiration for the young emperor. It is difficult to judge his success. Gratian almost certainly reached Rome, but there is no evidence that his attitude and the attitude of Rome changed dramatically as a result. Themistius' remarks on Gratian during the reign of Theodosius are of little help, since they are designed mainly to remind this emperor of his debt to Gratian in an effort to prevent strife between the two.[121] Moreover, his statement that Rome was grateful to Gratian for drawing Themistius to the city (31.354d) praises Themistius himself and says nothing of consequence about Gratian.

There is little evidence for Themistius' other activities in Rome, but he undoubtedly met some leading members of the senatorial aristocracy, including, perhaps, Symmachus and Vettius Agorius Praetextatus. Symmachus' *Relation* 3 on religious tolerance offers ideas also present in the panegyric of Jovian and the speech to Valens on religious persecution. Some may derive directly from Porphyry, but others may have emerged in a discussion with Themistius.[122] Praetextatus is reported to have translated the *Paraphrases* of Aristotle's *Analytics* into Latin (Boeth. *de interpret. ed. sec.* 1.289), perhaps because he met Themistius in 376.

More importantly, Themistius almost certainly held discussions with the Roman *princeps senatus*, the elder Symmachus, if the latter

---

120. Since Valentinian was involved with the Sarmatians at his death in 375 and the Goths began to create trouble in 376, a very short period is available for this speech. The Sarmatians do not cause trouble after the death of Valentinian, though the solution to the previous problem is unknown. Cf. A. Mócsy, *Pannonia and Upper Moesia* (London, 1974), 294–96.

121. See chapter 8.

122. See chapter 1 for this suggestion. The visit to Rome in 357 provided another occasion for this interchange of ideas.

was still alive.[123] The philosopher's own position as *princeps senatus* may have been a reason for his selection as ambassador. The younger Symmachus' frequent visits to emperors on behalf of the Senate and his father's visit to both Constantius and Julian in 361, indicate that harmony between Senate and emperor was a responsibility of the *princeps senatus*. By 376, good relations with Gratian had not yet been established. The Roman *princeps senatus* was unable to achieve them, even though he had been designated for the consulship of 377; he had perhaps been too much involved in the disturbances that led to the friction. He had also become unpopular with the urban population and was forced to leave the city in 375, though he returned to acclaim in 376; he probably died later in that year, before he could assume his consulship. Themistius, a *princeps senatus* himself, was perhaps asked to do what he could to guarantee a favorable reception for Gratian in Rome. If Symmachus had recently died or was ill, the mission was even more important. In any case, this visit indicates that Valens, as senior emperor, took concern for his nephew in the West.

During the reign of Valens, Themistius remained an important figure in the political life of the East. He did not add any position to those he was already holding at the beginning of the reign, though he may have been asked to become city prefect.[124] His influence with Valens was nevertheless considerable. In many ways, he matured as a philosopher and politician during this reign, becoming even more independent while still playing an active role. He himself later notes, that Valens was from time to time persuaded to heed his advice (31.354d). The philosopher's rebukes and warnings, couched in the form of panegyric, and the fact that his relations with Valens were not entirely harmonious, caused him to be attacked less virulently than before. Traces of the debate about Themistius' position appear from time to time, but the attacks were not severe enough to demand specific response or the philosopher did not deign to refute them.

---

123. Cf. A. Chastagnol, *Les fastes de la préfecture de Rome au Bas-Empire* (Paris, 1959), 159–63, on his career.

124. Themistius notes at 34.13 that he was often asked to assume this office.

8

Themistius and Theodosius

During the reign of Theodosius, Themistius reached the second peak of his political career. For the first time, he held office, as prefect of Constantinople in 384. This success renewed attacks against him by contemporaries. Earlier, he had defended himself against charges of sophistry, but at this late stage in his life, he was accused of debasing philosophy with his tenure of the city prefecture and the concomitant presidency of the senate. His relations with Theodosius were cordial and free from the disharmony occasionally evident during the reign of Valens. As usual, the philosopher praised some of the emperor's actions or promoted imperial policy in an effort to ensure continued acceptance of his own views or to effect a slight shift in policy.

The details of Theodosius' accession can no longer be recovered.[1] In the standard view which follows Pacatus (*Pan. Lat.* 2[12].10 ff.), Gratian summoned Theodosius from exile after the defeat of the Roman army and the death of Valens on 8 August 378 near Hadrianople. The situation demanded an experienced commander who was familiar with the Goths and their tactics. Theodosius, who had fled from Illyricum to Spain following the execution of his father in late 375 or early 376, was such a man. Friends at court, like his uncle Fl. Eucherius and Fl. Syagrius,[2] convinced Gratian to rehabilitate him. In the autumn of 378, the emperor appointed him *magister*

---

1. Earlier treatments in Seeck, *Geschichte*, 5:123–25, nn. at 477–79; W. Enßlin, "Die Religionspolitik des Kaisers Theodosius d. Gr.," *SitzBayAkadWiss* (1953), Heft 2, 5–7; N.Q. King, *The Emperor Theodosius and the Establishment of Christianity* (London, 1960), 17–18; A. Lippold, "Theodosius (1)," *RE* Suppl. XIII (1973), 837–44; and A. Lippold, *Theodosius der Große und seine Zeit*, 2nd ed. (Stuttgart, 1980), 12.

2. Seeck, *Geschichte*, 5:124, 479; Lippold, *RE* Suppl. XIII, 840–41; Matthews, *Western Aristocracies*, 94–96.

equitum et peditum[3] to lead the Romans against the Goths. After a victory later in the year, Theodosius left the front and traveled to Gratian at Sirmium. There, on 19 January 379,[4] the young emperor made his general Augustus of the East, because he was unable to rule the empire alone.[5]

Difficult to explain here is the sudden recall of Theodosius from exile and his selection first as a military leader of high rank and subsequently as coruler. If the death of the elder Theodosius resulted from the sudden accession of Valentinian II and the influence of his court officials,[6] Gratian was nevertheless a member of the college, with sufficient time to stop the investigation or execution order before it was too late. It is possible, too, that Gratian issued the order.[7] In either case, Gratian cannot be absolved of responsibility. Any suggestion that the elder Theodosius was the victim of false accusations is invalid. The *conspiration du silence*[8] of the sources guarantees his guilt, on charges that must have included treason.[9] No source, Christian or pagan, even when describing the accusations as malicious court intrigue, states that the charges were false, even after Theodosius rehabilitated the memory of his father.[10] Some writers do not even note the elder Theodosius' existence: the *Epitome* (48.1), relying on earlier

---

3. Also called *magister militum*. Cf., on his office, W. Enßlin, *Klio* 24 (1931): 137. Seeck, *Geschichte*, 5:124, 479, suggests *magister equitum* because Themistius (15.198a) calls him ἱππάρχων, but cf. W. Enßlin, *Klio* 23 (1930): 319, who notes that *magister equitum* appears elsewhere for *magister militum*.

4. Seeck, *Regesten*, 250, cites the evidence. Soc. *HE* 4.2.3, gives the date as 16 January.

5. The view of those who accept what is implied by Pacatus, *Pan. Lat.* 2[12].10 ff., and Theod. *HE* 5.5–6; cf. e.g., Seeck, *Geschichte*, 5:124–25; Enßlin, *SitzBayAkadWiss*, Heft 2, 7; King, *Emperor Theodosius*, 17–18; Lippold, *RE* Suppl. XIII, 840–41; Matthews, *Western Aristocracies*, 91.

6. Cf., e.g., W. Enßlin, *RE* X, A (1934), 1943–44; A. Lippold, *Riv. stor. dell' Ant.* 2 (1972): 197; Lippold, *Theodosius der Große*, 13; Matthews, *Western Aristocracies*, 64.

7. So R. Egger, *Byzantion* 5 (1930): 25–26, and A. Demandt, *Historia* 18 (1969): 602–5, 624–25.

8. A. Hoepffner, *REL* 14 (1936): 120, n. 1, first applied this unhappy phrase.

9. Thompson, *Historical Work of Ammianus Marcellinus*, 94–96; Demandt, *Historia* 18 (1969): 605–16.

10. On the rehabilitation, cf. Egger, *Byzantion* 5 (1930): 27–32.

sources, calls the new emperor the son of Honorius, who was his grandfather.[11]

Theodosius' return was probably not the result of a reinvestigation of the charges against his father.[12] More likely, relatives and friends at the court of Gratian[13] convinced the emperor that Theodosius had not been involved, that his parentage ought not to override his ability and experience, and that the flight to Spain resulted from a fearful expectation that his father's enemies, themselves later removed for treason, would persecute their victim's son as well.[14] The resignation could be excused on these grounds.[15] All this may explain a return from retirement; it does not date it or justify selection as Augustus.

The demands of empire did not force Gratian to appoint an emperor, since his young half brother Valentinian was a member of the college. Quite conceivably, one could establish a presence in the East, while the other remained in the West. Each had a court, with its civil and military bureaucracies. No compelling reason for a third emperor exists.[16] Not even military needs suffice: Gratian required a military leader, not an emperor.[17]

---

11. Seeck, *Geschichte*, 5:123, 478; Enßlin, *RE* X, A, 1937; Enßlin, *SitzBay-AkadWiss*, Heft 2, 5; and K.F. Stroheker, *Madr. Mitt.* 4 (1963): 110, consider Honorius the new emperor's grandfather. J.R. Martindale, *Historia* 16 (1967): 254–56, with stemma on 256; *PLRE*, 1:904; and Matthews, *Western Aristocracies*, 108, n. 3, advance the claim of an uncle named Honorius.

12. Demandt, *Historia* 18 (1969): 615–16, 625.

13. On these, cf. Stroheker, *Madr. Mitt.* 4 (1963): 113, and Matthews, *Western Aristocracies*, 93–96. Matthews notes (95) that Theodosius would have required wide support at court and especially in the army.

14. So Ambr. *de obitu Theod.* 53: *portauit iugum graue Theodosius a iuuentute, quando insidiabantur eius saluti, qui patrem eius triumphatorem occiderant.* Cf. Enßlin, *SitzBayAkadWiss*, Heft 2, 6, and Seeck, *Geschichte*, 5:124, 479.

15. Matthews, *Western Aristocracies*, 93, correctly sees Theodosius' sojourn in Spain as retirement, not exile.

16. The view that Valentinian was a weak emperor effectively relegated to third place in the imperial college, discussed at several points in this chapter, is irrelevant at this juncture: it is a consequence of, not a reason for, Theodosius' accession.

17. Cf., for a different view, Matthews, *Western Aristocracies*, 91: ". . . it was clear that a new emperor would have to be found at once—an effective general, and, if possible, one whose military reputation was not compromised by the disaster of Hadrianople. Such a consideration might undermine the claims of some likely candidates among the generals of Valens."

The sources suggest that Gratian summoned Theodosius after the battle of Hadrianople on 8 August 378, and only when the gravity of the situation became clear. After the summons reached him and before his official *dies imperii*, 19 January 379, Theodosius traveled to Thrace, conducted a campaign, won a victory, and reported to Sirmium, almost certainly before the end of December.[18] The period seems too short,[19] and the view requires active fighting in Thrace in winter as well.[20] It is more likely that Gratian recalled Theodosius shortly after Maximinus, the chief enemy of Theodosius the Elder, was put to death in 376.[21] If so, Theodosius could have served in Gratian's campaigns as early as 377. At the latest, he was with the forces that traveled toward the East in 378.[22]

Reasonable inferences to support this claim may be drawn from scattered fragments of evidence. Themistius states that Gratian raised Theodosius to the throne after continuous service as a company commander and general (15.188c). This may be an attempt to ignore an embarrassing retirement, but other writers mention Theodosius' absence. An obvious conclusion is that Theodosius was not in Spain for a long period.[23] His earlier positions include service with his father[24]

---

18. The exact date when he reached Sirmium is unknown, but it was almost certainly before the end of December, since Gratian had time to investigate Theodosius' claim of a victory.

19. Not, however, regarded as a problem by Seeck, *Geschichte*, 5:124; Enßlin, *SitzBayAkadWiss*, Heft 2, 7; Matthews, *Western Aristocracies*, 91; and others.

20. In other years, emperors campaigning in Thrace frequently returned to winter quarters by September; cf. Seeck, *Regesten*, 255, 259, 265. The victory of Theodosius in 379 was perhaps a little later: the news reached Constantinople on 17 November (*Chron. min.* 1:243).

21. On Maximinus, see Demandt, *Historia* 18 (1969): 616–25.

22. Lippold, *Theodosius der Große*, 12; not, however, at *RE* Suppl. XIII, 840.

23. Themistius is the earliest source to treat the theme, and Theodosius was more secure by 389, when Pacatus (*Pan. Lat.* 2[12].10.2) refers to a short retirement. Theodosius probably married Aelia Flacilla during this period; cf. Matthews, *Western Aristocracies*, 93–94; K. Holum, *Theodosian Empresses: Women and Imperial Dominion in Late Antiquity* (Berkeley, 1982), 22. Only a short period is required to ensure the birth of Arcadius and the conception of Pulcheria. The exact year of Arcadius' birth is unknown, but the evidence of Socrates (*HE* 6.23.7) suggests 377; cf. *PLRE*, 1:99; Holum, *Theodosian Empresses*, 22. On Pulcheria, cf. Lippold, *Theodosius der Große*, 12; Holum, loc. cit.

24. Cf. Lippold, *Riv. stor. dell' Ant.* 2 (1972): 195–200; A. Demandt, *Hermes* 100 (1972): 81–113.

and, just before his resignation, an appointment as *dux Moesiae*, where he enjoyed some success against the Sarmatians (Am. Mar. 29.6.15).

On his return, because it can hardly have occurred earlier, Theodosius was sent to Thrace by Gratian (Theod. *HE* 5.5), who needed capable generals in various places. Theodosius soon reported a victory over the Sarmatians,[25] who inhabited an area near Pannonia and Upper Moesia.[26] He began in the summer of 378, with a promotion (Pacat. *Pan. Lat.* 2[12].10.3) from *dux* to *magister equitum* (Them. *Or.* 15.198a: ἱππάρχων), before assuming command on the lower Danube after Hadrianople. His accession is more difficult to explain than his return and promotion, but the sources permit a possible reconstruction that can resolve some of the difficulties.

The series of events leading up to the accession finds its genesis in the last months of Valens' reign. Valens left Antioch in the spring of 378 and, on his journey to Thrace, reached Constantinople on 30 May. During his twelve days in the capital, he became extremely enraged with its citizens, who implored him to remove the Gothic threat from the walls of the city. Incensed, the emperor threatened to overturn the city and plough the site on his return from battle against the Goths (Soc. *HE* 4.38.5). The city had become disenchanted with Valens, and perhaps with the dynasty as a whole.[27] Though Valens died, the citizens of Constantinople took his threats seriously. At the end of his first speech to Theodosius, Themistius as civic orator asks the new emperor to uphold and confirm the privileges of the city:

> The great city begs of both [Theodosius and Gratian], you as lord to grant it, he as the one who made you lord, first, that it receive its champion as soon as possible and meet him before the rest of the East, and second, that all the gifts remain confirmed that your forefathers voted to it. By your forefathers I do not indiscriminately name all earlier emperors, but those highly esteemed

---

25. For the Sarmatian campaign: Them. *Or.* 14.182c, 15.198a; Auson. *grat. act.* 2.7–8.

26. Cf. Mócsy, *Pannonia and Upper Moesia*, 342.

27. Probably on religious grounds as well. Ammianus (31.11.1) remarks only that Valens experienced some popular discontent.

for mildness and philanthropy, of whom indeed you show your-
self a legitimate heir. (14.183a–b)

The city, moreover, laid claim to special consideration, or so Themistius implies:

> [The city] is present not only to ask for the things that it needs, but
> as the first to confirm the vote of the accession. . . . Of the two
> *métropoleis* of the world—I mean that of Romulus and that of
> Constantine—I would say that ours is more fit for you. (14.182a–b)

Textual problems prevent certainty about this passage and its immediate context, but the main point of what is not quoted seems to be that
emperor and city were both selected for prominence because of their
virtue.

Though his claim that Constantinople quickly supported the selection of the new emperor can bolster an argument that the city was
receptive to the accession, the statements do not indicate that Theodosius had engineered his rise to power by appealing to the city.
Themistius implies, but only implies, that Theodosius had been declared emperor before his official *dies imperii* and that he had support
at Constantinople, and probably in much of the East, as a suitable
replacement for Valens. If Theodosius recognized the possibilities and
made overtures to the East, especially the disaffected citizens of the
capital, by promising to disregard the threats of Valens, Themistius'
request is polite fiction, but important nevertheless, since emperors
most often granted privileges after specific requests.[28]

In this connection, the entry for 378 in the *Chronicon Paschale* is
interesting and problematic. The notice states that Valentinian died of
disease at Brigetio (an event of 375),[29] that Gratian named his mother
Marina Augusta (probably false),[30] that Theodosius was made Augustus on 19 January by his brother-in-law Gratian (a family relation only
true after the marriage to Galla, when Gratian was dead), and that

---

28. F. Millar, *The Emperor in the Roman World* (London, 1977), 420–34.
29. Perhaps confusing the date of Valens' death with that of Valentinian;
cf. M. Whitby and M. Whitby, *Chronicon Paschale 284–628 A.D.* (Liverpool,
1989), 49, n. 152.
30. Cf. Holum, *Theodosian Empresses*, 31, with n. 91.

Theodosius entered Constantinople on 24 November (the date given by Socrates [*HE* 5.6.6], but for the year 380). The entry is a confused composite from various sources,[31] and other problems occur in the vicinity. This text places Theodosius' expulsion of Arians, which Marcellinus Comes dates to 380 (*Chron. min.* 2:61), in 379. Nevertheless, the confusion and the indication in the *Consularia Constantinopolitana* (s.a. 380) that 14 November[32] was the day of Theodosius' entry into the capital are intriguing and may suggest a visit to the capital in November 378. Though this is beyond proof, a visit by a general after a campaign could hardly be thought unreasonable.

Another incident is equally intriguing. While waiting for Gratian to reach a decision, Theodosius dreamt that Meletius, a claimant to the episcopal throne at Antioch who had been exiled by Valens, crowned him emperor (Theod. *HE* 5.6). While the story may reveal a desire of Meletius for support from the new emperor, the opposite is more likely, since Theodosius, not Meletius, had the dream. From this, it is arguable that Theodosius appealed to certain bishops in the East, probably by promising to fight against Arianism.[33] He may have met Meletius previously at the Council of Sirmium in 375, shortly before his retirement, and later gave him the presidency of the Council of Constantinople in 381.[34]

One piece of evidence suggests that Gratian sought to undermine the support for his erstwhile general. Socrates reports that Gratian proclaimed toleration after the death of Valens. The edict was aimed at the East[35] rather than the entire empire and restored

---

31. It incorporates some statements found under the year 379 in the *Cons. Const.*

32. Different, however, only by the difference of "X."

33. Note the reference to Theodosius' expulsion of Arians in the entry for 379 in the *Chron. Pasch.* Clearly, the chroniclers are somewhat confused about the events of 378–380. On Theodosius' attempt to eliminate Arianism, cf. now J.H.W.G. Liebeschuetz, *Barbarians and Bishops: Army, Church and State in the Age of Arcadius and John Chrysostom* (Oxford, 1990), 157–54.

34. Cf. King, *Emperor Theodosius*, 36–38, for brief discussion. Holum, *Theodosian Empresses*, 18, n. 47, citing A.-M. Ritter, *Das Konzil von Konstantinopel und sein Symbol* (Göttingen, 1965), 38–40, points out that most of the bishops at the Council were adherents of Meletius, who had perhaps helped Theodosius with the list of invitations.

35. *HE* 5.2.1: Γρατιανὸς . . . καταγνούς τε θείου Οὐάλεντος τῆς περὶ τοὺς Χριστιανοὺς ὠμότητος. For discussion, cf. G. Gottlieb, *Ambrosius von Mailand*

all religious exiles with the exception of Eunomians, Photinians, and Manichees. Though Valens is credited with a similar measure in other sources,[36] Socrates places it before his account of Theodosius' accession, allowing a conclusion that Gratian attempted to lure the support of the East. He too may have traveled to Constantinople (Joh. Ant. fr. 185). Socrates also confirms the impression given by Themistius that Theodosius was judged worthy of the throne before Gratian proclaimed him.[37] This raises the question of Theodosius' responsibility. Once again, though Sozomen offers a similar statement (*HE* 7.2), the evidence does not allow certainty. The remarks, combined with Theodosius' dream, suggest intrigue, with both Gratian and Theodosius vying for support in the East. The unpopularity of Valens at Constantinople[38] and Antioch offered sufficient scope. It is not surprising to discover that religious opposition to Valens was involved.

This evidence may indicate that Theodosius presented himself to Gratian in the winter of 378 with a power base in the major cities of the East. Even if he did not engineer an acclamation as Julian had done,[39] Theodosius perhaps attempted to force Gratian's hand by consolidating his support in the brief period between his military success in 378 and his accession in 379. The attribution of his acces-

---

und Kaiser Gratian. Hypomnemata 40 (Göttingen, 1973), 71–80, who also points out that this edict is not the rescript from Sirmium that Gratian annulled on 3 August 379 (*CTh* 16.5.5).

36. Cf., for discussion, R. Snee, *GRBS* 26 (1985): 395–419, who, however, denies Socrates' ascription of such a measure to Gratian. It is possible that Valens' supposed edict was actually a pronouncement by Theodosius between the death of Valens and his accession. Sources, noting the date of Theodosius' official proclamation as emperor, might then credit an eastern edict to the previous emperor.

37. *HE* 5.2.3: Θεοδόσιον, ἄνδρα ἐκ τῶν εὐπατριδῶν τῆς Ἰσπανίας καταγόμενον πολλά τε κατὰ τοὺς πολεμίους ἀγωνισάμενον, καὶ διὰ τοῦτο ἄξιον τῆς βασιλείας ἤδη πάλαι καὶ πρὸ τῆς Γρατιανοῦ χειροτονίας ὑπὸ πάντων κριθέντα.

38. During Valens' brief visit to Constantinople in 378, the citizens, enraged at his failure to protect the suburbs of the city from the marauding Goths, had shouted in the Hippodrome, "Give us weapons and we ourselves will fight" (Soc. *HE* 4.38.4).

39. There is nothing to indicate that Theodosius had been acclaimed by his troops, but this is not impossible.

sion to Gratian would then reveal Theodosius' concern for apparent due process. His attempt to retain support in the East is indicated by religious toleration early in his reign. His first rescripts do not touch on religion, but focus instead on finance and administration, except for *CTh* 10.1.12, which allows Antioch to plant sacred cypress trees and to cut down a tree already standing. Theodosius announced his intention to accede to *mos uetus* and *constituta maiorum*, which reflect pagan propaganda and suggest that in public at least he was favorably disposed to pagan demands, as Gibbon and others have seen,[40] and to the injunctions of *paideia*.[41]

Themistius's first speech to Theodosius reflects the concerns of the early months of the reign. The orator had been ill when the first embassy from Constantinople traveled to Sirmium or Thessalonica to congratulate the new emperor and joined his compatriots later (14.180b–c). Though the oration cannot be dated precisely, it belongs to spring 379,[42] after Theodosius had left Sirmium, but before his campaigns. This is evident from the statement that the emperor had not yet begun to fight:

This army, which has not tasted pleasure, already has streamed in together voluntarily and has learned to acquire benefits by labors. It was not a poet's fable that Achilles by shouts alone threw confusion into the barbarians who were victorious earlier. For if you have not yet drawn up in battle against the guilty and have hindered their presumption simply by camping nearer and blockading them, what in all probability will those about to perish utterly endure, when they see you brandishing the spear and swaying the shield and the lightning flash of your helmet shining near? (14.181b–c)

After leaving Sirmium, Theodosius had traveled to Thessalonica, which he reached by 17 June 379 (*CTh* 10.1.12), before beginning his

40. A. Ehrhardt, *JEH* 15 (1964): 5–6. Jovian too was at first favorable to pagans in public; see chapter 6 above.

41. This treatment of Theodosius' accession is a refinement of views first outlined in my Ph.D. thesis, completed in 1989 (cf. T.D. Barnes, in *Grace, Politics and Desire. Essays on Augustine*, ed. H.A. Meynell [Calgary, 1990], 161–62, with 172, n. 26).

42. So Scholze, *Temporibus*, 50; Dagron, *Thémistios*, 23.

campaigns no later than 6 July, when he appears at Scupi (*CTh* 6.30.2). This last date is the *terminus ante quem* for *Oration* 14. No greater precision can be achieved. *CTh* 10.1.12 concerns cypress groves at Antioch and may be a response to another embassy. If so, Theodosius was still entertaining delegations in June.[43] Themistius' speech might then comfortably be dated about the same time, in May or early June.

Themistius begins by describing the effect of the accession on his illness: it immediately restored his health and drove away the weariness of old age. In fact, all citizens were looking to the new emperor as the cure for the troubles in the empire, since they expected him to restore to full health the areas devastated by the Goths. The emperor had already begun this task by moving his base of operations nearer the front, and the Goths were less presumptuous than they had been (14.180b–181c), abandoning Thrace for Illyricum.[44]

Constantinople owes the new emperor two crowns, the orator states, one of gold, which will be delivered when the emperor visits the city with the trophies of his victory against the barbarians, the other of goodwill, which remains at the capital and is also with the embassy of a city that was the first to accept Theodosius' accession. Since it became the second capital because of its virtue,[45] Constantinople is more suitable than Rome for an emperor whose accession was also based on virtue. Gratian acted like a wise old man, not a youth,[46] when he bypassed his relatives in favor of the best candidate (14.181d–182c).

Theodosius based his claim to legitimacy on the view that Gratian

43. Theodosius may have been annoyed by the number of delegations: *CTh* 12.12.7 (27 July 380) orders communities to send joint embassies of only three men.

44. For Theodosius and the Goths generally, cf. M. Pavan, *La politica gotica di Teodosio nella publicistica del suo tempo* (Rome, 1964), and Heather, *Goths and Romans*, 147–92 (150–51 for the campaign of 379).

45. I.e., it was selected and not simply the ancestral seat of Roman power.

46. It is tempting, given later comparisons of Theodosius to Trajan (cf. esp. *Epit.* 48.8), to think that Themistius is equating Gratian's selection of Theodosius to Nerva's of Trajan. This would then be the earliest comparison of the new emperor to his Spanish predecessor. Otherwise, the earliest reference is 16.205a, in 383. Note, however, that Gratian is credited with the virtue of age in his youth at 13.165d.

had selected him. Themistius accepted this, as his remark about Gratian's wisdom indicates, and mentions it a second time:

> But an emperor crowns an emperor and is not weakened in giving, but profits. For in giving honor, he acquires a partnership for his anxieties. For this reason, Gratian, seeing your virtue, did not look on age with suspicion and take into account that he as a younger would crown an older man, but that the father deliberately chosen by reason is more noble than the father by nature. Both deserve equal praise, one because he proclaimed an older man, the other because, being older, he was believed to have goodwill toward his son in the future. (14.182d–183a)

Themistius ends on a somewhat ominous note. He does not state unequivocally that Theodosius had goodwill toward Gratian, only that this existed in the popular conception. In and of itself, the statement is innocuous, but it contains a hint that Theodosius was unwilling to be anything but the leading emperor. Elsewhere, Themistius pleads with Theodosius for harmony between emperors (15.198b), implying that the opposite existed. Here, he is speaking with double intent, informing the audience that Gratian was responsible for the accession and promoting harmony by reminding Theodosius of a legitimacy based on acceptance by the senior emperor.

In the context of these two passages, Themistius discusses Theodosius' military success, in particular his success against the Sarmatians who had been ravaging the Roman side of the Danube. He states that citizens of the empire called Theodosius to the throne from the moment that he achieved this military success, noting that Gratian accepted a decree which the "occasion put to the vote in anticipation" (14.182c). The precise meaning of this phrase is difficult to determine. It recalls the words used of Jovian's accession (5.65d), where some doubts about initial legitimacy are possible.[47]

The importance of legitimacy can still be seen some years later, when Themistius refers again to the instrumental role of Gratian:

---

47. See chapter 6 for discussion.

When nearly all, both the generals and soldiers, are disheart-
ened in their minds at so many frictions of this sort and contem-
plating how this evil will turn out, and when no one is attempting to prevent it, God calls to authority the only one who is able
to hold out in such a cataclysm of evil. And Gratian is announcing the vote from above. (16.207a–b)

Theodosius' military ability and Gratian's selection are important, but
the divine now plays an important role. The necessity of Gratian's
action is no longer dictated by support from the East, but by a command from God, inherently a stronger claim and Themistius' usual
view after an emperor has successfully reached the throne.

The orator's requests, addressed, as was proper, to both emperors,[48]
follow this brief discussion of legitimacy. The first is the traditional
request that the new emperor visit the city (14.183a). Secondly, he
asks the imperial college to confirm the gifts conferred upon the city
by earlier emperors, in terms that damn Valens as an emperor without
mildness and philanthropy (14.183b) and contrast sharply with remarks made while Valens was alive.[49] Finally, the city asks Theodosius to enlarge the Senate. By granting this request, the emperor
will increase, not diminish, his treasury. Other emperors granted pil-
lars, statues, and fountains. The city is proud of these, but prefers
intangible honors. By making the city loftier with honors than Constantine had with buildings, the emperor will be in no way inferior to
the city's founder. Thus too at Rome true honors took root with the
inhabitation of the city (14.183b–d). Granting these requests, Themistius informs the emperor, will ensure that "your city will be a
second Rome, if indeed a city is men. Since now at least, we do not
very suitably receive honor for this name" (14. 184a). This last statement is uncomplimentary to Valens, typically enough at the beginning of a new dynasty, while the reference to Constantine suggests
that Themistius knew the religious views of the new emperor. The
emperor's apparently favorable attitude toward pagans in the early
years of his reign must consequently be regarded as one dictated by

48. On the complete lack of importance assigned to the younger Valentinian by Theodosius (and consequently Themistius), see later in this chapter.
49. See chapter 7.

political necessity. The case of Jovian is instructive. As for the request that the Senate be increased, Themistius was perhaps a suitable ambassador. He had held a commission to appoint new members to the Senate in the reign of Constantius and was *princeps senatus*. As so often in the past, Themistius was once again representing his city on an important embassy and performing his civic duty. Nothing is known about the outcome of this request nor why Constantinople asked for more senators. Presumably, given Themistius' continual attempts to ensure that the city's status equaled that of Rome, the number of eastern senators had fallen below the western total. Possibly, though this cannot be proved, Valens had refused to allow new senators to replace members who had died.

During the first two summers of his reign, Theodosius campaigned against the Goths and spent the intervening winter at Thessalonica. On 24 November 380, he entered the capital of the East and remained until mid 381.[50] According to Zosimus (4.33.1), he entered the city as if celebrating a triumph, and he may have been acclaimed by the population of the city.[51] Themistius did not deliver his second oration to Theodosius until 19 January 381 at the earliest. This is clear from his remark, when praising the emperor's frequent commutation of the death penalty, that the reign was in its third year (15.190b). The speech has accordingly been dated to the *dies imperii*.[52] Other indications of date offer support. At 15.185b–c, the orator notes that Theodosius was not on campaign due to the season. More importantly, he refers to a Gothic chieftain who joined Theodosius at table, submitting to the emperor's capacity for drawing Goths to himself like a magnet (15.190c–d). Constantine had honored this chieftain's father with a statue in the capital (15.191a). Themistius is the only source to mention the statue, but the Goth can only be Athanaric.[53] He had previously been hesitant to sit at the imperial

50. Seeck, *Regesten*, 255–57. Because CTh 10.10.15 dates to 16 November 380 at Thessalonica, Theodosius could not have entered Constantinople on 14 November, the date at *Cons. Const.* s.a. 380.

51. According to one manuscript of Hydatius, "*Theodosius secondo regni sui Agustus [sic] appellantur.*" Cf. Burgess, *The* Chronicle *of Hydatius and the* Consularia Constantinopolitana, 7, apparatus.

52. Scholze, *Temporibus*, 51.

53. See Thompson, *Visigoths*, 54.

table because of jealousy (15.190c), no doubt directed at Fritigern, his opponent in a recent civil war, and also a dining companion of the emperor. But Athanaric did not long eat imperial food. He entered the capital of the East on 11 January 381 and died in the city two weeks later, on 25 January (*Chron. min.* 1:243, 2:61). He was still alive when Themistius mentions him. Within the limits established by Athanaric's presence in the capital, Theodosius' *dies imperii* is the most suitable occasion for *Oration* 15.

Themistius begins his second speech for Theodosius by declining to chronicle wars, choosing instead to speak words "more peaceful than those of Homer, more imperial than those of Hesiod." As is his custom, by "plucking pure flowers from the meadows of Plato and Aristotle,"[54] he will "weave a crown of human happiness for the emperor" (15.185a). With his intention thus announced, the orator begins to work toward his theme that justice is the greatest of imperial virtues. He devotes a long section to a discussion of the dual role of rulers. They must protect the borders from external threats and the inhabitants from internal disharmony (15.185b–190a). In the process, Themistius does not fail to comment on the military prowess of both Gratian and Theodosius (15.187d), but remarks that Homer already had separated the functions of a ruler, applying military epithets to heroes like Achilles and Hector, but divine epithets, such as "nourished by Zeus," and "born of Zeus" (15.188b), to kings. After remarking that Theodosius, raised to the throne because of his military skills, knew that similarity to God was the distinguishing mark of a good emperor, Themistius points to his conclusion by quoting Homer, *Odyssey* 19.109, 111–114:[55]

> Just as, he says, of some blameless king, who, fearing god,
> upholds justice. And the black earth bears
> wheat and barley. The trees are heavy with fruit,
> it bears all things without fail, the sea provides fish
> because of good government. The people prosper under him.

---

54. Cf. 4.54b for similar flowers in 357.

55. In line 113, Themistius has πάντα instead of μῆλα. He may be quoting from Plato, *Rep.* 363b, who omits line 110, but does not have the alternate reading.

Justice and fairness, then, are the business of this art, particularly when it is godlike and divine in form (15.189a).[56] He exhorts the emperor to practice justice and mentions one further benefit. The practice of justice is a better safeguard of his throne than all the soldiers at court (15.189c–190a).[57]

Themistius has now stated his thesis and offers a greater proportion of historical material as he seeks to fulfill his dual purpose. His first goal is, as usual, to inform the audience that Theodosius was performing his duties in accordance with the philosophical position advocated in the speech. His second is directed at the emperor. By pointing out the benefits inherent in the practice of justice and fairness, Themistius hopes to induce Theodosius to continue in the same vein. The lack of emphasis on the military at a time when the emperor was celebrating his successes against the Goths is striking and suggests that Themistius was not ready to swallow wholesale the imperial propaganda on this point.[58] The orator is pointing out, as he had done during the reign of Valens, that the military function of the emperor, to which Theodosius had devoted most of his attention, was important, but should not exclude other activity. As usual, he is also attempting to attract the emperor's attention to a suggested change of policy, by treating other aspects of the reign favorably. Themistius moves back and forth between his two purposes, linking them by means of philosophical threads woven into his discourse.

He begins by pointing out that Theodosius had commuted all capital punishments meted out by the courts during the first two years of his reign (15.190b–c), an indirect, or perhaps a direct, attack on Valens. This generosity was noticed not only by subjects, but also by former enemies of the empire who now voluntarily cease their plundering and eat at the imperial table (15.190c–d). This praiseworthy disposition has led to benefits for the empire, including a possibility of avoiding combat. To secure his point, the orator refers to the emperor Antoninus Pius (in fact, Marcus Aurelius), whose practice of

---

56. Cf. *Risâlat*, pp. 103–5, for similar remarks.

57. Cf. 5.67a–b, probably based on Ael. Arist. *Or.* 35.15–19 Keil (see chapter 1).

58. Heather, *Goths and Romans*, 167, remarks this as well, but has Themistius preparing "public opinion for a change in imperial policy." He is rather alerting the emperor to another possible approach to the Gothic question.

justice gave him enough influence with God to be rewarded with rain on request when his army was dying of thirst (15.190d–191c),[59] and discusses the consequences of injustice. The plague that struck the Greek army at Troy affected the guiltless dogs and mules first, making it clear that the errors of rulers affect subjects as well (15.191c–192b).

Theodosius' justice and fairness lead to beneficence towards his subjects, including commutation of sentences of exile and execution (15.192d). Inevitably, Themistius mentions, but improves upon, the statement of Titus that he had not ruled one day because he had not done some good, suggesting that Theodosius was striving to do this each hour (15.193a). For Theodosius, the kindnesses will be as steps toward heaven, and he will receive such divine eponyms as "Savior," "Founder of cities," and "Friend to strangers and of suppliants," more worthy titles than "Germanicus" and "Sarmaticus," which derive from fear and war (15.193b–194a). Theodosius had won only one of these victory titles personally; the other is Gratian's. The sequence suggests that the college had earned the title "Germanicus" before "Sarmaticus." In 379, Gratian campaigned near the Rhine (Auson. *Act. grat.* 18.22) and probably assumed a victory title. Theodosius also fought that year, and news of victories over the Goths, Huns, and Alans reached Constantinople on 17 November 379 (*Cons. Const.* s.a. 379). Gratian had returned to Trier by 14 September (*CTh* 13.3.12), and his victory is listed first.[60]

Themistius continues his praise by providing examples of Theodosius' beneficence toward his subjects:

> The name of orphan has vanished and at present no one is fatherless, but indeed the helpless on whom some ill-starred necessity has fatefully decreed this misfortune have acquired an emperor in place of their ordinary father. You allow children to inherit all the other possessions of their ancestors; the accusations alone you do not permit, but they die with the offenders and do not outlive the fallen, nor do you exact penalties from those to be punished for earlier wrongdoings. (15.194c–d)

---

59. Cf. A. Birley, *Marcus Aurelius. A Biography,* 2nd ed. (New Haven and London, 1987), 171–74; G. Fowden, *Historia* 36 (1987): 83–95.

60. On the principle, cf. T.D. Barnes, *Phoenix* 30 (1976): 174–93; idem, *ZPE* 21 (1976): 149–55.

This passage reflects legal measures promulgated early in the reign, but, for the most part, comments on the emperor's attitude toward his subjects. Two rescripts, issued on 17 June 380 at Thessalonica, address inheritance by relatives of condemned individuals. The first, *CTh* 9.42.8, discusses persons sentenced to deportation. The fiscus was to claim half the estate of an individual with children or grandchildren. The condemned party retained one-sixth, and his descendants received one-third. Concern for children is evident in the next provision. In a case of a deportee with no children, but surviving parents, the fiscus claimed two-thirds, with the remainder divided between the individual and his parent(s). When no relatives survived, the fiscus absorbed five-sixths. In cases of treason, the fiscus appropriated five-sixths, with the remainder for children and grandchildren. The second rescript, *CTh* 9.42.9, discusses estates of persons condemned to capital punishment. Many provisions are the same, particularly when no children or grandchildren survived, that is, the fiscus received five-sixths, except in special cases. The important difference lies in the provision for children and grandchildren in the first and second rank, who would receive the entire estate. If only children of the third rank, in the male line, survived, half the estate would devolve to the fiscus.

The key to Theodosius' commutation of capital sentences lies in these rescripts. In those cases where individuals convicted of capital crimes had children, the lighter sentence of exile would guarantee the fiscus one-half the estate. Imperial kindness was thus profitable and, in effect, sold the lives of the convicted to their descendants for part of the inheritance. Though the orator pays scant attention to economic matters here, the treasury was hard pressed by the need to purchase peace from the barbarians, a policy that lies behind the orator's brief statement that the emperor sent gold to his creditors (15.192b).[61] Despite this background, the regular practice of commutation is praised by an orator who was probably aware of its economic implications. For the majority of his subjects, the emperor's new policy must have seemed generous. With one brilliant stroke, he received both honor and gold.

The rest of *Oration* 15 is devoted to the state of the empire.

---

61. On Theodosius' purchase of peace, cf., most recently, Heather, *Goths and Romans*, 158–75.

Themistius notes that the ship of state, with its two helmsmen, needs considerable knowledge and skill for guiding it in stormy waters. Obedience of rowers and all others in the ship, including the one standing in the stern, is also needed (15.194b–195c). This reference to Valentinian indicates that he did not command much respect from Theodosius. Near the end, Themistius notes that a pair of emperors, accompanied by an outrider, have a single soul and a single mind (15.198b).[62] As emperor, Valentinian was senior to Theodosius, though he was a mere boy. He was not, however, mentioned in *Oration* 14, and is unimportant in *Oration* 15. Obviously, Theodosius disregarded Valentinian from the beginning, despising him for his youth and for the Arianism of his mother Justina, the force behind the throne,[63] even after he married Galla.[64]

Themistius states that the emperors also require men who think correctly, as well as many eyes and ears, which must be healthy (15.196c–197a). These eyes and ears are not the *agentes in rebus* and informers, since Theodosius had limited their numbers CTh 6.27.3: 16 June 380) and had expressed a negative view on informers (*CTh* 10.10.12, 13: 30, 31 January 380). Rather, they are governors and other administrators. Because the emperor had addressed the question of corrupt officials (*CTh* 9.27.1; 8.15.6; 3.6.1; 9.27.2; 3.11.1: 15 January–17 June 380), Themistius' statement reflects Theodosius' practice. Before he closes the speech, Themistius refers twice to the healthy rivalry between emperors and once to Gratian's wisdom. He points to a reason for hope, since the order of the empire had not yet been overcome by the disorder of the barbarians and urges the emperors to take thought for the borders of the empire. The orator closes with a reference to philosophy, which will permit success on the Danube (15.197a–199b).

Themistius' last words indicate that the victory celebrated by Theodosius when he entered Constantinople was just that, a victory: he had not yet won the war.[65] Nearly two years later, on 3 October 382

---

62. For the theme, cf. 6.75d–76d, and Ael. Arist. *Or.* 27.22–39 Keil.

63. Theod. *HE* 5.15, states that Theodosius later wrote a letter to Valentinian advising him that his troubles with Maximus were a result of his Arianism.

64. S.I. Oost, *Galla Placidia Augusta: A Biographical Essay* (Chicago, 1968), 46–51, esp. 47, is inclined to allow Theodosius some feeling toward Valentinian.

65. So Matthews, *Western Aristocracies*, 92; and cf. the discussion by Heather, *Goths and Romans*, 165–68.

(*Cons. Const.* s.a. 382), Saturninus concluded terms of peace with the Goths. For this, he was rewarded with the consulship for 383. On 1 January 383, Themistius delivered *Oration 16*, a *gratiarum actio* for the peace and for the consulship of the general.[66] The consulship and the opportunity for the speech provided Themistius with an occasion to pay in full a debt he had owed to the new consul for more than thirty years (16.199c–200c). Saturninus, it appears, had introduced Themistius to the emperor, just as he had done in the reign of Constantius.[67] The speech, delivered on behalf of the Senate in its chambers, was attended by Theodosius, Saturninus, and Richomeres, the praetorian prefect Postumianus, the *magister officiorum* Palladius, the *comes sacrarum largitionum* Cynegius,[68] and some quaestors[69] (16.201b).

Themistius begins with the remark that he had been inclined to put down his pen because of weariness and old age. The achievement of peace, however, presented an opportunity that could not pass unnoticed (16.199c–d). Theodosius' peace treaty with the Goths allowed barbarians to settle in Roman territory, following his policy of dividing and assimilating them. Many Romans were as displeased with this arrangement as they had been during the reign of Valens, preferring instead to see the enemy totally defeated.[70] Themistius had argued for more humane measures in the previous reign, and it is possible that he was called out of semiretirement to promote Theodosius' interests on a subject which he had addressed previously. His friendship with the architect of peace suggests that the force behind any such summons was Saturninus himself.

Themistius praises Theodosius' selection of Saturninus, emphasizing the surprising proclamation of a private citizen in a year for which the emperor was widely expected to hold the office personally (16.203a) or, following the practice of recent emperors with infant children, to grant it to Arcadius (16.204b–c), who was to

66. For the date, Scholze, *Temporibus*, 52–54.
67. See chapter 4.
68. On whom, cf. J.F. Matthews, *JTS* 18 (1967): 438–46.
69. Cf. Scholze, *Temporibus*, 53–54, on the presence of these court officials.
70. On Theodosius' arrangements, cf. E.A. Thompson, *Historia* 12 (1963): 107–9 = *Romans and Barbarians* (Madison, 1982), 40–42. On the different responses, cf. Pavan, *La politica gotica di Teodosio*; Dagron, *Thémistios*, 95–119; and the more recent treatment by Heather, *Goths and Romans*, 158–75. On Themistius' views, cf. also Daly, *Historia* 21 (1972): 351–79.

become Augustus on 19 January 383.[71] Theodosius had already honored several relatives with the consulship, including his uncle and another kinsman, in 381 and 382,[72] with no break between them and Saturninus, as Themistius remarks (16.203d). Since he states that earlier emperors were often consuls during anniversary years (16.205b), Themistius' expectation of an imperial consulship is perhaps based on the practice of Valens and Valentinian, who held the office twice in each five-year period, but were careful to hold office in quinquennial and decennial years. Valens and Valentinian established a pattern broken by Theodosius when he gave the consulship to Saturninus. Interestingly, Theodosius was never consul more than once in a quinquennial period and sometimes not at all, holding the office in 380, 388, and 393.[73]

The next considerable portion of the speech is a discussion of the merits of Saturninus as general, with an emphasis on the benefits of peace. After noting that the jealousy that normally barks at those in positions of power had not afflicted Saturninus at all, Themistius indicates his desire, as a lover of peace, to omit the details of the general's actions (16.205d–206d).[74] He describes the situation in Thrace at the beginning of the reign and mentions the emperor's view that Roman strength lay not in the apparatus of war, but in divine wisdom and the ability to persuade the enemy to make peace. For this reason, he sent Saturninus, who had a similar attitude, to this theater of war, equipped

---

71. Themistius calls Arcadius "the esteemed light of the world" and an "Alexander" (16.204c). The infant consuls in question are Varronianus, son of Jovian, in 364, and Valentinianus Galates, son of Valens, in 369. On those occasions, Themistius was considerably more generous to infants as consuls than he is here.

72. There is some dispute about these consulships. Fl. Eucherius, cos. 381, was the uncle of Theodosius, with a Syagrius as colleague. In the following year, Claudius Antonius and Fl. Syagrius were the consuls, one a kinsman of Theodosius. Two questions have been raised. First, which of the consuls in 382 was the kinsman of the emperor? Second, which of the Syagrii was the consul in 381 and which in 382? Cf. for recent discussions with different solutions and references to earlier treatments, Martindale, *Historia* 16 (1967): 254–56; A. Demandt, *BZ* 64 (1971): 39–45; and R.S. Bagnall et al., *The Consuls of the Later Roman Empire* (Atlanta, 1987), for the years in question.

73. For similar remarks on quinquennial consulships, cf. Burgess, *NC* 148 (1988): 77–96.

74. See chapter 7 for this attitude during the reign of Valens.

with forbearance, mildness, and philanthropy (16.207b–208d). The general's appearance convinced the barbarians to cease their plundering and to follow him to the emperor, drawn by Saturninus' ability to persuade, which Themistius compares favorably to Orpheus's music (16.208d–209c). The orator naturally includes Theodosius in this discussion, commenting on his philanthropy and its salutary effect on the empire and the barbarians (16.209c–211a).

Themistius closes the section on benefits of peace with an eloquent reiteration of his view on warfare against barbarians:

> Grant that it was possible to destroy with ease and to do everything that might be possible for us and not experience any harm in return. . . . Would it be better to fill Thrace with bodies or farmers? To show it full of graves or of men? To walk through wild or cultivated fields? To number the slain or the ploughmen? To resettle the Phrygians and Bithynians, if it comes to this, or to cohabit with those whom we have subdued? I hear from those who come from there that they have now made the iron of their swords and armor into mattocks and sickles,[75] and that they greet Ares at a distance and worship Demeter and Dionysus. (16.211a–b)

The philosopher points out that assimilation of enemies was standard practice. Gauls can no longer be called barbarians, but are Romans, and Massinissa was preserved alive after his capture and lived to help Rome against other enemies.[76] Moreover, the achievement of peace has returned prosperity to the empire (16.211c–212c). These remarks are similar to some points in *Oration* 10.[77]

Themistius closes *Oration* 16 with a few words about the justice and mildness of the emperor, repeating some of the themes of *Oration* 15. He encourages Theodosius to feel confident that the remaining problems, with Persia and Armenia, can be resolved in the same way as

---

75. Almost certainly an allusion to the Old Testament (Joel 3.10; Micah 4.3), not registered by Downey, *Stud. Pat.* 5 (1962): 480–88.

76. Themistius uses Massinissa at 7.94d as an example in his plea for clemency for the followers of Procopius. Themistius is the only source to state that the Numidian was ever captured.

77. See chapter 7. Cf. Heather, *Goths and Romans*, 159–60, for the Goths' contribution of taxes and soldiers by the terms of the treaty of 382.

those in Thrace had been. Circumstances on the eastern borders bore
out Themistius' prediction. In 379, Shapur II had died and was succeeded by his brother Artaxerxes, whose unpopularity may have been
known to Themistius. A revolt of nobles in 383 removed Artaxerxes in
favor of Shapur III, son of the previous king.[78] In the following year,
Shapur sent an embassy to Theodosius (*Cons. Const.* s.a. 384). Themistius' final remarks refer to a desire to teach the lessons of *Oration*
15 to Arcadius and to be his Phoenix (16.212c–213b).[79]

The speech is largely a reiteration of themes found in earlier panegyrics. Naturally, Themistius' philosophical positions are adapted to
the new historical situation. The orator did not, however, exercise his
ingenuity to find new items to praise. More importantly, he did not
find it necessary to change imperial policy, as he had done in the
previous reign. In particular, his views on the benefits of peace allowed him to promote the treaty with the Goths enthusiastically. A
combination of old age and his agreement with Theodosius' policies
lies behind the lack of originality.

For about a year after the delivery of *Oration* 16, Themistius was
silent. Early in 384, however, a flurry of activity begins when the
philosopher held the urban prefecture briefly. His tenure of office
forced Themistius once again to defend himself and perhaps to re-
sign, though short terms were not unusual. His first speech of this
period, *Oration* 17, expresses his gratitude for the prefecture and must
date to his first few days in office. The speech concentrates on the
high position granted to philosophy, but notes as well that a true
philosopher does not refuse suitable office. He states that he had
undertaken ten embassies outside the city and gives examples of
other philosophers active in the political arena, including Arrian, Rusticus, Thrasea, Priscus, Bibulus,[80] Favonius, Xenophon, Socrates,
Plato, Pittacus, Bias, Cleobulus, and Archytas of Tarentum (17.215a–
c). These remarks represent a stance vis-à-vis some contemporaries

---

78. Cf. *PLRE*, 1:111, 803.

79. Cf. Themistius' similar remarks about Apollo and Achilles to Valentinianus Galates (9.123c) and Gratian (13.173d). There is no evidence that
Themistius ever taught Arcadius.

80. A conjecture of Harduin for Βίβος, accepted by Dindorf in his edition.

who accused him of debasing his profession by involving himself in political life.

The dates of both the prefecture and the speeches relevant to it are problematic. Seeck places the beginning of the prefecture in autumn 384.[81] Others propose dates earlier in 384[82] or even in 383.[83] Clearchus, Themistius' predecessor, was in office in September 384, if a date in the subscription to *CTh* 6.2.14 was read correctly by Cuiacius,[84] though this assumption can be avoided by postulating that another Clearchus,[85] or the same Clearchus for a second time, became prefect when Themistius left office, or that the rescript offers other problems.[86]

The speeches themselves offer sufficient indications of date. While in office,[87] the philosopher felt a need to defend, with *Oration* 31, his position as president of the Senate. This position was held by the urban prefect ex officio and is not the same as *princeps senatus*, which Themistius had been since the reign of Constantius.[88] He delivered the speech in the Senate, at the request of senators to discuss the accusations in public (31.352a–b). To answer the charges, he chose a time when the law provided an armistice to individuals harshly disposed toward each other, "the holy month of the year" (31.352b: τὴν ἱερομηνίαν τοῦ ἔτους). While this "holy month" could be the beginning of the calendar year,[89] reference to judicial inactivity probably indicates Lent. In 380, Theodosius had given a rescript prohibiting the investigation of criminal cases during the forty days (Quadragesima) before the Paschal season (*CTh* 9.35.4), and other rescripts, admittedly later, close the courts entirely during the seven days before and after Easter (e.g., *CTh* 2.8.19: 7 August 389).[90] If "holy month" means this period, as is

81. *Briefe*, 305–6.

82. Dagron, *Thémistios*, 11–12.

83. Scholze, *Temporibus*, 54–56; Schneider, *Die 34. Rede des Themistios*, 42–53.

84. The basis for Seeck's view.

85. So Scholze, *Temporibus*, 58.

86. As Seeck, *Geschichte*, 5:514, later did.

87. Seeck, *Briefe*, 306; Scholze, *Temporibus*, 57; Dagron, *Thémistios*, 26.

88. For discussion, see chapter 4.

89. Harduin, p. 703 Dindorf; Scholze, *Temporibus*, 57.

90. So Seeck, *Briefe*, 306, pointing out that the festival can hardly be pagan; cf. Dagron, *Thémistios*, 26, n. 136. Constitutions 2–17 (between 3 July 321 and November 386) of this title of the *Codex Theodosianus* on holidays are not extant.

likely,[91] the philosopher delivered the speech in February or March 384. Since Themistius refers in *Oration* 18 to the sixth year of the reign (18.217d) and is in office, *Oration* 31 cannot be as late as Lent 385.[92] In the speech, Themistius explains his choice of a political expression for his philosophy and lists precedents from history, as he had done often. He mentions his relations with emperors from Constantius to Theodosius, Jovian excepted, emphasizing the effect of philosophy and the honors that he received from emperors and colleagues.[93]

Oration 31 is weak and does not answer the charges. Themistius soon made a second attempt with *Oration* 34, but first delivered *Orations* 18 and 19. The context of these two speeches is the emperor's apparent attempt to deal with Maximus, who had forcibly replaced Gratian in the West. *Oration* 18, delivered while Themistius was in office,[94] refers to this "campaign" of summer 384, and it is clear that Themistius was to become the "guardian" of the emperor's son, whom, at the end of the speech, he invites to receive him (18.224b–225c). Because the "campaign" is complete (18.220d), the speech may postdate the emperor's return on or before 16 September (*CTh* 7.8.3).[95] Alternatively, the emperor, attested at Beroea[96] on 31 August (*CTh* 12.1.107), need only have been on a journey back from the feint at Maximus, without necessarily intending to return to the capital immediately. Since Theodosius is attested at Heraclea from 10 June to 25 July and was not at the capital after 6 May 384, the "campaign" may have occurred in May/June 384, with a visit to the Danubian regions thereafter. This chronology would allow a date for the speech in June, July, or August. The invitation to the emperor's son makes a date early in the summer more likely, since guardianship of the boy was probably limited to the period of the emperor's absence. The son in

---

91. The word ἱερομηνίαν refers to the Easter period at Greg. Nyss. *Ep.* 4 (= *PG* 46, 1025), but to the beginning of the calendar year at Soz. *HE* 2.3.

92. So Seeck, *Briefe*, 306. Bouchery, "Contribution," 207–8, who disputes the relevance of *CTh* 9.35.4, dates the speech to Lent 385, but for different reasons and thinks that Themistius was no longer in office.

93. For discussion of the speech, cf. Méridier, *Le philosophe*, 93–100.

94. So Scholze, *Temporibus*, 55, citing 18.224a–b.

95. So Seeck, *Briefe*, 305, who, however, places the campaign in November/December 384.

96. A reasonable and probably necessary emendation for the transmitted Verona; cf. T.D. Barnes, *JRA* 2 (1989): 257.

question must be Arcadius and cannot be Honorius:[97] the philosopher refers to only one son and calls him the "eponym of the god skilled in words" (18.225b), a reference to Arcadian Hermes. The speech was probably delivered before Honorius' birth on 9 September 384.[98]

Beginning from the argument that a good practitioner of any skill needs to follow that pursuit, Themistius notes that Theodosius had not been pleased with a Boeotian orator,[99] who had omitted philosophy in his speech. In contrast, the emperor had the seeds of philosophy within himself; this allowed him to conquer the Goths not with weapons, but with counsel alone,[100] and to practice good deeds for the empire and its subjects. This attention to philosophy gave Themistius two reasons for joy. First, the emperor had entrusted his son to him. Second, philosophy had been granted a lofty position (18.216d–219d).

The emperor's good deeds were so continuous, Themistius states, that he cannot include them in speeches before new deeds must take their place. On some occasions, the thought alone was worthy of praise, even if the action was not completed. Such is the case in the recent campaign toward the Rhine to avenge the death of Gratian and recover his remains. In the view of some contemporaries, nothing had been done, but the intention was splendid and royal. Achilles, by merely raising the war cry, achieved results (18.219d–221a). Themistius is referring here to a westward journey by Theodosius, who had been at the capital since autumn 381,[101] in summer 384, as a show of force against Maximus, with whom he

---

97. As Seeck, *Briefe,* 305, thinks, placing too much literal emphasis on the remark (18.224c) that the son was to come to the philosopher directly from the birth pains of his mother, his cradle, and his baby clothes.

98. So Harduin (pp. 634–35 Dindorf). Seeck, *Briefe,* 305; Bouchery, "Contribution," 206, n. 9, (who points out that Honorius does not appear in *Or.* 19 either); and Dagron, *Thémistios,* 24, do not feel that this is important and date the speech to the winter of 384/5. None of these interpretations note the reference to Hermes. Since Themistius mentions the winter sailing of the corn ships (18.221b–c), the earlier date may be thought problematic.

99. This orator cannot be identified. This reference need not indicate that Theodosius had returned.

100. One might compare the somewhat similar praise of Constantius for his victory over Vetranio; see chapter 4.

101. In fact, other than a brief campaign in 381, since November 380; cf. Seeck, *Regesten,* 255–65.

soon came to terms.[102] It is likely that Theodosius had no intention of removing Maximus at this time. Coins of Maximus minted at Constantinople permit no alternative to the view that Theodosius accepted Maximus as a legitimate emperor[103] and suggest that he was not dismayed by the death of Gratian. Further, Theodosius did not adopt measures to protect Valentinian, challenged by Maximus in 387,[104] until desire for his colleague's sister Galla, cleverly inflamed by her mother Justina, forced him to avenge Gratian as the price of her hand.[105] On no other occasion did Valentinian and his court, or even the dynasty, exercise any influence on Theodosius after his return from retirement.

The philosopher next briefly treats the emperor's policy on finance. He indicates that taxes had not increased and that the emperor was not ashamed to undertake responsibility for the corn supply. In addition, Theodosius had beautified the city with a variety of works, which were not yet complete, and had enlarged the circuit circumscribed by the city wall, rivaling Constantine's original expansion of Byzantium (18.221a–223b).[106] Themistius also remarks that Theodosius' attention to philosophy drove the effects of old age from the philosopher's limbs and stirred him to assume the city prefecture, not for personal honor, but to show that the emperor felt about human

---

102. On Theodosius' relations with Maximus, cf. Matthews, *Western Aristocracies*, 172–82, and C.E.V. Nixon, *Pacatus: Panegyric to the Emperor Theodosius* (Liverpool, 1987), 72–91.

103. Cf. Grumel, *REB* 12 (1954), 19–25; J.W. Pearce, in *RIC*, 9:xxii–xxiii, 233; and most recently, H.R. Baldus, *Chiron* 14 (1984): 175–92.

104. Zos. 4.44.1, makes it clear that Theodosius still had no intention of removing Maximus when he conferred with Valentinian and Justina at Thessalonica; cf. Paschoud's comments ad loc.

105. Oost, *Galla Placidia Augusta*, 46–48, and Holum, *Theodosian Empresses*, 45–46, put greater emphasis on political considerations than on the story retailed by the hostile Zosimus (4.43.2–44.4), but Galla was incontestably Arian, and passion must have played an important part in Theodosius' willingness to marry her. Holum (48) remarks that Galla at least must have renounced her Arianism before her marriage; Enßlin, *SitzBayAcadWiss* (1953), Heft 2, 56, converts the whole family.

106. For a brief discussion of Theodosius' building program, cf. Matthews, *Western Aristocracies*, 118–19; cf. also the works of Mango and Dagron cited in chapter 3.

happiness as Plato did. He closes the speech with the invitation to Arcadius, whom he asks to accept him as a guide to the teachings of Plato and Aristotle (18.223c–225b).

The last of Themistius' panegyrics is *Oration* 19, delivered in the Senate. The speech offers little evidence for its date, but does not mention Honorius, whose omission in a speech that promoted dynastic policy would be beyond forgiveness.[107] Themistius seems not to be prefect, and Theodosius was probably in the audience. This dates the speech to the very brief period between Theodosius' return and Honorius' birth. The orator does not mention his duties as the guardian of Arcadius, whom he mentions twice, each time in connection with the empress Flacilla, who had become Augusta before the death of Gratian (19.231a, 228b).[108] Thus, Themistius, who held the prefecture for only a few months (34.11), left before 9 September 384 the office he had assumed early in the year. The prefecture itself was largely uneventful, except for an unproved accusation that Themistius was responsible for a food shortage in the capital (34.13).

Uncharacteristically, Themistius is silent on the West, other than a remark that the East bows down to Theodosius and the West is not disturbed (19.227c).[109] Valentinian, it is true, does not appear in *Oration* 18, but this emperor is never given any significance, and that speech does mention the death of Gratian and the show of force that lay behind Theodosius' journey toward the Rhine. Themistius could hardly have failed to do so when the emperor was away. In *Oration* 19, Theodosius and his family are the only members of the imperial college to appear, and the others, Valentinian and Maximus, do not seem to exist, omissions due to Theodosius' dynastic policy. It was impossible to mention any conclusion of terms with Maximus, since the failure to avenge Gratian would place Theodosius' dynastic plans in a

---

107. Seeck, *Briefe*, 304, followed by Dagron, *Thémistios*, 24, dates the speech to the first eight months of 384, but had dated the beginning of the prefecture to the autumn of 384, eliminating the problem of the orator's failure to mention his office. At *Regesten*, 153, Seeck makes Themistius prefect in August. Scholze, *Temporibus*, 62–66, dates the speech to the winter of 385/6, as does Stegemann, "Themistios," 1646.

108. For discussion, Holum, *Theodosian Empresses*, 29–42

109. On the reasons for the omission of Constans in *Or.* 1, see chapter 4.

negative light. After his return, the emperor made it clear that he did not want the subject mentioned.[110]

The speech is devoted to philanthropy and offers little that is new. The orator begins from a different stance, quoting the oracle that indicated confusion about the mortal or divine status of Lycurgus of Sparta and making the same point about Theodosius (19.225c–228a). As usual, he offers a catalog of virtues headed by philanthropy, which alone makes an emperor similar to God (19.226d–227a). After briefly noting that Theodosius had honored his wife Flacilla and son Arcadius, the orator returns to his main theme before once again commenting on the dynastic policy of the emperor (19.228b–231a).[111] The rest of the speech is a discussion of the good qualities of Theodosius' reign (19.231b–233c).

It is perhaps fitting that the last of Themistius' extant speeches is *Oration* 34, his own summary of his life and career. No longer prefect (34.11), Themistius felt a need to answer his critics again, in a final attempt to justify his tenure of the prefecture and especially to respond to an epigram of Palladas (*AP* 11.292) directed against him.[112] The speech, whose date is not certain, but which probably belongs to the early months of 385,[113] reviews concepts that allowed him to hold office despite the view in some quarters that philosophers were to avoid politics. In his old age, Themistius is clearly proud of his career and perhaps a little weary of the complaints about the role that he had played in the political life of the empire for thirty years: he offers no new arguments. At the age of about sixty-eight, he felt no need to exercise his ingenuity in his own defense. He could hardly expect to be asked to serve the emperors once more. Indeed, his remarks on his own weakness and old age from the beginning of the reign may mean

110. In *Or.* 18, Themistius points out that the trip to the West might *seem* to have accomplished nothing.

111. 19.230b–c appears to refer to a conspiracy against Theodosius; cf. also Lib. *Or.* 1. 241. On this, cf. Barnes, *HSCP* 79 (1975): 331; and Norman, *Libanius' Autobiography*, 218–19.

112. On whom cf. A. Cameron, *CQ* 15 (1965): 215–29, esp. 219–25.

113. Seeck, *Briefe*, 306; Méridier, *Le philosophe*, 101 (in the early months of the year); and Dagron, *Thémistios*, 26, propose 385. Scholze, *Temporibus*, 58, and Stegemann, "Themistios," 1646, suggest the autumn of 384. The former group thinks that *Or.* 34 is the philosopher's last extant speech; the others do not. Schneider, *Die 34. Rede des Themistios*, 42–53, also discusses the date of the speech, concluding (53) that it belongs between 7 February and 6 June 384.

that his entire service under this emperor was more a duty than a pleasure.

As he had done many times before, Themistius discusses the history of philosophy and its necessity for the human race. He concludes this discussion with some remarks about Aristotle and Plato, pointing especially to Aristotle's views on philosophy and actions (34.1–6). His attitude at the end of his life's work has not changed from that expressed in his *protrepticus* to Julian.[114] Moreover, he reiterates the point that philosophers may legitimately serve good emperors. He notes that Theodosius brought philosophy into the palace, as Hadrian, Marcus Aurelius, and Antoninus Pius had done, and asked philosophers to follow the examples of Arrian and Rusticus, leave their books, and serve the state (34.7–10). Themistius also explains his acceptance of the city prefecture, which he had rejected in previous reigns,[115] on the grounds that Theodosius was a good ruler. Throughout this section, he discusses his relations with emperors and lists the honors received from them and from his senatorial colleagues (34.11–16).

The rest of the speech (34.17–30) is, in effect, another panegyric of Theodosius, designed to support the argument already stated. For example, the emperor commutes sentences of death and is beneficent, and orphans are no longer fatherless.[116] The main purpose of this list of imperial virtues, which goes on for some time, occurs early in the discussion. Themistius insists (34.19) that he had not lowered philosophy by association with the emperor, but raised it. This is a direct response to the epigram of Palladas, who had accused the philosopher of dragging philosophy down by using the silver-plated carriage that city prefects used.[117] In the final analysis, Themistius is attempting to portray the unity of his life and work as a politician and as a philosopher. Nothing is known about Themistius for the next few years, but he appears once more in a letter of Libanius to Calliopius (*Ep.* 18), which dates to about April or May of 388 and indicates that the philosopher was still alive. That Themistius is not mentioned

---

114. See chapter 5 for discussion.
115. For discussion, see chapter 4.
116. See the discussion of *Or.* 15 in this chapter for these items.
117. Cf. Dagron, *Thémistios*, 50–51.

again[118] does not preclude the possibility that he lived for a few more years, but it is likely that he died soon after Libanius wrote these words. The sophist wrote often to friends at the capital during the next few years, and a reference to Themistius might be expected. Conversely, the death of an acquaintance and sometime friend ought to have occasioned a remark. The only certainty is that Themistius lived to his early seventies, an old man who had lived a full life as one of the leading figures in the East for some forty years, attaining the second peak of his career during the reign of Theodosius, only a few years before his death. His life was a combination of philosophy and politics, a combination that he saw as a unified whole, though contemporaries did not always agree.

---

118. Cf. Seeck, *Briefe*, 306.

9

Epilogue

Graecus rhetor, quod genus stultorum amabilissimum est, Seneca the Elder once wrote (*Contr.* 10.5.25) when discussing a remark of an orator named Aemilianus. Some of Themistius' contemporaries probably thought of him in this way. Yet it is by now clear that Themistius was hardly a fool. He had thought very carefully about the changes in the empire, about the consequences of the new stability established by Diocletian and the Christian empire of Constantine, and attempted to reconcile the transformed Roman world with the injunctions of *paideia*. His response, not unreasonably, was to eliminate religion as an essential part of the cultural heritage, since religion, above all else, separated one group in late imperial society from the other. Language, literature, the philosophical heritage, and other traditions were the same for Christian and non-Christian alike in the Roman East, and, Themistius thought, a consensus of the elite, and of the governed, was possible on that basis.

To promote this concept as best he could, Themistius chose to operate in the public sphere. Unlike contemporary philosophers, he delivered speeches to large audiences, on philosophical and imperial topics. He addressed emperors frequently, with panegyrics designed as much to elicit responses as to flatter rulers for the sake of personal gain. Indeed, he refused, whenever he could, the tangible expressions of gratitude offered on a number of occasions. Not that Themistius cared nothing for himself. He is not averse to reminding audiences from time to time of the high esteem in which the emperors held him and exhibited considerable pride in his various accomplishments. But Libanius, for example, is far more boastful in his *Autobiography (Or.* 1) and rather more abrasive in his claims for his, it must be admitted, rather minor successes. The sophist achieved little for his city and nothing for the empire; he was, in fact, a drain on the treasury or wanted to be, by attempting to collect an official salary from Constantinople while teaching at Antioch. He is a considerably less sympathetic figure than Themistius, who was not always successful either, but nevertheless gained many advantages for his city and perhaps for the empire; the latter depends heavily on the interpretation of the history of the East in the fourth century.

It is beyond doubt that Themistius was influential in the transformation of Constantinople from an important imperial city to the new capital of the East. Though the impetus for this metamorphosis did not come from him alone, he was the most eloquent ambassador, as well as the chosen representative, of the city's elite. This fact alone makes his importance and influence certain; his fellow senators would not have selected him unless they had confidence in his ability to achieve their goals or to make the best attempt possible. Debates with opponents are thus only part of the story. A considerable portion of the pre-357 Senate must have supported him, if only because Constantius, in his letter to senators, had seemed amenable to Themistius' influence. The larger Senate of the late 350s must have been even more supportive, especially in the early stages, since many members were chosen by Themistius himself.

In short, the philosopher was highly regarded in his own day, and this is more important than modern attitudes. If his views and actions do not accord well with modern tastes, Themistius cannot be held responsible. Panegyrics were a fact of life in the fourth century and endemic; even governors of provinces were touted on every possible occasion as quintessential examples of humanity. Modern students of the period are perhaps fortunate that the extant corpus of literature does not include every panegyric ever delivered. Conversely, however, the survival of a larger body of these speeches would put Themistius' work into a different perspective, and he could more easily be judged by the standards of his own generation. Dissidence and the attempt to effect changes would be more visible. Themistius' panegyrics are in fact no more flattering than those delivered by Julian or Libanius, Mamertinus or Pacatus, though his topics differ in many ways.

A fair assessment of Themistius must pay tribute to his intent. For Themistius was above all a humanitarian. All his precepts, on philanthropy, peace, generosity, religion, and administration, urge moderation from emperors and from his contemporaries. With flattery that was both expected of him and designed to engage the attention of emperors, Themistius actively attempted to change their views. He was not always successful, but the expectation of total success is unrealistic. He should be given credit for his successes, and for the attempt to achieve positive results even when he failed. This does not mean that a reader cannot be frustrated by his speeches from time to time or see flattery where it does exist. But an understanding of his intent and the recognition that his speeches reflect the practice of his age should do much to mitigate the harshness so typical of assessments of Themistius in the past. Not only in the past, but also in the present: the most recent (brief) discussion of Themistius suggests that he was basically a propagandist for a series of regimes and a dissembler of that fact.[1]

Without detailed information about Themistius' detractors in the fourth century, it is difficult to decipher their motives. Jealousy of his success no doubt played a part, but the role he was playing at Constantinople was more provocative. Sophists and philosophers had always been expected to represent their cities, but Themistius was doing something more. As Constantinople became the eastern capital, civic duty mingled with imperial politics, and the independence of other cities was threatened. These were the most important issues in the early debate. Themistius cooperated with the emperors and their courts; his opponents disapproved, and on one point at least, they were correct: philosophers had rarely cooperated with emperors as harmoniously as Themistius was doing. But the reality had changed; the second century had long since disappeared. Philosophers, sophists, and the curial class of the cities could not turn back time. Some chose instead to oppose what they could, others to withdraw from society. Themistius opted for involvement and a voice, not always a powerful one, in the process of change. Opponents objected more to this choice than to Themistius' philosophical views on other issues, at least in the early stages of his career. He was, from their perspective, abandoning the old *paideia*. Themistius himself rejected this charge. For him, *paideia* was alive, renewed in its transformation to take account of the new reality. In the final analysis, he was more successful than they, but even he could not stem the Christian usurpation and, ultimately, rejection of *paideia*.[2]

---

1. Heather and Matthews, *Goths*, 13–26.

2. Cf. my review of Brown, *Power and Persuasion*, to appear in *Studies in Medieval and Renaissance History*, for the suggestion that Christians in the end transformed *paideia* beyond recognition or simply abandoned it.

With the exception of a short term as city prefect twenty-five years after the founding of the office at Constantinople, Themistius eschewed positions in the bureaucracy. His forum for prominence was the Senate, the institution he himself perhaps created and certainly enlarged. As was the case even with such prominent representatives of the Second Sophistic as Herodes Atticus and Aelius Aristides, interaction with the emperors was inevitable. Themistius' relations with the imperial court were at first the interactions of a leading civic politician with the central government. Because his city, Constantinople, became a capital after 357, his speeches, his ideas, and his private discussions with emperors and their advisers took on a wider imperial significance. Consequently, he was occasionally able to carry some influence with his emperors. More often, his civic status fell prey to the imperial status of officials like praetorian prefects, *magistri officiorum*, and *comites*, who counseled emperors on every aspect of the empire. In the final analysis, Themistius as civic politician did what he could for his city and the empire. The importance of his role in the events of the fourth century should not, on that account, be minimized. On the contrary, in thirty years, Themistius achieved for Constantinople what few civic politicians had accomplished for their own cities during the entire history of the empire. In the same vein, his influence on imperial politics, often less than that of others at any given moment, extended over a long period. In some important ways, he was thus the most significant politician outside of the emperors and their court officials during the period of his active service as a senator.

Throughout the entire period, Themistius remained a philosopher. Unlike his contemporaries and, indeed, most others in this profession since the beginning of the empire, he chose to operate in the public domain. The preceding chapters have concentrated more on his activity as a public figure and less on his philosophy per se. But the philosopher always lies behind the public figure and at no great distance. Philosophy is implicit everywhere in his speeches and explicit often, and the repetition of his views from reign to reign is evidence more of consistency than of some limited range of perspectives. He could adapt when the situation demanded it, but even then his basic stance did not change.

We may end where we began, with the author of the hypothesis to

Oration 4. Themistius was a *politikos philosophos*, that is, a philosopher engaged in public life. He was true to both occupations, but has generally been appreciated for neither. This book has attempted to redress the balance.

Appendices

Appendix 1

The Philosophical Works and Extant Speeches of Themistius

Themistius' purely philosophical work is not important to an understanding of his political career. The intricacies of his views on the intellect, for example, are significant to a history of philosophical inquiry,[1] but help little in depicting Themistius as philosopher and politician simultaneously in late imperial society. Instead, his vocation as a philosopher is the salient point. Nevertheless, a brief description of his philosophical works and of his speeches may be useful.[2] According to Photius (*Bibl.* Cod. 74), Themistius wrote two kinds of works on Aristotle; he describes these as ὑπομνήματα and μεταφράσεις, the latter on the *Analytica posteriora*, the *de anima*, the *Physica*, and others. In addition, he mentions exegetical works on Plato. The *Souda*, s.v. Θεμίστιος, calls the works on Aristotle παραφράσεις, listing the *Physica*, the *Analytica posteriora*, the *de anima*, and the *Categoriae*, and does not include treatments of Plato. Themistius at one point calls his writings συγγράμματα (23.294d) and refers to his work on the *Categoriae*, *Physica*, and *Analytica priora*. *Paraphrases* of the *Analytica posteriora*, *De anima* and *Physica* are extant in Greek versions,[3] but the

1. Themistius is, however, not mentioned in A.H. Armstrong, ed., *The Cambridge History of Later Greek and Early Medieval Philosophy* (Cambridge, 1970). For Themistius' views on the soul and intellect, cf. Blumenthal, *Phronesis* 21 (1976): 82–83; idem, in *Arktouros*, 391–400 (revised in *Aristotle Transformed*, 113–23); G. Verbeke, *Thémistius: Commentaire sur le traité de l'âme d'Aristote; Traduction de Guillaume de Moerbeke.* Corpus latinum Commentariorum in Aristotelem Graecorum 1 (Louvain, 1957), ix–lxii; and Schroeder and Todd, *Two Greek Aristotelian Commentators*, 37–39, with literature at 37, n. 123. Professor Todd has kindly sent me a draft of a complete translation of the *Paraphrase* of the *de anima*.

2. For a fuller account, Dagron, *Thémistios*, 14–16, on which the rest of this paragraph is based.

3. All edited by L. Spengel, *Themistii Paraphrases Aristotelis Librorum quae supersunt*, 2 vols. (Leipzig, 1866), and in *CAG*: *Analytica posteriora*, V, 1

Categoriae is lost, as is the *Topica*, attested in the *Paraphrase* of the *Analytica*.⁴ *Paraphrases* of the *de caelo* and Book 12 of the *Metaphysica* are extant in Hebrew, with the latter and parts of *de anima* preserved in Arabic as well.⁵ Another group of *Paraphrases* preserved under the name of Themistius was probably written by Sophonias much later.⁶

On the easy assumption that Photius' μεταφράσεις mean the *Paraphrases*, his ὑπομνήματα and references to exegetical works on Plato remain problematic, since no trace of these has survived. Photius is probably mistaken⁷ about works he had not read.⁸ The commentaries on Aristotle are similarly outside his personal knowledge (εἰς πάντα τὰ Ἀριστοτελικὰ φέρονται ὑπομνήματα), though the remark may refer to *Paraphrases* he had not seen. In short, it seems clear that Themistius wrote only *Paraphrases*.⁹ The solution to Photius' remarks may lie elsewhere. In *Oration* 4, Themistius praises Constantius for expanding the library at Constantinople by providing funds for the

---

(ed. M. Wallies); *Physica*, V, 2 (ed. H. Schenkl); *de anima*, V, 3 (ed. R. Heinze).

4. H.J. Blumenthal, *Hermes* 107 (1979): 174, with n. 27, expresses doubts about the *Paraphrase* of the *de sensu*, to which some have found reference in the *de anima*.

5. The Hebrew versions have been edited in *CAG*, V, 4 and 5, by S. Landauer, with Latin translations. For the different Arabic editions, cf. Dagron, *Thémistios*, 16.

6. Spengel, however, included these *Paraphrases* of portions of the *parva naturalia* as genuine. For discussion, cf. the preface of P. Wendland in *CAG*, V, 6. J.N. Mattock, *Akt. VII Kong. Arabis. u. Islamwiss.*, *AbAkadWissGött, PhilHistKl*, Folge 3, 98 (1976): 260–67, points out that the Arabic epitome by "Thamasitus" is not the work of Themistius.

7. Dagron, *Thémistios*, 16, suggests that he was misled by the obvious familiarity with Plato in the speeches. Todd, in Schroeder and Todd, *Two Greek Commentators*, 34, with n. 113, and in a letter to me, suggests that Photius may be referring to exegetical discussions of Platonic texts and Neoplatonic issues at various points in the *Paraphrases*, e.g., on the *Timaeus* in the *de anima*. Although this solution is attractive because of its simplicity, Photius seems quite clearly to separate the works on Aristotle from treatments of Plato.

8. For the speeches, Photius wrote ἀνεγνώσθη, and for the *Paraphrases*, he has εἴδομεν, but for the works on Plato he states, εἰσὶ . . . ἐξηγητικοὶ πόνοι.

9. So Blumenthal, *Hermes* 107 (1979): 168–82, against C. Steel, *Rev. phil. Louvain* 71 (1973): 669–80. Professor Todd suggests to me that the ὑπομνήματα may represent the youthful συγγράμματα of 23.294d. I am inclined to think that Themistius is referring to prepublication versions of some *Paraphrases*, if any distinction is to be made at all.

copying of manuscripts.[10] He talks of donating his own work (4.6c–d) and of other writers soon to be represented, including χοϱούς τε ὅλους ἐκ Λυκείου καὶ ᾿Ακαδημίας (4.60c).[11] This collection would include commentaries and might easily become associated with Themistius as the collector or perhaps as the donor of a family library, resulting eventually in Photius' mistake.[12]

Themistius insisted that his *Paraphrases* represented the culmination of family tradition and were not entirely his own creation (23.294d), but some false modesty may be assumed.[13] Whatever their origin, the *Paraphrases* were famous by the time Themistius reached the age of forty. He remarks in 358/9 that he had published authorized editions of the *Paraphrases* because unauthorized copies were circulating (23.294d). Fame, however, does not translate into importance as a philosopher, since his main importance for the history of philosophy rests in the fact that he was in some ways the last of the true Peripatetics[14] and not much influenced by Neoplatonism.[15] Though

---

10. See the discussion in chapter 4.

11. This would appear to represent a relatively complete collection of the writings of later adherents of the Lyceum and Academy. Themistius unfortunately gives no examples of authors included.

12. Cf. Vanderspoel, *Phoenix* 43 (1989): 162–64. R.B. Todd, *per litt.*, suggests to me that Photius' πάντα is a serious problem if it is taken to refer to commentaries of whatever kind on the entire corpus of Aristotle's work by Themistius and prefers to regard Photius' meaning as "all aspects of Aristotle," based on the vague language of 23.294d. I am not certain that this solves the problem, since Themistius was not concerned with all aspects of Aristotle's writings. While some works were generally ignored by commentators, Themistius' association with the entire output of the Lyceum as a library collection could explain the remark. Worth noting is the *Epitome* of Aristotle's zoological works extant in Arabic under the name "Thamasitus" (cf. n. 6 in this appendix), apparently linked to Themistius, but not by him.

13. So Dagron, *Thémistios*, 7. On family tradition, see chapter 2.

14. It may be more accurate to omit reference to Peripatetics, since this implies adherence to a specific school; cf. Schroeder and Todd, *Two Greek Aristotelian Commentators*, 34, n. 113. Here, as elsewhere, I mean that Themistius' thought is more "purely" Aristotelian, or for that matter, Platonic, than that of contemporaries and later writers.

15. Blumenthal, in *Arktouros*, 391–400 (revised, accepting a somewhat greater influence of Neoplatonism, in *Aristotle Transformed*, 113–23, esp. at 119–20); G. Verbeke, in *Dictionary of Scientific Biography* (New York, 1976), 13:307–8; Dagron, *Thémistios*, 43–44. On Themistius' attitude to Porphyry and Iamblichus, see chapter 1.

contemporaries read and attempted to interpret Aristotle, they did so
from the perspective of Plato or, more accurately, from their own
conception of Plato's meaning.[16] By Themistius' own design, the *Paraphrases* represent a new form of commentary on Aristotle.[17] Their
originality and importance lies in form, which was unique in the
fourth century, not in content,[18] and they were intended to be useful
in the understanding of Aristotelian philosophy, a goal that permeates the entire corpus.[19] In addition to the *Paraphrases*, Themistius, in
keeping with his view that philosophers ought to address the public,[20] delivered orations on philosophical themes, including speeches
περὶ ψυχῆς, possibly preserved in fragments,[21] and περὶ φρονήσεως.
A speech περὶ ἀρετῆς survives in Syriac,[22] and *Oration 22*, περὶ φιλίας,
is extant in Greek and Syriac.[23]

To this brief outline of Themistius' philosophical works may be
added a short account of his speeches. Photius opens his discussion
of Themistius with the remark that he had read thirty-six speeches,
which he terms political (*Bibl.* Cod. 74: λόγοι πολιτικοὶ λϛ'). The
Souda, s.v. Θεμίστιος, simply mentions speeches (καὶ διαλέξεις).[24]
Editors recently have tended to divide the speeches into two groups,
political (λόγοι πολιτικοί) and private (λόγοι ἰδιωτικοί). The first includes *Orations 1–11* and *13–19*, while the second comprises *Orations*

16. Wallis, *Neoplatonism*, passim.

17. Cf. his opening remarks in the *Paraphrase* of the *Analytica*, and on the
question of precedents, Blumenthal, *Hermes* 107 (1979): 174–76, with 175, n.
28.

18. Cf. the comments of Dagron, *Thémistios*, 7.

19 On Themistius' philosophy, cf. also E.R. Zeller, *Die Philosophie der
Griechen*, 5th ed. (Leipzig, 1923), III, 2, 797–801.

20. See chapter 2 for discussion of this view.

21. Blumenthal, *Hermes* 107 (1979): 174, with n. 26, doubts its authenticity.

22. All these items can be found in vol. 3 of the Teubner edition, the last
with a Latin translation by R. Mach.

23. *Or.* 22 is perhaps undatable. It may, however, be close in time to *Or.* 20
(355): of 11 references to Heracles, 3 occur in *Or.* 20 and 5 in *Or.* 22. Méridier,
Le philosophe, 9–14, places it in the reign of Constantius; Scholze, *Temporibus*,
78–79, during the reign of Valens. Dagron, *Thémistios*, 24, does not date it at
all. Scholze, loc. cit., suggests that Themistius would not repeat the thought
of 1.17c in almost exactly the same words at 22.266d–267a in the same reign. I
do not find this convincing.

24. Dagron, *Thémistios*, 16–17, with nn. 80–81, points out that the terms
used by Photius and the *Souda* mean different things.

20–34.[25] This division is somewhat arbitrary and artificial. Some of the so-called private speeches are political in nature, even if they were not delivered for a political occasion.[26] It is unclear whether Photius, who mentions Constantius, Valens, the young Valentinianus (Galates), and Theodosius, knew a speech to Julian, since he also omits Jovian and Gratian. In any case, it is evident that Photius found more speeches than those now extant in Greek. If the fragmentary περὶ φρονήσεως, the fragments[27] of the περὶ ψυχῆς, and Constantius' letter to the Senate at Constantinople, the Κωνσταντίου Δημηγορία, may be added to the thirty-three extant in Greek, Photius' statement that he knew thirty-six speeches can be regarded as correct,[28] without recourse to lost orations or those preserved in Arabic or Syriac and perhaps unavailable to him.[29] From Julian's *Letter to Themistius*, it is clear that Themistius wrote a *protrepticus*, extant only in the few fragments that Julian quotes,[30] less a speech than a treatise and included here for completeness. Finally, a scholion on a letter of Libanius (*Ep.* 241) quotes a fragment of a letter of Themistius.[31]

---

25. The Teubner text divides the speeches between vol. 1 and 2 on this basis. On *Or.* 12, see chapter 7. For a list of editions, cf. Downey's preface in vol. 1:XIII-XIV. On the work of Petau and Harduin, cf. R. Maisano, *Archivum Historicum Societatis Iesu* 43 (1974): 267–300.

26. Esp. *Or.* 31 and 34. Cf. Dagron, *Thémistios*, 17, with n. 81.

27. Even if these are not authentic, Photius need only have thought that Themistius wrote the treatise.

28. Dagron, *Thémistios*, 17–18, proposes to add four speeches to the extant thirty-three. He does not mention the letter of Constantius, but includes the περὶ ἀρετῆς. On the other hand, Photius mentions the Δημηγορία separately.

29. All edited in vol. 3 of the Teubner edition. On the textual tradition of the *Risâlat*, see appendix 3. For possible lost speeches on peace with the Goths, see chapter 7 (Themistius may be referring to discussions only). Dagron, *Thémistios*, 18, adds a lost speech of 357, in which Themistius reported on his embassy to Rome (chapter 4) and omits a speech delivered for the first consulships of Valentinian and Valens in 365 (chapter 7).

30. For detailed treatment, see chapter 5 and appendix 3, where I suggest that it was known to Arab scholars.

31. Not included in the Teubner edition, but it can be found in Bouchery, *Themistius*, 125, n. 2, and is translated in chapter 4.

Appendix 2

Themistius on His Contemporaries

Oration 28: The Character of Sophists and Philosophers

Translation

Note: In the notes, I offer only some brief remarks to clarify the translation or give parallels from Themistius himself.

(341b) Not only philosophers, but poets and rhetors as well, give birth to a great many speeches. Some, however, exult in this branch of learning and, taking great personal pride in it, communicate it to humanity, (c) often going forth to the theaters and festivals, decked out in gold and purple, reeking of perfumes, with painted eyelids, rubbed down with unguents, and crowned with floral garlands. Besides this adornment, so brilliant and extravagant, their speeches too are wily and exceed all boundaries in their cleverness and love of mankind (φιλανθρωπία),[1] glorifying, exalting, and greeting the spectators, emitting all kinds of sounds and singing songs filled with pleasure,[2] just like the Sirens. Since, then, they are so clever and obedient,[3] men also greet and praise them in return, and, as a consequence, (d) the whole earth is filled with these men, and the whole sea as well.[4]

Others,[5] of the race of Socrates, as is fitting and just,[6] have died and waned at the present time. For I do not know why they shudder with

---

1. Themistius is not referring to the virtue found so often in the panegyrics; rather, he means that the sophists display great affection for their audiences.
2. For speeches as songs, cf. 24.301a; 27.336c.
3. I.e., they do what is expected of them.
4. The whole paragraph amplifies 24.302a.
5. The contrast is with "some" in the previous paragraph; Themistius now discusses contemporary philosophy.
6. Given what follows, Themistius is probably sarcastic here.

fear and are wary of the marketplaces, in which, the poet says,[7] splendid men are brought to their maturity; they are unable[8] to peep out
from the pallet and the corner.[9] So completely have they forgotten their
ancestors, because these had discussions with the general population,
in the workshops, (342a) in the colonnades, in the baths, and in the
theaters.[10] For this reason, they not only drew to themselves and took
in hand those who were attending their schools, but also released the
cobbler from his leather, the pawnbroker from his table, and the lover
from the brothel. Out of their love of the human race,[11] they traveled to
Olympia, the Isthmus, Aegina, and Eleusis, and themselves performed the mysteries, with the favor of the gods, ***** for many men.[12]
But since then, like thieves and robbers, they flee the crowded areas (of
the city) *****[13] (b) not unsuitably do they distrust the instrument, in
order not to destroy their tongue because of their wisdom.[14]

But I, gentlemen, am making an eager attempt to lead them back to

---

7. *Iliad* 9. 441. Themistius refers to this again at 22.265c. At 27.334c, he
quotes a poet (either Simonides [so Am. Mar. 14.6.7] or Euripides [or whoever
it was; so Plut. *Dem.* 1]) to the effect that a man must live in a famous city to
engage in politics. Lib. *Or.* 2.2, alludes to this saying as well.

8. Through fear.

9. At 22.265a, he states that philosophers whisper to youths (i.e., students) in a single corner; and at 2.30b–c, he speaks of old philosophers who
cannot peep out of their houses due to their weakness and who converse with
three or four students.

10. Curiously, Libanius, *Or.* 1.55, states that he gave his lessons in the
baths, and in the whole city, when he was at Nicomedia, a city that loved
rhetoric.

11. Themistius' normal view of philanthropy is operative here.

12. Various supplements have been proposed; none is satisfactory. μετὰ of
the manuscript has generally been replaced with μητρὶ, "to the mother of the
gods." This emendation hardly seems appropriate, given the places mentioned. Presumably, something like "expiatory prayers" is required, since the
emphasis in what follows is on the philosophers' more recent silence.

13. This lacuna is evidently larger than the last. τὰ μέσα are clearly the
crowded areas of the city; cf. 22.265c: φεύγειν δὲ τὰ μέσα τῆς πόλεως. After the
lacuna, the topic is the philosophers' silence and distrust of their tongues.
The destruction of the tongue because of wisdom is a difficult concept; it may
mean that philosophers were too wise to speak with sophistic eloquence or
that their terminology was too obtuse. A scholiast suggests that speaking
wisdom not to be divulged (ἀπαρρησιάστου) would result in a loss of the
power of speech or debate. This is reasonable in the context of Eleusis.

14. This paragraph and part of the next amplifies 24.302a–b.

their earlier state.[15] On the other hand, I fear and suspect that, in attempting to speak with you, we may seem more absurd than the silent ones. For I know their nature exactly, that it is austere, stubborn, and unyielding. They do not even endure to give words to humans without restraint, but because of their lack of polish,[16] are more sparing of words than of money; (c) they scrutinize carefully and take great care that they do not give to anyone either more or less than is suitable. Consequently, it happens that they have very few acquaintances and friends because of their stinginess. Nevertheless, such is their willfulness that they themselves believe and insist to others that the praise that they give is natural human praise, but that the praise of those exquisite and sumptuous speakers is foreign and in no way suitable. And you could not discover from this (type of praise)[17] who was being praised, unless the name were written on the flattery, (d) just as the pictures of bad painters are known not by their skill, but from the inscription. True fame is alive and has more spirit than the works of Daedalus, so that even if it is thrown into the midst (of a gathering), it would spring forward and fasten on to whom it belonged. Even if the speaker cast his eyes in a different direction while delivering praise, the audience would immediately turn to look at him (343a) to whom the word, falling from the mouth, attached and fastened itself.

Look then, as I send my praise into the assembly, because that ruler seems to me to verify the name of his office, the one who is hard to overcome by gold, but easily persuaded by speech, a lover of freedom who praises greatness of mind while keeping guard against the stubbornness that lies close to it.[18] I do not name about whom I am speaking, I am not looking at him or smiling at him, I am not pointing him out with my finger, (b) nor have I stood up to touch his hands. But you know him immediately, and your eyes are carried in that direction, and so strong is the truth that you have not stopped shouting and calling out and springing out of your rocks.[19] And yet I have delivered plain words, and they were simply at random and rather

---

15. At 22.265c, Themistius states, "They must be allowed to remain where they want to remain," and mentions the need for him to speak in public.

16. ἀγροικίας. Themistius means that they are not urbane.

17. I.e., that of the sophists.

18. I.e., greatness of mind leads easily to singleness of mind.

19. I.e., seats.

antiquated, neither wrapped up nor embellished. But you seemed to admire not the words but the man whom the words shone upon and brought to light. And I know well that you swear, as regards this speech, (c) that it did not deceive or flatter, but sitting on high like a noble athlete, it shouted out, stirred forward, taught what it is necessary to guard against, and exhorted him to remain of good courage.

Discussion

In this short speech, Themistius inveighs against the practices of contemporary sophists and philosophers and offers his solution. His views are treated elsewhere; there is no need to repeat them here. More interesting in this context is the date and occasion of the speech, variously dated to the reign of Constantius or Theodosius,[20] when disputes with contemporaries are most evident. There is no direct evidence, but a careful study of the speech allows a preference for the early date.

Several remarks in the speech seem to reflect the situation late in the reign of Constantius. The most obvious is the statement by Themistius that his speech exhorted the emperor to "remain of good courage" (343c). He notes as well that his audience would swear that the speech did not "deceive or flatter" (343c). This comment may be a reply to a complaint by Julian in his *Letter to Themistius* that it was unlawful for a philosopher to "flatter or deceive" (254b, though the Greek words are different in the two texts). Julian released his treatise in 360, after his acclamation as Augustus, to undermine the influence of Themistius, or perhaps to capture his allegiance.[21] It would not be surprising if the philosopher felt it useful to display his veracity shortly after he saw Julian's remarks. In the same document, Julian informs Themistius that he could do as much good by teaching a few individuals as by taking an active part in public life (266a–b). Themistius' remark that contemporary philosophers could only have a few acquaintances and friends because of their laconic nature (342c)

---

20. Méridier, *Le philosophe*, 10–14, finds similarities to speeches during the reign of Constantius. Scholze, *Temporibus*, 66–67, finds references to Theodosius, and Norman, in the Teubner edition, vol. 2:160, apparatus, dates it after 381. Dagron, *Thémistios*, 25, is cautious.

21. On the date, Barnes and Vanderspoel, *GRBS* 22 (1981): 187–89; for remarks about Julian's intent, chapters 4 and 5.

might be a reply to this advice. These statements echo in many ways
the other speeches on the attitude toward rhetoric and philosophy
during the reign of Constantius; opponents in the reign of Theodosius, and Themistius in response, focused on the question of a
philosopher in political office. On a different issue, Themistius in his
panegyrics of Constantius, comments on the high spirit of the emperor,[22] but insists that it was of the right kind. The same praise
appears in *Oration* 28 (343a).

The sum of these points suggests that Constantius was emperor
when Themistius delivered the speech and that it was delivered late
in the reign. If the emperor was present, as seems to be required, it
should fall within the limits of his visit to Constantinople in 359/60.
He spent the winter at the capital, but was already on his way to the
Persian front when the envoys of Julian reached him at Caesarea with
letters to explain the events at Paris in February 360 (Am. Mar. 20.9.1).
Constantius had been at Constantinople as late as 14 March.[23] While
Ammianus states that the emperor became angry at the content of the
letters, he perhaps already knew of Julian's usurpation. Indeed, Julian wrote precisely because he thought that the emperor had heard
about the events from others (Am. Mar. 20.8.4: Decentius returned to
the East before Julian sent his envoys).[24] A speech in March 360 is not
impossible. Alternatively, it could be argued that Themistius traveled
with the emperor as far as Cappadocia and delivered the speech
there. One final point can be made: if *Oration* 28 is indeed a response
to the *Letter to Themistius*, Julian released his reply to Themistius'
earlier *protrepticus* immediately after the acclamation.

Oration 21: The First Reply to Contemporaries

Themistius begins "The Touchstone or The Philosopher," delivered in
late 355 or 356,[25] with a brief history of his life and education, topics

22. Especially in *Or.* 1.7c; see chapter 4 for discussion.
23. Accepting Seeck's emendation (*Regesten,* 207) of the date of *CTh* 7.4.5.
24. News of this type could travel fast: after Constantius' death on 3 November 361 in Cilicia, the news reached Julian quickly enough for a journey
from Naissus to Constantinople by 11 December, when he entered the city. In
addition to Decentius, Florentius' family preceded Julian's envoys (Am. Mar.
20.9.1).
25. For the date, see chapter 4.

addressed only a few months earlier in *Orations* 20 and 27. He sarcasti-
cally remarks that, on the basis of his mother's statements (i.e., that
his father was in fact his father), he was the son of a noble philosopher (21.244a), but does not consider himself a philosopher: his mind
had not been properly shaped by teachers, and he gave speeches
often.[26] The lengthy prologue (21.243a–247d) precedes a discussion of
the true philosopher.

The rest of the speech, one of his longest,[27] is a treatment of touchstones for a true philosopher.[28] The theme is the difference between
himself and contemporaries who approached philosophy differently.
On their view, Themistius was not a philosopher, but a sophist, since
philosophers rarely delivered speeches.[29] He denies the charge of
sophistry, but admits a failure to meet standards imposed by contemporaries. His remarks are ironic and indicate a rejection of these standards, and he asks his audience to judge for themselves. The touchstones derive directly from Plato; it would be sophistic to propose his
own (21.246b).

The first requirement is that the true philosopher be the offspring
of a holy marriage (γάμος ἱερός) between the best man and woman to
ensure good breeding,[30] a feature as characteristic of a philosopher as
the ivory shoulders of the Pelopidae (21.248a–250b).[31] The second is
that philosophers have knowledge of the eternal essence (τὴν οὐσίαν

---

26. He does note his training under his father and father-in-law (21.244b–
d).

27. S. Oppermann, *I. ΕΙΣ ΤΟΝ ΑΥΤΟΥ ΠΑΤΕΡΑ II. ΒΑΣΑΝΙΣΤΗΣ Η
ΦΙΛΟΣΟΦΟΣ* (20. und 21. Rede) (Göttingen, 1962), XL–XLII, offers an outline of this speech. The brief commentaries that accompany his introduction,
texts, and translations are primarily literary and are generally unhelpful for
the historical interpretation of both speeches. Méridier, *Le philosophe*, 1–8, is
more penetrating.

28. Themistius uses the concept of touchstones in *Or.* 2 when he examines
whether Constantius is a philosopher, again suggesting a date in 355/356.

29. Themistius himself had made this last point at 24.302a–b; see also *Or.*
28.

30. Plato, *Resp.* 458e. At 8.119d–120a, Themistius unabashedly proclaims
that the young Valentinianus Galates is this kind of offspring.

31. Greg. Naz. *Ep.* 38, perhaps knew this passage, since he writes that
oratory was as characteristic of Themistius as were the ivory shoulders of the
Pelopidae.

τὴν ἀεὶ οὖσαν)[32] and work at philosophy alone, since individuals can be skilled only at their own craft (21.250b–254b). The third proof is kindness toward those who seek wisdom and learning (21.254b–257c). A fourth is absolute hatred of falsehood and deceit in all their forms (21.257c–259d). Another item, not listed as a touchstone, but certainly a requirement, is that the true philosopher is not mercenary (21.259d–262a). Themistius mentions Thersites in his discussion of the fifth item, which leads him to his final point: the true philosopher is not a meddler, boaster or worker of evil (21.262a–264b). Under each head, Themistius offers examples of ways that the requirement was sometimes broken. Since he has proposed an examination of philosophy at Constantinople (21.248a), he is clearly indicting false philosophers. He is also defending himself against their charges.

Orations 23, 26, and 29: The Charges of Sophistry

In *Oration* 23,[33] Themistius defends himself against the accusation that he was a sophist. He refers to specific charges against him and points out, in a speech titled "Sophist," that he did not have the characteristics of a true sophist. He paints a picture of such a sophist, which was interpreted as an attack against a specific individual and necessitated the explanatory *Oration* 29, where he points out that not just one, but most philosophers at Constantinople fell into this category.

He begins with a discussion of the situation. He has entered the theater as if it were a law court, with his audience as jurors for his defense against accusations. While he does not know the identity of accusers who act in secret, he hopes to discover their names in their arrows, just as Philip of Macedon found the name of the archer Aster burned into the shaft of his arrow (23.282d–284c). After noting the opposition to philosophy from its very beginnings (23.284d–286d), Themistius discusses the laws that govern the conduct of philosophers and separate them from sophists, though these vary with the different schools (23.286d–287d). To this end, he cites Plato's description of the sophist:[34]

---

32. The concept and words derive directly from Plato, *Resp.* 485a–b.
33. On the date of these speeches, see chapter 4.
34. Drawn from Plato, *Soph.* 231d, 235a–c, 266b.

He depicts, first, a paid hunter of rich youths, second, a mer-
chant in the training of the soul, third, a huckster in these same
matters, fourth, an aggressive promoter of himself, fifth, a con-
testant with the skill of disputing in speeches. And indeed he
has capped these with a final summary, that is, an individual
who makes guesses about what does not exist, a copyist through
images, a craftsman in images of truth, and a conjurer of words.
(23.288a–b)

Themistius asks the jurors to judge him by these laws and points out
that he has never exacted payment for instruction (23.288c–294c).[35]
During the defense, the philosopher turns to the real reason for his
fame, his *Paraphrases* (23.294d–297a).

He denies that his visits to other cities convict him as a sophist on
Plato's fourth point, since he had undertaken these journeys, especially his recent visit to Rome, on behalf of the city, not for self-
promotion. As evidence he cites an emperor whose view had been
read to the senate, that is, Constantius and his letter to the Senate
(23.297b–299b). At the end, Themistius denies that he sells the training of the soul and is a boaster and deceiver, Plato's second and third
points (23.299c). The text apparently breaks off here, since he has left
other points unaddressed.

In *Oration* 26, delivered to a select group of individuals gathered in
some location other than the Theater of the Muses,[36] Themistius excuses his behavior. The summary, clearly written by Themistius and
perhaps delivered as a preface,[37] mentions a recent speech and corre-
lates this particular audience to the one in the theater as the Areopagus to the courts (26.311c–d). The identity of his audience and the

35. For his refusal to accept gifts from the emperor, see chapter 4.

36. Scholars, while admitting that Themistius may have used some arguments prevalent in the fourth century B.C., have not accepted the view of
H. Kesters, *Antisthène, étude critique et exégetique sur le XXVIᵉ discours de Thémistius* (Louvain, 1935), and *Plaidoyer d'un socratique contre le Phèdre de Platon*
(Louvain, 1959), that the philosopher simply made a few changes to a speech
of Antisthenes. Dagron, *Thémistios*, 44, n. 54, remarks that this view dispos-
sesses Themistius of one of his poorer works a little too quickly. On this
speech, cf. P.G. Grisoli, *RFIC* 95 (1967): 303–21.

37. He refers to himself and addresses his audience in the second person
plural.

place of delivery cannot be determined. They may have been persons of importance or people who customarily listened to his speeches, and Themistius perhaps delivered the speech at his own or a friend's house.[38] The orator implies that the audience may have been or may have considered themselves philosophers (26.313b) and notes that he is attempting to establish principles for them as well as for himself (26.313a).

As his first topic, he complains that rules concerning carpentry and other trades are left to practitioners of the trades. In contrast, individuals who are as ignorant as the population at large have taken responsibility for dictating rules to philosophy. Since philosophers must have the right to defend themselves, Themistius will undertake this defense on behalf of himself and the members of his audience (26.311d–313c). He will prove, just as he had recently done, that he is not a mercenary sophist and begins his defense by reading again (πάλιν) the charges against him. He has been accused of innovation, of failing to remain at home with a few students, of bringing philosophy into the open, of announcing speeches three days before they are to take place, and of catering to his audience for the sake of applause. Because former students have left him to join the enemy, he must contend alone with enemies and former friends (26.313c–314c).

The charge of innovation surprised him most. Using Plato's division of orators into three categories, the politician, the demagogue, and the sophist,[39] he insists that he is not a sophist, because he does not contest with a single opponent, nor is he a demagogue, since he enjoys applause only because it reveals appreciation of his words. Rather, he is the politician, because his speeches are useful.[40] On the charge of innovation, he admits guilt, but notes that he is not the first to do so and lists philosophers who held different views, for example, Thales, Anaximander, and others. Socrates, he remarks, did not follow tradition, but asked new questions, and did this in public. Both Plato and Aristotle were innovators, and the latter did not think that the same speeches were useful to both populace and philosophers. Themistius suspects that his revelation of the beauty of philosophy to

---

38. The suggestions of Méridier, *Le philosophe*, 33.
39. *Soph.* 268a–b.
40. The utility of his speeches is a recurring theme; cf. *Or.* 24 and chapter 2.

the masses was the basis for charges of innovation. Unlike medicine, which helps only individuals, philosophy is useful to all (26.320b–323a). Ideas ought to be exchanged through oratory. If philosophy remains hidden, the people will wonder why they are not worthy of knowledge, while the refusal of philosophers to take part in politics leaves government in the hands of the ignorant, similar to life in an Athens controlled by Anytus rather than Socrates. In this vein, Themistius complains that his contemporaries refused to engage in disputation publicly in the Senate, his pride and joy (26.326c).

Themistius notes his lack of concern for the philosophy of the movements of the stars and emphasizes his attempts to help humanity reach the ideal. He accuses philosophy of mocking bad orators and developing rhetorical theory without practicing the trade. The population is unfortunate, if it can only hear defenders of Nicias (declamation) and praises of spring, swallows, and nightingales.[41] Complaining that philosophers find error in Homer's views about the gods without offering a corrective, Themistius asks them to imitate Apollo in giving answers not only to individuals, but also to groups. People will listen with pleasure and heed the advice of philosophers (26.327a–331c).

Themistius addresses only the question of innovation and does not reply to the other charges. He insists that he is doing nothing new and attempts to reverse the charges with the accusation that his opponents have turned a dynamic tradition into a static one. In the end, he abandons his defense in favor of a plea to his contemporaries to become more like himself. It is not clear that he was successful. During the reigns of Julian, Jovian, and Valens, there are fewer traces of disputes with contemporaries, but Themistius' different role in politics, more than any change of opponents' attitude, was probably the cause.

Oration 29 replies to criticism for *Oration* 23. Themistius was accused of attacking all sophists, and one in particular, but replies that he had merely claimed not to be a sophist. In general, sophists were not angry, just as doctors would not be if he claimed to be a citharist. And he had not attacked any specific individual. If a sophist at Constantinople resembled the picture painted in *Oration* 23, he was convicted by Plato, whose laws had been the basis of Themistius' remarks (29.343d–348a). *Oration* 29 appears to be directed mainly against an

---

41. I.e., the type of speeches delivered by orators like Himerius.

individual who had deliberately misinterpreted his earlier speech, to cast further reproach on him (cf. 29.345b–c).

The five orations from the reign of Constantius discussed in this appendix reveal the nature of the opposition to Themistius. In essence, his unnamed and unknown opponents regarded his activities as unsuitable for a philosopher. Themistius responded with the claim that philosophers had been actively involved in public life long before the fourth century. Other speeches from this reign—*Orations* 20, 24, 27, and even 32, all discussed elsewhere—address many of the same topics from a different angle, but his point is always the same: philosophers had not only the right, but the obligation to take part in public life.

Arabic Authors on Themistius' Works
to Julian

The extant works of Themistius include a treatise called a *Risâlat*, which is preserved in two Arabic manuscripts. The texts are similar, but not precisely the same.[1] The first, mentioned in 1897, but not published until 1920,[2] is titled *Epistula Damistiyus, ministri (wazir) Ilyan, qui est Iulyanus rex, de re publica gerenda. Versio e lingua Syriaca ab Ibn-Zur'a facta*.[3] The second offers the title *Epistula Thamistiyus philosophi ad regem Ilyan de re publica gerenda, item de regno gubernando*, but is signed by a another translator as *Epistula Thamistiyus ad Ilyan regem missa; versio facta ab Abu 'Uthman Sa'id Ibn-Ya'qub al-Dimashqi*.[4] M. Bouyges discovered the second manuscript and, though he saw it only briefly, suggested translations of a Syriac original by different

1. Much of the following information derives from M. Bouyges, *Archives de Philosophie* 2.3 (1924): 15–17, who also offers a summary. I have been unable to obtain some of the literature to which Bouyges refers; some references consequently derive from his. I. Shahîd has published a critical text and Latin translation of the work in vol. 3 of the Teubner edition of Themistius' works. This Latin translation was done some years before its eventual publication in the Teubner text. Professor W.E. Kaegi has kindly lent me an English translation done by A.A. Vasiliev for G. Downey in 1949.

2. By L. Cheikho (who had discovered the text), *Al-Machriq* 18 (1920): 881–89. The manuscript was in the possession of Ahmad Pasha Taymur. The other manuscript is preserved at Constantinople (= Köprülü 1608, fol. 138–145). Cf. Shahîd, p. 75.

3. Because I do not read Arabic, I quote the text in Latin. The entry on Ibn Zur'a in the *Fihrist* of Ibn al-Nadîm (B. Dodge, ed. and trans., *The Fihrist of al Nadim* [New York, 1970]) 2:632, reads, in part: "He is contemporary with our time, and one of the leaders in the science of logic as well as in the philosophical studies. He is also one of the accurate translators. . . . Among his books there were: . . . what he translated from the Syriac; . . ."

4. According to Ibn al-Nadîm (Dodge, *Fihrist*, 2:700), "he was one of the good translators."

hands.[5] Cheikho, who announced the first manuscript, identified "Damistiyus" with Themistius; "Thamistiyus" in the second confirms the identification.

Arab encyclopedists elsewhere mention works to Julian. Ibn al-Nadîm lists two, a *Kitâb ilâ liyoûliyânos fi't-Tadbîr* and a letter to Julian the emperor,[6] while Ibn al-Qiftiy refers to a *Kitâb liyoûliyânos fi't-Tadbîr*. Ibn al-'Ibri (= Ibn Hebrei), a Syriac writer, has a longer title for, apparently, the same work: *Kitâb liyoûliyânos fi't-Tadbîr wasiyâsati'l-Mamâlik*, translated as "Lettre à Julien sur la Politique," by Leclerc, who notes that Ibn al-'Ibri wrote that "Thémistius, dans sa lettre à Julien, l'aurait détourne de persécuter les chrétiens." Bouyges points out that this is inexact: Ibn al-'Ibri in fact wrote that Themistius "composa un *Kitâb liyoûliyânos* . . . et une *Risâlat* adressée à lui, encore, dans laquelle il le détourné de persécuter les chrétiens." In the view of Arab scholars, Themistius thus addressed two works to Julian, a *Kitâb* and a *Risâlat*.[7]

If the author of the extant *Risâlat* is Themistius, the identity of the recipient, which has been disputed,[8] can only be Julian in the Arabic tradition: both Ibn al-'Ibri and Ibn al-Nadîm list two items addressed to him. According to Ibn al-'Ibri, one was designed to stop persecution of Christians, and, if this is reliable, no other emperor during the lifetime of Themistius could have been the addressee.[9] Errors, including the remark about persecution, are possible. Some Byzantine scholars wrongly thought that Themistius held office under Julian,[10] a view shared by Ibn Zur'a, who calls the philosopher a *wazir Ilyan*.[11] Because

5. Bouyges, *Archives de Philosophie* 2.3 (1924): 16, who also notes Cheikho's identification with Themistius.

6. The transliteration of the titles derive from Bouyges, *Archives de Philosophie* 2.3 (1924): 17, who does not note that Ibn al-Nadîm records a second work. For this, cf. al-Nadîm (Dodge, *Fihrist*, 2:611), where the works of Themistius include "Book to Julian, Administration; . . . Epistle [= *Risâlat?*] to Julian the Emperor." The first of these seems to be the *Kitâb* mentioned in the text, while the second may be the *Risâlat* referred to by Ibn al-'Ibri.

7. For the bibliographical details, see Bouyges, *Archives de Philosophie* 2.3 (1924): 17.

8. Cf. Stegemann, "Themistios," 1667, and Shahîd's introduction, pp. 76–80. Theodosius is the alternative.

9. Themistius did rebuke Valens' religious intolerance; see chapter 7.

10. *Souda*, s. v. Θεμίστιος. Phot. *Bibl.* Cod. 74, puts the floruit under Valens.

11. Shahîd, p. 77, points out that this translator refers to Julian only in the subordinate clause that names the emperor under whom Themistius held

both groups may be establishing a floruit under a single emperor, the only firm evidence for the addressee is the text itself.

Arabic sources thus suggest that Themistius twice offered his views to Julian, in a *Risâlat* and in a *Kitâb*. In the extant text, the Arabic title is *Risâlat*. Of the items by Themistius that Ibn al-'Ibri mentions, this is the title of a work written to stop persecution of Christians. The extant work offers no evidence of this theme. Rather, its content reveals an affinity to the *Kitâb*, translated as *"Lettre"* (Leclerc) and "Book" (Dodge). *Risâlat* normally has the same meaning, but can also designate a treatise.[12] Shahîd notes that the word means either *epistula* or *dissertatio* and that in the text, the work is called a *qaul*, undoubtedly λόγος in Greek, which can indicate an *epistula* or an *oratio*. He entitles his translation *Epistula Themistii de re publica gerenda*, relying on one standard translation of the Arabic to suggest a letter, not a speech or treatise.[13]

Two possible conclusions emerge. First, the similarity of meaning between *Kitâb* and *Risâlat* has allowed the *Kitâb* of Arab scholars to become *Risâlat* in the manuscripts, since the extant treatise more or less fulfills the requirement of a book or letter on politics or administration. Second, it is possible that Ibn al-'Ibri erred when he wrote that the treatise was designed to stop Julian from persecuting Christians, an intention not known to al-Nadîm. The second possibility is more economical. It seems likely, therefore, that the extant *Risâlat* is the *Risâlat*, or letter, of the Arab scholars. In chapter 5, I argue that this *Risâlat* is a translation of Themistius' panegyric of Julian or of an epitome of this panegyric. Ibn al-'Ibri's view that Themistius was attempting to persuade Julian to cease persecution of Christians may simply derive from the philosopher's frequent attempt to promote religious toleration. The nonextant *Kitâb* can, in turn, be regarded as the *protrepticus* sent to Julian in Gaul.

---

office and is therefore not reliable evidence for the addressee. The Arabic word *wazir* need not indicate an office, but could simply mean a favored counselor. For refutation of the view that Themistius held high office under either Constantius or Julian, see chapter 4.

12. *Kitâb* is often used of longer works, such as books, while *Risâlat* frequently denotes shorter works, particularly letters, but the terms are interchangeable in certain situations. The core meaning of each is a written composition. I am grateful to Professor Andrew Rippin of the Department of Religious Studies at the University of Calgary for discussing these terms, and *wazir*, with me.

13. Shahîd, p. 83, n. 1.

Appendix 4

The Addressee of the *Risâlat*

The main problem for interpretation of the *Risâlat* is the identity of the addressee. The treatise was addressed to an emperor during Themistius' career,[1] with Julian and Theodosius as the favored candidates. The main arguments for Theodosius are the references to God, which could reflect Christianity, to peace, amplified by two references to the concord between the emperor and other kings, and a possible reference to the author's own career under Theodosius, as urban prefect and as tutor of the emperor's son. The case for Julian rests on the statements of the scribes, not to be trusted entirely, though Arab encyclopedists clearly refer to a work of this nature addressed to Julian, and on the view that the arguments for Theodosius present too many difficulties.

The case for Theodosius is not solid,[2] since the required conditions did not occur during his reign. Themistius refers to a single emperor throughout. In almost every political speech delivered when more than one emperor occupied the throne,[3] he mentions the entire imperial college, doing so even when Julian was Caesar (*Or.* 2, 3, 4). Theodosius was never sole emperor, though only his sons were additional members of the college after Valentinian II died in 392. While the philosopher pays scant tribute to the existence of the younger Valentinian in panegyrics of Theodosius,[4] the young emperor always appears before 384, when dynastic policy forced his elimination from speeches and the inclusion of Arcadius instead. If Themistius followed normal practice, the only possible emperors are Julian as sole emperor and Jovian.

The time of peace that Themistius describes does not accord well

1. Cf. p. 99: *id quod tibi, o rex felicissime, accidit*.
2. For a summary of the arguments, cf. Shahîd's introduction in the Teubner edition, vol. 3:76–81.
3. *Or.* 1 is a notable exception. On the reason for this, see chapter 4.
4. See chapter 8 for discussion.

with the reign of Theodosius. Though discussing the rule of an ideal emperor, he talks of a number of nations and enemies brought back under imperial control, of kings who entrusted their fate to his care, and of peace and treaties.[5] He continues with a list of the benefits of peace, including the cessation of ignorance, increased education, commerce and fertility, cheaper grain, justice, security, lack of fear, and the vanishing of dissension.[6] He refers to the fact that everyone, soldiers included, lives at peace and knows his station.[7]

The statements "bonds formed between themselves" (p. 103: *corda inter se coniuncta*) and "with harmonious thoughts every dissension has vanished" (p. 105: *sententiis concordibus dissensio omnis euanuit*) do not refer to the Council of Constantinople in 381.[8] The "bonds" are placed between "wars" and "fires of evil" and have nothing to do with religion, while "harmonious thoughts" follow a reference to prevailing security and precede a statement on the lack of military activity. Both statements refer to military rather than religious harmony, which the Council in question did not in any case ensure. The tenor of the passage suggests that, when these words were written, a civil war had been raging and that the opposing sides had reached agreement. The possibility of a reference to the acceptance of Magnus Maximus as a legitimate emperor is excluded by the appearance of only one emperor. These phrases and their context best describe the situation after the death of Constantius, when the eastern and western armies amalgamated under the single authority of Julian. In the winter of 382/3, the Gothic king Athanaric reported to Theodosius at Constantinople.[9] In the *Risâlat*, "kings" had submitted, a claim that better describes the Germanic kings who surrendered to Julian. As Caesar, Julian brought

---

5. *ex quo factum est, ut nationibus omnibus et regnis in dicionem eius redactis et hostibus deuictis potentes demissi sint et reges in fidem eius se tradiderint. eius enim auctoritate et summa dignitate bella composita sunt, corda inter se coniuncta, ignes malitiae exstincti* (p. 103).

6. *cessit ignorantia, studium doctrinae auctum; uiis quoque patefactis commercia augentur, fecunditas in maius producta, annona uilior facta et, iustitia latius diffusa, res correctae sunt et, securitate praevalente, metus dissipatus et sententiis concordibus dissensio omnis euanuit* (pp. 103–5).

7. *miles nullus iniuriam uel intulit uel fecit; in statione sua quisque mansit, sub umbra eius delituit, locum suum cognouit nec modum excessit* (p. 105).

8. Cf. Shahîd, p. 79, reporting, not necessarily accepting, the argument.

9. Cf. *Or.* 15. 190d–191a, on which chapter 8.

back under imperial control various peoples in Gaul and Germany and accepted the submission of several kings, including Suomarius (Am. Mar. 17.10.3), Hortarius (17.10.7–8), Macrianus, Hariobaudus, Vadomarius, Urius, Ursicinus and Vestralpus (18.2.15–19), all of whom he had conquered.[10]

The argument that Themistius is referring to his own career in the passages about imperial advisers and officeholders is difficult to accept. He mentions positions that he himself never held, but his purpose is to outline the type of individual suitable for various offices (p. 109).[11] While Themistius may have felt that he fulfilled the requirements, the discussion is abstract, and his advice is applicable to any emperor. He intended his establishment of the ideal as praise of the current emperor,[12] in the clear understanding that he appointed his officials from this perspective.

Later, Themistius refers to an individual "by whose care and tutelage the king himself has been brought up" (p. 111: *cuius cura atque tutela rex ipse sit educatus*). As the context indicates, Themistius is discussing the individuals from whom the emperor ought to choose his personal servants. He is not referring to his guardianship of Arcadius. This does not rule out Theodosius as the addressee, since the passage gives advice. If it reflects court reality, it could refer to Theodosius,[13] or any other emperor.

Finally, possible reflections of Christianity and a Christian emperor do not strengthen a case for Theodosius. References to God take a form that may emerge from Christianity. Shahîd (p. 78) translates the Arabic as follows: "*Deus Optimus Maximus* (lit., *qui benedictus et super omnes exaltatus est*)" and "*Deus Summus Omnipotens* (lit., *cui sunt et potestas et maiestas*)." While these and the other references appear to derive from Christianity, Shahîd points out that the process of several translations, including Syriac Christianity and Arabic Islam, may have added them.[14] In any case, much of late antique paganism had

---

10. On Julian in Gaul, cf. Bowersock, *Julian the Apostate*, 33–45.

11. See below for further discussion of this and the next point.

12. Note p. 105: *Et hactenus in oratione mea locutus, ea demonstrabo, domino nostro imperanti obsecutus, quae Augusto inesse necesse est, . . .*

13. Cf., for Spaniards at the court of Theodosius, Stroheker, *Madr. Mitt.* 4 (1963): 115 ff. (= *Germanentum und Spätantike* [Zurich, 1965], 65 ff.); Matthews, *JTS* 18 (1967): 438–46; idem, *Western Aristocracies*, passim.

14. Shahîd, p. 78.

adopted the concept of a single, all-powerful God, and Christian concepts were liberally applied. In other speeches, albeit to Christian emperors, Themistius shows familiarity with Christian writings, but uses these to support philosophical, not religious, ideals.[15] Many ideas that in the third century would need to be seen as peculiar to Christianity can in the fourth be regarded as common to Christianity and paganism.[16] Julian's own views provide sufficient evidence that pagans sometimes used Christian ideas to promote and revive their own religious perspectives.[17]

Upon close inspection, the arguments for Theodosius vanish. There is reason to prefer Julian.[18] While Themistius' speeches are quite philosophical in content, he nowhere else sets out social and philosophical foundations of kingship before suggesting practical approaches to rule. Elsewhere, he mentions philosophical points as they are necessary for his purpose. His practice in the *Risâlat* suggests an addressee who was himself a philosopher. Themistius considers most emperors philosophers, but only Julian was interested in philosophy as a discipline. Only he could fully understand the implications of the treatise, whose form might be part of a continuing philosophical debate between the two.

One argument for Julian as addressee is not the thematic material included, but the topics omitted.[19] For Themistius, the most important virtue was philanthropy, which subsumes all others and makes an emperor similar to God.[20] Constantius (*Or.* 1), Valentinian and Valens (*Or.* 6), and Theodosius (*Or.* 19) receive panegyrics on this theme, and the concept occupies an important place in the speech to Jovian (*Or.* 5). That it does not appear in the *Risalât*[21] is unusual and irregular and may reflect the difference of opinion on this topic between emperor and philosopher.

---

15. Cf. Downey, *Stud. Pat.* 5 (1962): 480–88.

16. Cf. G. Downey, *HTR* 50 (1957): 259–74.

17. Julian often expresses the need for pagans to emulate Christians in, e.g., charity; cf. e.g., *Ep.* 89b, 305b–c; *Ep.* 84, 430d–431b; *Miso.* 363a–c. Cf. also Greg. Naz. *Or.* 4.111, and Soz. *HE* 5.16, for Julian's actions in this regard.

18. Denied by Criscuolo, *Koinonia* 7 (1983): 93, n. 19.

19. So J. Croissant, *Serta Leodiensia*, 26.

20. For discussion, see chapter 4.

21. Croissant, *Serta Leodiensia*, 20; Dvornik, in *Late Classical and Mediaeval Studies*, 78.

The practice of philanthropy, Themistius states at various points, raised an emperor out of the material world to a medial stage between humanity and divinity. An underlying assumption is that divine or semidivine status was desirable. Julian's view of philanthropy is less abstract and rather similar to earlier, that is, second-century, views. He emphasizes the status of humanity rather than that of the ruler himself. His goal in philanthropy is the amelioration of the human condition, not the enhancement of imperial honor.[22] While acknowledging that philanthropy reflects divinity,[23] Julian cannot endure the idea that humanity in general and emperors in particular could achieve divine status.[24] Humans might imitate God, but could never be God.

Julian had informed Themistius of his view in his *Letter to Themistius*. After quoting the description of a true king from the *Laws* of Plato, he interprets the passage:

> Do you understand that, although a ruler is human by nature, he must be divine and semidivine in conduct, and banish from his soul everything that is mortal and savage except what must remain for physical preservation? (259a–b; trans. Wright)

A little later, he remarks:

> It seems to me, at any rate, that the task of reigning is beyond human capability and that a ruler requires a more divine nature, as indeed Plato also used to say. (260c–d; trans. Wright)

Julian uses these statements to explain a reluctance to serve as emperor. Underlying them, however, is the assumption that he was not divine and could not perform his duties properly. For Themistius, divinity and philanthropy were inseparably linked. Presumably, he bypasses this virtue in the *Risâlat* to avoid conflict with Julian's views. Further, while he discusses humanity's need for rulers and offers

---

22. For Julian's different goals within the practice of philanthropy itself, cf. Kabiersch, *Untersuchungen zum Begriff der Philanthropia*, passim.

23. Julian and Themistius do agree on some points; cf. Kabiersch, *Untersuchungen zum Begriff der Philanthropia*, 54–61.

24. Cf. Dvornik, in *Late Classical and Mediaeval Studies*, 71–81.

advice on a number of topics, the philosopher does not consider some
other elements of *Herrscherideal*, the nature of kingship. He omits
discussion of the emperor as law incarnate (*nomos empsychos*), remarking that a ruler was guardian of the laws.[25] These omissions probably
reflect the same purpose of avoiding conflict: Julian held the view that
he was not above the law.[26] All in all, the *Risâlat* is much more likely to
have been addressed to Julian.

---

25. Croissant, *Serta Leodiensia*, 20–25; Dvornik, in *Late Classical and Mediaeval Studies*, 78. For a brief discussion of the concept, see chapter 6.

26. For brief discussion, Athanassiadi-Fowden, *Julian and Hellenism*, 92–
93. Themistius twice states that Theodosius is "law incarnate": 16.212d,
19.227d.

Appendix 5

The Chronology of Themistius' Speeches

For the following chronology of Themistius' speeches, it seems unnecessary to provide a concordance to the chronologies of others. Instead, the first list refers to the place where the dates are discussed and references to earlier work can be found. Items no longer extant are placed in brackets. The second list includes only the extant speeches.

In Chronological Order

Date	*Oration*	Location	Reference
341/343	24	Nicomedia	chap. 2
March 347	1	Ancyra	chap. 4
autumn 348	33	Constantinople	chap. 2
autumn 349	32	Constantinople	chap. 2
early 350s	30	Constantinople	chap. 4
Sept./Oct. 355	20, 27	Paphlagonia	chap. 4
? 355	22	?Constantinople	app. 1
Nov./Dec. 355	2	Constantinople	chap. 4
[355/356	*Kitâb*	Sent to Julian	app. 3]
355/356	21	Constantinople	chap. 4
1 January 357	4	Constantinople	chap. 4
May 357	3	Rome	chap. 4
[summer 357	report	Constantinople	chap. 4
358/359	23, 26, 29	Constantinople	chap. 4
March 360	28	Constantinople	app. 2
[361/363	persecution	?	chap. 5; app. 3]
late 362	*Risâlat*	sent to Julian	chap. 5; app. 3
1 January 364	5	Ancyra	chap. 6
winter 364	6	Constantinople	chap. 7
[1 January 365	consulship	Constantinople	chap. 7]
winter 366/7	7	Constantinople	chap. 7

Date	Oration	Location	Reference
28 March 368	8	Marcianopolis	chap. 7
[368/369	discussions	Marcianopolis	chap. 7]
1 January 369	9	?Constantinople	chap. 7
369/370	10	Constantinople	chap. 7
28 March 373	11	Antioch	chap. 7
[375/376	persecution	Antioch	chap. 7]
375/376	25	Antioch	chap. 7
spring 376	13	Rome	chap. 7
spring 379	14	?Thessalonica	chap. 8
19 January 381	15	Constantinople	chap. 8
1 January 383	16	Constantinople	chap. 8
early 384	17	Constantinople	chap. 8
spring 384	31	Constantinople	chap. 8
summer 384	18	Constantinople	chap. 8
summer 384	19	Constantinople	chap. 8
384/385	34	Constantinople	chap. 8

In Numerical Order

Oration	Date	Oration	Date
1	March 347	20	Sept./Oct. 355
2	Nov./Dec. 355	21	355/356
3	May 357	22	? 355
4	1 January 357	23	357/359
5	1 January 364	24	341/343
6	autumn 364	25	375
7	winter 366/7	26	357/359
8	28 March 368	27	Sept./Oct. 355
9	1 January 369	28	March 360
10	369/370	29	357/359
11	28 March 373	30	early 350s
13	spring 376	31	spring 384
14	spring 379	32	autumn 349
15	19 January 381	33	autumn 348
16	1 January 383	34	384/385
17	early 384		
18	summer 384		
19	summer 384		

Bibliography

Except for items listed in the Abbreviations, the bibliography in principle contains full citations of all items that appear in the notes, including those that I mention, but have not seen, and encyclopedia articles. In general, I do not include items on Themistius that I have not used, but some exceptions can be found. For sources, I have included only some of the major items, rather than a complete list of all texts used, and texts with commentaries that I have used.

Aalders, G.J.D. "ΝΟΜΟΣ ΕΜΨΥΧΟΣ." In Politeia und Res Publica. Palingenesia, Monographie und Texte zur klassische Altertumswissenschaft 4 (1969): 315–29.

Alföldi, A. A Conflict of Ideas in the Late Roman Empire: The Clash between the Senate and Valentinian I. Oxford, 1952.

Armstrong, A.H., ed. The Cambridge History of Later Greek and Early Medieval Philosophy. Cambridge, 1970.

Athanassiadi-Fowden, P. Julian and Hellenism. Oxford, 1981.

Austin, N.J.E. "A Usurper's Claim to Legitimacy. Procopius in A.D. 365/6." Rivista Storica dell' Antichità 2 (1972): 187–94.

Bagnall, R.S., et al. The Consuls of the Later Roman Empire. Atlanta, 1987.

Baldus, H.R. "Constantius und Constans Augusti: Darstellungen des kaiserliches Brüderpaares auf Prägungen der Jahre 340–350 n. Chr." Jahrbuch für Numismatik und Geldgeschichte 34 (1984): 77–106.

———. "Theodosius der Große und die Revolte des Magnus Maximus—das Zeugnis der Münzen." Chiron 14 (1984): 175–92.

Ballériaux, O. "Le ΜΕΤΡΙΟΠΑΘΗΣ Η ΦΙΛΟΤΕΚΝΟΣ (Discours XXXII) de Thémistius." Byzantion 58 (1988): 22–35.

Barnea, I. "Themistios despre Scythia Minor." Studii şi Cercetări de Istorie Veche 18 (1967): 563–73. In Romanian, with French summary on pp. 573–74.

Barnes, T.D. "Porphyry Against the Christians: Date and the Attribution of Fragments." Journal of Theological Studies 24 (1973): 424–42.

———. "A Law of Julian." Classical Philology 69 (1974): 288–91.

———. "Constans and Gratian in Rome." Harvard Studies in Classical Philology 79 (1975): 325–33.

———. "Imperial Campaigns, A.D. 285–311." Phoenix 30 (1976): 174–93.

———. "The Victories of Constantine." *Zeitschrift für Papyrologie und Epigraphik* 21 (1976): 149–55.

———. "Emperors and Bishops, A.D. 324–344: Some Problems." *American Journal of Ancient History* 3 (1978): 53–75.

———. "A Correspondent of Iamblichus." *Greek, Roman and Byzantine Studies* 19 (1978): 99–106.

———. *Constantine and Eusebius.* Cambridge, Mass., 1980.

———. "Imperial Chronology, A.D. 337–350." *Phoenix* 34 (1980): 160–66.

———. *The New Empire of Diocletian and Constantine.* Cambridge, Mass., 1982.

———. "Himerius and the Fourth Century." *Classical Philology* 82 (1987): 206–25.

———. "Regional Prefectures." In *Bonner Historia-Augusta-Colloquium, 1984/85*, 13–23. Bonn, 1987.

———. "Emperors on the Move." *Journal of Roman Archaeology* 2 (1989): 247–61.

———. "Religion and Society in the Age of Theodosius." In *Grace, Politics and Desire: Essays on Augustine*, ed. H.A. Meynell, 157–75. Calgary, 1990.

———. *Athanasius and Constantius: Theology and Politics in the Constantinian Empire.* Cambridge, Mass., 1993.

Barnes, T.D., and J. Vanderspoel. "Julian and Themistius." *Greek, Roman and Byzantine Studies* 22 (1981): 187–89.

Barrow, R.H. *Prefect and Emperor.* Oxford, 1973. Text, translation and commentary on Symmachus' *Relationes*.

Bastien, P. *Le monnayage de Magnence (350–353).* 2nd ed. Wetteren, 1983.

Baynes, N.H. "The Early Life of Julian the Apostate." *Journal of Hellenic Studies* 45 (1925): 251–54.

Behr, C.A. *Aelius Aristides and the Sacred Tales.* Amsterdam, 1968.

———. *P. Aelius Aristides: The Complete Works.* 2 vols. Leiden, 1981–86.

Béranger, J. *Recherches sur l'Aspect idéologique du Principat.* Schweizerische Beiträge zur Altertumswissenschaft 6. Basel, 1953.

Bidez, J. *La tradition manuscrite et les éditions des Discours de l'Empereur Julien.* Gand, 1929.

Bidez, J., G. Rochefort, and C. Lacombrade, eds. and trans. *L'Empereur Julien: Œuvres Complètes.* 2 vols. Paris, 1932–64.

Bidez, J., and F. Winkelmann, *Philostorgius Kirchengeschichte.* 2nd ed. Berlin, 1972.

Birley, A. *Marcus Aurelius: A Biography.* 2nd ed. New Haven and London, 1987.

Bloch, H. "A New Document of the Last Pagan Revival in the West, 393–394 A.D." *Harvard Theological Review* 38 (1945): 199–244.

Blockley, R.C. "The Panegyric of Claudius Mamertinus on the Emperor Julian." *American Journal of Philology* 93 (1972): 437–50.

———. *Ammianus Marcellinus: A Study of His Historiography and Political Thought.* Collection Latomus 141. Brussels, 1975.

———. *The Fragmentary Classicising Historians of the Later Roman Empire.* 2 vols. Liverpool, 1981–83.

Blumenthal, H.J. "Neoplatonic Elements in the De Anima Commentaries." *Phronesis* 21 (1976): 64–87.

———. "Photius on Themistius (Cod. 74): Did Themistius Write Commentaries on Aristotle?" *Hermes* 107 (1979): 168–82.

———. "Themistius. The Last Peripatetic Commentator on Aristotle?" In *Arktouros: Hellenic Studies Presented to Bernard M.W. Knox on the Occasion of His 65th Birthday*, ed. G.W. Bowersock, W. Burkert, and M.C.J. Putnam, 391–400. Berlin, 1979. Revised version in *Aristotle Transformed: The Ancient Commentators and Their Influence*, ed. R. Sorabji, 113–23. London, 1990.

Booth, A.D. "Elementary and Secondary Education in the Roman Empire." *Florilegium* 1 (1979): 1–14.

———. "À quel âge Libanius est-il entré à l'École du Rhéteur?" *Byzantion* 53 (1983): 157–63.

Bouyges, M. "Notes sur des Traductions arabes d'Auteurs grecs." *Archives de Philosophie* 2.3 (1924): 1–23.

Bowersock, G.W. *Greek Sophists in the Roman Empire*. Oxford, 1969.

———. *Julian the Apostate*. Cambridge, Mass., 1978.

———. *Hellenism in Late Antiquity*. Ann Arbor, 1990.

Bradbury, S.A. *Innovation and Reaction in the Age of Constantine and Julian*. Ph.D. diss., University of California, Berkeley, 1986.

———. "The Date of Julian's *Letter to Themistius*." *Greek, Roman and Byzantine Studies* 28 (1987): 235–51.

Brauch, T. "The Prefect of Constantinople for 362 A.D.: Themistius." *Byzantion* 63 (1993): 37–78.

———. "Themistius and the Emperor Julian." *Byzantion* 63 (1993): 79–115.

Brown, P. *Power and Persuasion in Late Antiquity: Towards a Christian Empire*. Madison, 1992.

Burgess, R.W. "Quinquennial Vota and the Consulship in the Fourth and Fifth Centuries." *Numismatic Chronicle* 148 (1988): 77–96.

———. *The* Chronicle *of Hydatius and the* Consularia Constantinopolitana: *Two Contemporary Accounts of the Final Years of the Roman Empire*. Oxford, 1993.

Burns, T.S. *The Ostrogoths: Kingship and Society*. Historia Einzelschriften 36. Wiesbaden, 1980.

Cameron, Alan "Notes on Palladas." *Classical Quarterly* 15 (1965): 215–29.

———. "Wandering Poets: A Literary Movement in Byzantine Egypt." *Historia* 14 (1965): 470–509. Reprinted in *Literature and Society in the Early Byzantine World*. London, 1985.

———. "The Date of the Anonymous *de rebus bellicis*." In *De Rebus Bellicis*. BAR International Series 63, 1–10. Oxford, 1969. Revised and reprinted in A. Cameron, *Literature and Society in the Early Byzantine World*. London, 1985.

———. "Julian and Hellenism." *The Ancient World* 24 (1993): 25–29.

Cameron, A., and J. Long. *Barbarians and Politics at the Court of Arcadius*. Berkeley and Los Angeles, 1993.

Cameron, Averil. *Christianity and the Rhetoric of Empire*. Berkeley and Los Angeles, 1991.

Cameron, A., and J. Herrin. *Constantinople in the Early Eighth Century: The PARASTASEIS SYNTOMOI CHRONIKAI*. Columbia Studies in the Classical Tradition 9. Leiden, 1984.

Češka, J. "En marge de la visite de Constance à Rome en 357." *Sborník prací filosofické Fakulty Brněnské University*, Ser. E, 10 (1965): 107–15.

Charlesworth, M.P. "Imperial Deportment: Two Texts and Some Questions." *Journal of Roman Studies* 37 (1947): 34–48.

Chastagnol, A. *Les fastes de la préfecture de Rome au Bas-Empire*. Paris, 1959.

———. *La préfecture urbaine à Rome sous le Bas-Empire*. Paris, 1960.

———. "Remarques sur les sénateurs orientaux au IVe siècle." *Acta Antiquae Academiae Scientarum Hungaricae* 24 (1976): 341–56.

Cheikho, L. "Risâlat de Damistiyos vizir d'Elyan, c'est-à-dire le roi Youliyanos, sur la Politique, traduite du syriaque par Ibn Zour'at." *Al-Machriq* 18 (1920): 881–89.

Clark, C.U., ed. *Ammiani Marcellini Rerum Gestarum Libri Qui Supersunt*. 2 vols. 1910. Reprint Berlin, 1963.

Classen, C.J. "Nec spuens, aut os aut nasum tergens vel fricans (Amm. Marc. XVI 10, 10)." *Rheinisches Museum für Philologie* 131 (1988): 177–86.

Colpi, B. *Die paideia des Themistios: Ein Beitrag zur Geschichte der Bildung im vierten Jahrhundert nach Christus*. Bern, 1988.

Corsi, P. "Costante II in Italia, I." *Quaderni Medievali* (1977): 32–72.

Courcelle, P. "Du nouveau sur la vie et les œuvres de Marius Victorinus." *Revue des Études Anciennes* 64 (1962): 127–35.

Courtonne, Y. *Saint Basile: Lettres*. Vol. 1. Paris, 1957.

Criscuolo, U. "Sull'epistola di Giuliano imperatore al filosofo Temistio." *Koinonia* 7 (1983): 89–111.

Croissant, J. "Un nouveau Discours de Thémistius." *Serta Leodiensia*. Bibliothèque de la Faculté de Philosophie et Lettres de l'Université de Liége 44 (1930): 7–30.

Cumont, F. *Sur l'authenticité de quelques Lettres de Julien*. Université de Gand, Recueil de Travaux 3. Gand, 1889.

Dagron, G. *Naissance d'une capitale: Constantinople et ses institutions de 330 à 451*. Paris, 1974.

———. *Constantinople Imaginaire: Études sur le recueil des Patria*. Bibliothèque Byzantine, Études 8. Paris, 1984.

Daly, L.J. "Themistius' Plea for Religious Tolerance." *Greek, Roman and Byzantine Studies* 12 (1971): 65–79.

———. "The Mandarin and the Barbarian: The Response of Themistius to the Gothic Challenge." *Historia* 21 (1972): 351–79.

———. "Themistius' Concept of *Philanthropia*." *Byzantion* 45 (1975): 22–40.

———. "'In a Borderland': Themistius' Ambivalence Toward Julian." *Byzantinische Zeitschrift* 73 (1980): 1–11.

———. Themistius' Refusal of a Magistracy." *Jahrbuch der österreichischen Byzantinistik* 32/2 (1982): 177–86. Abstract of a paper delivered at the XVI. Internationaler Byzantinistenkongress, Vienna, 4–9 October 1981.

——. "Themistius' Refusal of a Magistracy (*Or.*, 34, cc. XIII-XIV)." *Byzantion* 53 (1983): 164–212.

Defourny, M. "The Aim of the State: Peace." In *Articles on Aristotle*, vol. 2, *Ethics and Politics*, ed. J. Barnes, M. Schofield, and R. Sorabji, 195–201. London, 1977.

De Lacy, P. "Plato and the Intellectual Life of the Second Century A.D." In *Approaches to the Second Sophistic*, ed. G.W. Bowersock, 4–10. University Park, Penn., 1974.

Demandt, A. "Der Tod des älteren Theodosius." *Historia* 18 (1969): 599–626.

——. "Die Konsuln der Jahre 381 und 382 Namens Syagrius." *Byzantinische Zeitschrift* 64 (1971): 39–45.

——. "Die Feldzüge des älteren Theodosius." *Hermes* 100 (1972): 81–113.

de Tervarent, G. "Eros and Anteros or Reciprocal Love in Ancient and Renaissance Art." *Journal of the Warburg and Courtauld Institutes* 28 (1965): 205–8.

Dilke, O.A.W. *Greek and Roman Maps*. London, 1985.

——. "Itineraries and Geographical Maps in the Early and Late Roman Empires." In *The History of Cartography*, vol. 1, *Cartography in Prehistoric, Ancient, and Medieval Europe and the Mediterranean*, ed. J.B. Harley and D. Woodward, 234–47. Chicago, 1987.

Dillon, J. *The Middle Platonists*. London, 1977.

Dindorf, W. *Themistii Orationes*. Leipzig, 1832. Reprint Hildesheim, 1961. Includes the notes of Harduin and Petau.

Dodge, B., ed. and trans. *The Fihrist of al-Nadim: A Tenth Century Survey of Muslim Culture*. 2 vols. New York, 1970.

Dodgeon, M.H., and S.N.C. Lieu. *The Roman Eastern Frontier and the Persian Wars (A.D. 226–363): A Documentary History*. London and New York, 1991.

Downey, G. Translation of Themistius' *Orations*. Photocopy made available to me by Professor W.E. Kaegi.

——. "Education and Public Problems as Seen by Themistius." *Transactions of the American Philological Association* 86 (1955): 291–307.

——. "*Philanthropia* in Religion and Statecraft in the Fourth Century after Christ." *Historia* 4 (1955): 199–208.

——. "Themistius and the Defense of Hellenism in the Fourth Century." *Harvard Theological Review* 50 (1957): 259–74.

——. "Themistius' First Oration." *Greek [, Roman] and Byzantine Studies* 1 (1958): 49–69. Translation of *Oration* 1, with brief notes.

——. *A History of Antioch in Syria from Seleucus to the Arab Conquest*. Princeton, 1961.

——. "Allusions to Christianity in Themistius' Orations." *Studia Patristica* 5 (1962): 480–88.

Downey, G., and A.F. Norman. *Themistii Orationes*. 3 vols. Leipzig, 1964–74. Vol. 3 contains translations into Latin of the περὶ ἀρετῆς by R. Mach and of the *Risâlat* by I. Shahîd.

Duval, Y.M. "La venue à Rome de l'empereur Constance II en 357, d'après Ammien Marcellin (XVI 10, 1–20)." *Caesarodunum* 5 (1970): 299–304.

Dvornik, F. "The Emperor Julian's 'Reactionary' Ideas on Kingship." In *Late Classical and Mediaeval Studies in Honor of Albert Mathias Friend, Jr.*, ed. K. Weitzmann, 71–81. Princeton, 1955.

————. *Early Christian and Byzantine Political Philosophy: Origins and Background.* 2 vols. Washington, D.C., 1966.

Eadie, J.W., ed. *The Breviarum of Festus: A Critical Edition with Historical Commentary.* London, 1967.

Edbrooke, R.O. "Constantius and Hormisdas in the Forum of Trajan." *Mnemosyne* 28 (1975): 412–17.

————. "The Visit of Constantius II to Rome in 357 and Its Effect on the Pagan Roman Senatorial Aristocracy." *American Journal of Philology* 97 (1976): 40–61.

Egger, R. "Der erste Theodosius." *Byzantion* 5 (1930): 9–32.

Ehrhardt, A. "The First Two Years of the Emperor Theodosius." *Journal of Ecclesiastical History* 15 (1964): 1–17.

Enßlin, W. "Kaiser Julians Gesetzgebung und Reichverwaltung." *Klio* 18 (1922): 104–99.

————. "Zum Heermeisteramt des spätrömischen Reiches. I. Die Titulatur der magistri militum bis auf Theodosius I." *Klio* 23 (1930): 306–25.

————. "Zum Heermeisteramt des spätrömischen Reiches. II. Die magistri militum des 4. Jahrhunderts." *Klio* 24 (1931): 102–47.

————. "Theodosius (9)." *RE* X, A (1934): 1937–45.

————. "Die Religionspolitik des Kaisers Theodosius d. Gr." *Sitzungsberichte der Bayerischen Academie der Wissenschaften, Philosophisch-historische Klasse* (1953), Heft 2.

Fedwick, P.J. "A Chronology of the Life and Works of Basil of Caesarea." In *Basil of Caesarea: Christian, Humanist, Ascetic*, 2 vols., ed. P.J. Fedwick, vol. 1, 3–19. Toronto, 1981.

Foerster, R. "Andreas Dudith und die zwölfte Rede des Themistios." *Neue Jahrbucher für Pädagogik* 6 (1900): 74–93.

————. *Libanii Opera.* 12 vols. Leipzig, 1903–23.

Fowden, G. "The Pagan Holy Man in Late Antiquity." *Journal of Hellenic Studies* 102 (1982): 33–59.

————. *The Egyptian Hermes: A Historical Approach to the Late Pagan Mind.* Cambridge, 1986.

————. "Pagan Versions of the Rain Miracle of A.D. 172." *Historia* 36 (1987): 83–95.

Gärtner, H. "Einige Überlegungen zur kaiserzeitliche Panegyrik und zu Ammians Characteristik des Kaisers Julian." *Akademie der Wissenschaften und der Literatur in Mainz, Abhandlungen der geistes- und sozialwissenschaftlichen Klasse* (1968), Abh. 10, 499–529 [3–33 paginated separately].

Garzya, A., ed. *In Themistii Orationes Index Auctus.* Hellenica et Byzantina Neapolitana 11. Naples, 1983–89.

Geffcken, J. *The Last Days of Greco-Roman Paganism.* Trans. by S. MacCormack of *Der Ausgang des griechisch-römischen Heidentums*, 2nd ed. (1929). Amsterdam, 1978.

Goffart, W. "Did Julian Combat Venal *Suffragium*? A Note on *CTh* 2.29.1." *Classical Philology* 65 (1970): 145–51.

Goodenough, E.R. "The Political Philosophy of Hellenistic Kingship." *Yale Classical Studies* 1 (1928): 55–102.

Gottlieb, G. *Ambrosius von Mailand und Kaiser Gratian*. Hypomnemata 40. Göttingen, 1973.

Griffin, M.T. *Seneca: A Philosopher in Politics*. Oxford, 1976.

Grisoli, P.G. "«Filosofia» nel XXVI Discorso di Temistio." *Rivista di Filologia Classica* 95 (1967): 303–21.

Grumel, V. "L'Illyricum de la mort de Valentinien Iᵉʳ (375) à la mort de Stilicon (408)." *Revue des Études Byzantines* 9 (1951): 5–46.

———. "Numismatique et Histoire: L'Époque Valentinienne." *Revue des Études Byzantines* 12 (1954): 7–31.

Hadot, P. *Porphyre et Victorinus*. Paris, 1968.

Hahn, I. "Zur Frage der sozialen Grundlagen der Usurpation Procopius." *Acta Antiquae Academiae Scientarum Hungaricae* 6 (1958): 199–210. In Russian, with German summary on p. 211.

Hamblenne, P. "Une «Conjuration» sous Valentinien?" *Byzantion* 50 (1980): 198–225.

Hamilton, W., ed. and trans. *Ammianus Marcellinus: The Later Roman Empire* (A.D. 354–378). London, 1986. Includes an Introduction and Notes by A. Wallace-Hadrill.

Heather, P.J. *Goths and Romans 332–489*. Oxford, 1992.

Heather, P.J., and J.F. Matthews. *The Goths in the Fourth Century*. Liverpool, 1991.

Hoepffner, A. "Le Mort du «magister militum» Théodose." *Revue des Études Latines* 14 (1936): 119–29.

Holum, K. *Theodosian Empresses: Women and Imperial Dominion in Late Antiquity*. Berkeley and Los Angeles, 1982.

Hussey, R. *Socratis Scholastici Ecclesiastica Historia*. 3 vols. Oxford, 1853.

Jacoby, D. "La population de Constantinople à l'époque byzantine: un problème de démographie urbaine." *Byzantion* 31 (1961): 81–109.

Jones, C.P. "Aelius Aristides, ΕΙΣ ΒΑΣΙΛΕΑ." *Journal of Roman Studies* 62 (1972): 134–52.

———. "The Reliability of Philostratus." In *Approaches to the Second Sophistic*, ed. G.W. Bowersock, 11–16. University Park, Penn., 1974.

———. *The Roman World of Dio Chrysostom*. Cambridge, Mass., 1978.

———. *Culture and Society in Lucian*. Cambridge, Mass., 1986.

Jülicher, A. "Basileios (15)." *RE* III, 1 (1899): 52–54.

Kabiersch, J. *Untersuchungen zum Begriff der Philanthropia bei dem Kaiser Julian*. Wiesbaden, 1960.

Kaegi, W.E. "Domestic Military Problems of Julian the Apostate," *Byzantinische Forschungen* 2 (1967): 247–64. Reprinted in *Army, Society and Religion in Byzantium*. London, 1982.

———. "The Emperor Julian at Naissus." *L'Antiquité Classique* 44 (1975): 161–71. Reprinted in *Army, Society and Religion in Byzantium*. London, 1982.

———. "Constantine's and Julian's Strategies of Strategic Surprise against the Persians." *Athenaeum* 69 (1981): 209–13. Reprinted in *Army, Society and Religion in Byzantium*. London, 1982.

Kaster, R.A. "The Salaries of Libanius." *Chiron* 13 (1983): 37–59.

———. *Guardians of Language: The Grammarian and Society in Late Antiquity.* Berkeley and Los Angeles, 1988.

Kelsen, H. "Aristotle and Hellenic-Macedonian Policy." In *Articles on Aristotle*, vol. 2, *Ethics and Politics*, ed. J. Barnes, M. Schofield and R. Sorabji, 170–94. London, 1977.

Kennedy, G.A. *Greek Rhetoric Under Christian Emperors.* Princeton, 1983.

Kesters, H. *Antisthène de la dialectique: Étude critique et exégetique sur le XXVIᵉ discours de Thémistius.* Louvain, 1935.

———. *Plaidoyer d'un socratique contre le Phèdre de Platon.* Louvain, 1959. Includes a French translation of *Oration 26*.

King, N.Q. *The Emperor Theodosius and the Establishment of Christianity.* London, 1960.

———. "*Compelle Intrare* and the Plea of the Pagans." *The Modern Churchman*, n.s., 4 (1961): 111–15.

Klauser, T. "Aurum Coronarium." *Gesammelte Arbeiten zur Liturgiegeschichte, Kirchengeschichte und christlichen Archäologie. Jahrbuch für Antike und Christentum*, Ergänzungsband 3 (1974): 292–309.

Klein, R. *Constantius II. und die christliche Kirche.* Impulse der Forschung 26. Darmstadt, 1977.

———. "Der Rombesuch des Kaisers Konstantius II. im Jahre 357." *Athenaeum* 57 (1979): 98–115.

Lacombrade, C. "L'empereur Julien émule de Marc-Aurèle." *Pallas* 14 (1967): 9–22.

Lampe, G.W.H. *A Patristic Greek Lexicon.* Oxford, 1961.

Levi, A., and M. Levi. *Itineraria picta: Contributo allo studio della Tabula Peutingeriana.* Rome, 1967.

Liebeschuetz, J.H.W.G. *Antioch: City and Imperial Administration in the Later Roman Empire.* Oxford, 1972.

———. *Barbarians and Bishops: Army, Church and State in the Age of Arcadius and John Chrysostom.* Oxford, 1990.

Lieu, S.N.C., ed. *The Emperor Julian: Panegyric and Polemic.* Liverpool, 1986.

Lightfoot, C.S. "Fact and Fiction—The Third Siege of Nisibis (A.D. 350)." *Historia* 37 (1988): 105–25.

Lippold, A. "Kaiser Theodosius d. Gr. und sein Vater." *Rivista storica dell'Antichità* 2 (1972): 195–200.

———. "Theodosius (1)." *RE* Suppl. XIII (1973): 837–961.

———. *Theodosius der Große und seine Zeit.* 2nd ed. Stuttgart, 1980.

MacCormack, S. "Latin Prose Panegyrics: Tradition and Discontinuity in the Later Roman Empire." *Revue des Études Augustiniennes* 22 (1976): 29–77.

———. *Art and Ceremony in Late Antiquity.* Berkeley and Los Angeles, 1981.

Maisano, R. "La critica filologica di Petau e Hardouin e l'Edizione Parigina del

1684 delle Orazioni di Temistio." *Archivum Historicum Societatis Iesu* 43 (1974): 267–300.

———. "La *Paideia* del *Logos* nell' Opera Oratoria di Temistio." *Koinonia* 10 (1986): 29–47.

Mango, C. *Le développment urbain de Constantinople (IVe-VIIe siècles)*. Travaux et Mémoires, Monographies 2. Paris, 1985.

Martindale, J.R. "Note on the Consuls of 381 and 382." *Historia* 16 (1967): 254–56.

Matthews, J.F. "A Pious Supporter of Theodosius I: Maternus Cynegius and His Family." *JTS* 18 (1967): 438–46. Reprinted in *Political Life and Culture in Late Roman Society*. London, 1985.

———. *Western Aristocracies and Imperial Court A.D. 364–425*. Oxford, 1975.

———. *The Roman Empire of Ammianus*. London and Baltimore, 1989.

Mattock, J.N. "The Supposed Epitome by Themistius of Aristotle's Zoological Works." *Akten des VII. Kongresses für Arabistik und Islamwissenschaft. Abhandlungen der Akademie der Wissenschaften in Göttingen, Philologisch-historische Klasse*, Folge 3, 98 (1976): 260–67.

Mazzarino, S. *Aspetti sociale del quarto secolo*. Rome, 1951.

McCormick, M. *Eternal Victory: Triumphal Rulership in Late Antiquity, Byzantium and the Early Medieval West*. Cambridge, 1986.

Mesk, J. "Dion und Themistios." *Philologische Wochenschrift* 54 (1934): 556–58.

Millar, F. *The Emperor in the Roman World*. London, 1977.

Miller, K. *Itineraria Romana: Römische Reisewege an der Hand der Tabula Peutingeriana*. Stuttgart, 1916. Reprint 1964.

Mócsy, A. *Pannonia and Upper Moesia*. London, 1974.

Mommsen, T., ed. *Chronica minora*. 3 vols. Monumenta Germaniae Historica, Auctores Antiquissimi 9, 11, 13. Berlin, 1892–98.

Moraux, P. *Une imprécation funéraire à Néocésarée*. Bibliothèque archéologique et histoire de l'Institut française d'Archéologie d'Istanbul 4. Paris, 1959.

Müller, C. *Fragmenta Historicorum Graecorum*. Vol. 4. Paris, 1851. Reprint Frankfurt/Main, 1975.

Müller-Seidel, I. "Die Usurpation Julians des Abtrünnigen im Lichte seiner Germanenpolitik." *Historische Zeitschrift* 180 (1955): 225–44.

Neri, V. "Ammiano Marcellino e l'elezione di Valentiniano." *Rivista Storica dell' Antichità* 15 (1985): 153–82.

Nixon, C.E.V. *Pacatus: Panegyric to the Emperor Theodosius*. Liverpool, 1987. Includes introduction, translation, and notes.

Norman, A.F. *Libanius' Autobiography*. Oxford, 1965. Includes introduction, text, translation, and commentary.

———. *Libanius: Selected Works*. Vol. 1. Loeb Classical Library. London and Cambridge, Mass., 1969.

———. *Libanius: Autobiography and Selected Letters*. 2 vols. Loeb Classical Library. London and Cambridge, Mass., 1993.

Oost, S.I. *Galla Placidia Augusta: A Biographical Essay*. Chicago, 1968.

Oppermann, S.I. ΕΙΣ ΤΟΝ ΑΥΤΟΥ ΠΑΤΕΡΑ II. ΒΑΣΑΝΙΣΤΗΣ Η ΦΙΛΟ-

ΣΟΦΟΣ (20. UND 21. REDE). Göttingen, 1962. Texts, German translations, and commentary.

Paschoud, F. *Zosime: Histoire Nouvelle*. 3 vols. Paris, 1971–89.

Pavan, M. *La politica gotica di Teodosia nella publistica del suo tempo*. Rome, 1964.

Pelikan, J. *Christianity and Classical Culture: The Metamorphosis of Natural Theology in the Christian Encounter with Hellenism*. New Haven, 1993.

Penella, R.J. *Greek Philosophers and Sophists in the Fourth Century A.D.*: Studies in Eunapius of Sardis. Liverpool, 1990.

Petit, P. *Libanius et la vie municipale à Antioche au IV e siècle après J.-C.* Paris, 1955.

————. "Les sénateurs de Constantinople dans l'œuvre de Libanius." *L'Antiquité Classique* 26 (1957): 347–82.

Pharr, C. *The Theodosian Code*. Princeton, 1952.

Philippart, L. "A propos d'un prétendu discours perdu de Thémistius." *Serta Leodiensia*. Bibliothèque de la Faculté de Philosophie et Lettres de l'Université de Liége 44 (1930): 269–75.

Piganiol, A. *L' Empire chrétien*. 2nd ed. Paris, 1972.

Portmann, W. *Geschichte in der spätantiken Panegyrik*. Frankfurt am Main, 1988.

————. "Die 59. Rede des Libanios und das Datum der Schlacht von Singara." *Byzantinische Zeitschrift* 82 (1989): 1–18.

Prato, C., and A. Fornaro. *Giuliano Imperatore: Epistola a Temistio*. Studi e Testi Latini e Greci 2. Lecce, 1984.

Rees, D.A. "Bipartition of the Soul in the Early Academy." *Journal of Hellenic Studies* 77 (1957): 112–18.

Richard, G. "Les Obstacles à la Liberté de Conscience au IVe siècle de l'Ere chrétienne." *Revue des Études Anciennes* 42 (1940): 498–507.

Rist, J.M. *Stoic Philosophy*. Cambridge, 1967.

————. "The Stoic Concept of Detachment." In *The Stoics*, ed. J.M. Rist, 259–72. Berkeley, 1978.

Ritter, A.-M. *Das Konzil von Konstantinopel und sein Symbol*. Göttingen, 1965.

Robert, J., and L. Robert. *Bulletin Épigraphique*, 1960.

Robert, L. *À travers l'Asie mineure*. Bibliothèque des Écoles françaises d'Athènes et de Rome 139. Paris, 1980.

Rolfe, J.C. *Ammianus Marcellinus*. 3 vols. Loeb Classical Library. London and Cambridge, Mass., 1935–40.

Ruether, R.R. *Gregory of Nazianzus: Rhetor and Philosopher*. Oxford, 1969.

Russell, D.A., and N.G. Wilson. *Menander Rhetor*. Oxford, 1981. Text, translation, and commentary.

Salzman, M.R. *On Roman Time: The Codex Calendar of 354 and the Rhythms of Urban Life in Late Antiquity*. Berkeley and Los Angeles, 1990.

Šašel, J. "The Struggle between Magnentius and Constantius II for Italy and Illyricum." *Živa Antika* 21 (1971): 205–16.

Scharold, J. *Dion Chrysostomus und Themistius*. Burghausen, 1912.

Schemmel, F. "Die Hochschule von Konstantinopel im IV. Jahrh. p. Ch. n." *Neue Jahrbucher fur Pädagogik* 22 (1908): 147–68.

Schenkl, H. "Die handschriftliche Überlieferung der Reden des Themistius."

Wiener Studien 20 (1898): 205–43; 21 (1899): 80–115, 224–63; 23 (1901): 14–25.

———. "Beiträge zur Textgeschichte der Reden des Themistios." *Sitzungsberichte der Akademie der Wissenschaften zu Wien* 192 (1919), Abh. 1, 1–89.

Schneider, H. *Die 34. Rede des Themistios.* Winterthur, 1966. Includes text, German translation, and commentary.

Schroeder, F.M., and R.B. Todd. *Two Greek Aristotelian Commentators on the Intellect.* Toronto, 1990.

Schwarz, W. *De vita et scriptis Iuliani imperatoris.* Bonn, 1888.

Seeck, O. *Q. Aurelii Symmachi Quae Supersunt.* Monumenta Germaniae Historica, Auctores Antiquissimi 6, 1. Berlin, 1883.

———. "Zur Inschrift von Hissarlik." *Hermes* 18 (1883): 150–53.

———. "Die Münzpolitik Diocletians und seiner Nachfolger," *Zeitschrift für Numismatik* 17 (1890): 116–42.

———. *Geschichte des Untergangs der antiken Welt.* 6 vols. Berlin, 1897–1921.

Seeck, O., and H. Schenkl. "Eine verlorene Rede des Themistius." *Rheinisches Museum für Philologie* 61 (1906): 554–66.

Shahîd, I. *Byzantium and the Arabs in the Fourth Century.* Washington, D.C., 1984.

Sievers, G.R. *Das Leben des Libanius.* Berlin, 1868.

Sivan, H. *Ausonius of Bordeaux: Genesis of a Gallic Aristocracy.* London and New York, 1993.

Snee, R. "Valens recalls the Nicene exiles and anti-Arian propaganda." *Greek, Roman and Byzantine Studies* 26 (1985): 395–419.

Solari, A. "La Elezione di Gioviano." *Klio* 26 (1933): 330–35.

Soraci, R. *L'Imperatore Gioviano.* Catania, 1968.

G. Sotiroff. "The Language of Emperor Valentinian." *Classical World* 65 (1972): 231–32.

Spengel, L. *Themistii Paraphrases Aristotelis Librorum quae supersunt.* 2 vols. Leipzig, 1866.

Steel, C. "Des commentaires d'Aristote par Thémistius?" *Revue philosophique de Louvain* 71 (1973): 669–80.

Stertz, S.A. "Themistius: A Hellenic Philosopher-Statesman in the Christian Roman Empire." *Classical Journal* 71 (1975/76): 349–58.

Straub, J. *Vom Herrscherideal in der Spätantike.* Stuttgart, 1939. Reprint 1964.

Stroheker, K.F. "Spanische Senatoren der spätrömischen und westgotischen Zeit." *Madridischer Mitteilungen* 4 (1963): 107–32. Reprinted in *Germanentum und Spätantike,* 54–87. Zurich, 1965.

Sundwall, J. *Weströmische Studien.* Berlin, 1915.

Szidat, J. "Zur Ankunft Julians in Sirmium 361 n.Chr. auf seinem Zug gegen Constantius II." *Historia* 24 (1975): 375–78.

Tassi, A.M. "Costanzo II e la difesa della maestà imperiale nell'opera di Ammiano Marcellino." *Critica Storica* 6 (1967): 157–80.

Teall, J.L. "The Grain Supply of the Byzantine Empire, 330–1025." *Dumbarton Oaks Papers* 13 (1959): 89–139.

Thompson, E.A. *The Historical Work of Ammianus Marcellinus.* Cambridge, 1947.
———. *A Roman Reformer and Inventor.* Oxford, 1952. Introduction, text, translation, and commentary on *de rebus bellicis.*
———. "The Visigoths from Fritigern to Euric." *Historia* 12 (1963): 105–26. Reprinted in *Romans and Barbarians: The Decline of the Western Empire,* 38–57. Madison, 1982.
———. *The Visigoths in the Time of Ulfila.* Oxford, 1966.
Toynbee, J.M.C. "Roma and Constantinoplis in Late-Antique Art from 312 to 365." *Journal of Roman Studies* 37 (1947): 135–44.
Turcan, R. "L'abandon de Nisibe et l'opinion publique (363 ap. J.C.)." *Mélanges A. Piganiol* (Paris, 1966), 2:875–90.
Valdenberg, V. "Discours politiques de Thémistius dans leur rapport avec l'antiquité." *Byzantion* 1 (1924): 557–80.
Vanderspoel, J. "The Fourth Century Philosopher Maximus of Byzantium." *The Ancient History Bulletin* 1.3 (1987): 71–74.
———. "Themistios and a Philosopher at Sikyon." *Historia* 36 (1987): 383–84.
———. "Themistius, *Or.* 4.58c: An Emendation." *Mnemosyne* 40 (1987): 149.
———. "Themistios and the Origin of Iamblichos." *Hermes* 116 (1988): 125–28.
———. "The 'Themistius Collection' of Commentaries on Plato and Aristotle." *Phoenix* 43 (1989): 162–64.
———. "The Background to Augustine's Denial of Religious Plurality." In *Grace, Politics and Desire: Essays on Augustine,* ed. H.A. Meynell, 179–93. Calgary, 1990.
———. "Review of Peter Brown, *Power and Persuasion in Late Antiquity: Towards a Christian Empire.*" To appear in *Studies in Medieval and Renaissance History.*
van Geytenbeek, A.C. *Musonius Rufus and Greek Diatribe.* Trans. and rev. B.L. Hijmans. Assen, 1973.
Vasiliev, A.A. "Themistius' Address to the Emperor Julian." Unpublished translation of the *Risâlat* prepared for G. Downey in 1949. Photocopy made available to me by Professor W.E. Kaegi.
Verbeke, G. *Thémistius: Commentaire sur le traité de l'Ame d'Aristote, Traduction de Guillaume de Moerbeke.* Corpus Latinum Commentariorum in Aristotelem Graecorum 1. Louvain, 1957.
———. "Themistius." In *Dictionary of Scientific Biography,* 13: 307–8. New York, 1976.
Vigneaux, P.E. *Essai sur l'histoire de la praefectura urbis à Rome.* Paris, 1896.
von Haehling, R. "Ammians Darstellung der Thronbesteigung Jovians im Lichte der heidnisch-christlichen Auseinandersetzung." In *Bonner Festgabe Johannes Straub zum 65. Geburtstag am 18 Oktober 1977,* ed. A. Lippold and N. Himmelmann, 347–48. Bonn, 1977.
von Petrikovits, H. "Fortifications in the North-Western Roman Empire from the Third to the Fifth Centuries A.D." *Journal of Roman Studies* 61 (1971): 178–218.
Waites, M.C. "Some Features of the Allegorical Debate in Greek Literature." *Harvard Studies in Classical Philology* 23 (1912): 1–46.

Wallis, R.T. *Neoplatonism*. London, 1972.

Weber, E. *Tabula Peutingeriana: Codex Vindobonensis 324*. 2 vols. Graz, 1976.

Whitby, M., and M. Whitby. *Chronicon Paschale 284–628 A.D.* Liverpool, 1989.

Wilhelm, F. "Zu Themistios, Or. 27.400 Dind." *Byzantinische-neugriechische Jahrbuch* 6 (1929): 451–89.

Wirth, G. "Themistios und Constantius." *Byzantinische Forschungen* 6 (1979): 293–317.

———. "Jovianus. Kaiser und Karikatur." *Vivarium: Festschrift Theodor Klauser zum 90. Geburtstag, Jahrbuch für Antike und Christentum*, Ergänzungsband 11 (1984): 353–84.

Wolf, P. *Vom Schulwesen der Spätantike: Studien zu Libanius*. Baden-Baden, 1950.

Wright, W.C. *The Works of the Emperor Julian*. 3 vols. Loeb Classical Library. London and New York, 1913.

———. *Philostratus and Eunapius: Lives of the Sophists*. Loeb Classical Library. London and Cambridge, Mass., 1921.

Zeller, E.R. *Die Philosophie der Griechen*. 5th ed. Leipzig, 1923.

Index

The index includes most individuals and places mentioned in this book. Ancient authors simply cited as evidence are not included, nor are some items only introduced into the text incidentally; treatments of the speeches of Themistius can be located by the use of appendix 5; and references to footnotes are not added when items are already indexed for that page. The index includes references to predecessors and *exempla* cited by Themistius insofar as they appear in this book; though not complete for Themistius' work, they provide a representative sampling. The entry for Themistius is selective, but both it and the index as a whole attempt to identify major concepts and ideas as well as people and places.